−**273** Publishers

Social

work

Saatchi & Saatchi's Cause-Related Ideas

Published 2000 by –273 Publishers
23–24 Margaret Street, London W1N 7LB, UK
email@minus273publishers.com

Edited and designed by Mark Thomson

Additional design: Samantha Finn
Translation editor: Christiane Blass, Cologne
German translation: Annette Wiethüchter, Berlin
French translation: Philippe Keyvân Safavi, Paris
Spanish translation: Manners, Barcelona
Chinese translation: Accent on type Ltd., London
Production: David Grover
Printed by Conti Tipocolor, Calenzano, Italy
Printed on totally chlorine-free bleached paper from
renewable sources

ISBN 0–9538128–0–4

–273

content

If you're offended by this advertisement, you should be.

Nobody should be treated like this.

Yet unfortunately, there are millions of people around the world who are.

For many, a verbal lashing is the very least they have to worry about.

In Brazil, for example, Amazonian estate workers face a punishment called 'the trunk'.

A man who hasn't felled his quota of trees, is stripped, tied up and left in a hollowed out tree-trunk for three days.

As if that isn't punishment enough, the trunk is first smeared with honey to attract ants and other insects.

In India, children face similar horrors. Kids as young as six are sold to work in carpet factories.

When the loom-masters can't find enough children to buy, they kidnap them.

The kids are made to work all day. If they slow down at all, they are not allowed to sleep at night. If they make a mistake, they are beaten.

One child was doused with paraffin and set ablaze because he asked for time off. Six others were so viciously beaten for just playing, one of them died.

In Nepal, slavery is just as widespread. Ten year old girls are abducted and sold into prostitution in India.

First, they have to go through a 'grooming' period. Stripped naked, they are locked in a tiny room for days at a time without food.

They are burnt with cigarettes, beaten and raped until eventually they become totally submissive. Only then will they fetch the highest prices from Bombay's brothel keepers.

Just as prostitution can be a form of slavery, so can marriage.

In many parts of the world parents still control who their daughters wed. Who they choose very much depends on what the groom's family offers in exchange. The bride's welfare matters little.

Consequently, there are many women forced to marry against their will. Some even as young as nine. One twelve year

old Nigerian girl hated her husband so much, she kept trying to run away from him.

To stop her, he hacked off both her legs. As you can see, slavery isn't a thing of the past.

Nor is it just a problem of the Third World.

In Britain alone, there have been 1700 cases of abused domestic servants reported since 1987. Most of them are young girls from poor backgrounds overseas. They see working in Britain as an answer to their problems.

But when they get here, they are often treated no better than animals. Many are made to sleep on the floor and just fed scraps. They have to work an 18 hour day. If they complain, they're beaten or caned. Some aren't even allowed out. Some are raped.

The list of atrocities goes on and on.

There are still over 100 million slaves in the world. Each one probably has a story as pain-filled as these.

Anti Slavery International campaigns for the abolition of slavery. We know that it's only by making the facts of these people's lives known and by bringing slavery out into the open that we'll ever destroy it.

Indeed, by lobbying and by raising world awareness of these issues, we've persuaded governments and the UN to tackle the problem.

In some countries like Thailand, India and Pakistan we've even pushed them into changing the law.

None of this would have been possible without the help of our supporters. They have sent letters and asked questions of individuals, companies and governments all around the world.

To keep the pressure on them, we need your help in our forthcoming campaigns.

If you'd like to be involved, fill out the coupon below and become a member. In time, we'll make sure no one knows what it feels like to be treated as a slave.

ANTI-SLAVERY
INTERNATIONAL

Anti-Slavery International, Stableyard,
Broomgrove Rd, London SW9 9TL.
Tel: 0171-924 9555. Fax: 0171-738 4110.

I would like to join ASI: £15 Individual membership ☐ £5 Student, Unwaged ☐ I would/would not like more information. Name _____

Address _____ Postcode _____ I would like to donate £____ Payment can be made by cheque or postal order (payable to Anti-Slavery International) or by credit card. Mastercard ☐ Visa ☐ Amex ☐ Diners ☐ Number ☐☐☐☐☐☐☐☐☐☐☐☐☐☐☐☐ Expires ☐☐☐☐

Saatchi & Saatchi's social work
by Ed Jones

Social advertising is in the genes of Saatchi & Saatchi.

It has always been a continuous thread in the agency's work.

So much so that, some years ago, Paolo Ettorre and his team at Saatchi & Saatchi in Italy assembled an exhibition of the company's cause-related ideas.

There's now a new travelling exhibition, Saatchi & Saatchi & Social, to which this book is a companion piece.

The many outstanding campaigns for serious human issues in both vividly demonstrate the agency's focus on world-changing ideas.

A fascinating aspect of the work is how it functions as a form of social history, charting the changes in public concerns over the years.

For example, in relation to sex as a public health issue, less is heard now about contraception and more about AIDS.

On road safety, there is less about injury and more about pain.

Executionally, there is less use of two dimensions and more use of events and installations, or 'ideas bigger than ads'.

In style, there is today less stark shock and more lingering inference.

Shock is now considered an approach to be used with caution, for fear of 'compassion fatigue', the reasoning being that too-painful images will be counter-productive in gaining the audience's sympathy.

But sometimes this tactic seems unavoidable.

Italy's Greenpeace ad, Women and Children First, 1996 (p. 24) was produced by Stefano Maria Palombi and Luca Albanese to coincide with nuclear tests in the Pacific.

It shows a baby with hydrocephalus, his head hideously deformed as a result of his mother having been exposed to 'harmless' radiation fallout from earlier tests in Soviet Kazakhstan.

So horrifyingly bizarre is the image that it is necessary for the first line of copy to make it clear that this is a real documentary photograph, not a computer-generated distortion.

This is an interesting illustration that, although there are some cultural differences, the work here generally has a universal intelligibility, whichever country originated it.

Advertising has become the world's *lingua franca*.

That's why, everywhere, it is now increasingly possible to approach an issue with subtle implication rather than head-on.

In the UK campaign for the National Society for the Prevention of Cruelty to Children (NSPCC), Can't Look, 1999 (p. 26), there are no violent adults or abused children to be seen.

Consciously avoiding shocking imagery, creative team Kes Gray and Dennis Willison decided to use the most powerful tool possible.

The viewer's imagination.

So they set themselves a rule: show nothing, imply everything.

Thus there are no live people at all in the spot, only static depictions of children's icons – the Spice Girls, footballer Alan Shearer, Rupert The Bear and Action Man – all shielding their eyes from the painful events that we can hear.

Less is chillingly more.

The American novelist John Updike has invented an amusing phrase in talking of 'the oxymoronic concept of truth in advertising', but actually this is an outmoded misconception.

In fact, a very striking feature of the work in this book is the remarkable degree to which it does employ the power of truth.

Anyone who has ever written an ad knows that, in the face of the towering suspicion and scepticism of the average reader or viewer, lies and half-truths are startlingly ineffective.

At the same time, people who've worked on social campaigns will tell you they are often told true stories so horrible they could not be published.

More and more commercial advertisers are also realising that the way to gain the trust, loyalty, respect and affection of their audience is simply to tell the truth.

Of course, for this to be an effective commercial strategy, you will require a product whose truth, if told, is persuasive.

But why produce any other kind of product?

In social advertising, it's impossible to lie.

On any contentious issue (which is almost all of them), the smallest inaccuracy will be seized upon by opponents and used to discredit the entire argument.

To pre-empt this, every claim is carefully checked.

As a result, the long-copy ads in this book are as informative as most rigorously researched editorial articles on the same subject.

And, incidentally, better written.

As an example, take the NSPCC's Raped as a 3 Year Old, 1992 (p. 58), with its picture of a middle-aged man whom one initially assumes to be the perpetrator.

This ad is an outstanding example of how cool, matter-of-fact language, every trace of indignation and anger deliberately excluded by creative team Mike Boles and Jerry Hollens, can be enormously powerful.

It doesn't tell the reader how to think.

In the simplest, almost laconic terms, virtually devoid of adjectives, it reports the facts.

The anger the issue undoubtedly merits is produced entirely in the conclusions drawn by the reader.

Creative director Richard Myers recalls that when this poster ran in the stations of London's underground railway, its arresting headline and almost 500 words of copy stopped such large numbers of people, many missing trains to finish the text, that it had to be moved along the platforms to minimise the safety risk.

It would scarcely have been to the public good if anyone had fallen under a train in order to read even the most elegantly-written advertisement.

Another ad for the same client, showing a pregnant girl contemplating her bulging belly, and the headline We Both Have The Same Father, 1995 (p. 30), seems for a moment to have no edge to it, until the incestuous implications sink in.

This is just one example which illustrates that advertising and communications skills themselves have no inherent ideology.

They reflect their culture, not invent it.

And we live in a culture where social causes, as much as commercial products, require effective communications.

For not all social clients are non-commercial.

Road safety, anti-racism and anti-drug campaigns, recruitment for nurses and teachers, and social advertising supported by existing commercial clients are usually gained in competition with other agencies and paid for in the normal way.

More important, though, is the fact that social advertising focuses on ideas which achieve some kind of transformation of perceptions and attitudes on issues of serious public interest and importance.

Big ideas that turn small budgets into powerful campaigns.

Actual behaviour may be difficult to change immediately but at the very least an intrusive and dramatic idea can kick-start the raising of awareness that a problem exists.

There are numerous examples where a provocative and adventurous idea, supported by a minimal media budget, has generated many times more its value in column-inches of unpaid-for media coverage.

One example is the series for the UK's Commission for Racial Equality.

Here the headline puns by Chris Kirk and Giles Montgomery impart a bleak, gallows humour that was deliberately designed to evade the accusation of ranting.

In the Worst Marks poster, 1997 (p. 50), this enabled the ad to hint also at the issue of the academic performance of ethnic minorities.

In the case of Asian pupils, it is in fact above average.

Personal knowledge, as so often, illuminated the Junk Mail execution, 1997 (p. 171), one of several in the series which was art-directed by Ajab Samrai Singh who, as a 6-year-old growing up in a poor area of the English West Midlands, experienced petrol being poured through the letterbox of his parents' home.

A campaign like this appears as part of a continuing flood of fact and opinion in every medium and, for that matter, every type of workplace and social gathering.

But as with many social campaigns, despite a relatively small media budget, the striking content of the ads maximized exposure by generating huge amounts of editorial and public debate.

This led to awareness of the CRE and its objectives rising from 35 per cent to 50 per cent in the space of two years.

A great idea is revered for its wit, its pungency and originality, its impact or vibrant memorability.

It's what gets advertising people up in the morning, what provokes the most heated debate in the office or, late at night, in their corporate cups, the most enthusiasm, glee and affection.

For those whose talents, personal ambitions and professional preoccupations are focused every day on finding ways of changing minds and influencing behaviour, the Holy Grail is discovering world-transforming ideas.

Who said 'We are most true to ourselves when praising others'?

I have met few advertising people who do not admire the anti-drinking and driving ad, Glasses, 1993 (p. 140), from Singapore, created by Dean Turney and Francis Wee.

The idea is such a stunningly simple demonstration, the response of almost every copywriter and art director is, first, 'Why did nobody think of that before?'

And then, 'Why didn't I think of that before?'

From inside a car driving through a city, we see successive empty beer glasses placed in centre-screen, each obscuring the view slightly more.

After the fourth glass, when the view ahead is really unclear, the car smashes into the back of a bus.

So economical, in all senses, and so brilliant.

Jaw-dropping clarity of argument is also to be found in the poster for the UK's Gun Control Network, 1997 (p. 68).

Following the massacre of a class of schoolchildren in Dunblane, Scotland, the British government was introducing a law to ban certain firearms.

But the law excluded .22 handguns.

Amazed and angry, a creative team in London, Bill Gallacher, Robin Murtough and Keith Terry, had no money and no time, as the debate to approve the flawed law was imminent.

Having discovered that Robert Kennedy had been assassinated with a .22 handgun, they used a stock shot, improvisation and a Mac to create a billboard to be displayed on a truck outside parliament on the day of the debate.

It read: 'If a .22 handgun is less deadly, why isn't he less dead?'

The stunning impact of these few words helped get a ban on .22 handguns included in the firearms law.

As Tom Cordner, creative director in Los Angeles puts it, 'An ad may even be a great one, but you see it and it's gone. It's somewhat fleeting. But a great idea finds a place to linger in your soul. It stays with you.'

The background to this observation is that Saatchi & Saatchi believe the world is rapidly developing an attention-economy.

And in the attention-economy, as the worldwide creative director of the company, Bob Isherwood, says, 'Ideas are the currency of the future'.

If that's true, the biggest investment should not be in media but in ideas.

The American Advertising Agencies' Association estimates that US citizens are exposed to 3,000 commercial messages each day, in some form or another.

TV commercials, posters, press ads, logos, bus sides, supermarket floor stickers, product packaging: it's everywhere.

Of these, consumers say they have some sort of reaction to just... twelve.

When the welter of trash and trivia is so pervasive, and the background din of our communications culture so deafening, how can a message make itself heard?

Whether for a commercial client or on a social issue, this is clearly something of a challenge.

In fact even more so for a social client because the media budget available is always a fraction of that for commercial campaigns.

Therefore, if the ideas created for social clients can somehow successfully cut through the ambient racket, with all these attendant disadvantages, might they not also have some lessons for the communications problems of a wider range of clients?

Saatchi & Saatchi think it is possible to demonstrate that they have created a number of ideas which achieved transformations on various social topics.

One illustration of the sheer pleasure to be had in being persuaded to consider a serious issue comes from New Zealand.

Out-and-out hilarity is an unusual and tough angle to pull off in a road safety ad, but Glen Wood and Peter Force in the Grunge Angels TV spot, 1995 (p. 70) manage it with apparent ease.

The most at-risk target audience is represented by two young men.

To the sound of an angelic chorus, they find themselves in the clouds.

On the celestial PA system comes the announcement: 'For your entertainment this afterlife, we bring you Whitney Houston's Greatest Love Songs...'

They understandably regard an eternity of that as a fate worse than death.

The titles point out that 'Death Sucks' and it might be wise to wear seat belts.

Humour with a gloriously absurdist cast finds itself leavening another grim issue in Italy's War on Hunger ad for the UN Food & Agriculture Organisation, 1998 (p. 134).

It opens with monochrome documentary footage of an army in battle.

But it is soon revealed that their rockets are dayglo sweetcorn, their helicopters tomatoes.

Soldiers crawl through the undergrowth toting bananas for machine-guns.

A mortar barrage is fired with artichokes.

It's a crazy world.

The observation is appropriate when the global military budget spent differently would solve most of the world's problems with hunger.

It may be worth mentioning that many of the ads shown in this book have won the top creative awards in the world's leading competitions at Cannes, London, New York and elsewhere.

Awards may be the highly-prized fetish of the advertising business but being the best in the judgement of one's peers is hardly grounds for apology.

Apart from being more familiar with the competitive genres, the judges' response to an eloquent appeal is no different from that of any other human being.

It only illustrates that these ideas and executions have outstanding drama, excitement and potency, often achieved while addressing new and difficult types of challenge.

There is a myth entertained by some who are interested in advertising industry creative competitions that social and charity ads are some kind of soft option for winning awards.

In fact the opposite is true, the relevant categories invariably being the most heavily-subscribed.

All entries benefit equally from the same types of emotive subject matter.

Contrary to popular belief, however, it is very hard to get it right and very easy to get it wrong.

In most respects, social and commercial advertising present similar problems.

But in one respect, they differ.

A basic challenge that makes social communications so difficult but so rewarding if done successfully, is that the aim is to transform first the perceptions, then the attitudes of an audience on a subject they would probably prefer not to think about at all.

Unlike conventional commercial advertising, there is little prospect of offering the audience much self-gratification if they accept your argument.

If it is true, as Dr. Johnson said, that 'the soul of an advertisement is promise, big promise', what is the 'promise' of social advertising?

As we slump over our Sunday coffee and croissants, we really don't want to think about AIDS or landmines or cruelty to children.

We don't want to regard ourselves as perhaps part of the problem of racism, road accidents or environmental destruction.

We certainly don't want to face the fact that by simple inaction we may be contributing to the plight of hungry children, refugees or oppressed minorities.

'We're all guilty', they say.

Do we really have to talk about that now?

Well, yes actually, if we're to try to make the world a slightly better place.

In the social field advertising people have to discover a point of access to the audience's sympathies when there is little possibility of appealing to the self-interested or acquisitive impulse.

In seeking this, a helpful paradigm devised in the early 1940s by an American academic, A H Maslow, is proving to be useful in explaining why consumers, especially in wealthier societies, are increasingly turning away from crudely materialistic appeals to their self-interest.

Maslow's hypothesis is that humans have a 'Hierarchy of Needs', usually illustrated by a pyramid, at the base of which are the Physiological needs of overcoming hunger and thirst.

Above these are the Safety needs of security and protection.

Next are the Social needs of a sense of belonging and love.

One step higher are the Esteem needs of recognition, self-esteem and status.

Finally, at the apex of the pyramid, are the Self-actualization needs of self-development and realization.

This hypothesis is consistent with the frequently-made observation that, throughout the world, traditionally-respected pillars of society are today held in measurably lower regard than before.

Governments, churches, police, armed forces, in Britain the monarchy and in the USA the presidency, have all been shown to share the same human failings as the rest of us.

On the other hand, certain companies and brands have been increasing their perceived levels of public trust and confidence.

There is concrete evidence for this.

People are increasingly responding to banks and investment funds which firmly state an ethical policy of avoiding shareholdings in environment-unfriendly companies, or in corporations whose prosperity depends on damaging their customers' health, or in companies which exploit Third World suppliers.

Investors are willing to do this even though they know it is likely to reduce the rate of return on their savings.

The financial pages of the newspapers now list significant numbers of ethical investment funds.

The Co-operative Bank in Britain has a markedly lower turnover of account holders than other banks and is now the largest issuer of Gold VISA cards in the whole of Europe.

In fashion and cosmetics Liz Claiborne and The Body Shop have both prospered on an ethical stance.

In addition, many commercial organisations are discovering that, when making choices between products or services of more or less parity, consumers are increasingly favouring those which identify themselves with a relevant non-commercial cause.

Doing this has become known as Cause-Related Marketing.

For example, Procter & Gamble in Australia is linked with the Save The Children Fund. Even in an economically emerging market like India, Procter & Gamble is already working with UNESCO to bring child workers back into schools.

The Tesco supermarket chain in Britain supports Computers For Schools.

Harley-Davidson n the USA works with the Muscular Dystrophy Association.

American Express runs the Charge Against Hunger campaign.

For a fuller discussion of the topic of Cause-Related Marketing, I recommend the currently definitive book on the subject, the excellent Brand Spirit, by Hamish Pringle & Marjorie Thompson (John Wiley & Sons, UK, 1999).

Broadly speaking, the book's conclusion is that corporations which ignore the social dimension in their communications will increasingly tend to be rejected by consumers, although it must be recognised that not all types of social issue will attract corporate sponsorship.

In preparing this text, I have spoken to many of the people who created the work, and asked them why they find it professionally so interesting and personally so rewarding.

Most have a strong personal sympathy or even identification with the issue, which usually has a purpose which is self-evidently worthwhile.

Most causes themselves are inherently dramatic, so there is no need to borrow interest from outside.

The clients usually have a clear brief, a passion to communicate it, and a willingness to be brave in how they do so.

The customary limitations on what they have to spend commit them to supporting adventurous ideas which have a huge, immediate impact.

It must be said, however, that social clients are not reckless in what they approve.

Their campaigns often demand results that are clearly measurable, by popular response, or by government statistics, or monetary returns in fund-raising, or by the volume of public, political or media debate generated.

Much the same, in fact, as commercial clients demand.

There's no surprise in that.

Both operate in markets where there are many competing brands.

Both must overcome obstacles and resistance to their messages.

Both must find ways of getting under the radar of sceptical audiences.

Both need to get people talking about them.

Both need to be provocative in order to get a response at the lowest possible cost.

Yet both must do so in ways that preserve the integrity of their brands.

Both, it seems, need the power of simple ideas that translate into simple choices.

Both need ideas that can transform people's lives.

Ideas like those in this book.

18

Pram/Family Planning, The Health Education Council, UK, 1975

'You don't wanna be bothered with all that family plannin' stuff, love – Scott! Leave orf, will ya? – I mean, what can all them doctors and clinics tell ya that anyone with a bit of common couldn't work out for themselves? Or ask a friend. That's what I did – Anna! Leave that baby alone! 'ow many times I gotta tell ya? – If you don't wanna get pregnant, you should... y'know what I mean... be careful an' that. Just use your 'ead.'

VOICEOVER: Don't listen to old wives' tales about family planning. Your doctor or clinic will welcome you, married or single, with friendly and accurate advice. Look in the phone book under Family Planning.

'... Anyway – with this lot, 'ow could I afford contraceptives?'

VOICEOVER: It'll cost you nothing.

Pram/Family Planning, The Health Education Council, UK, 1975

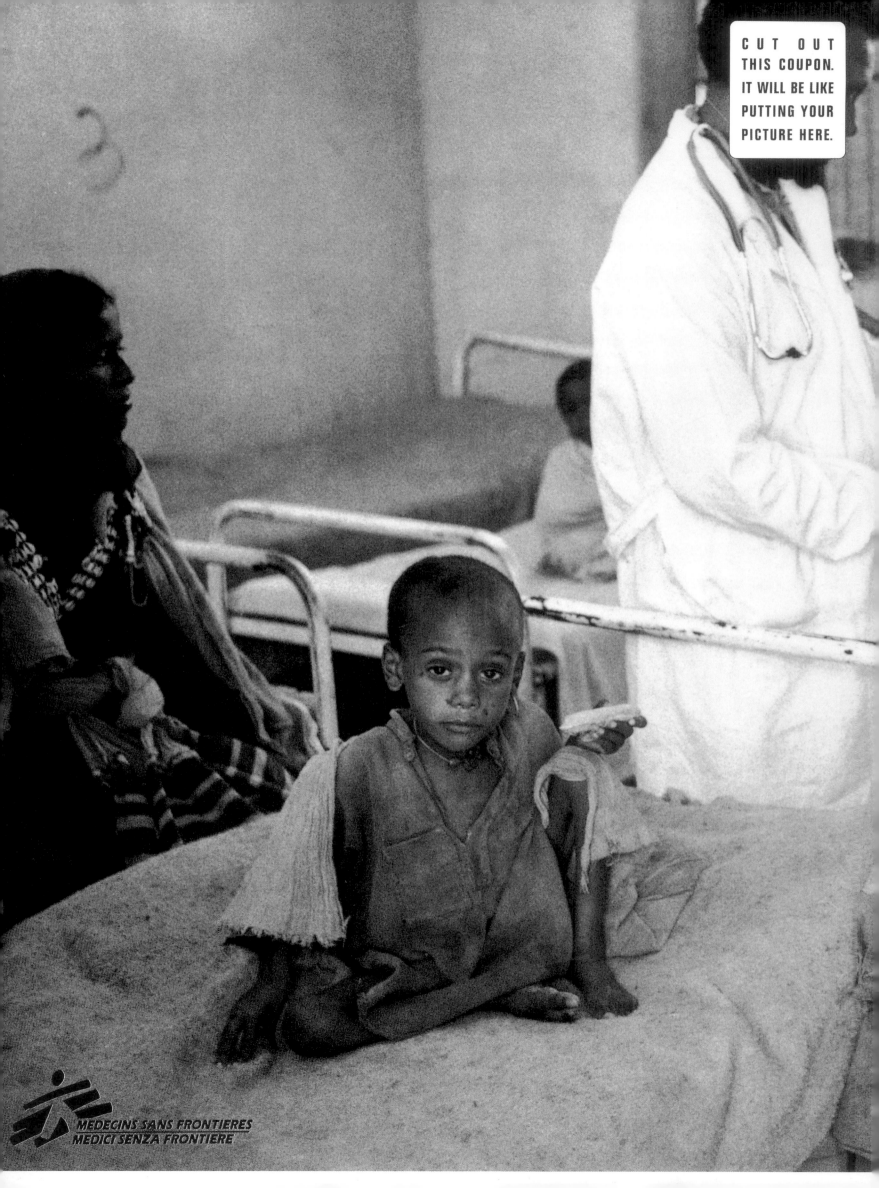

CUT OUT
THIS COUPON.
IT WILL BE LIKE
PUTTING YOUR
PICTURE HERE.

MEDECINS SANS FRONTIERES
MEDICI SENZA FRONTIERE

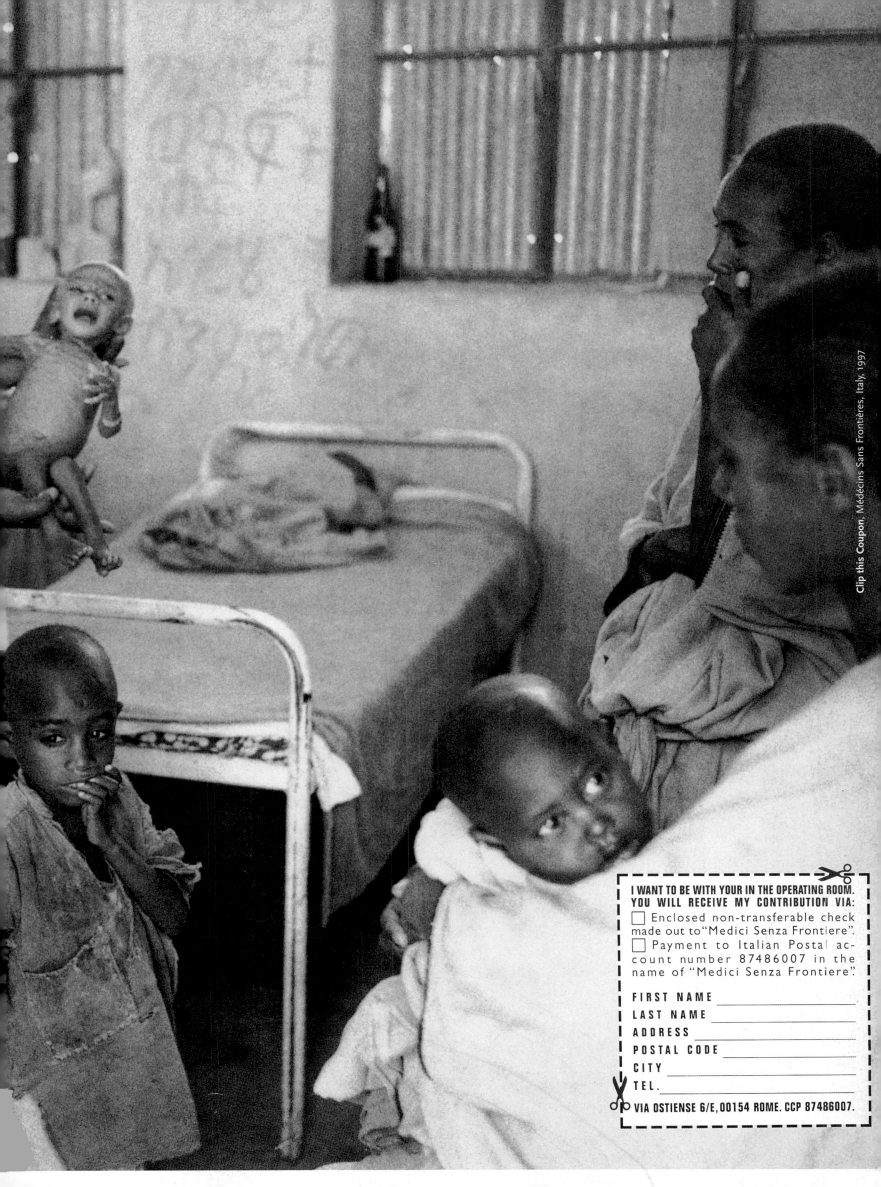

Clip this Coupon. Médécins Sans Frontières, Italy, 1997

And the Nuclear Powers said: women and children first.

No, this is not a graphic elaboration. It's a child from Kazakistan, born with hydrocephalus. This deformity is a result of the radiation the child's mother was exposed to. Now, don't get angry with us for showing to you, get angry with those who hid it from you, maintaining that nuclear tests are not risky.

GREENPEACE

Scene 1
WOMAN: Shut up!
I'm going to smack your face against that door if you don't stop that screaming now.

Scene 2
MAN: Come and sit over here.

Scene 3
MAN: You're brainless. You're stupid. You're no child of mine.

Scene 4
CHILD: Mummy, where are you?
I don't like being on my own.

Scene 5
MAN: Not a word to anyone. This is going to be our little secret.

VOICEOVER: Sometimes we can't bear to look either.
Cruelty to children can be stopped and with your help it can be stopped forever.
Please support the NSPCC Full Stop campaign.

TITLE: Cruelty to children must stop.
Full Stop.

Can't Look, National Society for the Prevention of Cruelty to Children (NSPCC), UK, 1999

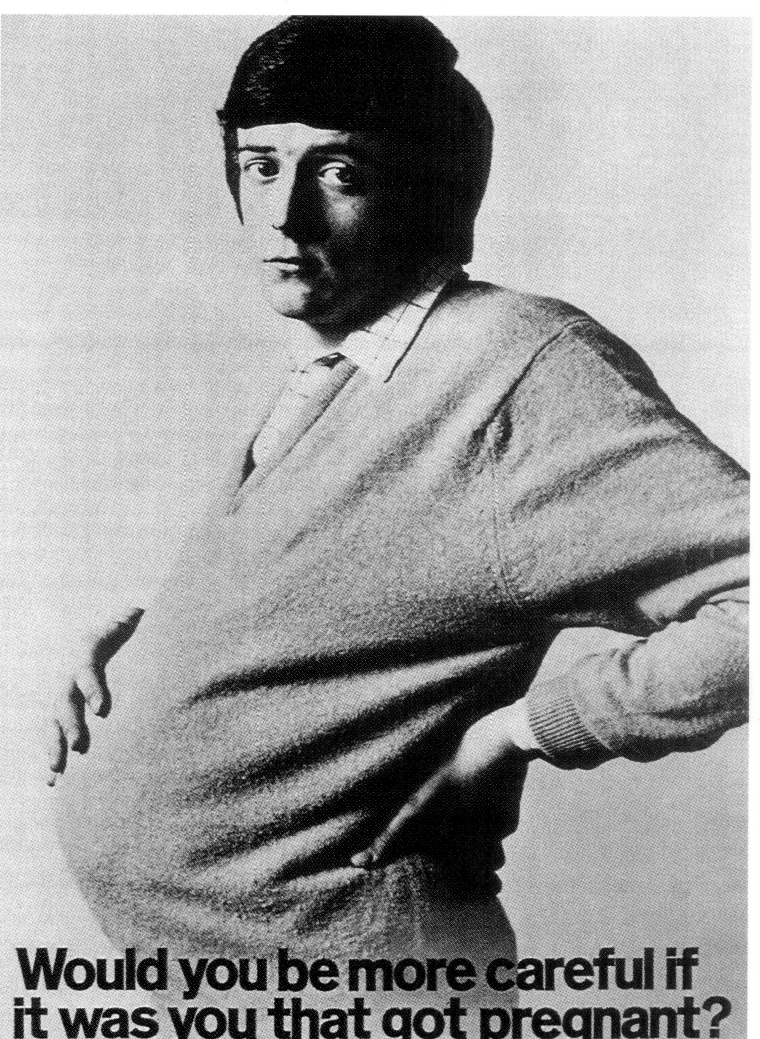

Would you be more careful if it was you that got pregnant?

Anyone married or single can get advice on contraception from the Family Planning Association. Margaret Pyke House, 27-35 Mortimer Street, London W1 N 8BQ. Tel. 01-636 9135.

The Health Education Council

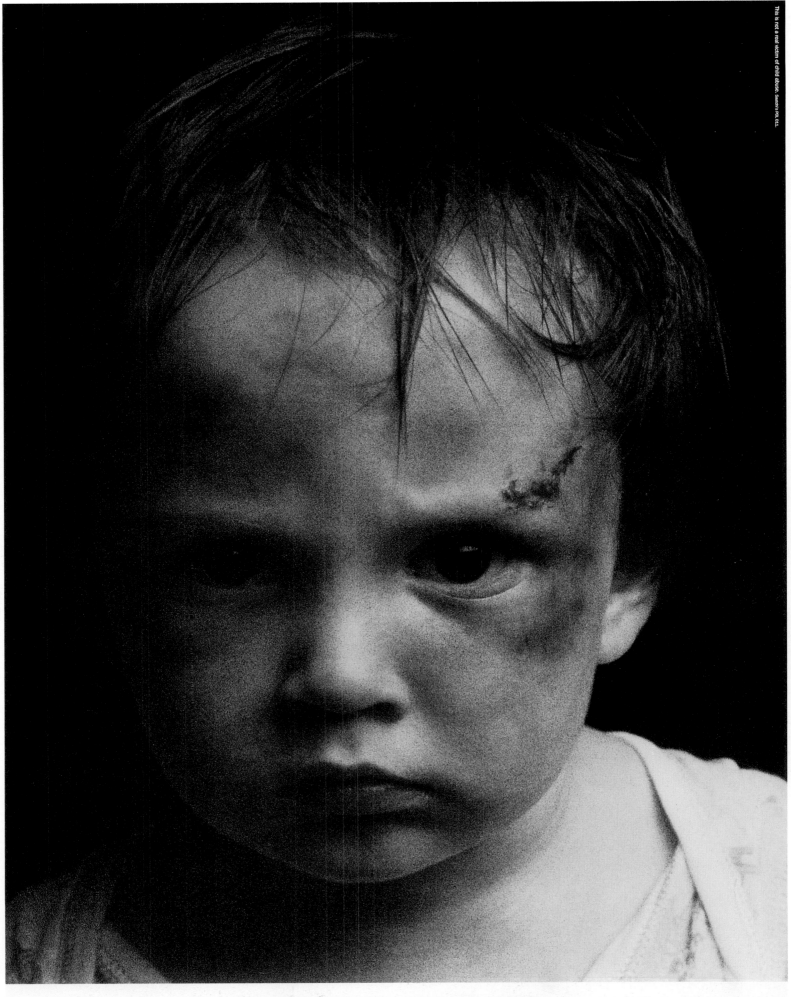

This is not a real victim of child abuse. *Sample is POL 011.*

REPORT IT
AND STOP IT.
NSW POLICE SERVICE

SOME FATHERS CHANGE THEIR BABIES.

You can see the damage that's been done to this child's head. Or can you?

The fact is that while the physical wounds will heal in time, the mental scars will last a lifetime.

Changing a happy well-balanced child into a nervous wreck.

Thousands of children are abused in this way each year. By their fathers and their mothers alike.

But if you suspect that a child is being abused by anyone, you're the one who's responsible.

Because, after all, if you're not reporting child abuse you might as well be doing it.

If you have any information about the abuse of children, please call us on Wednesday September 4th.

1 800 011 233
REPORT IT
AND STOP IT.
NSW POLICE SERVICE

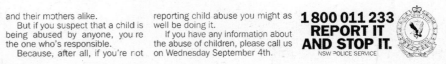

Some Fathers, NSW Police, Australia, 1996

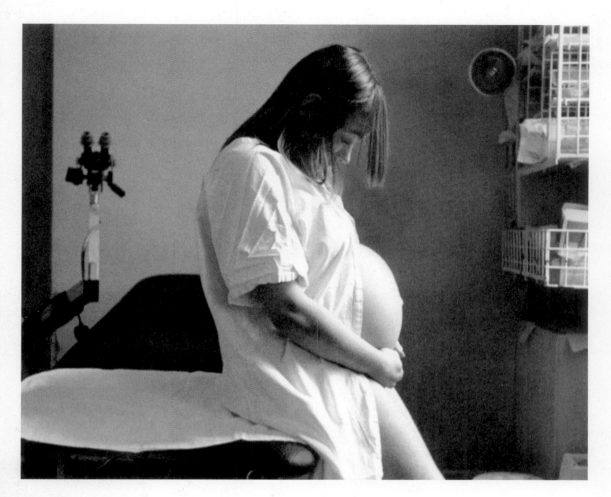

WE both have the same Father.

This is Sally's story.

'My mum died when I was twelve. One night when I had a bad dream my dad said I could sleep in his bed.

To start with he just cuddled me, but then he started doing other things. I wanted him to stop but he wouldn't. I hated it, it really hurt. He said it meant he loved me.

The next day when I was leaving for school he said I mustn't tell anyone about what happened. After that he wanted me to sleep with him every night. He called it our little secret.

Later, when my periods stopped my dad kept me off school. He told them that I was ill.

Sometimes I can feel the baby moving inside me, it feels horrible.'

Luckily Sally's school reported her absence and now she's getting all the support she needs.

Of course, there's more to her abuse than becoming pregnant.

She'll need long term counselling to tackle the emotional damage, such as feelings of guilt and an inability to form relationships.

In fact, all forms of abuse can cause emotional harm. Not just the more obvious forms involving sexual assault and physical brutality.

For example, withdrawal of any signs of affection, ignoring children, constantly criticizing or shouting at them can lead to emotional scars which last a lifetime. Sometimes, children can even be driven to commit suicide.

Because of all this, the NSPCC is launching 'A Cry for Children'. It's a cry to everyone to stop and think about their behaviour towards children.

To recognise the impact that any form of cruelty can have on a child. And to realise that the way children are treated affects their whole lives.

Please answer the cry.

If you, or someone you know is suffering abuse, call the NSPCC Child Protection Helpline on 0800 800 500.

Or if, after reading this, you would find more information helpful, please call us on 071 825 2775.

NSPCC
A cry for children.

Same Father, National Society for the Prevention of Cruelty to Children (NSPCC), UK, 1995

DOES THE WORLD HAVE ITS PRIORITIES RIGHT?

The State of the World Forum is bringing together many of the world's most influential people to debate vital issues facing humanity-----nuclear disarmament-----ending conflict-----the role of women and child development. Its about getting our future priorities right. Join the debate via our website between 27 October and 1 November.----- It's your chance to change the world.

STATE
of the
WORLD
FORUM

www.worldforum.org

STATE of the
WORLD
FORUM

www.worldforum.org

Astronaut, State of the World Forum, New Zealand, 1998

THIS GIRL WANTS A CHAT

LOST YOUR PATIENCE?

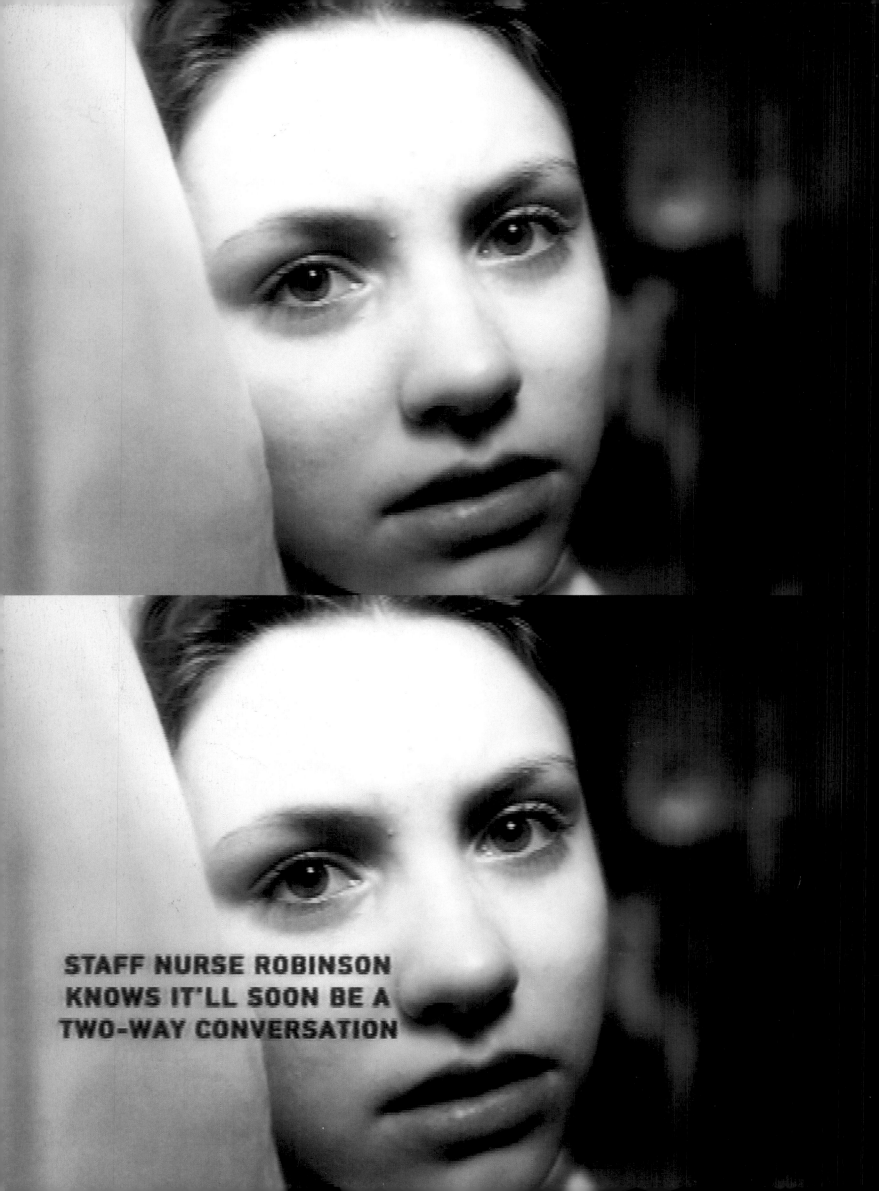

STAFF NURSE ROBINSON
KNOWS IT'LL SOON BE A
TWO-WAY CONVERSATION

NURSE ROBINSON'S VOICE: Hi Rachel, you've got me again. Another girls' night in eh?

TITLE: The New NHS needs more nurses.

VOICEOVER: Nurses make a difference. For information on nursing or returning to nursing with
improved pay and conditions call 0845 60 60 655

VOICEOVER: It's here where one in ten of all killings take place.

There are one to two deaths every week.

In a year there are over 5000 beatings, and over 1700 sexual assaults.

36

TITLE: In Britain, 36,000 children live with the threat of being abused every day.
NSPCC. A Cry for Children.

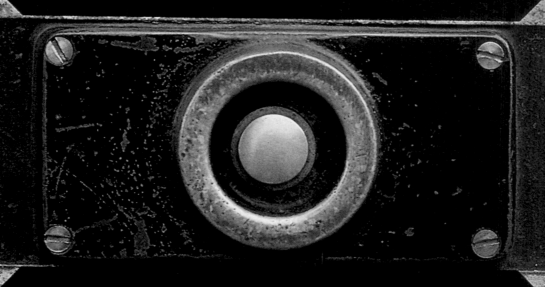

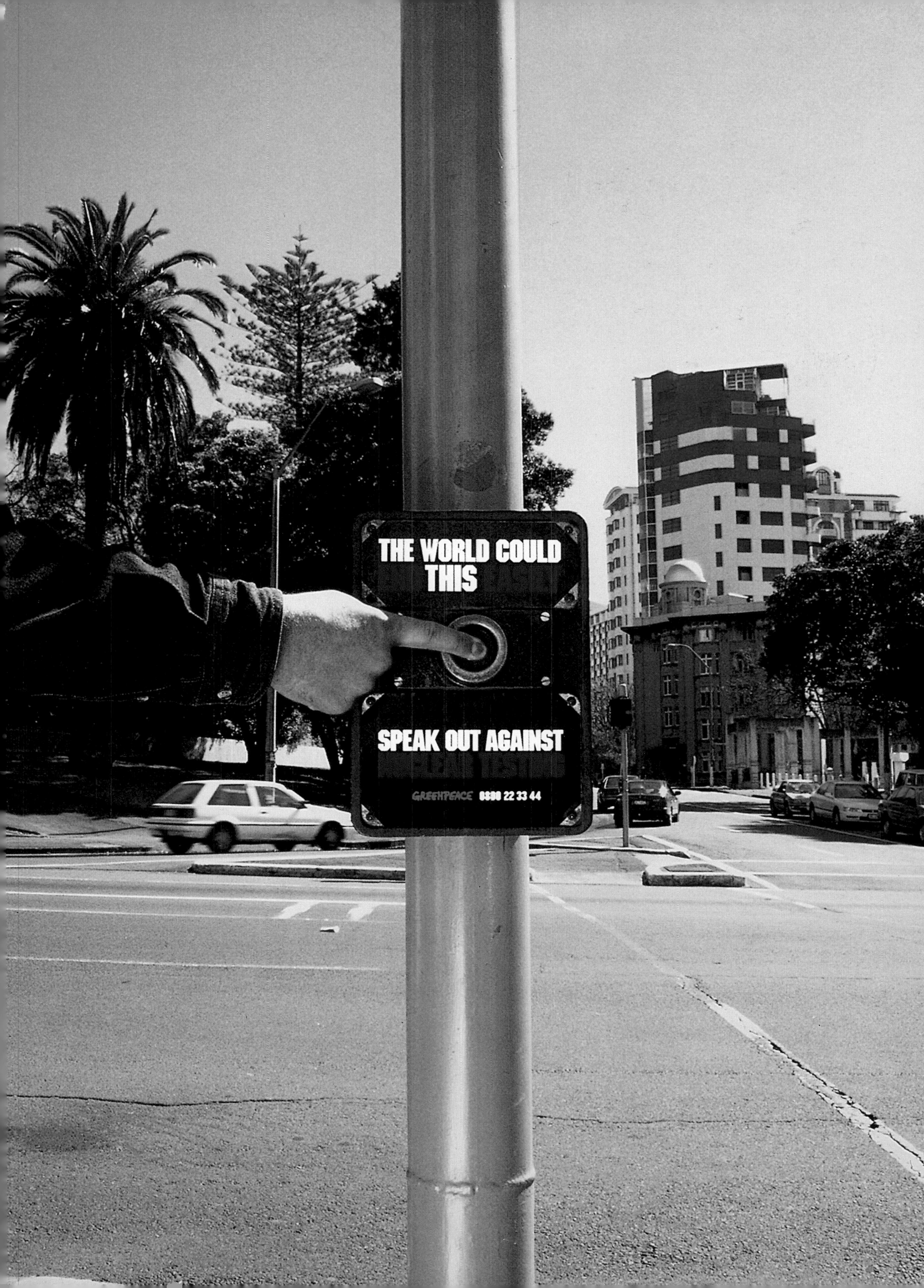

THE WORLD COULD
THIS
SPEAK OUT AGAINST
GREENPEACE 0800 22 33 44

The World Could End This Easily, Greenpeace, New Zealand, 1998

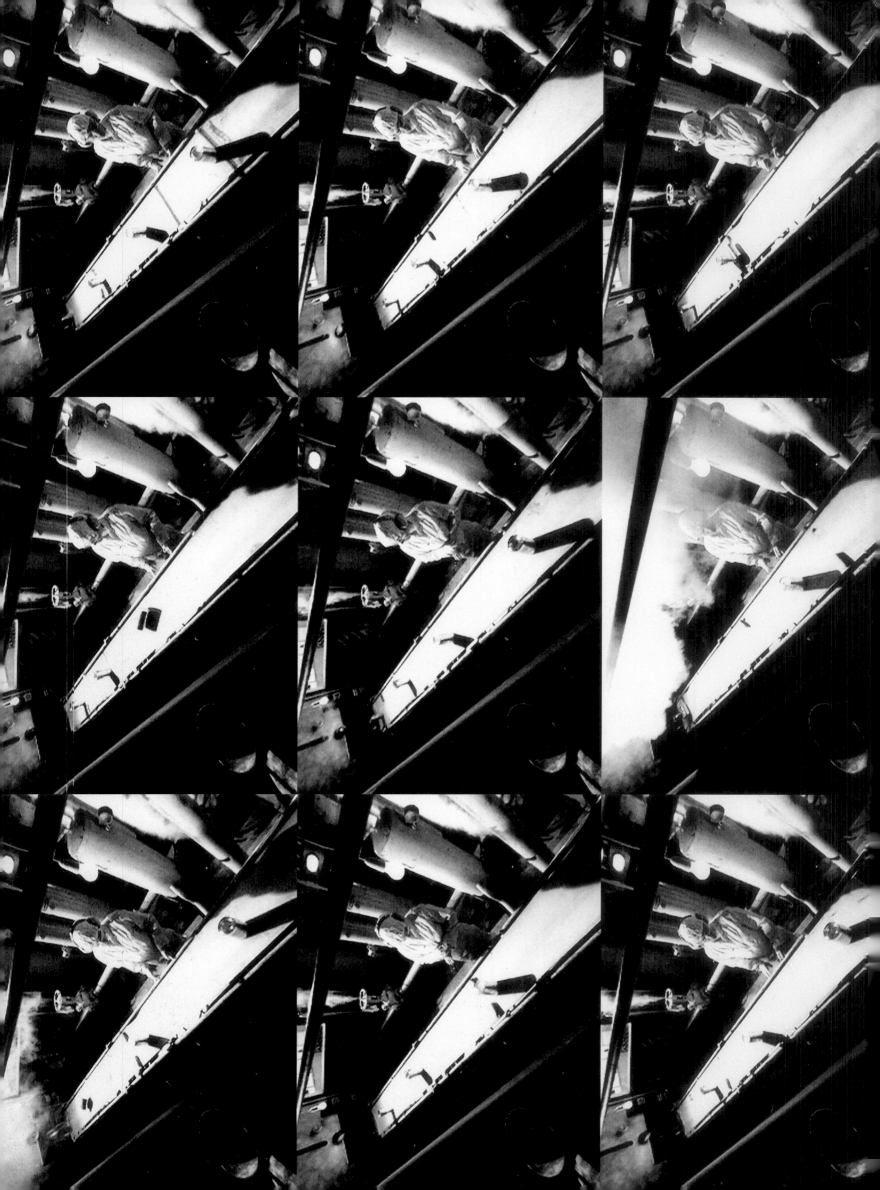

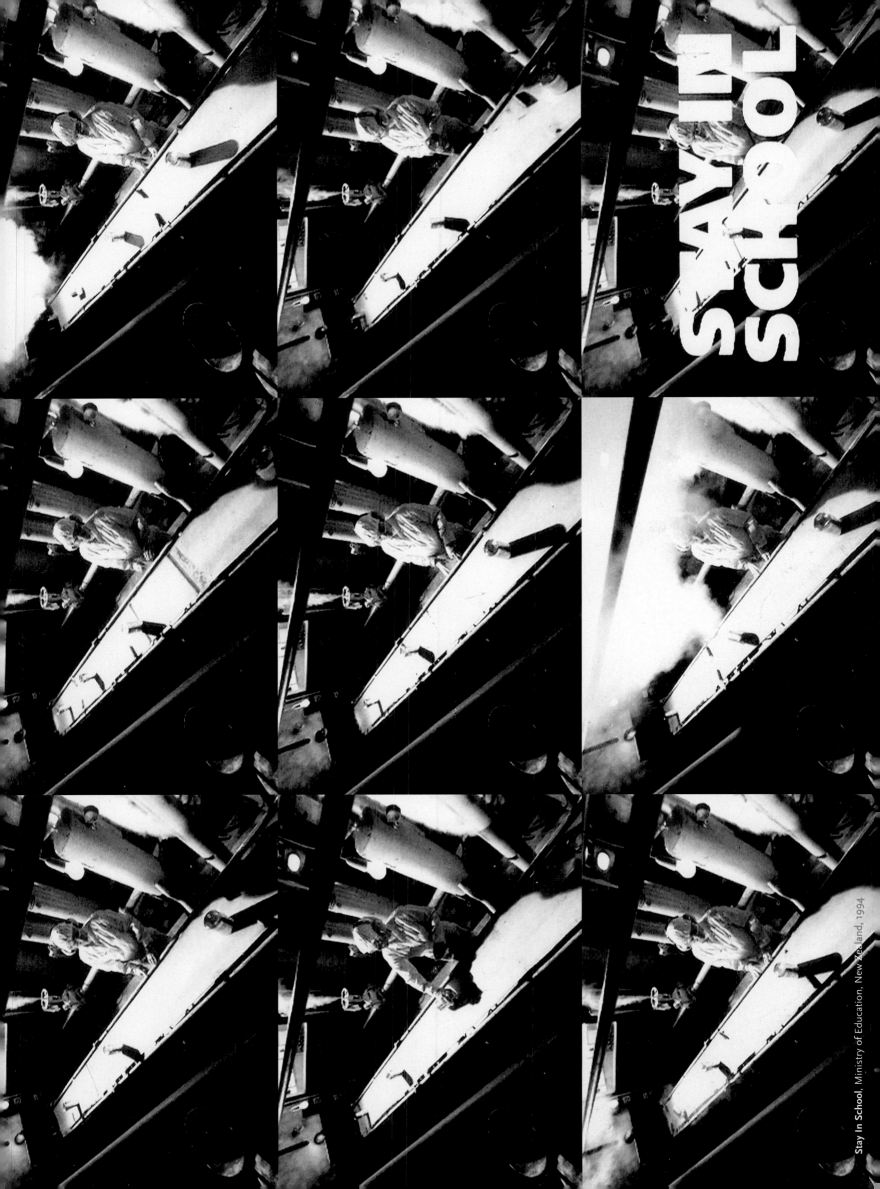

STAY IN SCHOOL

'If I said the word "fuck" it would probably bother you.
If I told you I was hungry, it probably wouldn't.
Fuck, I'm hungry.'

TITLE: Good food should never go to waste.

Hungry, Second Harvest, Canada, 1994

Day Against Violence. Italian Football Association, Italy, 1995

Day Against Violence, Italian Football Association, Italy, 1995

TITLES: It seemed impossible.
It happened on the 12th February 1995.
One billion seven hundred million people saw it all over the world.
For the first time ever.
The Italian football teams entered the field wearing the other team's shirts.
And they read a message, that football must unite, not divide.
Today, that idea belongs to everyone.
Nothing is impossible.

Worst Marks, Commission for Racial Equality, UK, 1997

He'd been struggling with multiplication. *He simply couldn't see how it worked until his teacher came up with a different way of explaining it.*

A TEACHER PASSING
AN EXAMINATION.

The moment when a pupil grasps a concept which has been proving difficult is probably one of the best things about teaching. It means that the teacher has found a way through that makes sense. It couldn't be more significant.

GETTING the penny to drop is at the very heart of teaching. It's the connection between knowledge being imparted and understood. For the teacher and the pupil it's a shared achievement.

It's the very thing that may draw you towards a career in teaching. If it does, you'll be pleased to learn that the other rewards are worthwhile too.

From December, there's a starting salary of around £14,000 for primary and secondary school teachers with a good honours degree in inner London (including inner London allowance and supplement).

The Head teacher of a large inner London secondary school could expect to earn up to £48,000.

It isn't easy money, of course. After all, teaching isn't a mechanical process. It can't be.

Each class is made up of pupils with a wide range of abilities, interests, attitudes and backgrounds.

As a teacher you have to learn about these differences, remember them and respond to them.

For instance, the speed at which children learn varies between individuals and between topics, yet the teacher has to reach them all.

Blank faces may call for an entirely novel way of explaining something, and an inventive approach can work wonders for classroom morale generally.

In a sense, a teacher sits an examination every day. And has to pass.

A daunting prospect or an invigorating challenge? If you think it's the latter, training can take your urge to teach and hone your natural skills to prepare you for the daily examination. And for a career that's doubly rewarding.

You can learn about becoming a teacher by ringing 0345 300121 quoting Dept. code IS/4/A or sending off the coupon below.

Teaching brings out the best in people.

Teacher Passing an Examination, Department of Education and Science, UK, 1992

Class, what's your New Year's resolution?

TITLE: In the Philippines, thousands of children spend New Year's Day in hospitals with fingers missing and hands blown off due to cheaply manufactured firecrackers.
This campaign aims to put an end to the vicious cycle.

Ma'am, I won't play with firecrackers anymore.

Resolution, Anti-Firecrackers, Philippines, 1995

TITLE: This New Year hands off Firecrackers.

Would you like to work in Europe as a PROSTITUTE?

There are millions of women who have no choice.

Like immigrant women who are deceived by international sex dealing organizations. They are victims of exploitation, and cannot make decisions regarding their own lives.

You will be surprised to learn about the methods used nowadays to diminish the human being.

Manos Unidas wants to end these ways of abuse. Help us abolish slavery.

Manos Unidas

BARQUILLO, 38 · 3º · 28004 MADRID · Tel. 91 308 20 20 · Fax: 91 308 42 08

As you can see from the page insert on the left, you can find this execution amongst the classified ads (job opportunities section) in the main Spanish newspapers.

E cosa posso farci?

Tutto, meno che ucciderla.

MAN 1:	Beautiful girl, eh?
MAN 2:	Is she a virgin?
MAN 1:	Sure, she's my daughter.
MAN 2:	How much?
MAN 1:	Only 100 Dollars.
MAN 2:	What does she do?
MAN 1:	Everything – but don't kill her
	... come along sweetheart.

VOICEOVER:	If it happened to your daughter, you'd be frightened, wouldn't you?
	When you're abroad, remember it. A child is a child all over the world.
TITLE:	Centro Italiano per L'adozione Internationale

Child Abuse, The Italian Centre for International Adoption (CIAI), Italy, 1997

What's it like to be raped as a 3 year old? A victim explains.

I FIRST remember being sexually abused by my father when I was about 3. It may have happened before, I don't know.

I can see it now, me lying in bed, with that big face coming towards me. He'd kiss me good-night, but he didn't stop at kissing.

He used to tell me it was our secret. And if I ever told anyone about it I'd be sent away.

But even as a child I knew something wasn't right. It was those words, "I'll protect you." How could he be protecting me? He was bloody hurting me.

It's strange really, he was my enemy, but at the same time my only friend in the world. He made me depend on him. He controlled me. My body was his toy for more than 9 years.

At school I found it hard to mix. I felt different. I'd never let anyone get close to me. In the changing rooms after P.E. I hated people seeing my naked body. I was so ashamed, thought they might be able to tell what had been happening to me and call me a poofter.

Even when I managed to find a girlfriend I still wasn't sure if I was heterosexual. I was terribly rough with her. I suppose I wanted to be in control of someone, like my father was with me.

Sex terrified me. Having an orgasm just made me think of what my father did inside of me. And that big smiling face.

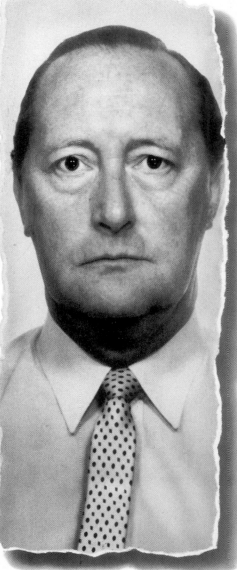

I met someone else eventually. We got married. After 2 years she left me. She said I was cold and didn't understand her.

But that's how I was. I just wasn't aware of causing or feeling mental or physical pain. Something inside me had been switched off long ago. There were times when I could actually cut myself with a knife and not feel a thing.

After the divorce, I turned to drink. It was a way of escaping. But I still suffered deep depressions.

Last year, my father finally died. I think that's what made me contact the NSPCC. I was 53 years old, and it was the first time I'd ever told anyone about my childhood.

Once a week for 6 months a Child Protection Officer worked with me. He got me to tell him everything about my experience. Talking about it was very painful. For over 40 years I guess I'd been trying not to think about it.

Eventually though, it started to work. He made me realise that what happened wasn't my fault.

For the first time I can ever remember I actually began to feel good about myself. It was just like being let out of a dark and lonely cell.

I'll never forget what happened to me. But at least I can start to live my life.

For further information on the work of the NSPCC, or to make a donation, please write to: NSPCC, 67 Saffron Hill, London, EC1N 8RS or call 071 242 1626.

To report a suspected case of abuse, call the NSPCC Child Protection Helpline on 0800 800 500.

NSPCC
Act Now For Children.

Raped as a 3 Year Old, National Society for the Prevention of Cruelty to Children (NSPCC), UK, 1992

DOCTOR JEKYLL.

MISTER HYDE.

You are a reliable, affectionate, and attentive family man. You have a beautiful wife and a lovely nine year old daughter. Your family's love is the greatest of all blessings to you. You would defend it against anything and anybody. Then, comes the time when you have to go away on business. You're going to an exotic destination, Bangkok for example, one of those countries where anything is tolerated, where 'they have quite different traditions and customs'. And there, together with shirts and souvenirs in an open-air market, they offer you a little girl. She is a pretty 9 year old girl who resembles your daughter a little, but actually looks more like a full-grown woman. You think that this is just the way they do things over there, and your quick-change starts: you are turning into a different person. The world paedophilia market, a rich and powerful market of death, is counting on another win. In fact, most of their profits do not come from criminals and perverts. They come from ordinary people, people like yourself. At CIAI (the Italian Center for International Adoption) they have been fighting to assert a very simple concept for many years, which no-one should ever forget, especially when travelling abroad: a child is a child, wherever you are in the world.

DONATIONS CAN BE CHARGED TO YOUR CREDIT CARD BY CALLING ON NUMBER +39-2-55.01.20.11 OR BY BANK TRANSFER TO A/C N. 10837 AT CARIPLO, BRANCH 15, MILAN, ITALY.

CIAI
CENTRO ITALIANO
PER L'ADOZIONE
INTERNAZIONALE
Via oltrocchi, 11 Milano

Dr Jekyll, Mr Hyde, The Italian Centre for International Adoption (CIAI), Italy, 1997

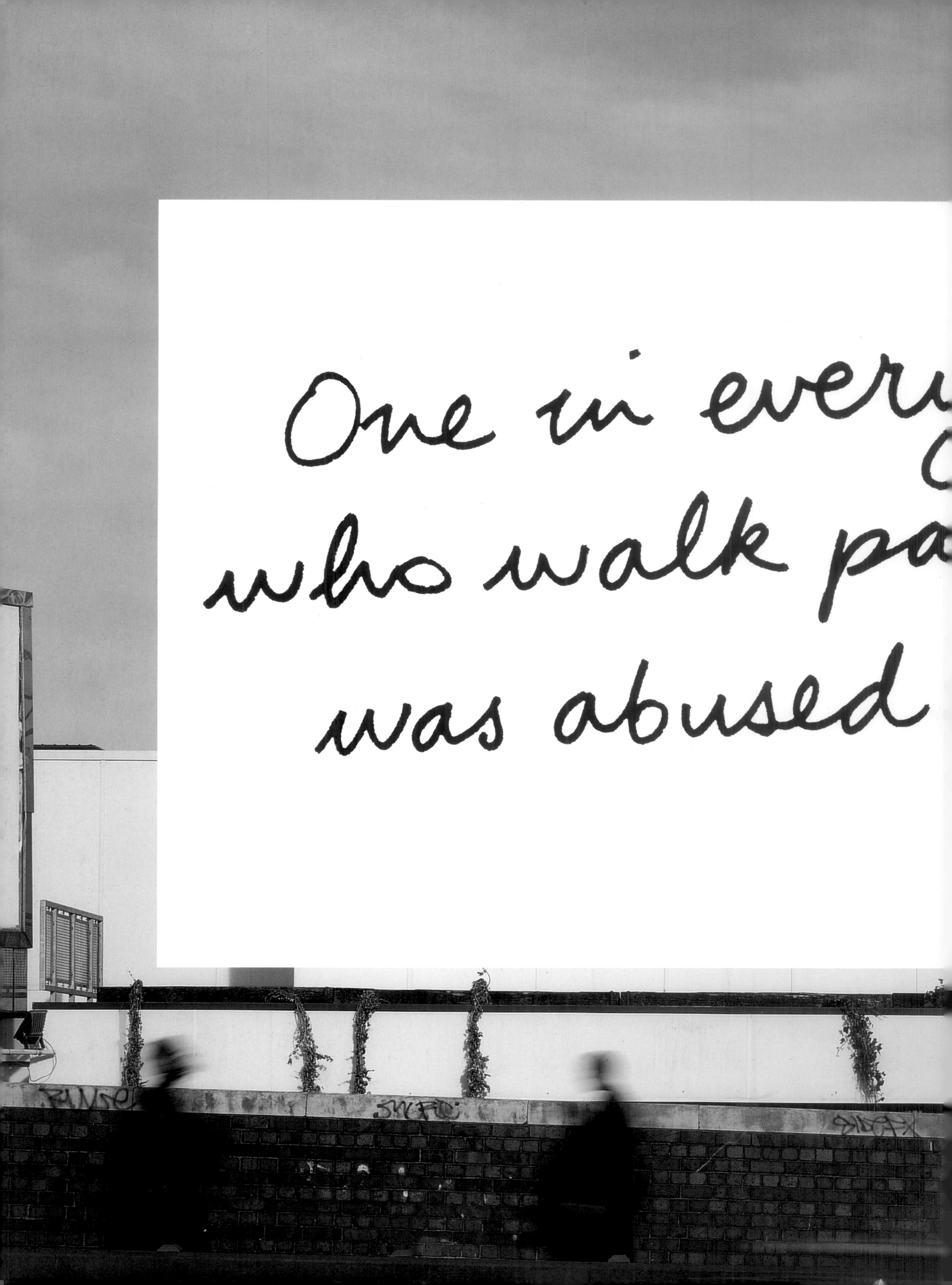
One in ever
who walk pa
was abused

NSPCC

A cry for children.

BanG
baNg
BANG
Gun
THANK YOU
OUTDOOR

Ph. 799·2547
BanG
Bang
BanG
BANG
Bang
BANG
baNg
BANG
Bang
Gun
THANK YOU
OUTDOOR PLUS

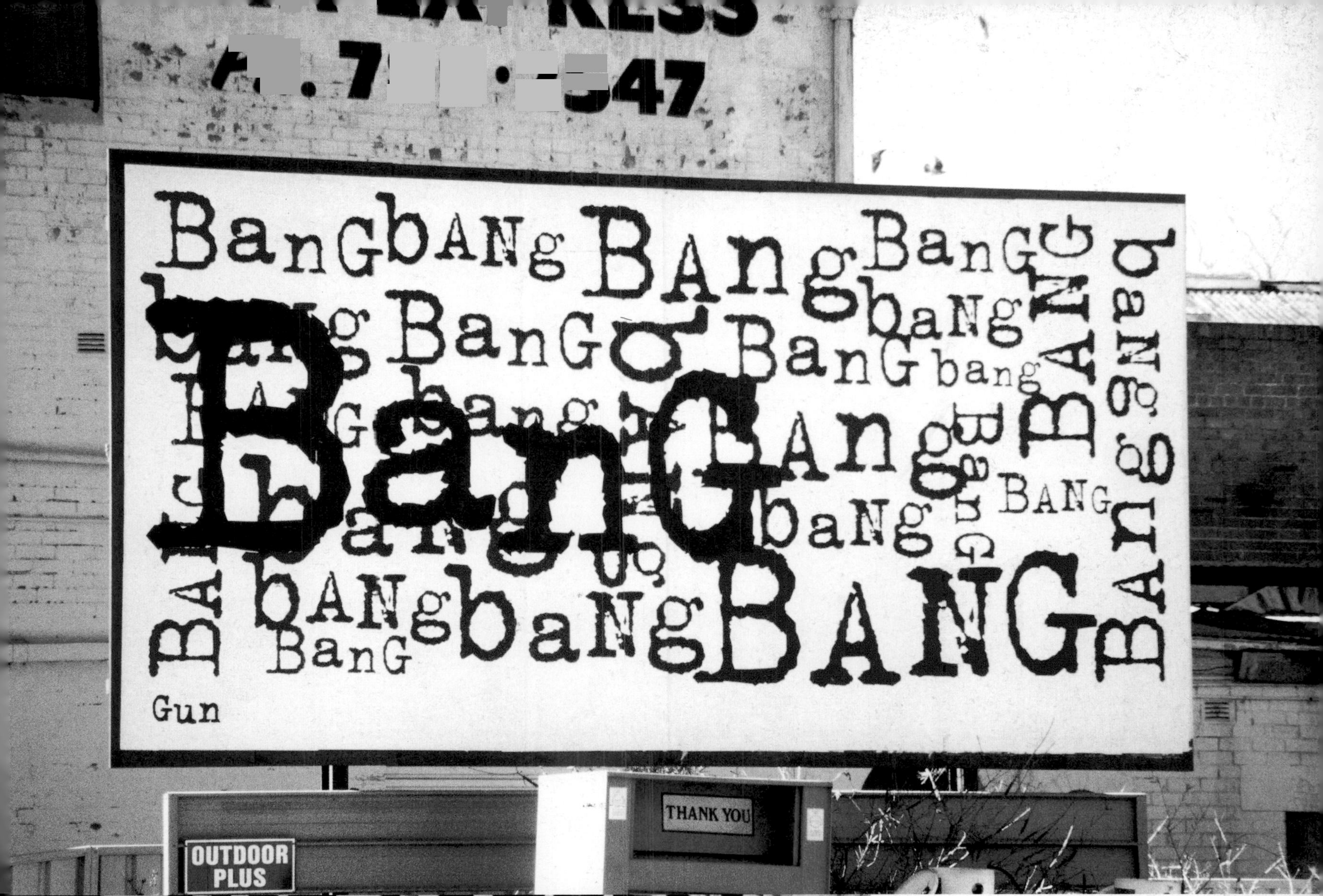

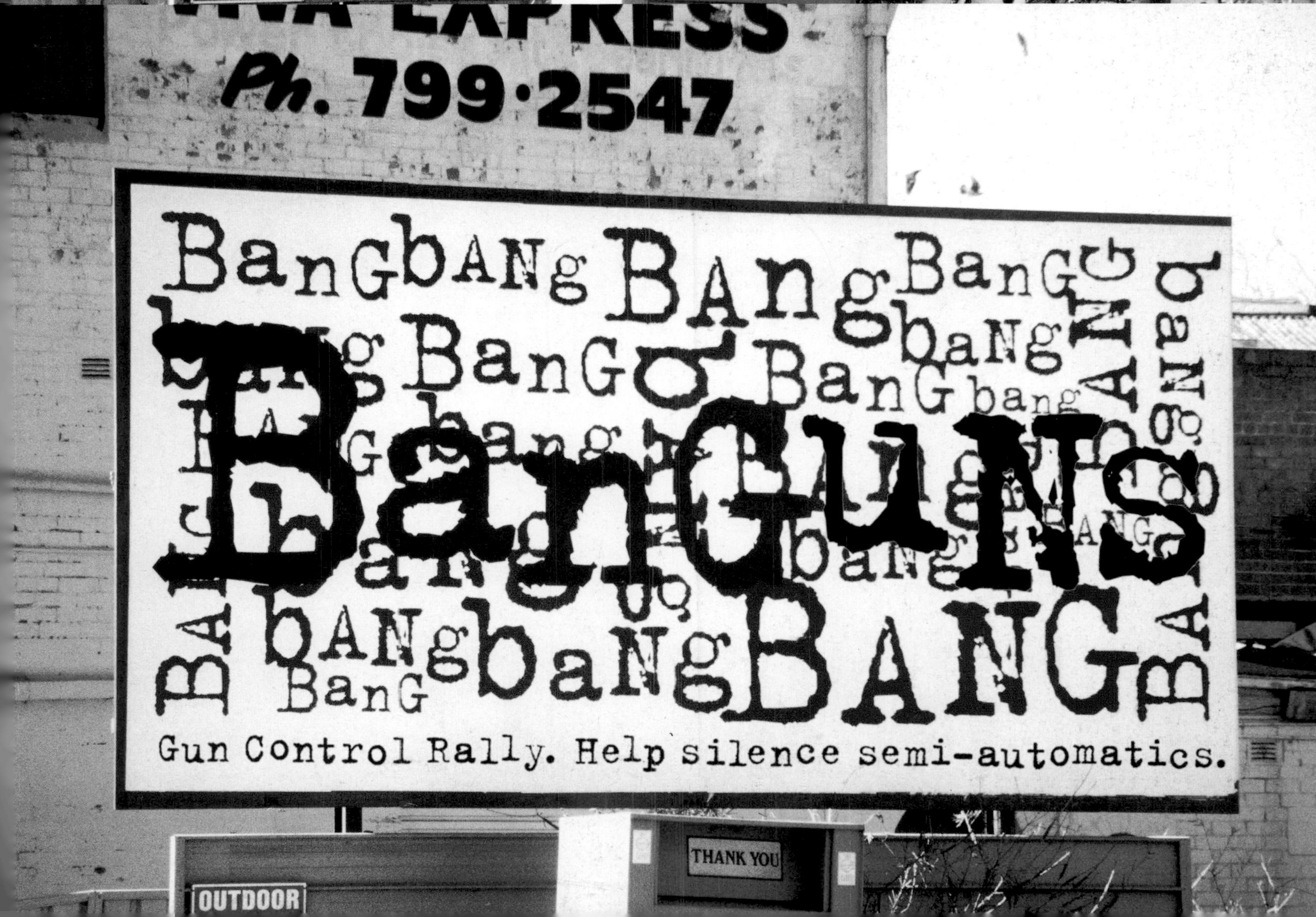

Ban Guns. Coalition for Gun Control, Australia, 1996

PENIS WITHOUT A
Get free ones by calling

ONDOM.
50-8629.

Iniciativa
Comunitaria

Bullet, Iniciativa Comunitaria AIDS/Condoms, Puerto Rico, 1999

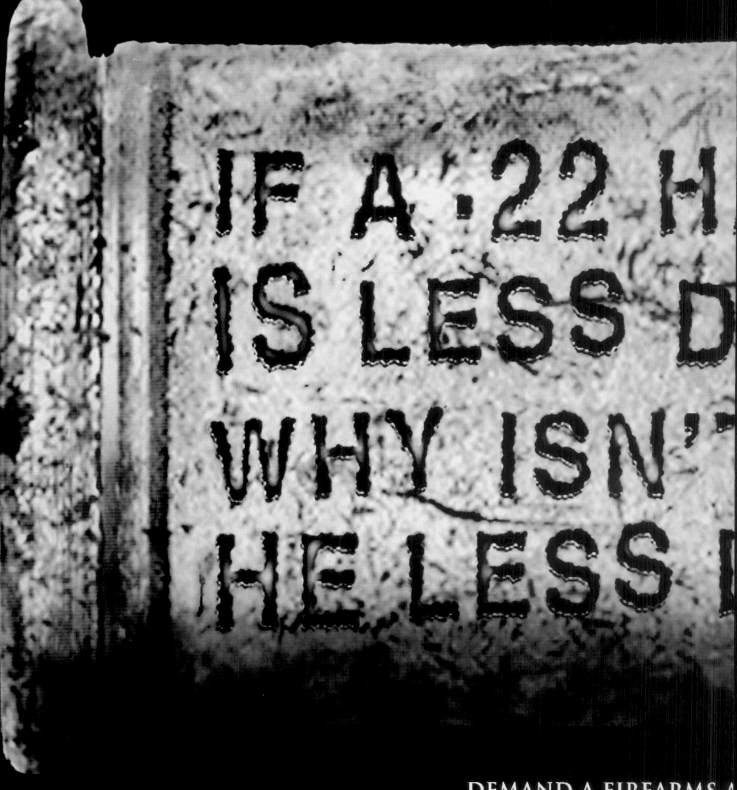

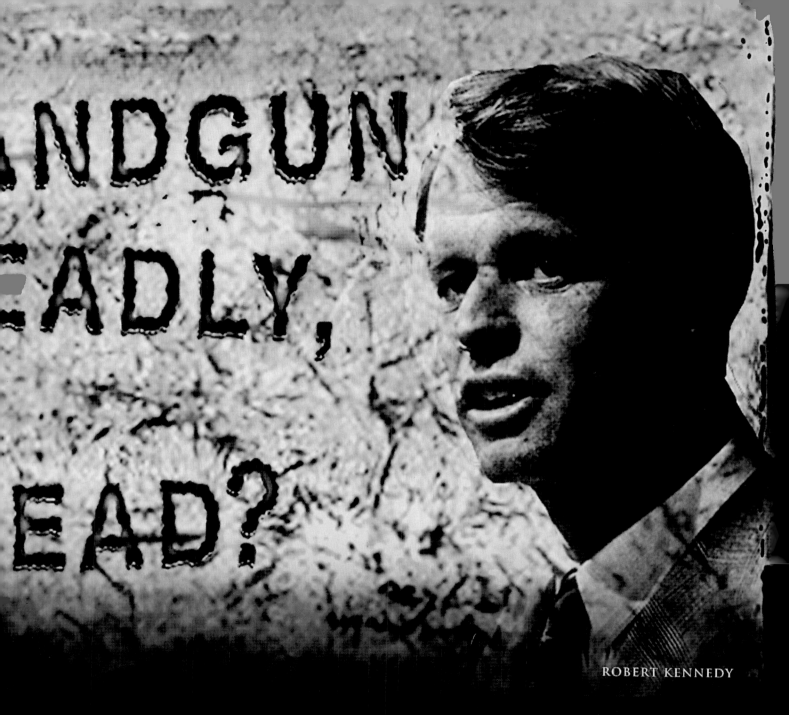

ROBERT KENNEDY

HAT KILLS THE ·22

Grunge Angels, The Health Sponsorship Council, New Zealand, 1995

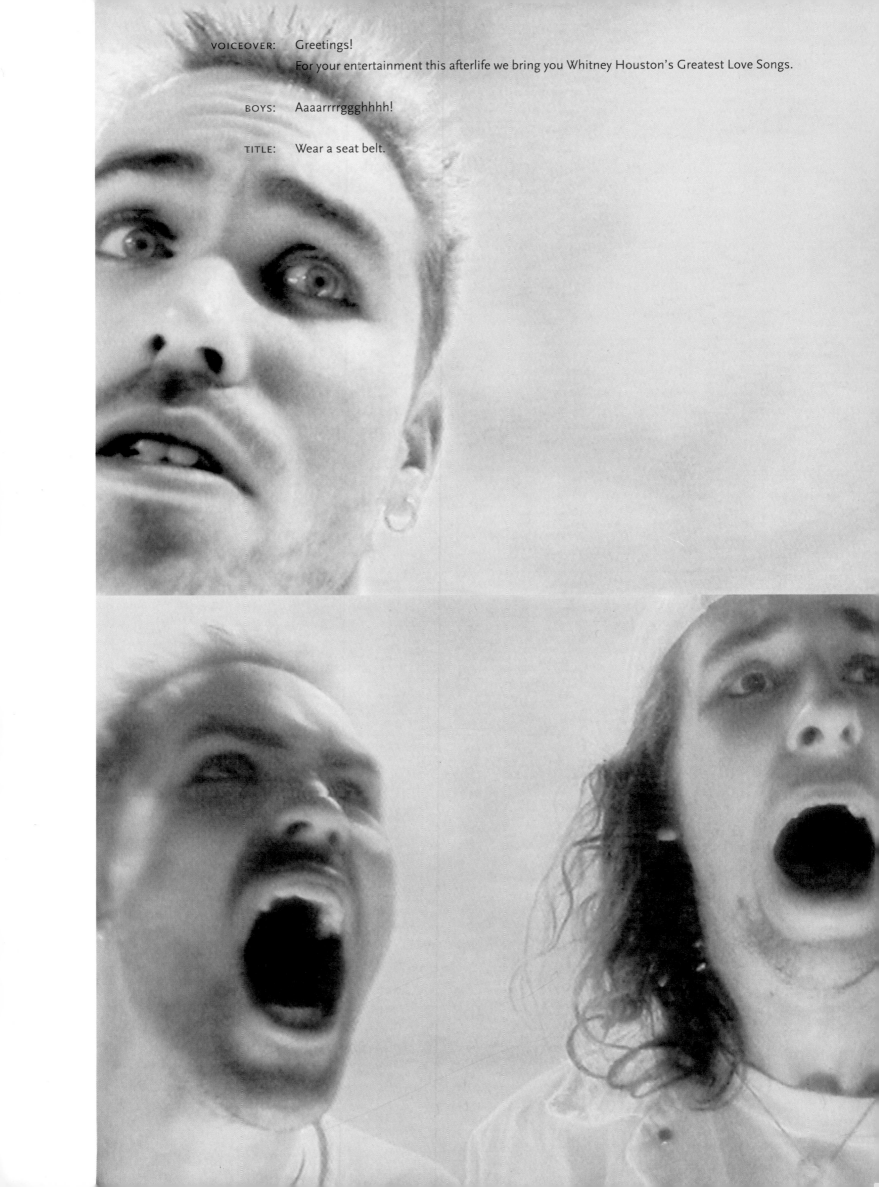

VOICEOVER: Greetings!
For your entertainment this afterlife we bring you Whitney Houston's Greatest Love Songs.

BOYS: Aaaarrrrggghhhh!

TITLE: Wear a seat belt.

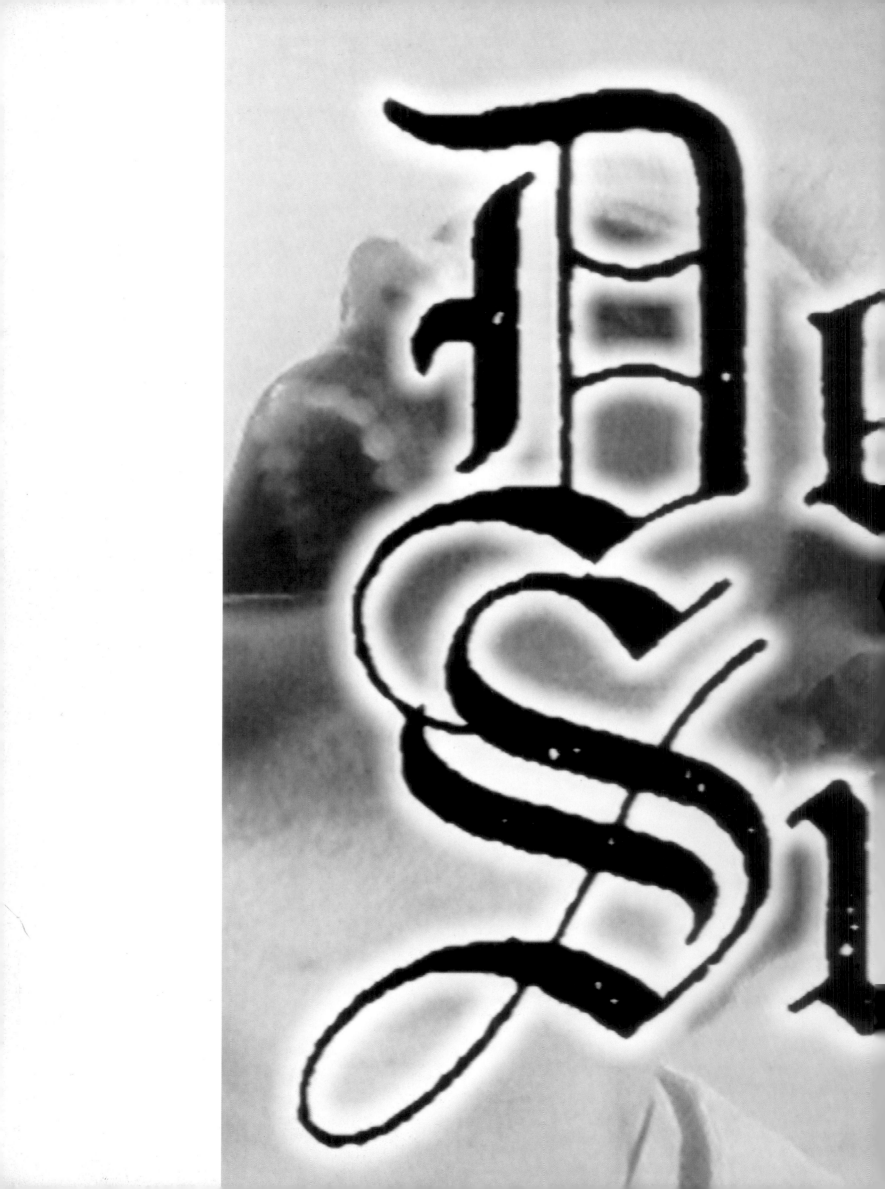

Grunge Angels, The Health Sponsorship Council, New Zealand, 1995

RUBBER. THE LATEST IN BEDROOM WEAR.

BOYS ALWAYS LOOK
BETTER IN RUBBER.

Rubber Man, Action for AIDS, Singapore, 1992

SHE WANTS TO PUT HER TONGUE IN YOUR MOUTH.

MAKE LEARNING CANTONESE OR MANDARIN EASY. CALL HONG KONG LANGUAGE LEARNING CENTRE 2385 5331

Tongue, Hong Kong Language Learning Centre, Hong Kong, 1995

TITLE: Warning. The following scene may disturb some viewers.

VOICECVER: What you're about to see will shock you.
It is the result of a seven year old girl in the back seat of a car travelling at 50 kilometres an hour without wearing a seat belt.
Please look closely at the wounds.

Mother, Ministry of Transport, New Zealand, 1990

VOICEOVER: No seat is safe without a seat belt.
Wear one always.

TITLE: The Road Toll Must Come Down.

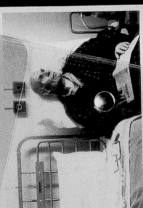
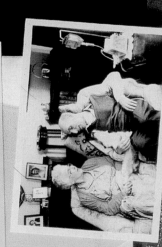

Thank You
To Allan

OXYGEN, MEDICATION AND ARTIFICIAL FEEDING GRADUALLY MADE ERIC FEEL MORE COMFORTABLE.

THE NURSE ALWAYS MANAGED TO FIND TIME FOR ERIC AND HIS FAMILY; TO ADVISE, REASSURE OR SIMPLY TO LISTEN.

AFTER THREE WEEKS HIS SYMPTOMS HAD STABILISED ENOUGH FOR HIM TO GO HOME.

WHEN ERIC AND HIS NURSE FINALLY SAID GOODBYE, THEY PARTED AS FRIENDS.

NURSING OLDER PEOPLE IS RARELY EASY. YOU NEED TO BE RESILIENT, COMPASSIONATE, WITH LOTS OF INITIATIVE.

BUT JUST THINK OF THE REWARDS. IMAGINE THE JOB SATISFACTION YOU GET FROM FULFILLING A DYING MAN'S LAST WISH.

NO OTHER CAREER COMES CLOSE. CALL 0345 645464 QUOTING 2J.

ANYTIME.

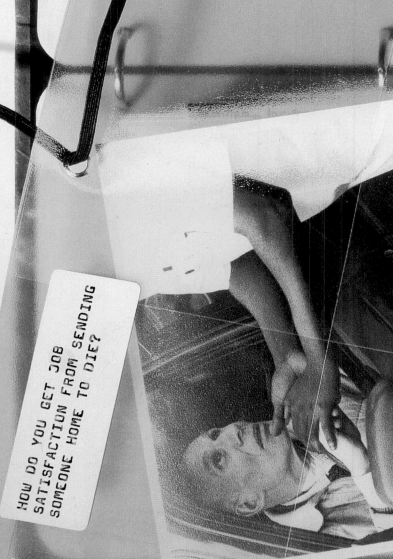

HOW DO YOU GET JOB SATISFACTION FROM SENDING SOMEONE HOME TO DIE?

SUN MON TUE WED THU FRI SAT

BY THE TIME HE GOT TO HOSPITAL, ERIC'S CHRONIC ILLNESS HAD NEARLY FINISHED HIM. BREATHING AND SWALLOWING WERE DIFFICULT AND PAINFUL.

ANYTHING MORE VIGOROUS COULD BE EXCRUCIATING.

DESPITE THIS, ERIC, WHO WAS 83, WAS DETERMINED TO END HIS DAYS AT HOME. BUT HE WASN'T GOING ANYWHERE UNTIL HIS NURSE HAD MADE HIM STRONG ENOUGH.

NURSING. HAVE YOU GOT WHAT IT TAKES?

On August 24, Danny will marry Tessa.

More later.

Episode 1

On August 24, Danny will marry Tessa.

Breakfast!

Yum! Bacon!

Can Tessa cook?

Of course she can cook.

That's funny – her mother can't.

Bruce!

If you were going to write this family a letter

you'd address it to the Carters, care of

Central Hawkes Bay.

This farm's been in the Carter family for over 80

years. Danny is next in line. And soon after the

wedding he and Tessa will share this house.

And another generation will be trained to work

this land. And so it will go on.

Dad, I'll, um, pick up those hinges before

footy training tonight if you like.

Yeah, that'd be good.

We'll leave about 4pm Pete.

Fine.

And don't be there all night.

More later.

THE OWL HOTEL

In four weeks, Danny will marry Tessa.

More later.

Episode 2

TITLE: In four weeks, Danny will marry Tessa.

VOICEOVER: As they have done over the last few years,
              Danny and Pete call into the drinkery on their
              way home from footy training.

BLUE: Hey – here comes Mr Four Weeks.

PETE: Gidday Pete.

BLUE: How are you this evening Blue?

DANNY: Look who's back.

MATTHEW: Hey Matthew. Where've you been?
              Oh went down Palmy man, look at that A & P
              show.

PETE: See anything good?

MATTHEW: Prize bull – fella from Waikato with a prize
              bull… charge $5 for a look.

DANNY: Did you get to see it?

MATTHEW: I said what about a concession man, for a
              family? He said to me 'How many of you's?'
              And I told him… just me and the missus and
              our 13 kids. He said to me 'Man, you stay
              right there. I'll get that bull to have a gawk at
              you!'

VOICEOVER: It's become a bit of a welcome habit this.
              Matthew has always returned from somewhere.
              And he's always got a story to tell. They reckon
              it's called The Owl because old Blue doesn't
              give a hoot if you stay there all night. But,
              probably there's another reason.

TITLE: More later.

A Country Story, Land Transport Safety Authority/NZ Police, New Zealand, 1999

In three weeks, Danny will marry Tessa.

A penny for your thoughts Danny.

Well little brother, I was just thinking how damn lucky we are. Not a care in the world. No rat race. No grasping for money.

That's very deep.

Forget that, brother – where's this penny you owe me?

Here!

They have always got on this well. Had to really. And now, in a few more weeks Pete will be best man at the wedding.

Give up?

Depends.

Depends on what?

Well, I'm best man right?

Right.

I make a speech right?

Right.

How much do you want me to say about that bird you met at Massey a few years ago?

Want a hand? Nice shirt.

What was her name again? Irene!

Forget the penny!

(Sings) Irene goodnight Irene, Irene good night...

More later.

Episode 4

TITLE: In two weeks, Danny will marry Tessa.

COACH: Okay boys, there's no way we're going to let
             those townies thrash us again. We have got to
             hit them hard by first whistle. You got to let
             them know who's boss.
             Speaking of which, there's a few beers on
             tonight on account of Danny and Tessa and
             all that.
             Okay that's it.

CAPTAIN: ... Yeah hang on a sec blokes, I would just like
             to say we wish you a lot of success... and...
             anyway here's to Danny and Pete....

CLUBMATE: Danny and Tess.

CAPTAIN: Oh yeah... Danny and Tess... good luck.

DANNY: Gidday!

MATTHEW: How long to go mate?

DANNY: Couple of weeks.

MATTHEW: My old uncle got married again the other day...

DANNY: How old is he?

MATTHEW: 91.

DANNY: 91! Why'd he want to get married at that age?

MATTHEW: He didn't want to Danny – he had to!

TITLE: More later.

A Country Story, Land Transport Safety Authority/NZ Police, New Zealand, 1999

Episode 5

TITLE: Next week, Danny will marry Tessa.

DANNY: Hi mum!

MUM: You're late. Try these... Tessa made them.

TESSA: Pete?

DANNY: Nice cakes, Tessa.

TESSA: Muffins.

DANNY: Nice cakes, muffins.

DAD: We had a visitor this morning boys.

PETE: Anyone important?

DAD: Yes, a very important young man, from the farm labourers' union. He wanted to know about wages and conditions of everyone.

So I told him about the head shepherd, you know, couple of hundred a week and free house and that.

Then there is the roustie, hundred and sixty and free house and that.

Then he says: any others? I said well then there's the half-wit – he does most of the work on the place and he gets about $40 a week.

So he says: forty dollars a week! That's the one I want to talk to. And I said you are. And he left.

TITLE: More later.

THE OWL HOTEL

This week, Danny will marry Tessa.

More later.

Episode 6

TITLE: This week, Danny will marry Tessa.

VOICEOVER: This week Danny and Tessa will become the new Mr and Mrs Carter... and once again the family farm will move on to younger, stronger hands.

BLUE: Hey Danny...
Hang on Matt...
Hey Danny, listen to this...
Go on Matt...

MATTHEW: I am just telling these fellas here about that day that townie bloke, you know that lifestyle bloke was asking Skinny. He said to him 'Excuse me Skinny... when that horse of yours was crook with the cough and that... what'd you give him?' And Skinny says 'I gave him the phenyl.' Anyway a couple of days later the townie bloke's back, and he bottles up Skinny and he says 'Hey Skinny I gave that horse of mine phenyl and he died!' And Skinny says 'Yeh... mine too'

BLUE: Hey Danny, message, Tessa is at your folk's place man... some detail about the big event.

DANNY: Oh yeah... okay, thanks, we'd better go. Come on Pete, want a lift?

MATTHEW: Too right – one more and we are off.

TITLE: More later.

A Country Story, Land Transport Safety Authority/NZ Police, New Zealand, 1999

THE OWL HOTEL

Danny will marry Tessa this week.

Episode 7

TITLE: Danny will marry Tessa this week.

BLUE: Hello, hold it boys... this could be the war office...

Hello. Owl... Gidday Bruce... no they were here all right.

DAD: Thank you Blue, thanks.

DAD: That's that... trouble with the Ute... I'll have to go out and get 'em.

MUM: Trouble with the Ute?... why didn't they phone?

DAD: Oh Mother, Oh Mother.

TITLE: Country people die on country roads.

TITLE: More later.

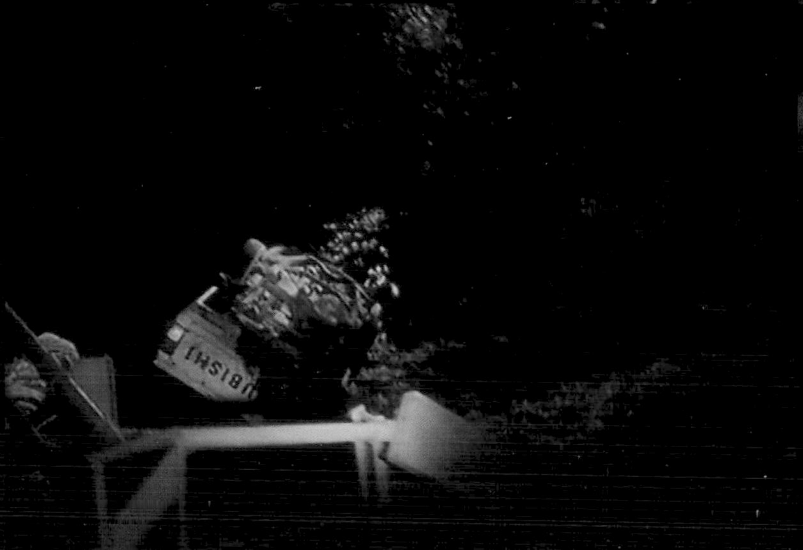

Episode 8

TITLE: Danny is dead.

VOICEOVER: Both Matthew and young Danny died in the crash that night. Country people do die on country roads. Pete will never be the same. He's in Christchurch. At the spinal clinic. He can't walk. And he never will.

TESSA: Have they come up with any offers on the farm yet Mum?

MUM: I think so.

DAD: One or two people interested.

MUM: Tell Bruce.

TESSA: I'm going away. Not forever. Just for a while. But I'll keep in touch

DAD: Whereabouts away?

TESSA: Stay up north with my Aunt in Piha.

DAD: Really.

MUM: She's going away Dad, she's having Danny's baby.

DAD: It never stops Mum, does it? It just never stops.

TITLE: No more ever.

& VOICEOVER: Country people die on country roads.

A Country Story, Land Transport Safety Authority/NZ Police, New Zealand, 1999

Flood level after
Hurricane Mitch

To help the survivors call 1800 025 192 unicef
AUSTRALIA

The Height of It, UNICEF, Australia, 1999

You have to tell me what street, because otherwise, if you go to sleep, I don't know where to take you.

'Oi. Taxi!'

'Yeah, you go to all these pubs and you never find them. Yeah you just...'

'And he holds up his arm and he's got this handcuff on it. Handcuff!'

'I'm not going home!'

'This is where you want to go. Woooo, we're here!'

'You order a bacon burger and all they give you is bloody rind.
You know? It's always the same.'

95

'One second he was behind me and the next he was gone...'

'Herne Bay thanks.'
'Herne Bay, whereabouts?'

'Is there the White Lady or something down here? It is.'
'Yeah, just down there.'

'You're looking really good tonight...'

'He goes to these overseas pubs and he always get lost.'
'No, no, no, because it's not there. It's not where we're going...
 it's where we came from.'

If you drink then get a taxi, you're a bloody genius.

Taxi Confessions, Land Transport Safety Authority/NZ Police, New Zealand, 1996

Disaster. New Zealand Red Cross. New Zealand, 1996

ALL'S FAIR IN LOVE AND WAR? NO IT ISN'T. EVEN IN BATTLE THERE ARE RULES. IN THE COURSE OF HUMANITARIAN WORK IN WAR ZONES ALL OVER THE WORLD, THE RED CROSS ENCOUNTERS SOLDIERS WHO HAVE NO IDEA WHAT THEIR OBLIGATIONS ARE TO PRISONERS, TO CIVILIANS OR TO THE ENEMY.

IF WE CAN TEACH THOSE SOLDIERS ABOUT THE CONDUCT REQUIRED OF THEM BY THE GENEVA CONVENTIONS, THEN WE CAN SAVE LIVES. YOU MAY BE SURPRISED BY SOME OF THE WORK RED CROSS DOES, BUT WHATEVER IT IS AND WHEREVER IT TAKES US WE STILL NEED YOUR HELP TO DO IT.

Fight, New Zealand Red Cross, New Zealand, 1996

THE IDEA FOR THE RED CROSS EMBLEM WAS BORN ON A BATTLEFIELD IN SOLFERINO IN 1859. TODAY IT STILL SEPARATES MEDICS FROM SOLDIERS, LIFE FROM DEATH. IT IS PROTECTED BY GENEVA CONVENTION AND TO MISUSE IT IS A CRIME UNDER LAW. IT DOESN'T BELONG ON A FIRST AID KIT. IT CAN'T BE USED BY VETS OR MEDICAL CENTRES. IT IS A SYMBOL OF PROTECTION, NEUTRALITY AND HUMANITY. THE NEW ZEALAND RED CROSS HAS A DUTY TO PROTECT IT, BECAUSE WITHOUT IT WE CAN'T PROTECT YOU.

350 Languages, New Zealand Red Cross, New Zealand, 1996

DON'T
FORGET
HOW
TO HAVE
SEX
AFTER
DRINKING

- Carefully remove from foil
- Squeeze end to remove air
- Gently unroll over entire length of penis
- Hold base and withdraw slowly after ejaculation
- Dispose of condom hygenically after use

THINGS SLIP YOUR MIND AFTER DRINKING. PROTECT YOURSELF FROM AIDS. USE A CONDOM. JUST REMEMBER WHERE YOU PUT IT.

ACTION FOR
AIDS

Don't Forget, Action for AIDS, Singapore, 1993

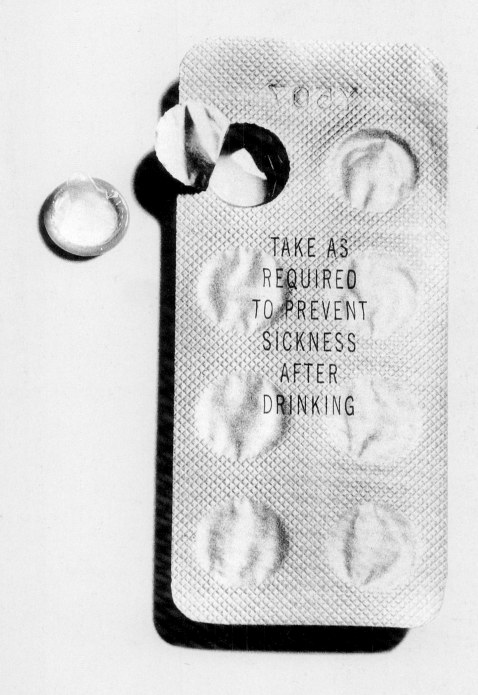

TAKE AS
REQUIRED
TO PREVENT
SICKNESS
AFTER
DRINKING

DRINKING CAN LEAD TO UNSAFE SEX. PROTECT YOURSELF WITH A CONDOM. BECAUSE AIDS WILL MAKE YOU SICK. PERMANENTLY.

ACTION FOR
AIDS

Prevent Sickness, Action for AIDS, Singapore, 1993

NO MATTER HOW MUCH YOU DRINK
REMEMBER TO HAVE A NIGHTCAP

THE MORE YOU DRINK, THE MORE YOU FORGET. REDUCE THE RISK OF GETTING AIDS. REMEMBER. WEAR A CONDOM TO BED.

Night Cap, Action for AIDS, Singapore, 1993

IF YOU WANT YOUR EMPLOYEES TO STAY LONGER, GIVE THEM THE RIGHT PACKAGE.

What your employees get up to in bed is none of your business. But it could have a disturbing impact on your company's business.

Suppose a member of your staff contracts the HIV virus.

Eventually, if they develop the AIDS illness, you'll have to replace them.

In the meantime, you and your other employees might worry about whether it's safe to have HIV infected people working in your midst. Fortunately it is safe.

You'll also want to know the legal implications. And whether the worker will be covered by insurance, or if your company is responsible.

It's important to find out the answers to these questions now. Because if your business isn't already affected by AIDS, it soon could be.

By the year 2000, the epidemic will be a bigger problem in Asia than it is in the currently worst-affected area, Africa. And by then, over 40% of new infections will be occurring here - unless you take action now to help prevent the spread of this disease.

Start by getting in touch with your local AIDS action group and government health authority. They should be able to answer your questions.

They'll also advise you on taking the necessary steps to help prevent AIDS from spreading in your company.

Such measures as having a health expert talk to your employees. Putting up posters about AIDS prevention on your notice boards. And even installing condom dispensing machines in your washrooms.

You can locate your nearest AIDS action group by inquiring at your local United Nations Development Programme office or at the UNDP in New Delhi (see address below).

Take action now. You'll boost staff morale by showing that you care.

And you'll avoid losing valuable employees to AIDS.

UNDP 55, LODI ESTATE, POST BOX NO. 3059, NEW DELHI-110003, INDIA FAX 91-11-4627612
THIS ADVERTISEMENT WAS PRODUCED AS A PUBLIC SERVICE BY SAATCHI & SAATCHI ADVERTISING

Right Package, Action for AIDS, Singapore, 1993

TITLES: We'll never get tired of repeating it.
The condom is the most reliable weapon against AIDS.
Convince your partner to use it.

ANLAIDS.

'Preservativo.'

'Pre...

'va...

'ti...

'Preservativo.'

Preservativo, ANLAIDS, Italy, 1995. The presenter is a famous Italian TV personality, Alba Parrietti. The commercial caused a scandal, the Catholic Church being opposed to condoms, and the word 'condom' being forbidden on state-owned AND Italian TV.

Strangers in the Night, AIDS Awareness, Yugoslavia, 1998. Music: Strangers in the Night transforming to Chopin's Funeral March as the notes become crucifixes.

VOLUNTARIS DE LA CREU ROJA.

VOICEOVER: Lots of people like these two will make love on the beach this summer.

Red Cross. Make love!

Love Story, Red Cross, Spain, 1987. Music: theme from Love Story.

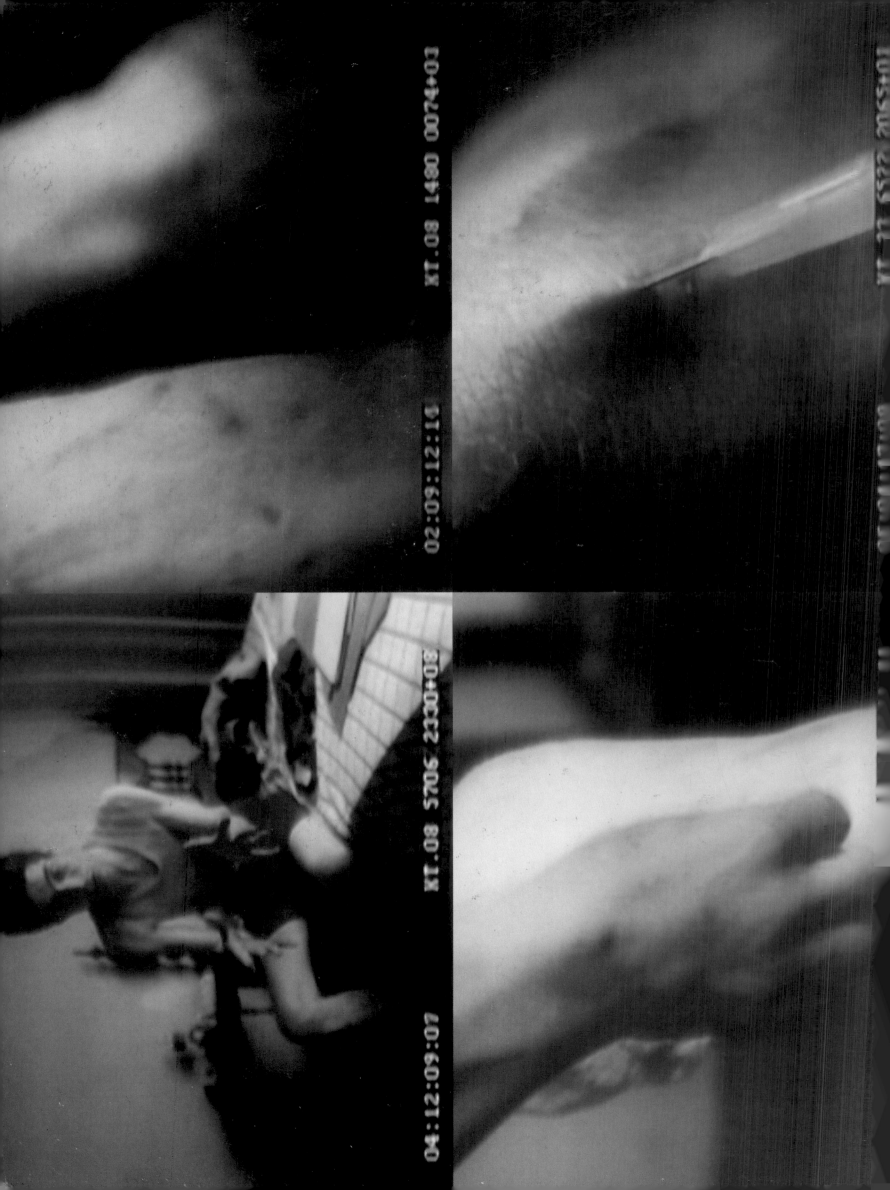

'...You know, I just felt, like, real good man.

Y'know, I wasn't like racing, I wasn't speeding, y'know, I was like mellow.

And I, like, I threw up the first time and everything and after when I threw up, man, I said Wow! This shit is fucking like – good.

Right...

Y'know, okay... oh y'know... oh you know when you used to go on a ride and, y'know, your adrenaline... pumps. Know what I'm saying?

That's the feeling.

Like that.

I had cellulitis in my thigh.

I got a scar so big. It's unbelievable, man.

I almost got er... I had gangrene on my foot, and that they almost took my foot off.

I consider myself pretty intelligent.

I can do whatever I want to do, man.

Whatever I want to do, I can do.

I threw up man, my guts.

And as I threw up, I'm like, Damn boy, this is fucking what I want, y'know?

I just want to be nice man – that's all I wanna do – that's it.

Why can't people just do that?

Maybe everybody should shoot up and mellow out.

I got these tracks man, all over my body.

The pus was coming out of the little hole here, like nothing.

I used to do a lot more things, y'know, like, I used to go to movies more and go out to restaurants, I use to go to Broadway shows, I like Broadway shows they're nice, man.

By the time 97 rolls around, 96 at this time, right 1996 August 17th, 18th – whatever it is – you will come here with your cameras and I'll be a totally different person.

I'll be successful.

And I'll bet my life on it.'

TITLE: Heroin. Want some?
Partnership for a Drug-Free America.

VOICEOVER: Once again folks item J343 is the Surfing Monkey coin bank. It's great for graduation, wedding gifts and I believe we sold out on this one last time so please don't let this one pass you by. Now let's go to caller Scott in Nashville... now Scott, I understand that you have just bought fifteen of the surfing monkey banks. Is that true?

'...Yeah!... (background noise & laughter) ...Shh, man... I'm on TV...'

TITLE: Marijuana. A very expensive habit.
Partnership for a Drug-Free America.

J - 343
Surfing
Monkey
Coin Bank

Retail Price:
~~$36.00~~

Our Price:
$19.95

S&H $4.25

Number Sold:
2

J - 343
Surfing
Monkey
Coin Bank

Retail Price:
~~$36.00~~

Our Price:
$19.95

S&H $4.25

Number Sold:
17

Jim Morrison 1943-1971

Janis Joplin 1943-1970

In advertising, they say one of the surest ways to get your message across is to put celebrities in your ad.

John Belushi 1949-1982

River Phoenix 1970-1993

Partnership for a Drug-Free America®

VOICEOVER:　One gram of cocaine costs as much as a boom box.

Three grams of cocaine costs as much as a TV.

Seven grams, a trip to Paris.

One gram a week for a year, a new car.

If you're on coke everything you work for is disappearing right under your nose.

TITLE:　Partnership for a Drug-Free America.

Nose, Partnership for a Drug-Free America, USA, 1988

VOICEOVER: One of these women showed her respect for nature by donating part of her pay cheque to
               the Environmental Federation of California.
               The other did not.

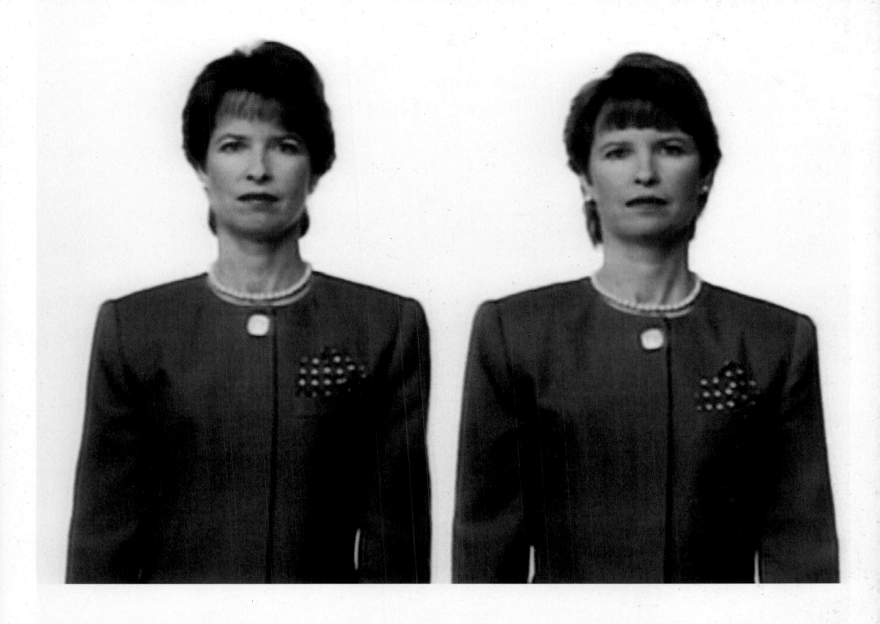

Elephant, Environmental Federation of California, USA, 1992

VOICEOVER: Now, you may not know which one gave to the environment but an elephant never forgets. Support nature at the office by donating to the payroll deduction plan for the environment.

TITLE: Environmental Federation of California.

VOICEOVER: Now, you may not know which one gave to the environment but an elephant never forgets. Support nature at the office by donating to the payroll deduction plan for the environment.

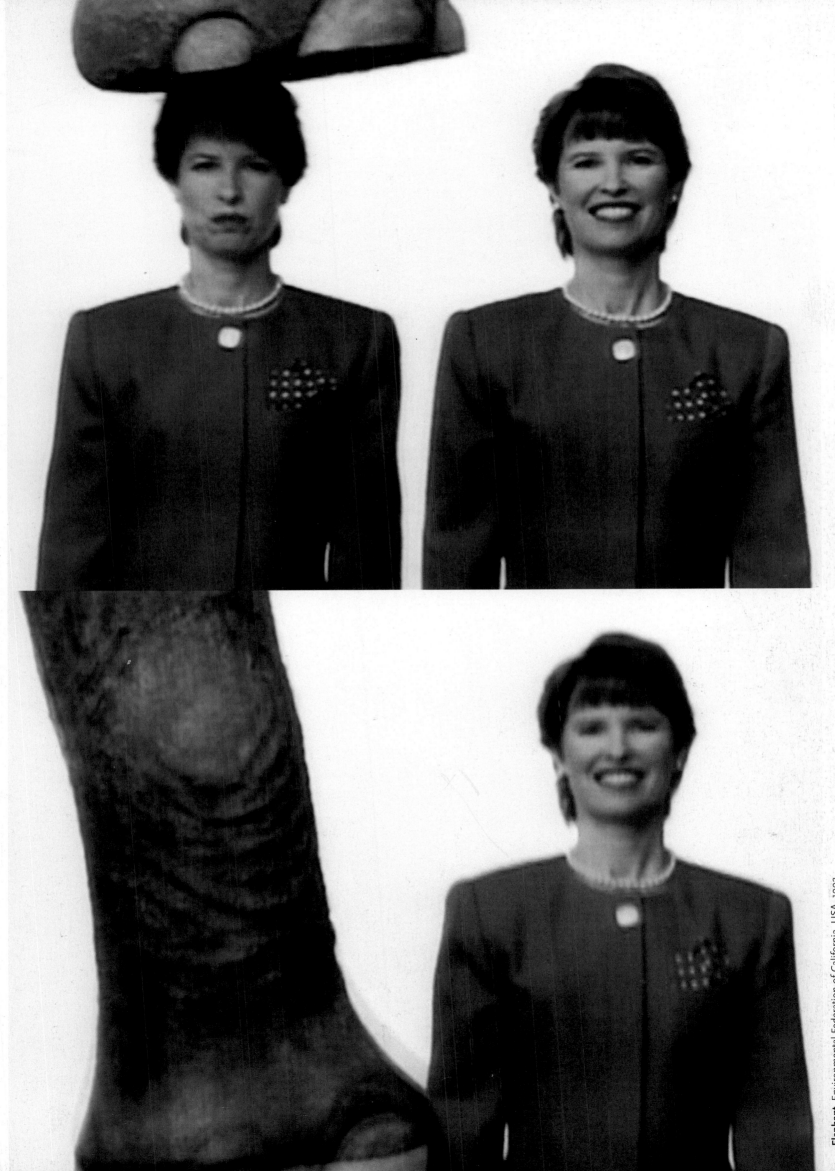

Elephant, Environmental Federation of California, USA, 1992

The only fur I'm not ashamed to wear.

The Only Fur, International Fund for Animal Welfare, Italy 1996. The model is the Marquise Marina Ripa di Meana. When this poster appeared, she was the Italian Ambassador for the International Fund for Animal Welfare.

Hatchet, Fundação S.O.S. Mata Atlântica, Rainforest Conservation, Brazil, 1999

Fundação
S.O.S. Mata Atlântica
www.sosmataatlantica.org.br

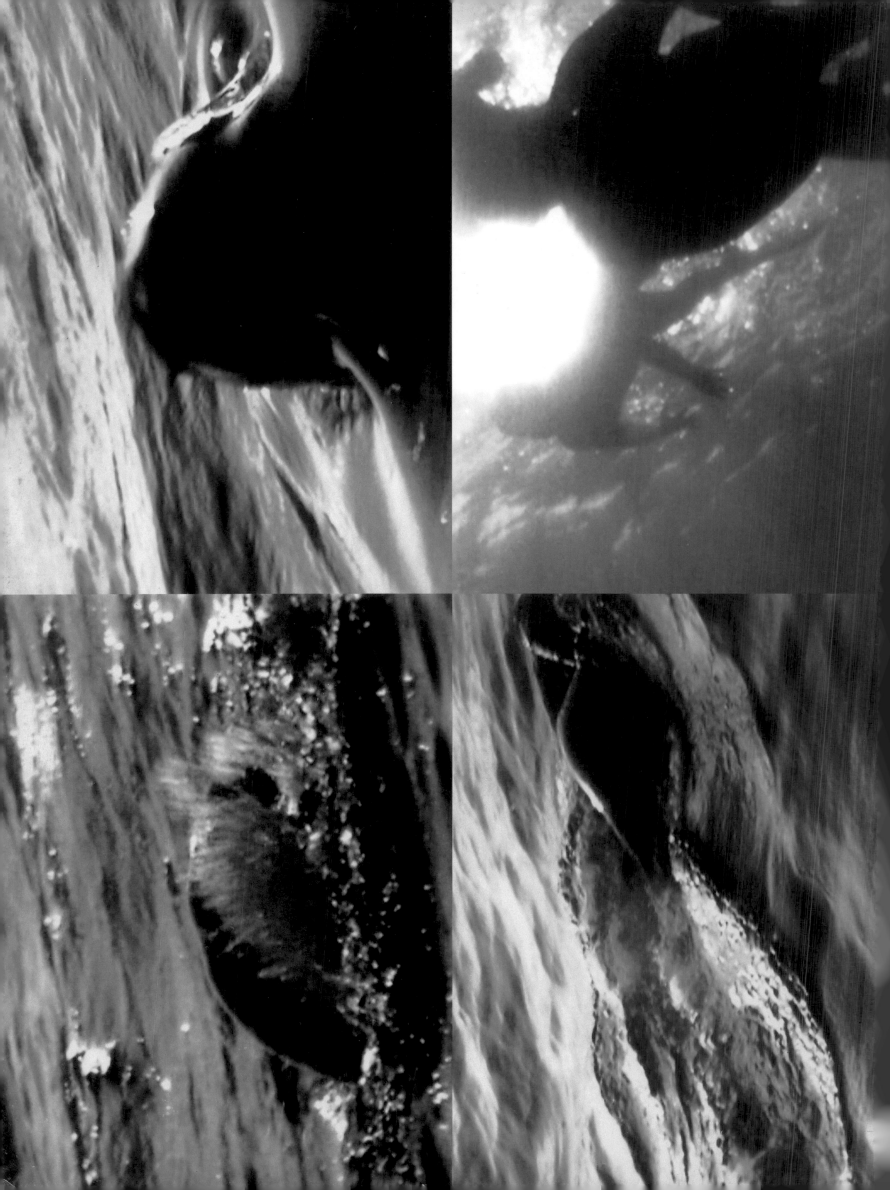

VOICEOVER: What whales want is just what we want. To be free to live in peace, to reproduce without
               problems. But today more than ever, their existence is in danger.

               Greenpeace has always fought to save them from extinction.
               Help Greenpeace.

Whales, Greenpeace, Italy, 1993

Save **100** Hurricane
Mitch victims from
dehydration for just **$12.**

HELP UNICEF HELP CHILDREN IN EMERGENCY SITUATIONS. CALL **1800 025 192**   unicef
AUSTRALIA

Water Cooler, UNICEF, Australia 1999

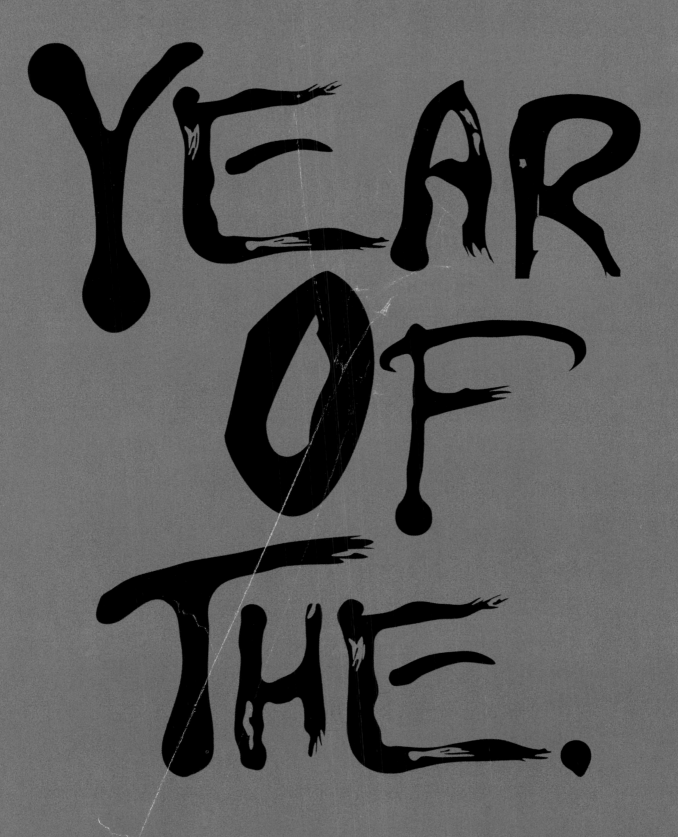

YEAR OF THE.

The tiger is being erased. Total extinction is now a very real danger. WWF, the World Wide Fund For Nature, is working vigorously to help protect tigers everywhere from deforestation and the illegal body part trade. In this, the Year of the Tiger, please do what you can to help us keep the tiger cause alive and back in the headlines.

For further details, please call 703 3772.

WWF

Year of the, World Wildlife Fund, Vietnam, 1998

Millions of Rwandan
refugees badly need
potable water, as they
need food, medicine
and air to breathe.

COMITATO ITALIANO
unicef

The only water left in Rwanda.

Last Water in Rwanda, UNICEF, Italy, 1994

Going, Going, Gone World Wildlife Foundation, Singapore, 1990

GOING

GOING

GONE.

DON'T LET IT HAPPEN.

EXTINCTION IS FOREVER.

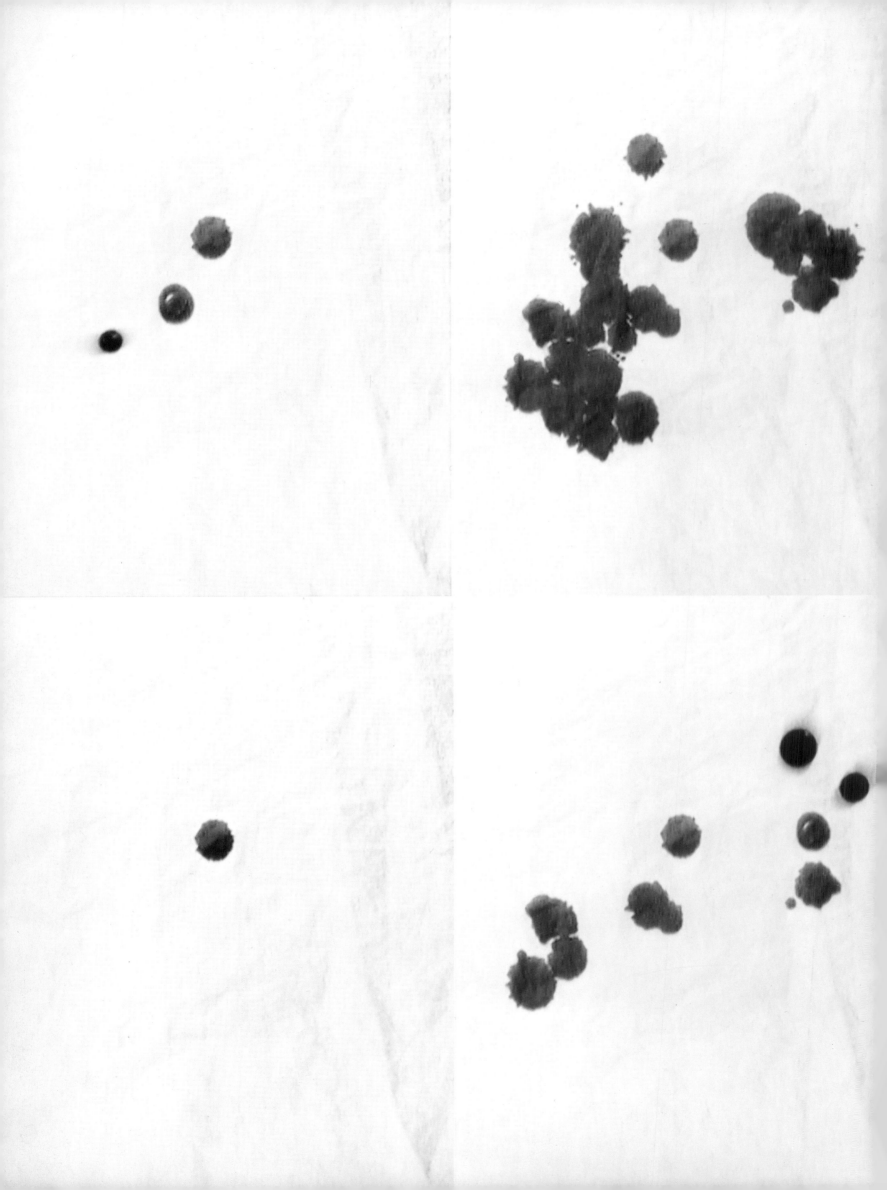

We are Doctors without borders. Support us.

Zair is bleeding.

Zaire, Doctors without Borders, Sweden, 1992

War on Hunger, FAO, Italy, 1998

Speed Kills, New Zealand Police, New Zealand, 1994

EACH DRINK YOU
HAVE BEFORE DRIVING
IMPAIRS
YOUR JUDGEMENT.

Glasses, Traffic Police, Singapore, 1993

THE ASHE
ONE CIG

 **DON'T TREAT THE ROA**

ROM JUST
ARETTE

DE LIKE AN ASHTRAY

JENOM VŮL NEDÁ PŘEDNOST ZEBŘE

ŘIDIČ, KTERÝ NEMYSLÍ, ZABÍJÍ.

BATES SAATCHI & SAATCHI ADVERTISING

Only an ox does not give way to a zebra. Thoughtless driving kills.
(Being called 'an ox' in Czech is equivalent to being called an asshole.)

Sit there all day every day.
That's what jail's like.

The Censor

MAN: Stop!
Show me that piece again.
Go on... hurry up.
No, no, no, no, leave that out.
You must not do that.
No, no, no. That is not allowed.
Stop that.
Omit that.
Omit it.
That's not allowed, you know that.
Omit that.
That... That... And that!
Go on... Go on, dance.
Stop! Why aren't you dancing?
You call that a dance?
Stop that! I will not have any innuendo.

VOICEOVER: This short play by the Czech writer Ivan Kraus, censored in his own country, was published
in Index on Censorship, a magazine which exposes the suppression of artists around the
world and offers them a platform.
Index is for the censored artist, and for you.
Index on Censorship.

THE CENSOR

The Censor, Index on Censorship, UK, 1986

FREE PRESS

Article 19

I will not lift my leg to your Mercedes Benz.

I will not bite the pizza delivery man.

I will not hide my bone under your pillow.

I will not dig under the pillow in the middle of the night to look for bones.

I will not lick your face immediately after licking my private parts.

Adopt a pedigree pet from the SPCA. Call 287 5355.

Spaniel, SPCA, Singapore, 1997

'How much is that doggie in the window...

'the one with the waggly tail...

'How much is that doggie in the window...

'I do hope that doggie's for sale...'

£1.05p a day.

£7.35p a week.

£29.40p a month.

Before you give someone a dog this Christmas...

£352.80p a year.

please count the costs. RSPCA.

£4,939.40p a lifetime.

Dog and Gun, Royal Society for the Prevention of Cruelty to Animals (RSPCA), UK, 1986

This can happen when you ride a bike and don't wear a helmet.

This can happen when you ride a bike and don't wear a helmet.

This can happen when you ride a bike and don't wear a helmet.

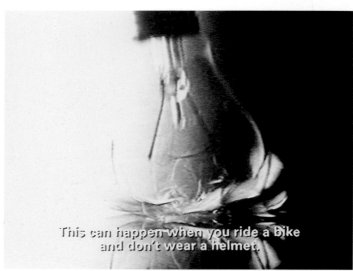

This can happen when you ride a bike and don't wear a helmet.

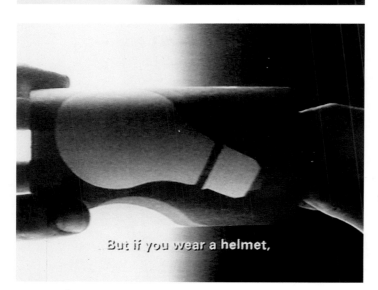

But if you wear a helmet,

it won't happen.

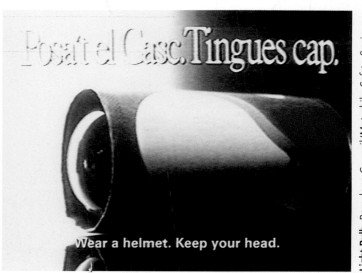

Posa't el Casc. Tingues cap.

Wear a helmet. Keep your head.

M 6 6 5 6 2 3 3 0 1 1 9-9 6

● METRO POLICE: JAIL DIV

Don't piss your life away.

MADD
CANADA ™
Mothers Against Drunk Driving

The No sky.

Look at it. This is the sky of those who kill thousands of animals each year, for sport. The sky of those who are trying to block the Referendum on hunting. But it is also the sky of all the lazy or indifferent people who do not vote on June 3. So take a good look at it. If a No vote wins today, this lifeless sky will be your sky tomorrow.

The Yes sky.

Vote yes, on June 3, to ban hunting. You will read the results in the sky.

Look at it. This is the sky of those who work each day to defend nature. The sky of those who understand that a ban on hunting in Italy means the opening of a wonderful new season. Give wings to the values you believe in: vote Yes on June 3. You will read the results in the sky. **WWF**

Vote No/Vote Yes, World Wildlife Fund, Italy, 1990

Poached Egg

TITLES: Poached Fish

Poached Elephant

Ivory.
Don't let the slaughter start again.
Don't buy it. Don't sell it. Don't wear it. Don't use it.

Poached Elephant, World Wildlife Foundation, Singapore, 1993

WHAT-IF-IT-WERE-THEM
WHO ABANDONED US ?

Chi abbandona gli animali
è una bestia.

WHOEVER ABANDONS ANIMALS
IS AN ANIMAL !

IF IT WERE THEM TO CONDEMN US TO
A SUMMER FIT ONLY FOR A DOG ?

Abbandono, Worldwide Fund for Nature, Italy, 1987

TITLES: Not so long ago, a woman from Alabama wanted to sit at the front of the bus.

And a gentleman from India wanted to raise consciousness without raising his voice.

In East Germany, a man wanted to break free.

And a woman travelled the world, giving hope to those who had none.

This is the power of one.

To protect your home in the Amazon.

To prevent poaching of the African mountain gorilla.

To rescue harp seals in Finland.

Or to care for the environment in our own backyard.

The power of one is to do something.

Anything.

Earth Communications Office.

Power of One, Earth Communications Office, USA, 1992

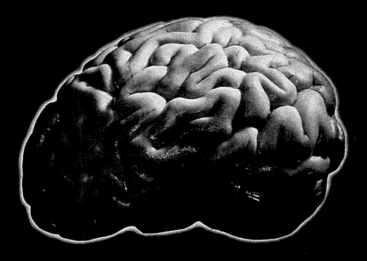

AFRICAN

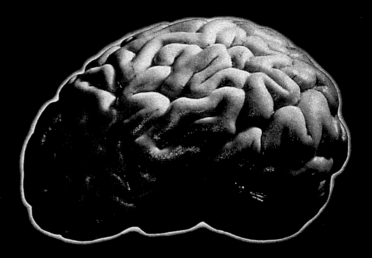

EUROPEAN

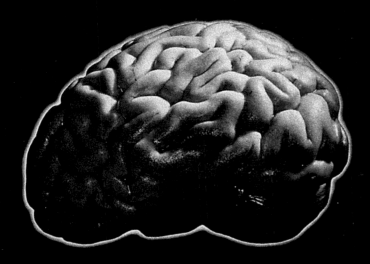

ASIAN

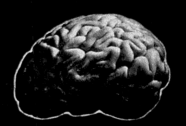

RACIST

Brains, Commission for Racial Equality, UK, 1995

all different all equal · EUROPEAN YOUTH CAMPAIGN AGAINST RACISM · SUPPORTED BY COMMISSION FOR RACIAL EQUALITY

CHILD.

In Africa.

In America.

In Europe.

MEDECINS SANS FRONTIERES
MEDICI SENZA FRONTIERE

Where there are wars, epidemics and natural disaster
Medici Senza Frontiere via Ostiense 6

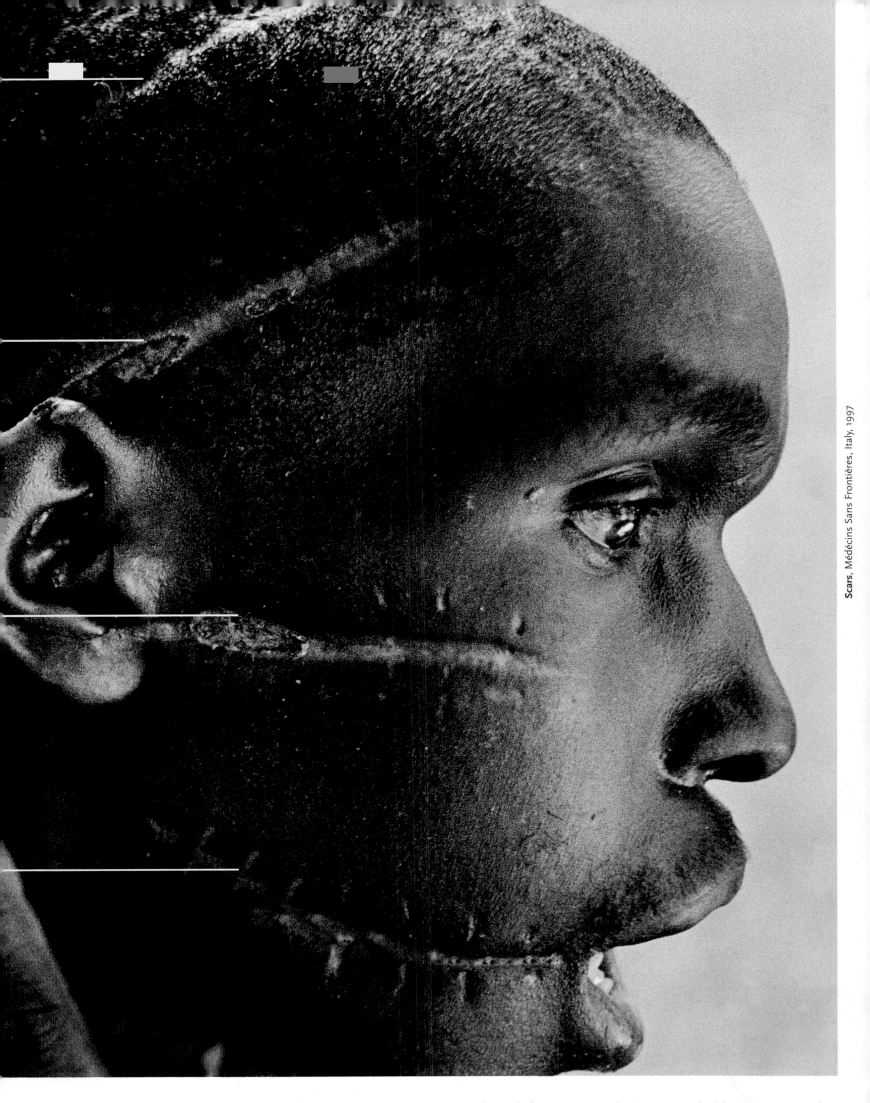

Scars, Médécins Sans Frontières, Italy, 1997

re there too. Every day, for 25 years, stitchin-up the world's wounds.
I.06-57300900 fax 06/57300902 Roma c.c.p. 87486007.

'I reckon we should just send them all back, don't you?...'

'...Pakis, Jews, Italian...'

Hundreds of 'them' leave journalism.

Thousands of 'them' close down their shops.

'That's alright mate.'

Thousands of 'them' leave the transport system.

Thousands of 'them' stop teaching.

'Sorry!'

VOICEOVER: Just this once we're going to grant him his wish, and see what happens to Britain when thousands of 'them' leave our hospitals.

Thousands of 'them' leave construction.

The thousands of 'them' leave the finance industry.

'Send them back home – that would be g...'
'Fancy a curry?'

Hundreds of 'them' stop competing for Britain.

Hundreds of 'them' close factories putting thousan...
on the dole.

CLOSED

And the sacrifices made by millions of 'them' will be forgotten.

THEY'RE US.

THEM?

Them, Commission for Racial Equality, UK, 1996

WHO SAYS ETHNIC MINORITIES CAN'T GET JOBS? THERE ARE OPENINGS EVERYWHERE.

Lavatory attendant. Office cleaner. Somebody has to do all the low-paid, menial jobs, but why is it so often people from ethnic minorities? Prejudice, racial discrimination and harassment are denying people the choice of job they deserve. It's unjust and unfair. More than that, it's a terrible waste of British talent.

Getting into a skilled profession is hard enough for anyone these days.

But it's even harder for ethnic minorities.

For a start, qualifications count, but most ethnic minorities are still more likely to be unemployed than white people.

They have to apply for more jobs before they get one. In a recent investigation, one in three companies who were tested refused interviews to black and Asian applicants.

But they did offer interviews to white applicants with the same qualifications.

If they do find a job, ethnic minorities often find promotion harder to achieve than their white colleagues.

There's a disproportionately low number of ethnic minorities at managerial level.

For example, in one large transportation company 30% of the workforce are from ethnic minorities, but they account for only 3% of the management.

On top of all this ethnic minorities face racial harassment in the workplace.

If they complain about it they are often

told to accept harassment as part of the job.

Sadly, most people do accept it.

Those who don't may have to take their employer to an industrial tribunal where hard evidence must be provided to support their complaint.

Whether or not they win their case they may well have to start the trying process of searching for a job all over again.

No wonder ethnic minorities have found it so difficult to make progress in Britain.

However, bad as the situation seems, some aspects have changed for the better.

A West Indian who came here in the fifties to work for British Rail remembers:

"It was hell. For the first ten years nobody would sit next to me in the lunch break. They gave you the worst job, paid you less, gave you no training.

They insulted you. There were 'No nigger' notices everywhere. It was very different then. There was no law against it."

Thankfully, the law has changed.

In 1976 the Race Relations Act was passed, making it unlawful for employers to discriminate on the grounds of colour, race, ethnic or national origin.

Those who do discriminate face hefty bills for compensation and legal costs, as well as having their guilt aired in public.

The Act certainly put an end to blatant discrimination like the 'No nigger' notices.

But it didn't put an end to the more subtle discrimination that still exists today.

Such as when an employer says "Sorry,

there's someone else more qualified for the job." when there isn't.

Or when a manager 'forgets' to mention an opportunity for promotion to someone.

This is discrimination.

It's subtle, perhaps even unintentional, but it can still be very demoralising.

Imagine being told over and over again that you are not qualified enough for a job when you know very well that you are.

What could you do about it?

If your case is strong enough you could

talk to the Commission for Racial Equality.

We are the independent body funded by the Home Office whose job it is to eliminate every kind of racial discrimination.

To this end we give support to victims of discrimination in industrial tribunals.

(It's not always ethnic minorities. We've dealt with cases of white workers being treated unfairly by black or Asian bosses.)

We're also working with trade unions to help them fight racial discrimination and harassment, within their own organisations as much as in the workplace.

Many trade unions now have specially designated officers who can give practical support and advice to people who have been discriminated against.

You'll find similarly qualified officers at your local Racial Equality Council and Citizens Advice Bureau.

What's more, with our help companies are adopting equal opportunity policies. These prevent discrimination before it can happen, giving everyone a fair chance.

If you'd like to talk to someone about implementing such a policy in your company, please write to us at the address below.

This is how we'll defeat racism.

Not by violence, but by accepting each other as equals. By opening our minds.

For the sake of ourselves and of the generation who are growing up now, this would be the most promising opening possible.

COMMISSION FOR RACIAL EQUALITY
CRE Information Section, Elliot House, 10-12 Allington Street, London SW1E 5EH.

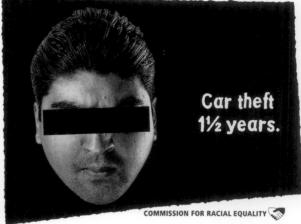

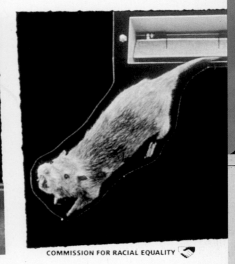

Les discours sur la purification ethnique,
ça ne vous rappelle rien ?

HALTE AUX CRIMES CONTRE L'HUMANITÉ DES NATIONALISTES SERBES

Ethnic Cleansing, Médécins du Monde, France, 1994

YOU MAY NOT CARE WHETHER JEWISH LIFE SURVIVES INTO THE NEXT GENERATION.

ENGLAND 1990 PHOTOGRAPHER LEO REGAN

BUT HE DOES.

Jewish life has survived for thousands of years. Fascism has survived for seventy. But in all that time it has been devastating. The warning signs are still here and every one of them carries the same message: don't become complacent. That's why the JIA has such a vital role to play. We need to be able to respond to the persecution of Jews anywhere in the world, at any time. We need to be alert to any threat. We respond to those threats by providing funds for the Jewish Agency, helping it to rescue Jews wherever they are, and to bring them to the safety of Israel. When they arrive, we help them to build new lives with new opportunities. Israel holds the key to all our futures.

Help us to teach the next generation the importance of Israel and the need for us to preserve Jewish life all over the world.

Show your commitment to the JIA by telephoning us on 0345 585004* today and we'll talk about how you can help.

You might not think that you're needed. But we do.

JIA
SAVING JEWISH LIFE

Not even a flag to wrap themselves in.

RED CROSS KURDISH APPEAL

Phone (01) 766877 or (01) 765135 with your pledges.

PRINTING DONATED BY PRINT & DISPLAY

No Flag, Red Cross Kurdish Appeal, Ireland

TITLES: Commission for Racial Equality.
1997 European Year Against Racism supported by the Home Office.

This is the product of 14 commercial directors each volunteering to be given a single word brief such as 'eating', 'work', 'religion', 'sleep' etc. They were asked to film in eight seconds, in black and white, their idea of what this word meant when applied to 'equality'.

Equals, Commission for Racial Equality, UK, 1997

You can do something about
domestic violence

call the Police

NSW POLICE SERVICE

Shattered Dreams, NSW Police Service, Australia, 1997. Music: Bach's Air on a G-string.

DAVID BRINGS ME FLOWERS.

AND TELLS ME HE LOVES ME.

AND I WANT TO BELIEVE HIM.

MY FRIENDS SAY I'M STUPID.

BUT THEY DON'T KNOW DAVID.

DAVID BRINGS ME FLOWERS.

AND TELLS ME HE'S SORRY.

WHEN HE LOSES HIS TEMPER.

AND ACCIDENTLY HITS ME.

MY FRIENDS SAY I'M STUPID.

BUT THEY DON'T KNOW DAVID.

DAVID HIT ME LAST NIGHT.

AND I THOUGHT HE WOULDN'T STOP.

IT ALL SEEMS LIKE A BLUR.

AND MY FRIENDS THEY WERE RIGHT.

BUT DAVID BRINGS ME FLOWERS

IF YOU'RE A TEEN IN AN ABUSIVE RELATIONSHIP, THERE'S SOMEONE YOU CAN TALK TO. JUST CALL 213-626-3393.
WE'RE THE LOS ANGELES COMMISSION ON ASSAULTS AGAINST WOMEN AND WE CAN HELP.

Flowers, Commission Against Assaults on Women, USA, 1996

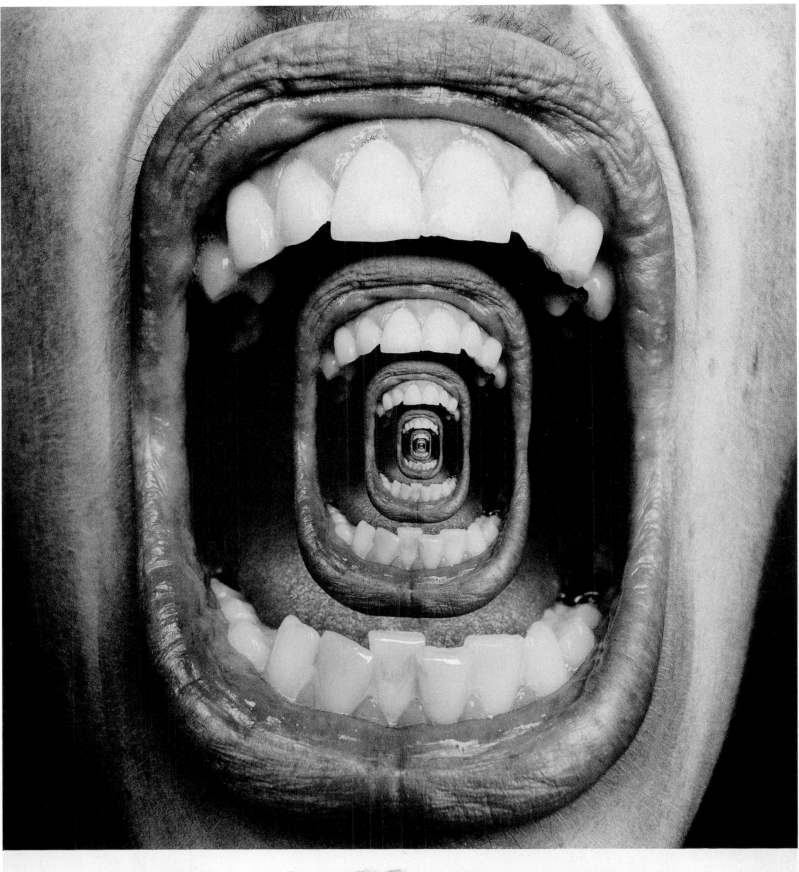

THE ABUSE YOU YELL AT YOUR KIDS STAYS IN THE FAMILY FOR GENERATIONS

You're useless. You're dumb. I wish you'd never been born. Shout verbal abuse like this at your kids and you don't just hurt them, you teach them to be abusive parents too. Break the cycle. Call 0800 222 999 for a free parenting booklet that will help.

NEW ZEALAND
CHILDREN & YOUNG PERSONS
SERVICE

Scream, NZ Children & Young Persons Service, New Zealand, 1996

Scene 1

MAN: Do you think I go out with my mates just to make your life a misery?

WOMAN: Shut up.

MAN: Do you?

WOMAN: Shut up.

MAN: When was the last time you put your arms around me?

WOMAN: Leave me alone.

MAN: Have I got a sign round my face that says I'm fucking invisible?

WOMAN: No.

No.

No.

MAN: Have I?

WOMAN: Leave me alone.

MAN: Am I invisible?

WOMAN: Shut up! Just shut up, just leave me alone.

MAN: Listen I'm going on the piss tonight.

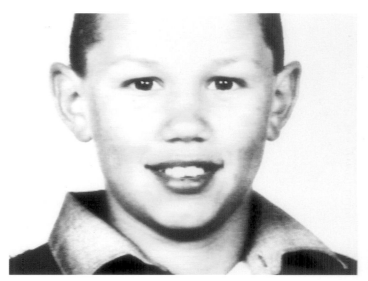

Scene 2

MAN:	Do you think I go out with my mates just to make your life a misery?
WOMAN:	Shut up.
MAN:	Do you?
WOMAN:	Shut up.
MAN:	When was the last time you put your arms around me?
WOMAN:	Leave me alone.
MAN:	Have I got a sign round my face that says I'm fucking invisible?
WOMAN:	No.
	No.
	No.
MAN:	Have I?
WOMAN:	Leave me alone.
MAN:	Am I invisible?
WOMAN:	Shut up!

Scene 3

MAN:	Do you think I go out with my mates just to make your life a misery?
WOMAN:	Shut up.
MAN:	Do you?
TITLE:	It's up to you to break the cycle.
	For more information 0800 222 999.

Vicious Circle, NZ Children & Young Persons Service, New Zealand, 1995

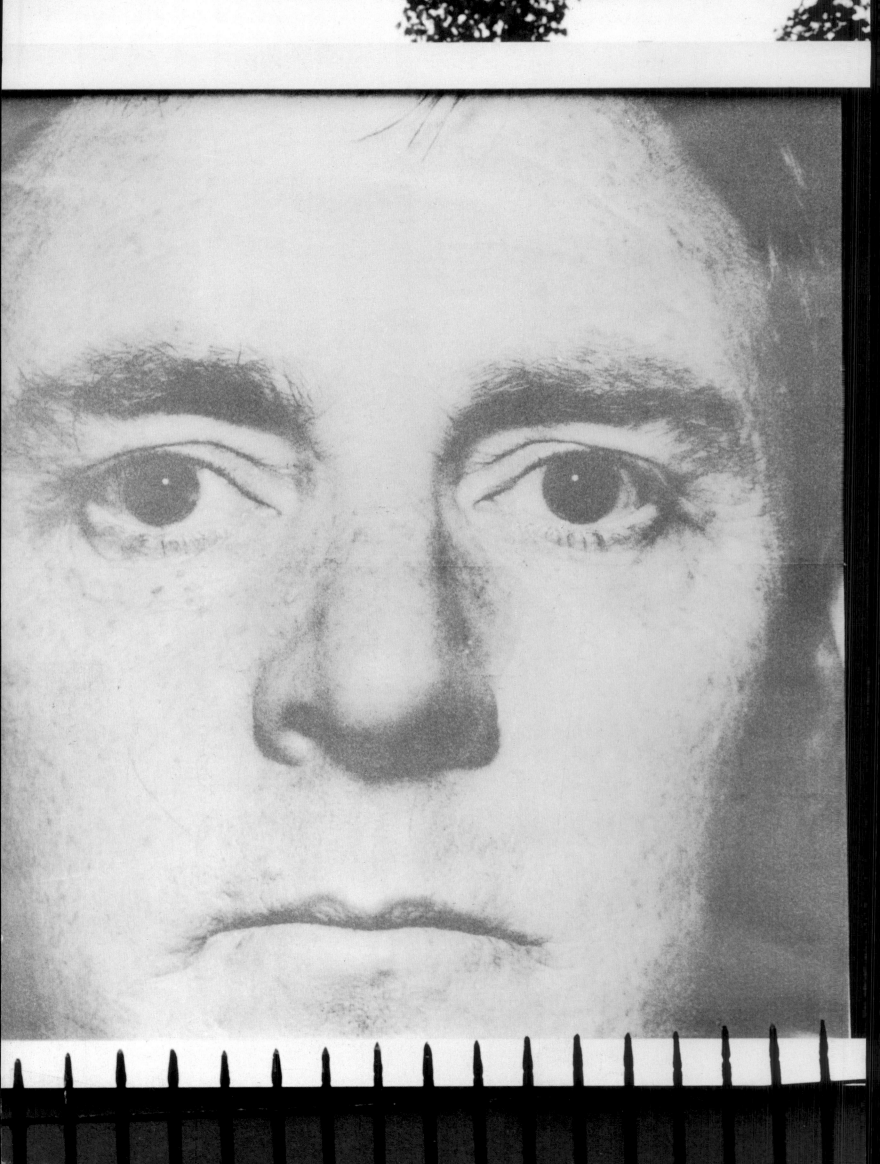

MY PICTURE IS FADING FAST.

Every day I am more helpless as my muscles waste away. There is no cure for my disease and hope for me but I want there to be hope for others. Please send a donation to help people live with MND and to pay for research.

SO AM I.

Motor Neurone Disease Association. Box 246, Northampton NN1 1TR. Registered Charity No 294354.

12570

MY PICTURE IS FADING FAST.

ery day I am more helpless as my muscles ste away. There is no cure for my disease and hope for me but I want there to be hope for ers. Please send a donation to help people live with MND and to pay for research.

SO AM I.

tor Neurone Disease Association.
Box 246, Northampton NN1 1TR. Registered Charity No. 204354.

'Come on!'

If you just went for a few good walks, that would be a start. The chances are you'll actually like it.

'Away you go!'

'Come along darling, walkies!'

VOICEOVER: It may come as a nasty shock, but people need exercising just as much as dogs.

Once you really get going, your heart, lungs and muscles all get stronger. You'll shake off depression, you'll feel a new man, or a new woman.

Come along, Roger.

'Here Roger, fetch!'

'Roger! Come back at once!'

And get a lot more out of it.

VOICEOVER: A few minutes' exercise every day could add so much more to your life.

...YOU'll put more effort into everything you do.

LOOK AFTER YOURSELF! The Health Education Council

Walkies, The Health Education Council, UK 1979

SCARRED FOR LIFE BY A CAR THAT MISSED HER BY MILES.

Naledi was safe in bed while her daddy was walking home drunk from the shebeen. He never knew what hit him, but she'll suffer for the rest of her life.

WATCH YOUR STEP.

Naledi/Crying Girl. Department of Transport, South Africa

Netanyahu may Barak with do rival oust to deal

Anwar's Malaysia democracy battle takes up wife for the

BY SARAH STRICKLAND
in Kuala Lumpur

BY PATRICK COCKBURN
in Jerusalem

ROME
EUROPEAN TIMES

BY FLORENCE KENNEDY

THE MS SOCIETY
PROVIDING THE

...something (some money) to help us fight this
During MS Week
To find out more
on 0808 800 8000.

It can disrupt e...
...unpredictable disease.

WHAT'S MS LIKE?

CLOSE YOUR EYES
AND STICK A PIN
IN THIS PAGE
EVERY DAY FOR THE
REST OF YOUR LIFE.

TODAY YOUR WHOLE BODY HURTS

TODAY YOU CAN'T FEEL YOUR FINGERS

TODAY YOU HAVE MUSCLE SPASMS

TODAY YOU CAN'T MOVE YOUR LEFT LEG

TODAY YOU CAN'T DRIVE

TODAY YOU CAN'T CLIMB THE STAIRS

TODAY YOU FEEL OK

TODAY YOU'RE IMPOTENT

TODAY YOUR VISION IS BLURRED

TODAY YOU HAVE NO BALANCE

TODAY YOU CAN'T MOVE YOUR RIGHT LEG

TODAY YOU CAN'T FEEL YOUR FINGERS

TODAY YOU CAN'T CONCENTRATE

TODAY YOUR WHOLE BODY HURTS

TODAY YOU FEEL GREAT

TODAY YOU FEEL LIKE YOU HAVE FISH SWIMMING AROUND INSIDE YOUR BODY

TODAY YOUR HEARING IS MUFFLED

TODAY YOU CAN'T MOVE

TODAY YOU CAN'T STOP SHAKING

TODAY YOU CAN'T TALK

TODAY YOU CAN'T FEEL YOUR TOES

TODAY YOU CAN'T MOVE YOUR RIGHT ARM

TODAY YOU'RE INCONTINENT

TODAY YOU'RE DEAF

TODAY YOU CAN'T FEEL YOUR FEET

TODAY YOU FEEL FINE

TODAY YOU CAN'T MOVE

TODAY YOU CAN'T STOP SHAKING

TODAY YOU CAN'T TALK

TODAY YOU CAN'T FEEL YOUR FINGERS

TODAY YOU FEEL TIRED

TODAY YOU CAN'T CLIMB THE STAIRS

MS is a disease that attacks the central nervous system. You never know from one day to the next which part of your body it will affect. and how severely.
Anyone can get MS and we want you to find out more about it. For more information or to make a donation please call us 24 hrs on 0800 100 133

THE MS SOCIETY
PROVIDING THE STRENGTH TO FIGHT MS

Pin, Multiple Sclerosis Society, UK, 1997

Barak may do deal with rival to oust Netanyahu

BY PATRICK COCKBURN

BENJAMIN NETANYAHU'S opponents may unite to back one candidate as a way of defeating the Israeli Prime Minister in next month's election.

The best – and perhaps only – chance of victory for Ehud Barak, the One Israel candidate, is to persuade Yitzhak Mordechai, the former defence minister, to stand down and join forces with him.

One Israel, the new name for the Labour party, would offer Mr Mordechai, the candidate of the newly created Centre party, four or five ministerial posts in a new government, according to Israeli press reports. Mr Mordechai himself would become the deputy prime minister and defence minister.

Mr Netanyahu is a little behind Mr Barak in the polls, but the large number of voters who are declaring themselves to be "undecided" traditionally swing to the right.

Mr Mordechai, whom polls show will win some 17 per cent of the vote on 17 May, has failed to make the breakthrough that would enable him to survive until the second round of balloting. This takes place on 1 June if no candidate wins half the vote in the first round.

The Centre party leadership largely comprises politicians and members of the Israeli establishment who have quarrelled with Mr Netanyahu. According to the daily *Maariv*, its leaders – with the exception of Mr Mordechai – are reconciled to doing a deal before the election, in which they are likely to fare badly.

Mr Barak needs to win in the first round of the election, because as many as a quarter of the Israeli-Arab community may not turn out for voting on 1 June.

In the first round, Israeli-Arabs will be attracted to the polls because that is the Knesset election, in which they will be voting for their own parties as well as the prime minister.

One Israel, advised by American political consultants, has run a better-organised campaign in recent weeks. But this may make only a limited difference because voter loyalty in Israel is often determined by membership of ethnic or religious communities, such as the ultra-orthodox Jews or Russian immigrants. In this way, One Israel is at a disadvantage and, under its old name of Labour, has won only one election outright since 1973.

Even with Mr Mordechai supporting him, Mr Barak faces a close race. He needs Azmi Bishara, the Arab candidate for the prime minister's office, to throw his support behind him.

Mr Bishara currently has the support of 4 per cent of voters.

By contrast, Mr Netanyahu wants Benny Begin, the candidate of the far right, not to drop out in case he should set a precedent for Mr Mordechai also giving up.

If Mr Mordechai does decide to back Mr Barak, the partnership will probably be agreed only a week before the election, thus allowing Mr Mordechai to maximise his demand for jobs in a new government.

Amnon-Lipkin Shahak, the former Israeli chief of staff and a founder of the Centre party, would reportedly be made ambassador to Washington and also put in charge of negotiations with Syria.

The inability of the Centre party to make a breakthrough confirms the diagnosis of Yossi Beilin, one of the leaders of One Israel, that Israeli politics has few centrist or floating voters. This is because normal political differences are reinforced by the various religious, ethnic and class loyalties.

Such floating voters as do exist are enthusiastically pursued by all parties.

This is particularly true of the Russian immigrants, whose voting patterns are considered more fluid than those of other communities. Party leaders were yesterday courting Igor Ivanov, the Russian Foreign

Anwar's wife takes up the battle for democracy in Malaysia

Dr Azizah Ismail: 'I will rise up and protect my family and that can be transformed into political change' *AP*

BY SARAH STRICKLAND
in Kuala Lumpur

AZIZAH ISMAIL is a tiny woman with a huge task on her hands. This time last year few people had heard of the softly spoken retired eye surgeon who entertained guests, looked after the children and attended party conferences with her husband, Malaysia's former deputy prime minister Anwar Ibrahim. She had certainly never made a public speech.

Now, she regularly draws crowds of up to 20,000 and is attempting to perform a miracle: unseat the powerful coalition that has ruled Malaysia since it gained independence from Britain in 1957. With only rudimentary weapons she is facing a Goliath in a battle that few expect her to win. But they are watching with fascination and growing respect.

Seated on a sofa in her spacious but modestly furnished house in one of Kuala Lumpur's leafy suburbs, she laughs when she recalls the moment she realised what her future might hold. "We were at a rally and my husband said, 'If anything happens to me, then Azizah will take over.' It was unreal to hear him say that, he hadn't really discussed it with me."

Anwar had been sacked by his former friend and mentor, the Prime Minister, Mahathir Mohamad. Anwar and his wife were touring the country, calling for *reformasi*, inspired by the uprising that had ousted President Suharto of Indonesia. A few months later, when Anwar was arrested, 46-year-old Dr Azizah took over the campaign, joining a long list of Asian women who have inherited a political role from their fathers and husbands.

A serene, warm-hearted woman, Dr Azizah has withstood much: allegations that her husband betrayed her with both sexes, his violent arrest by masked gunmen, the sight of his bruised and beaten face and the news last week that he will be behind bars for the next six years. She has remained dignified and calm throughout. "I controlled myself because I would have broken down," she said. "Anwar told me not to be sad, to be brave."

Her main selling point, she believes, is that she is both a trained doctor and an embattled mother. "I am seen as a maternal figure with a maternal instinct. I will rise up and protect my family and I think that can be transformed into political will to change. People have sympathy for me and my position translates into what is wrong with the system. I only wish I had more political acumen, could be a better orator. Caught unprepared I can only make the best of it, which I think is also my appeal. I speak from the heart and have even seen grown men cry."

Dr Azizah, who recently launched the National Justice Party, knows the odds are against her: she faces a huge political machine that has money, experience and a cowed media behind it. Her main weapon is public outrage at Anwar's treatment, which she says has opened people's eyes to injustice and corruption.

"Traditionally people would vote for the status quo and stability. We are going for a clean, effective government – not instability. The system has worked for us but we have to remove the repression." Her party has adopted a "multi-ethnic" label and its success depends on attracting votes from Malaysia's three main ethnic communities: Malays, Chinese and Indians. The two main opposition parties, one fiercely Islamic, the other mainly Chinese, are sharing a platform with her.

"We have not glossed over the differences, we accept they exist. The exciting thing is that we have come together on common ground, with common goals." Never seen without her headscarf, Dr Azizah describes herself as a pious Muslim, drawn to her husband by his deep religious convictions.

"He was very Islamic and I felt that we could have a good life together. My parents were not so happy because he was considered anti-government but they got over it."

The as yet unproven allegations of sodomy and adultery, which Anwar has been found guilty of trying to cover up, caused pain as they would in any household. "We are not angels, we are humans. I looked at my husband's relations with me and decided no letter should be used to destroy my happiness. I knew from then that they were trying to break us. I do not believe the allegations and nor do our children. They know their father."

Now Anwar sits in a jail that he helped to construct. "The irony is that he approved the allocation of funds for the building," says Dr Azizah, summoning a smile in the midst of her grief.

Italians open their eyes to spotless B&B

THE ITEM was thown away at that Italians are hygiene

EUROPEAN TIMES

ROME

the end of the regional television news, which follows the national bulletin. The Agency for Rome's Jubilee Year 2000 reported that 1,500 families in the capital had expressed interest in offering B&B accommodation to foreign guests. B&B is a totally new concept in Italy but with 30 million pilgrims and tourists expected to descend on Rome next year, its introduction is nothing if not timely. Hotels are expensive and there will not be enough to go round.

But the news set me thinking about how almost every aspect of domestic life is different in Italy compared with Britain, the United States, Australia – or, indeed, anywhere in the world. I remember when I first arrived here, the perplexity of my hostess when I politely declined her offer of *ciabatte*, a sort of shoe-cum-slipper. It was summer and the mock marble tiles were delightfully cool under my bare feet. She insisted, because I could have caught a chill, and even if her floors were cleaned daily my feet would inevitably get dirty.

Before I knew it, I was visualising all sorts of farcical scenes. Mrs Rossi's shocked face when Mr Smith presents her with a thank-you bouquet of chrysanthemums (they're strictly for graves and bringing them into a house courts bad luck). Mrs Smith asking Mr Rossi in her best Italian whether she could wash some smalls in the bidet. Wholesale panic when the Smith teenager innocently pulls a strap on the wall in the bathroom, not realising it's an alarm bell in case Grandma Rossi takes a bad turn in the bath. The apoplexy of Grandpa Smith as the Rossi's 16-year-old daughter nonchalantly lights up a Marlboro in the living room.

My curiosity sparked, I contacted the freephone lines about B&B set up by the chamber of commerce. It took me two days to get through, so presumably lots of Romans are similarly interested.

I was told that a regional law defined what B&B Italian-style should comprise. Those interested in B&B must live on the premises – which cuts out people wishing to put country houses to this use, and there is a limit of six guests. The tourism board inspects the premises before giving an OK, but there are no guidelines on price, which varies according to whether you are overlooking Piazza Navona or a car park.

One thing that is defined clearly is breakfast. Guests are forewarned there will be no point in complaining that there are no bacon and eggs or fresh croissants. Tea, coffee and milk are obligatory – food is left up to the proprietor on the condition that it be pre-packed, preferably in individual portions. You may be offered cheese and ham but it will not be freshly cut.

It's important to understand that this, from the point of view of Italian administrators, at least, is for your own good. One national trait that is frequently overlooked is freaks; this does not just mean enormous attention to their own cleanliness and the tidiness of their houses but also to what they eat. My babysitter will frequently leave a packet of lentils or baking powder on the table with an accusing note saying "*Scaduto!*" (past its use-by date) and my mother-in-law scrubs my chopping board with bleach. By ordering packed breakfasts, the authorities are simply avoiding the dire, though remote prospect, that someone's memory of Rome will be a stomach ache.

But this is Italy and you may well find someone prepared to break the rules.

The law stipulates that the paying guests will have use of the bathroom. Many Italians are convinced that foreigners, and Brits in particular, are not great washers and therefore long, hot showers won't send their power bill through the roof. My partner's teenage daughter had been pestering him for months about going on an exchange trip to Ireland this summer to improve her English. But when he finally agreed, she was having second thoughts. A girl from the next class up had, it seemed,

When in Rome, you may live where the Romans do

had a nightmare experience with "*una famiglia di Zulu*". Zulu is Italian yoof-speak for barbarians. The family in question were guilty of leaving a grubby ring in their bath. Their young Italian visitor had to apply some elbow grease and Jif before she could start her ablutions.

The Italian B&B will be a real novelty on the psychological front. Italians are not accustomed to opening their home to people other than extended family or close friends. The pervasive concept of *bella figura* – which is why Italians are always better groomed than most other Europeans – means their houses must be spotless, their meals impeccable, their linen whiter than white. And why would one go to that effort to impress someone you didn't know and might never see again?

It seems those interested in offering B&B are either Romans who have travelled or those who believe that new year 2000 is going to be such a nightmare in terms of traffic and crowd chaos, that they might as well try and make a few extra lire.

FRANCES KENNEDY

Registered charity 207495

MS SCRAMBLES MESSAGES BETWEEN THE BRAIN AND THE BODY.

t can disrupt every part of your body, every aspect of your life. At any time.
During MS Week, we are aiming to raise awareness (and ho y some money) to help us fight this unpredictable d
To find out more about Multiple Sclerosis, freefone the MS ne on 0808 800 8000.

MS WEEK APRIL 18-25
THE MS SOCIETY
PROVIDING THE STRENGTH TO FIGHT MS

Scrambled Page, Multiple Sclerosis Society, UK, 1999

NSW HEALTH
FOR A STATE OF BETTER HEALTH

Me No Fry, NSW Health, Australia, 1991

IT'S A ONCE IN A LIFETIME OPPORTUNITY.
MISS IT.

Eclipse, Action for Blind People, UK, 1999

Come and
see us.

The cure for breast can

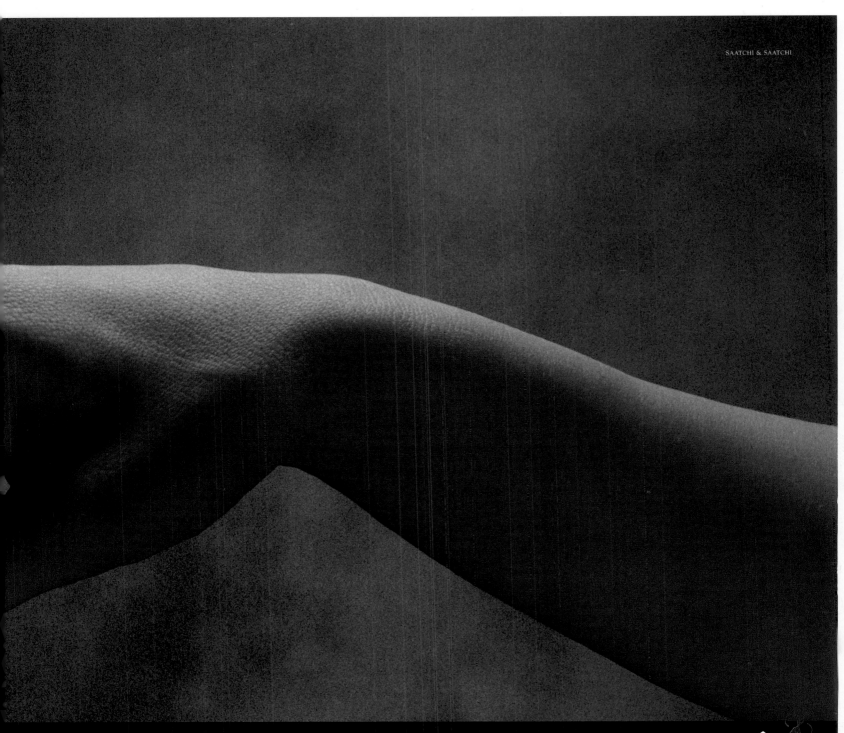

r is prevention. ITALIAN CANCER SOCIETY

Come and see us, Italian Cancer Society, Italy, 1999

This is what happens when a fly lands on your food.

Flies can't eat solid food, so to soften it up they vomit on it. Then they stamp the vomit in until it's a liquid, usually stamping in a few germs for good measure.

Then when it's good and runny they suck it all back again, probably dropping some excrement at the same time.

And then, when they've finished eating, it's your turn.

Cover food. Cover eating and drinking utensils. Cover dustbins.

The Health Education Council

Flies on Food, The Health Education Council, UK, 1970

You can't scrub your lungs clean.

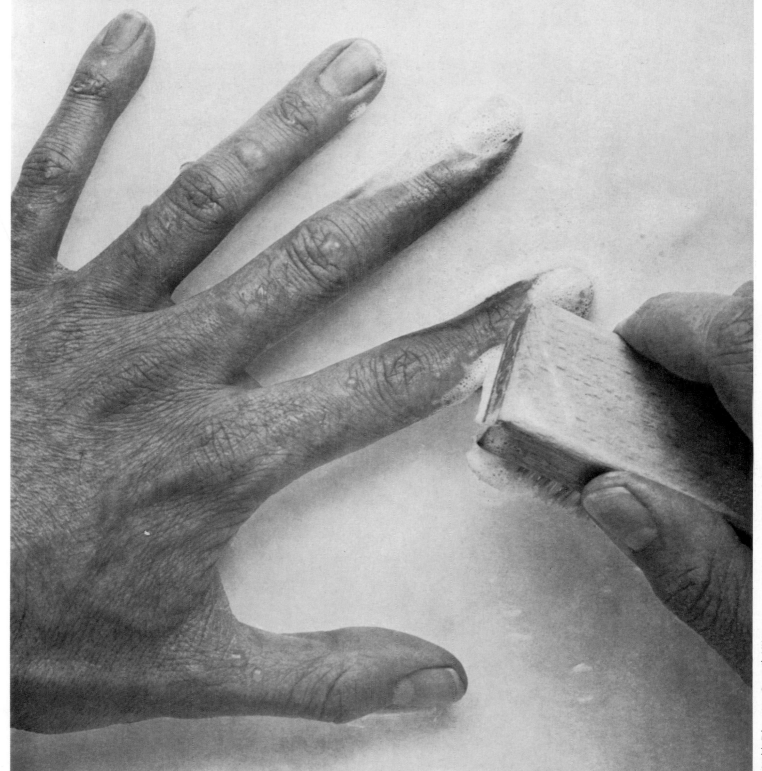

Lung cancer kills thirteen times more smokers than non-smokers.

The Health Education Council

Scrub your Lungs, The Health Education Council, UK, 1971

YOUR CAR IS A LETHAL WEAPON.

DRIVE CAREFULLY.

Published in the interests of road safety in the U.A.E.

Only three days left until "Anti-land mines day".

STATISTICS OF DESPAIR: *110 million landmines set in 64 countries around the world; a victim every 20 minutes; from 5 to 10 million mines produced each year; 100 million more ready in the world's arsenals; 90% of casualties to women and children.*
NUMBERS FOR HOPE: *Postal account N° 189241, Mani Tese, Italian Campaign Against Land mines, via Cavenaghi 4 - 20149 Milan.*
ON SATURDAY, APRIL 13, COME TO PIAZZA SANTI APOSTOLI TO SIGN OUR PETITION AND MAKE YOUR CONTRIBUTION.

ITALIAN CAMPAIGN AGAINST LAND MINES

Three More Days, Italian Anti-Landmine Association, Italy, 1996

CAN A $3 LANDMINE CRIPPLE A WHOLE ECONOMY?

It can when farmers are too afraid to plow their fields; when children are too scared to walk to school; when the simplest daily activities become a game of Russian roulette. Yet, in addition to the 110 million landmines still lying buried in the Third World, another 2 million are being planted each year. Help abolish landmines. It's the only way the Third World can make a step forward. To find out how you can help, please write to your local government or to the Mine Clearance and Policy Unit, Department of Humanitarian Affairs, United Nations, New York, N.Y. 10017.

UN
WE BELIEVE

DON'T PUMP OUR CHILDREN FULL OF LEAD.

USE UNLEADED PETROL.

Published in the interests of the environment in the U.A.E.

Unleaded. Government of Dubai, Dubai, 1997

It's even more disgusting on the pavement.

If your dog shits in the street, please clean it up.

BATES SAATCHI & SAATCHI ADVERTISING With thanks to: Gianfranco Pontillo · photo, B&B reklamní společnost · billboard space.

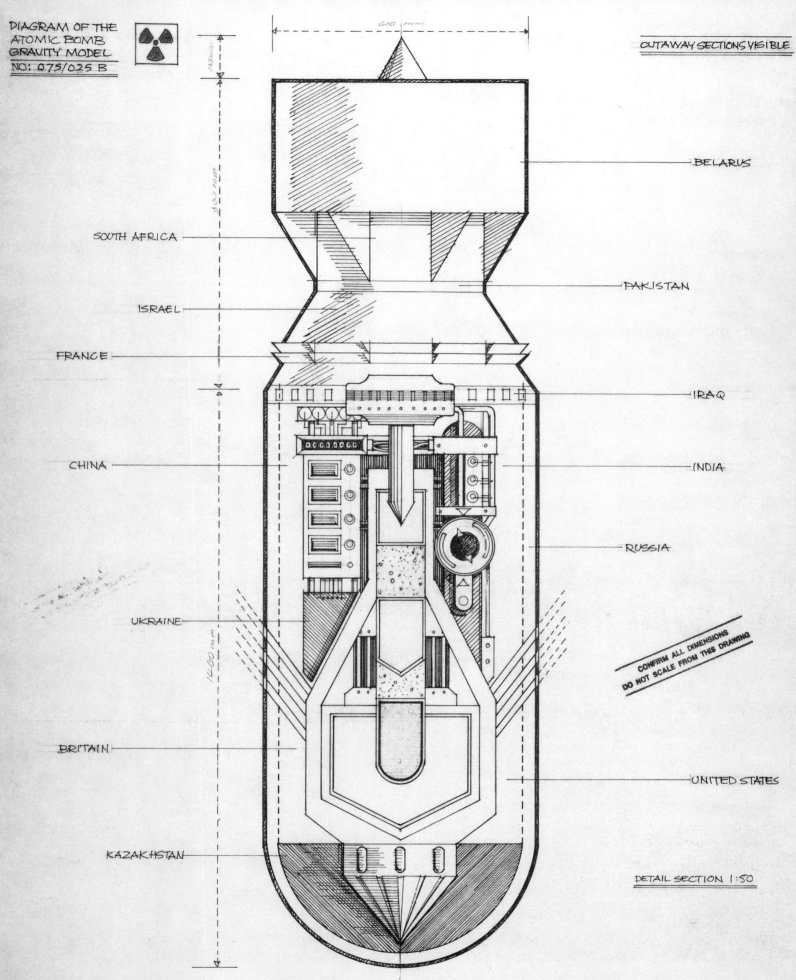

DIAGRAM OF THE
ATOMIC BOMB
GRAVITY MODEL
NO: 075/025 B

CUTAWAY SECTIONS VISIBLE

BELARUS

SOUTH AFRICA

PAKISTAN

ISRAEL

FRANCE

IRAQ

CHINA

INDIA

RUSSIA

UKRAINE

CONFIRM ALL DIMENSIONS
DO NOT SCALE FROM THIS DRAWING

BRITAIN

UNITED STATES

KAZAKHSTAN

DETAIL SECTION 1:50

FINALLY SOMETHING THE WHOLE WORLD CAN WORK TOGETHER ON.

INTERNATIONAL COOPERATION HAS DONE A REMARKABLE JOB OF
THREATENING US ALL WITH ANNIHILATION. NOW PERHAPS IT CAN DEFUSE THE SITUATION.
IF YOU EVER WANTED TO CHANGE THE WORLD THIS IS YOUR CHANCE.
JOIN THE DEBATE VIA OUR WEBSITE BETWEEN 27 OCTOBER AND 1 NOVEMBER.

WWW.WORLDFORUM.ORG

STATE
of the
WORLD
FORUM

Atomic Bomb, State of the World Forum, New Zealand, 1998

DON'T LEAVE
FIRE HAZARDS
LYING ROUND
THE HOUSE.

Leaf/Match, NRMA, Australia, 1997

We have been married for 18 years.

It has generally been a peaceful life.

We're busy with our own things.

Day after day, it's work , home, kid.
Nothing out of the ordinary.

When he was laid-off. . . .

It happened so suddenly.

My mind went blank.

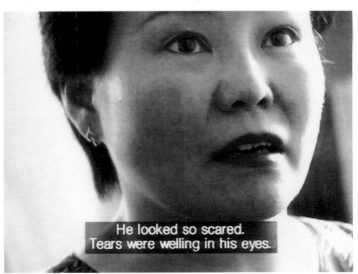

He looked so scared.
Tears were welling in his eyes.

Off Duty, CCTV, China, 1998

The first thing to go was my self-esteem.

I could only think of drowning my misery with alcohol.

He needs my support.

She's been so encouraging.

Don't worry. It will turn out well.

Being laid-off has been the best thing to happen to us for a while.

We've never been closer.

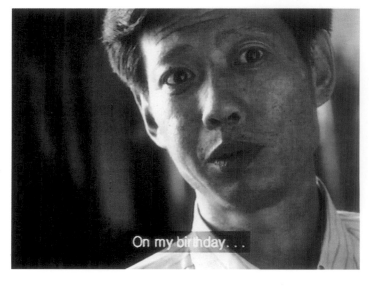

On my birthday. . .

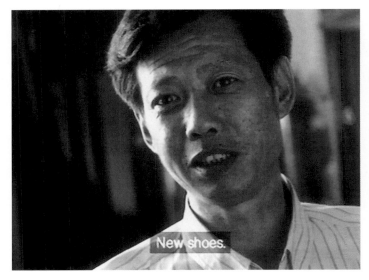

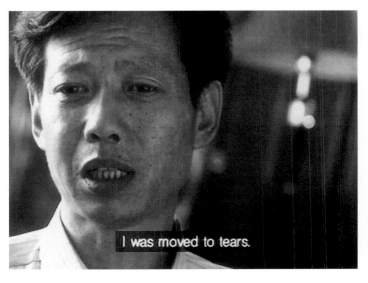

Off Duty, CCTV, China, 1998

Dear Eric,

There is a virus spreading through our community which is claiming a life every week. It is spread through contaminated blood or sexual contact. I'm sure you know what I'm talking about. HIV and ultimately AIDS.

The only way we can stop it spreading is to spread the word faster than the virus.

And the word is condoms. Practise safe sex and use them. It's that simple.

Now take this letter and copy it 6 times. Send them to people who you consider make the world a better place. Don't be embarrased, we could all do with a reminder.

If you send the letter on to six people this week, and each of these people do the same, by the end of the month 7,776 people will be better informed. If you choose to do nothing, by the end of the year several million people will have missed our message.

We owe it to everyone to spread the word and beat the virus.

SIGNED: Someone who cares

PS. If you could afford to send a donation to the Aids Foundation they would very much appreciate it. Their address is:

NZ AIDS Foundation.
PO Box 7287,
Wellington,
New Zealand.

Chain Letter, New Zealand AIDS Foundation, New Zealand, 1996

SLOW POISON.

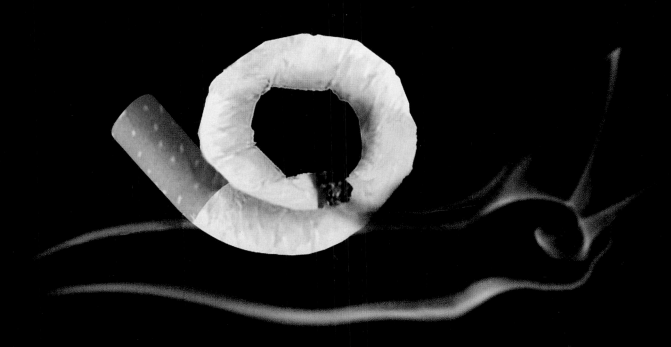

ISSUED IN THE PUBLIC INTEREST BY
TATA TEA LIMITED

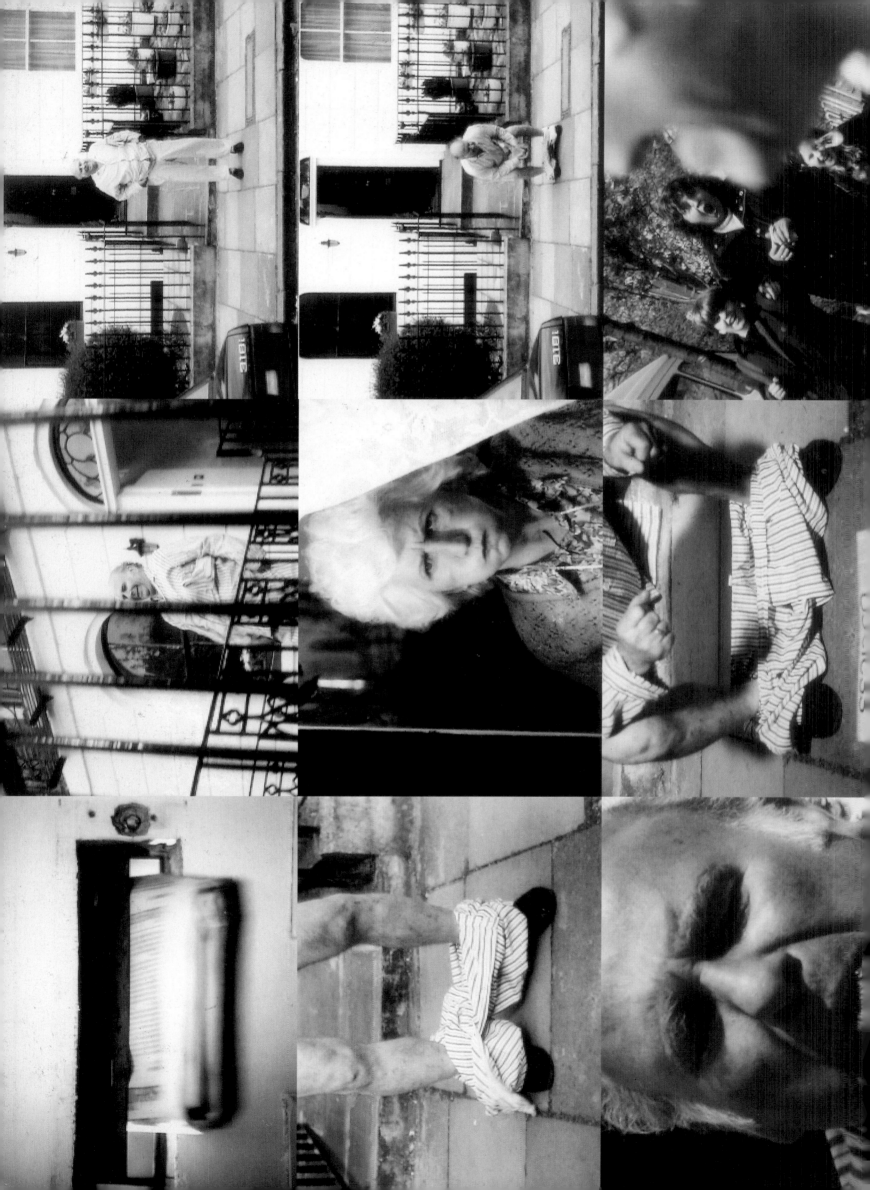

Morning! Turned out nice again...

LONDON BOROUGH OF ISLINGTON

DON'T
LET YOUR DOG N.7

LONDON BOROUGH OF ISLINGTON

YOU
WOULDN'T N.1

Clean-Up, Islington Council, UK, 1996. Music: Morning Mood from Grieg's Peer Gynt Suite.

VOICEOVER: Is there anybody out there?

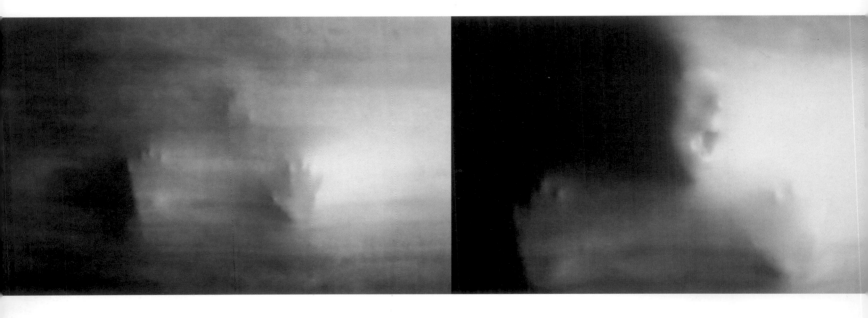

VOICEOVER: Is there anybody out there?

Is there anybody out there?

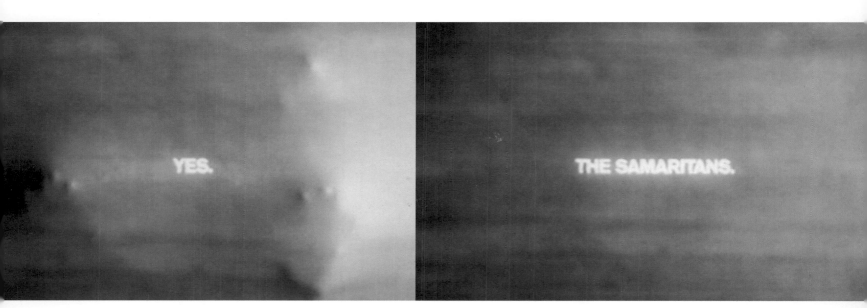

RON

WAS ALL SET TO DIE

THEN CAME THE WORST NEWS OF ALL.

Talk about gutted, well you would be wouldn't you? There you are, assured of having terminal cancer when, like a bolt from the blue, your doctor delivers the killer blow. "The treatment has worked. The cancer has been eradicated. You're going to live." Devastation hits. The outlook simply could not be worse.

Now you have to remember that Ron's story is fairly unique. Most people wouldn't react the way he did. But the thing about dying (or in Ron's case, not dying) is that no two people react the same way.

When he was first diagnosed with cancer, Ron, quite naturally, was shocked. It was the worst thing he'd ever heard. But over time his outlook changed. He accepted his fate. He even started to plan for it, his whole life becoming geared up to dying. And that's where the problems started. So prepared for death was Ron that he reached a stage of contentment. Normally in our field this is the best possible outcome. In fact it is good when a terminally ill patient reaches this phase, because it is so unusual. At Mary Potter Hospice we feel as if we've done our job to the best of our ability if we can help a patient reach this point.

"You're going to live Ron." Hold the wreaths. Cancel that hearse. Surely it's the best news he could ever get, right? Wrong. You see his life was so geared to dying that in a funny sort of way, it had become his reason for living. He'd started saying his goodbyes, everything was leading nicely towards a well plotted out conclusion, he was outta here.

And then in one cruel blow, that reason for living was taken away from him. Death's door was slammed in his face. Suddenly all the preparations and mental anguish he'd been through had been for nothing. Floundering around in his new lease on life Ron started to imagine illnesses. He got a heart condition. He was convinced of it. He didn't of course, in truth it was a head condition, and the mind being the most powerful organ of all did the rest for him. Ron became a man hell bent on finding an excuse for wallowing in imminent death. That was where he now felt the most comfortable. He'd come to rely on all the new found support services available to the dying. He'd adapted too well to all the attention and sympathy. That's not to say he enjoyed them, but he needed them. And it was in this state that he lived out his days.

Ron's tragic fate was largely self imposed. And although he was never a patient at Mary Potter Hospice, it is a true story from our head doctor (Ron was one of his patients when he worked in England) that highlights the sort of problems we regularly encounter.

And it has important ramifications for Mary Potter Hospice when it comes to how we handle patients. Because sometimes even when everything takes a turn for the best, the situation actually becomes much worse. That is how unpredictable our working day is. That's why we're constantly looking to learn from the Ron's of this world so that situations like his don't repeat themselves.

It's been said that only two things in life are certain: death, and taxes. While taxes are frighteningly predictable, death isn't. Ron's story is testament to that, and so is Nell's. But her story is right at the opposite end of the spectrum. Possibly the perfect death. Petronella, Nell to her friends, came from Kapiti way. She was

E.

...an inpatient at Mary Potter Hospice, but only very briefly. Nell was in her early 60's when she was first referred to us in May 1994. She had growths on her liver, kidney, pancreas and stomach. This wasn't her first brush with cancer, back in 1989 she'd had to have a kidney removed. But when she was diagnosed this time, she was told she had just two months to live. Nell came into the Hospice in tremendous pain and vomiting constantly.

We too were convinced that she was not long for this world, we wouldn't put a time limit on it though. If it's one thing we've learned it's that putting an expiry date on a person can be one of the worst things to do. For a start it is virtually impossible to be accurate. But more importantly, it can lead to situations like Ron's.

At first we thought Nell's cancer was raging out of control, but she didn't. She was sure she'd just pulled a muscle and that was causing the pain. She was wrong. But she also felt the drugs she was on could be causing the problems, and this time she was right. In the two weeks that she was in the Hospice we were able to get her onto a course of pain control which didn't cause her to vomit. She went home pain free and ready to get on with life. She still had cancer, it was still incurable, but she still had a lot of living to do.

More and more these days we're finding that our patients are happier to be treated away from the hospice building itself. They still come in, and our beds are still full, but they tend to come in periodically for treatment and pain control assessments, then they head back home, where they're most comfortable. We encourage this as much as possible. It's a risk that if patients check into the Hospice too soon, they may resign themselves to dying too soon. But at home, they tend to get on with life, as Nell did.

Two months went by, then three, then six. Nell just kept on lusting for life. She regularly consulted with her GP, and our Hospice doctor would visit her up the coast every couple of months. She used naturopathic remedies too. But it was her outlook that did the most good of all. If she'd believed her initial death sentence, if she'd decided to stay at Mary Potter, she could well have just stopped living. Thankfully she didn't. She wanted to stay at home with her husband.

She wanted to leave home with her husband too. Which they did often. They'd hook up the caravan and go for long trips all around New Zealand. Far from being like Ron, far from becoming consumed by death, Nell became even more consumed by life.

At the end of 1995 complications set in. Nell had a bowel blockage. But even this didn't stop her. She had an operation which fixed it, and led to an excellent recovery. She was still a box of birds some sixteen months after she was meant to die. By May 1996 though, her disease finally began to catch up with her. She became tired and pain again reared its head. Nell herself realised that her time was ending. She could no longer swallow her pills so pain relief had to be administered through a needle under her skin. Only at this point, some two years after her first diagnosis, did Nell decide to return to the Hospice to die.

As we said before, we try not to say when people are going to die. What often happens though, is that the patients themselves tell us. Something deep inside them lets them know it is about to happen. That's how it was with Nell. On the morning of the day she died she knew it would be her last. She called in all of her family one by one to say her goodbyes, and once that was completed, they all gathered around her, and she died peacefully.

Nell was an amazing woman, forever smiling and always positive, even though the threat of cancer hung over her for seven years. The memory of her still lingers strong in the minds of the staff at the Hospice, and with other terminally ill people that she gave support and encouragement to. In a strange way, far from finding her illness frightening, she found it liberating. She didn't know how long she had to live, but she was absolutely determined to make the most of it. As one of our staff remarked afterwards, she adopted the Frank Sinatra approach to dying. She did it her way.

At Mary Potter Hospice we have a mantra; making the most of life. As Nell showed, often this can be achieved away from the hospice building itself. That's why we're extending our services into the community. It's also why, with tremendous local support, we have just built an outpatient unit in the Kapiti region. And with your support during our street appeal this year we'll be able to do even more to help the dying (and those who find out they're not actually dying after all) to make the most of life.

YOU'RE GOING TO LIVE

A stroke isn't the end

YOU JUST HAVE TO START AGAIN.

You have a one-in-eight chance of suffering a stroke. Of course, if you are a smoker, your risk increases five times. High blood pressure, increases your chances four times. And if you are a smoker with high blood pressure, then you've hit the jackpot. Your chance of suffering a stroke is 18 times greater. A stroke results from a sudden interruption of the blood supply to part of your brain and it causes brain damage. You will suffer some or even all of the following symptoms: Death (the worst outcome, so we thought we would get it out of the way first) Loss of consciousness. Paralysis or weakness in your face, arm or leg on one side. You could well be unable to communicate. Perhaps you'll have difficulty swallowing or eating. You might have a loss of bladder or bowel control. Impairment to vision is on the cards. Loss of memory and loss of emotional control feature. Your earning potential could well go out the window. And depression, it goes without saying, is very common. Often you are left with a body that has two totally different halves

ONE SIDE CAN BE PRETTY MUCH AS IT WAS BEFORE. BUT YOU'LL NEED TO TEACH THE OTHER SIDE HOW TO MOVE, CO-ORDINATE, SPEAK, EAT, AND WALK FROM SCRATCH. AFTER ALL THAT, IT'S HARDLY SURPRISING THE COMMON PERCEPTION IS THAT IF YOU'RE LUCKY ENOUGH TO SURVIVE A STROKE YOU'RE ACTUALLY NOT VERY LUCKY AT ALL. IT'S WITH SOME PLEASURE THAT WE CAN TELL YOU THIS ISN'T SO. THERE'S A GOOD CHANCE THAT YOU'LL BE ABLE TO MAKE A PARTIAL, EVEN A FULL RECOVERY. INTENSIVE THERAPY, SKILLED NURSING, AND TIME CAN HELP YOU REGAIN FULL CONTROL OF THE BODY. ANOTHER POSITIVE SIDE OF STROKE IS THAT AS WE LEARN MORE ABOUT THE CAUSES WE CAN SIGNIFICANTLY LOWER THE CHANCES THAT YOU WILL SUFFER ONE. EXCESSIVE ALCOHOL, SMOKING, HIGH STRESS LEVELS, LACK OF EXERCISE, HIGH BLOOD CHOLESTEROL, HEART DISEASE, DIABETES AND OBESITY ALL PLAY A PART. MANY OF THESE CAN BE CONTROLLED THROUGH MEDICATION, CHANGES TO DIET OR WORK HABITS, OR IN THE CASE OF EXCESSIVE ALCOHOL FOR EXAMPLE, A HEALTHY DOSE OF SELF CONTROL (DON'T WORRY, WE'RE NOT BEING TOTAL WOWSERS, JUST ENCOURAGING A BIT OF MODERATION). THE STROKE FOUNDATION IS NEW ZEALAND'S ONLY BODY COMMITTED SOLELY TO HELPING THE VICTIMS OF STROKE, THEIR FAMILY AND FRIENDS. BUT, SURPRISE SURPRISE, WE ARE NOT A RICH ORGANISATION. IN ORDER TO CONTINUE OUR WORK, OUR RESEARCH, OUR SUPPORT SERVICES AND OUR PREVENTATIVE EDUCATION PROGRAMMES WE NEED YOUR HELP. YOU CAN MAKE A DONATION TO THE STROKE FOUNDATION. PO BOX 2320 WELLINGTON, OR PHONE YOUR DONATION TO 0800 STROKE (0800 787 653). ANY AMOUNT YOU CAN SPARE WILL HELP US TO SPREAD THE WORD ABOUT PREVENTING STROKE, AND ENSURE THAT MORE PEOPLE REALISE IT'S NOT A ONE-SIDED STORY.

STROKE
FOUNDATION

Enquiries may be directed to the Stroke Foundation of New Zealand Inc. PO BOX 2320, WELLINGTON. TELEPHONE (04) 472 8099, FAX (04) 472 7019.

Start Again, Stroke Foundation, New Zealand, 1997

blind /blaɪnd/ *adj., v., n., & adv. –* *adj.* **1** lacking the power of sight.

blind /blaɪnd/ *adj., v., n., & adv. –* *adj.* **2** (often foll. by *to*) unwilling or unable to appreciate (a factor, circumstance, etc.)

Spend a day with the blind. It'll make you see things differently.

Issued in public interest by TATA TEA LIMITED *Making a difference...differently*

SISTA SAATCHI & SAATCHI-105/98C A

Blind, Tata Tea Limited/Blind Campaign, India, 1999

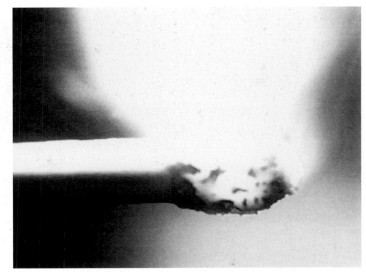
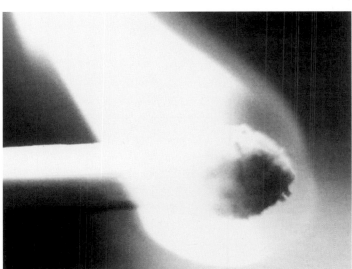

When one life is extinguished

something inside it

can light up another one.

LA VIDA TE LLAMA.
DONA TUS ORGANOS.

Life calls you
Donate your organs.

Matches, Antena 3 Television/Organ Donation, Spain, 1992

VOICEOVER: Some prisoners have electricity and three meals a day.
Some prisoners have hot running water and colour television.

230

VOICEOVER: Other prisoners don't...
And their only crime was to outlive their income.
So please, help Rand Aid make the difference. 011–882 2510.

Prisoner, Rand AID (Home of the Aged), South Africa, 1998

ANGRY, FRUSTRATED, CONFUSED?
PUNCH THESE.

THE SAMARITANS. PH 03 366 6676. 24 HOURS.

**Saatchi & Saatchis soziale Werbung
von Ed Jones**

Sozial engagierte Werbung liegt Saatchi & Saatchi in den Genen und zieht sich wie ein roter Faden durch ihre Arbeit.

Und das so sehr, dass Paolo Ettorre und sein Team von Saatchi & Saatchi in Italien vor einigen Jahren eine Ausstellung mit den der sozialen Idee verbundenen Kampagnen zusammengestellt haben.

Jetzt gibt es wieder eine Wanderausstellung, Saatchi & Saatchi & Social, die von diesem Buch begleitet wird.

Die vielen hervorragenden Werbekampagnen in Buch und Ausstellung, die sich beide mit wichtigen gesellschaftlicher Fragen befassen, zeigen klar, welche Bedeutung die Agentur weltbewegenden Ideen einräumt.

Ein faszinierender Aspekt dieser Arbeit ist, dass sie sich wie die Geschichte der Veränderungen im öffentlichen Bewusstsein unserer Zeit lesen lässt.

So wird zum Thema Sex im Hinblick auf die Volksgesundheit heute weniger über Empfängnis-Verhütung als über AIDS-Verhütung gesagt.

Wenn es um Verkehrssicherheit geht, wird heute weniger über Verletzungen als über Schmerzen geredet.

Bei der Umsetzung wird heute weniger auf zweidimensionale Medien gesetzt als auf multimediale Veranstaltungen und Installationen – auf „Ideen, die größer sind als Anzeigen".

Was den Stil betrifft, so findet sich heute weniger krass Schockierendes als vielmehr Nachklingendes, das zum Nachdenken anregt. Heute werden erschütternde Bilder nur behutsam eingesetzt, aus Angst vor einer „Mitleidsermüdung".

Wenn die Bilder zu sehr weh tun, erwecken sie schließlich nicht mehr das Mitgefühl des Publikums. Es gibt jedoch Momente, in denen diese Taktik unvermeidlich erscheint.

Zum Beispiel veröffentlichten Stefano Maria Palombi und Luca Albanese ihre Greenpeace-Anzeige für Italien Women and Children First (1996, S. 24) zeitgleich mit den Atombombentests im Südpazifik.

Das Plakat zeigt ein Baby mit grässlich deformiertem Wasserkopf, dessen Mutter während der Schwangerschaft „harmlosen" radioaktiven Niederschlägen von Atomtests in der Sowjetrepublik Kasachstan ausgesetzt gewesen war.

Das Baby ist so Furcht erregend hässlich, dass der Werbetext mit der Versicherung beginnen musste, es handle sich um eine echte Dokumentaraufnahme und nicht etwa um eine Computer-Retusche.

Diese Geschichte ist deswegen interessant, weil sie belegt, dass die Arbeit von Saatchi & Saatchi trotz einiger kultureller Unterschiede allgemein und international verständlich ist, egal in welchem Land die jeweilige Werbung produziert wurde.

Die Sprache der Werbung ist zur globalen Lingua franca geworden. Deshalb wird heute ein Thema immer öfter mit subtiler Hintergründigkeit statt im Frontalangriff angegangen.

In der englischen Kampagne Can't Look! (1999, S. 26) für die National Society for the Prevention of Cruelty to Children (NSPCC), den britischen Kinderschutzbund, tauchen zum Beispiel weder gewalttätige Erwachsene noch missbrauchte Kinder auf. Kes Gray und Dennis Willison entschieden sich nämlich bewusst gegen die Verwendung schockierender Bilder und für das wirkungsvollste Werbemittel überhaupt. Das Vorstellungsvermögen des Betrachters.

Ihre Regel hieß: Zeige nichts, impliziere alles.

Infolgedessen sind in ihrem Werbespot überhaupt keine handelnden Personen zu sehen, sondern nur Standfotos von den Idolen britischer Kinder und Jugendlicher – die Spice Girls, Fußballer Alan Shearer, Rupert The Bear und Action Man –, die sich alle die Augen zuhalten, um nicht sehen zu müssen, was die Zuschauer hören.

Weniger ist Furcht erregend mehr.

Der amerikanische Autor John Updike sprach vom Wahrheitsbegriff der Werbeindustrie als Oxymoron, das zwei sich widersprechende Begriffe miteinander verbindet. Der Gedanke ist zwar amüsant, aber dennoch eine falsche und längst überholte Einschätzung.

Tatsächlich ist eines der eindrucksvollsten und auffallendsten Merkmale der Arbeiten von Saatchi & Saatchi ja gerade, dass sie sich weitestgehend auf die Macht der Wahrheit verlassen.

Jeder, der auch nur einmal einen Werbetext verfasst hat, weiß, dass Lügen und Halbwahrheiten aufgrund des großen Misstrauens und der Skepsis des Durchschnittshörers oder -zuschauers in Wirklichkeit überraschend ineffektiv sind.

Gleichzeitig werden Mitarbeiter von Kampagnen für gemeinnützige Organisationen Ihnen sagen, dass sie häufig wahre Geschichten hören, die so grauenvoll sind, dass sie nicht publiziert werden können.

Immer mehr kommerzielle Werbeagenturen haben inzwischen auch erkannt, dass sie das Vertrauen, die Loyalität, Achtung und Zuneigung ihres Publikums nur gewinnen können, wenn sie schlicht und einfach die Wahrheit sagen.

Damit dies auch zur wirtschaftlich erfolgreichen Strategie wird, muss man natürlich ein Produkt haben, dessen Wahrheit in der Darstellung überzeugt.

Warum sollte man überhaupt irgendwelche „unehrlichen" Produkte herstellen?

In der Werbung für ein soziales Engagement kann man einfach nicht lügen, egal um welches umstrittene Thema es gerade geht – und umstritten sind fast alle –, denn bei der kleinsten Ungenauigkeit wird der Spieß sofort von den Gegnern umgedreht und die ganze Beweisführung zu Fall gebracht.

Um so etwas zu verhindern, überprüft man

sorgfältig jede Behauptung oder Feststellung. Aus diesem Grund sind die Textwerbungen im vorliegenden Buch ebenso informativ wie jeder sorgfältig recherchierte Leitartikel zum gleichen Thema. Und gelegentlich besser formuliert.

Nehmen wir zum Beispiel die NSPCC-Kampagne Raped as a 3 Year Old (Mit 3 Jahren vergewaltigt, 1992, S. 58) mit ihrem Bild eines Mannes mittleren Alters, den man, ohne den Text zu lesen, für den Täter halten muss. Diese Anzeige ist ein hervorragendes Beispiel für die sachlich-kühle Sprache der Werbedesigner (in diesem Fall Mike Boles und Jerry Hollens), die jede Spur von moralischer Entrüstung oder Wut strikt vermeidet und gerade deswegen umso eindringlicher sein kann.

Die Anzeige sagt dem Leser nicht, wie er denken soll. Wut über den Kindesmissbrauch ist zweifellos angebracht, sie entsteht jedoch ausschließlich aus des Lesers eigenen Schlussfolgerungen.

Creative Director Richard Myers weiß noch genau, dass dieses Anzeigenplakat mit seiner Überschrift und fast 500 Worten Text in Londoner U-Bahnstationen so große Menschentrauben anzog (wobei viele einen Zug fahren ließen, um den Text zu Ende zu lesen), dass es aus Sicherheitsgründen an anderen Stellen aufgehängt werden musste. Schließlich hätte es dem öffentlichen Wohl nicht gedient, wenn jemand beim Lesen eines, wenn auch noch so elegant formulierten, Plakattextes buchstäblich unter die Räder gekommen wäre.

Eine zweite Bildanzeige für den gleichen Kunden zeigt eine werdende Teenager-Mutter, die auf ihren dicken Bauch hinunterschaut. Die Überschrift lautet: We Both Have The Same Father (Wir haben beide denselben Vater, 1995, S. 30). Diese Zeile liest man zunächst wie eine sachliche Feststellung, bis man begreift, dass hier der Inzest angeprangert wird.

Das ist nur ein Beispiel dafür, dass Werbe- und Kommunikationsfachmänner und -frauen nicht a priori eine bestimmte Ideologie vertreten. Sie erfinden ihre Gesellschaft nicht, sondern reflektieren sie.

Wir leben in einer Kultur, in der soziales Engagement ebenso wie jedes kommerzielle Produkt wirkungsvoll beworben und gefördert werden muss. Bekanntlich sind nicht alle Sozialsponsoren gemeinnützig.

Die Agentur akquiriert Werbekampagnen für mehr Verkehrssicherheit, für Rassenverständigung und gegen Drogenmissbrauch, Plakate mit Ausbildungsangeboten für Krankenschwestern oder Lehrer von kommerziellen Kunden (normalerweise im Wettbewerb mit anderen Agenturen) und berechnet marktübliche Honorare.

Wichtiger ist aber die Tatsache, dass sich die Werbung für Sozialsponsoring schwerpunktmäßig mit Ideen befasst, die Anstoß zu einer Veränderung in der öffentlichen Wahrnehmung und Behandlung gesellschaftlich relevanter Fragen geben ... mit zündenden Ideen, die aus kleinen Budgets einflussreiche Kampagnen machen.

Das Verhalten der Menschen kann dadurch natürlich nicht auf die Schnelle geändert werden, aber ein eindringlicher, nachhaltig in Szene gesetzter Gedanke kann zumindest das Problembewusstsein wecken.

Es gibt zahlreiche Beispiele dafür, dass eine provozierende, „verrückte" Idee, unterstützt von einem minimalen Werbe-Etat, durch die kostenlose Zusatzwerbung in vielen Presseberichten und -kommentaren ihren ursprünglichen Wert um ein Vielfaches erhöht hat.

Ein Beispiel hierfür ist die Anzeigen- und Plakatserie der britischen Kampagne für Rassengleichheit. Mit ihren wortspielerischen Überschriften legten Chris Kirk und Giles Montgomery ganz bewusst einen rauen Galgenhumor an den Tag und entzogen sich so dem Vorwurf, schwülstig oder pathetisch zu sein. Dadurch konnten sie beim Plakat mit der Überschrift Worst Marks (engl. Wortspiel: schlechteste Noten oder schlimmste Wundmale, 1997, S. 50) auch auf die Frage der schulischen Leistungen ethnischer Minderheiten in Großbritannien hinweisen, die im Fall der aus Asien stammenden Schüler tatsächlich überdurchschnittlich gut sind.

Persönliches Erleben bildete – wie so oft – die Grundlage für die Gestaltung des Junk-Mail-Plakats (Unerwünschte Reklamesendung, 1997, S. 171): Art Director Ajab Samrai Singh wuchs in einer armen Gegend des westlichen Mittelenglands auf und erlebte als Sechsjähriger, dass jemand Benzin durch den Briefschlitz in der Haustür seines Elternhauses goss und anzündete.

Eine Kampagne wie diese geht durch alle Medien, begleitet von einer steten Flut von Fakten und Kommentaren, und wird an jedem Arbeitsplatz und auf allen möglichen Veranstaltungen diskutiert. Wie bei so vielen Sozialwerbekampagnen vervielfachte sich also ihre Wirksamkeit – trotz des begrenzten Etats – durch jede Menge Leitartikel und die öffentliche Diskussion. Der landesweite Bekanntheitsgrad der Commission for Racial Equality (Kommission für Rassengleichheit) stieg danach innerhalb von zwei Jahren von 35 auf 50 Prozent.

Eine zündende Idee wird bewundert, weil sie geistreich, scharfsinnig, originell, treffend oder eingängig ist.

Sie ist es, die die Werbeleute morgens aus dem Bett springen lässt, tagsüber im Büro heftige Diskussionen hervorruft und spät nachts die größten Stürme der Begeisterung, Heiterkeit oder Rührung in ihren Kaffeetassen auslöst.

Für diejenigen, die mit ihrem Talent und ihrem persönlichen Einsatz jeden Tag gezielt nach Wegen suchen, um Meinungen zu verändern und Verhalten zu beeinflussen, für diejenigen ist der Heilige Gral das Aufspüren von Ideen, die die Welt bewegen.

Wer hat gesagt: „Wir sind uns selbst am treuesten, wenn wir andere loben"?

Ich habe nur einige wenige Werbefachleute getroffen, denen Saatchi & Saatchis Werbung gegen Alkohol am Steuer mit dem Titel Glasses (1993, S. 140) nicht gefällt. Dean Turney und Francis Wee kreierten sie in Singapur. Ihre Grundidee ist so einfach, dass fast jeder Werbetexter oder Art Director sich spontan fragt: „Warum bin ich nicht darauf gekommen?"

Im Werbespot sitzt der Zuschauer in einem Auto, das durch die Stadt fährt. Die Sicht wird zunehmend durch leere Biergläser versperrt, die der Fahrer auf dem Armaturenbrett abstellt. Nach dem vierten Glas kracht das Auto in den davor fahrenden Bus.

So sparsam – in jeder Hinsicht – und einfach genial. Ein Aha-Erlebnis bietet auch das Plakat für das britische Gun Control Network (Less Dead, 1997, S. 68). Nach dem Massaker unter den Schülern einer Klasse im schottischen Dunblane legte die britische Regierung einen Gesetzentwurf zum Verbot bestimmter Faustfeuerwaffen vor. Ausgerechnet der Revolver mit dem Kaliber 22 sollte davon ausgenommen sein.

Bill Gallacher, Robin Murtough und Keith Terry, Mitglieder eines Londoner Creative Teams, waren entsetzt und empört, hatten aber weder Geld noch Zeit, da die Parlamentsdebatte über das Gesetz unmittelbar bevorstand. Sie wussten, dass Robert Kennedy mit einem 22er erschossen worden war, und improvisierten mithilfe eines ihrer Archivfotos und eines Mac eine Plakatwand, die sie am Tag der Parlamentsdebatte auf einem Lastwagen vor dem Parlament aufstellten.

Darauf stand zu lesen: „Wenn ein 22er weniger tödlich ist, warum ist er dann nicht weniger tot?"

Die bestürzende Wirkung dieser wenigen Worte trug dazu bei, dass auch der 22er-Revolver in das Feuerwaffengesetz einbezogen wurde.

Tom Cordner, Creative Director in Los Angeles, meint: „Eine Anzeige kann sehr gut sein, und trotzdem sieht man sie und hat sie im nächsten Moment vergessen. Eine wirklich große Idee dagegen findet ihren Weg in dein Innerstes. Man vergisst sie nicht."

Saatchi & Saatchi sind davon überzeugt, dass die Welt sich auf dem schnellsten Weg zu einer „Aufmerksamkeits-Wirtschaft" befindet. In dieser Weltwirtschaft – so Bob Isherwood, internationaler Creative Director der Agentur – „sind Ideen die Währung der Zukunft".

Wenn das stimmt, sollte man die größten Summen nicht in die Medien, sondern in Ideen investieren.

Der US-Verband der Werbeagenturen schätzt, dass die amerikanischen Bürger pro Tag mit rund 3.000 kommerziellen Botschaften aller Art überschüttet werden. Mit TV-Spots, Plakaten, Zeitungsanzeigen, Logos, Anzeigen auf Bussen, Supermarktfußböden und Verpackungen. Werbung ist allgegenwärtig.

Verbraucher sagen aber, dass sie nur auf ganze zwölf (!) dieser Tausenden von Botschaften irgendwie reagieren. Schund und Banalitäten zuhauf sind so überwältigend und die Hintergrundgeräusche unserer Kommunikationskultur so ohrenbetäubend – wie kann sich da eine Botschaft bemerkbar machen und Gehör verschaffen?

Das ist in jedem Fall eine Herausforderung, ob nun für einen kommerziellen Kunden gearbeitet wird oder für einen gemeinnützigen. Im letzteren Fall ist die Herausforderung noch größer, da der Werbe-Etat eines Vereins meist nur einen Bruchteil kommerzieller Budgets ausmacht.

Wenn also die für Sozialsponsoring-Zwecke entwickelten Ideen das allgegenwärtige Werbegetöse erfolgreich übertönen – könnten daraus nicht auch Lehren für die Kommunikationsprobleme eines größeren Kundenkreises gezogen werden?

Saatchi & Saatchi glauben aufzeigen zu können, dass sie eine ganze Reihe von Ideen entwickelt haben, die in bestimmten sozialen Fragen und Bereichen Veränderungen bewirkt haben.

Ein Beispiel für den Spaß, den ein Creative Team aus der Bearbeitung eines ernsthaften Themas ziehen kann, stammt aus Neuseeland.

Schreiende Komik ist ein ungewöhnlicher und brutaler Aufhänger, um vor Raserei im Straßenverkehr zu warnen, aber Clen Wood und Peter Force haben diese Gratwanderung in ihrem TV-Spot Grunge Angels (1995, S. 70) bravourös gemeistert:

Die am meisten gefährdete Zielgruppe wird von zwei Jugendlichen dargestellt, die sich – zum Klang süßer Engelschöre – in den Wolken wiederfinden.

Über die himmlische Lautsprecheranlage ertönt die Ansage: „Zu Ihrer Unterhaltung senden wir an diesem Nach-Leben Whitney Houstons beliebteste Liebeslieder …"

Natürlich finden die Jungs diese Ewigkeit noch schlimmer als den Tod, worauf eine Stimme aus dem Off „Tod ist Scheiße" sagt und es wäre wohl besser sich anzuschnallen.

Ein herrlich bizarrer Humor lockert auch eine andere schwerwiegende Problematik auf, und zwar im italienischen Werbespot War on Hunger (1998, S. 134) für die UN Food & Agriculture Organisation.

Er beginnt mit einem Streifen Dokumentarfilm in Schwarzweiß – eine Armee im Kampf. Bald erkennt man, dass die Raketen fluoreszierende Maiskolben und die Hubschrauber Tomaten sind. Soldaten robben – Bananen wie Maschinengewehre im Anschlag – durchs Unterholz. Granatwerfer spucken Artischocken aus.

Eine total verrückte Welt.

Aber ganz richtig beobachtet: Wenn die in jedem Land der Welt für den Militärhaushalt bereitgestellten Mittel anders verwendet würden, könnte der Hunger überall erfolgreich bekämpft werden.

Viele der in diesem Buch gezeigten Werbespots haben übrigens bei den international wichtigsten Wettbewerben in Cannes, London, New York und anderswo erste Creative Awards gewonnen.

Auszeichnungen sind wahrscheinlich die meist begehrten Fetische der Werbeindustrie, aber man muss sich wohl kaum dafür entschuldigen, wenn Kollegen und Konkurrenten einen im jeweiligen Genre als die Besten ansehen.

Schließlich reagieren sie, ganz abgesehen von ihrem Fachwissen, auf eine eloquente Darstellung so wie jeder andere Mensch auch.

Die Preise illustrieren nur, dass die derart ausgezeichneten Werbespots besonders dramatisch, spannend und wirkungsvoll sind, während sie gleichzeitig neue und schwierige, heikle Themen behandeln.

Einige Laien, die sich für die Kreativwettbewerbe der Werbeindustrie interessieren, sind der irrigen Meinung, Werbespots für soziale und wohltätige Zwecke seien so etwas wie Optionsscheine auf erste Preise. Das Gegenteil ist der Fall, da in diesen Kategorien immer die meisten Beiträge eingereicht werden.

Alle eingereichten Spots profitieren gleichermaßen von den gleichen emotionsgeladenen Themen.

Im Gegensatz zur weit verbreiteten Meinung ist es jedoch sehr schwer, die Sache gut und richtig auf den Punkt zu bringen, und sehr leicht, alles falsch zu machen.

Soziale und kommerzielle Werbung stehen in vielerlei Hinsicht vor den gleichen Schwierigkeiten – unterscheiden sich aber in einem Punkt:

Die grundlegend schwierige Herausforderung bei der Werbung für soziale Fragen – und zugleich das Lohnende einer solchen Aufgabe, wenn sie gut gelöst wurde – besteht darin, dass sie als Erstes die öffentliche Wahrnehmung eines unbequemen Themas und dann die innere Einstellung der Menschen zu einem Problem verändert, über das sie am liebsten überhaupt nicht nachdenken.

Anders als bei der kommerziellen Werbung besteht hier für die Betrachter wenig Aussicht auf eigene Genüsse, wenn sie sich das Argument der sozialen Werbung zu eigen machen.

Wenn Dr. Johnsons Behauptung stimmt – „Die Seele einer Werbung ist das Versprechen, ein großartiges Versprechen" –, was kann dann eine Werbung für gemeinnützige Zwecke „versprechen"?

Wenn wir sonntags noch müde über unseren Kaffetassen und Croissants hängen, haben wir wirklich keine Lust, an AIDS oder Landminen oder grausam misshandelte Kinder zu denken.

Wir wollen nicht zugeben, dass wir selbst an Problemen wie Rassismus, Verkehrsunfällen oder Umweltzerstörung nicht unbeteiligt sind.

Auf keinen Fall wollen wir der Tatsache ins Auge sehen, dass wir vielleicht allein schon durch Nichtstun zum Elend hungernder Kinder, verzweifelter Flüchtlinge oder unterdrückter Minderheiten beitragen.

„Wir sind alle mitschuldig", sagen sie.

Müssen wir jetzt wirklich darüber reden?

Ja, eigentlich schon, wenn wir die Welt wenigstens ein bisschen verbessern wollen.

Wenn sie soziale Fragen ansprechen, müssen Werbedesigner den Schlüssel zum Mitgefühl der Betrachter finden und können dabei wohl kaum an den Eigennutz oder das Gewinnstreben der Menschen appellieren.

Auf der Suche nach diesem Schlüssel ist eine These hilfreich, die der amerikanische Psychologe A.H. Maslow Anfang der vierziger Jahre aufstellte. Sie erklärt, warum Verbraucher (vor allem in wohlhabenden Ländern) sich zunehmend allen krass materialistischen Appellen an ihre eigenen Interessen verweigern.

Maslow stellte fest, dass die Menschen eine ganze „Hierarchie von Bedürfnissen" haben, meist in Form einer Pyramide dargestellt mit den Grundbedürfnissen Nahrung und Wasser als Basis.

Darüber steht das Bedürfnis nach Sicherheit und (Wetter-)Schutz.

Danach kommen die sozialen Bedürfnisse nach Liebe und Zugehörigkeit zu einer menschlichen Gemeinschaft.

Auf der nächsthöheren Stufe befindet sich der „Achtungsbedarf", das Bedürfnis nach Anerkennung, Selbstachtung und Status.

Und schließlich, an der Spitze der Pyramide, haben die Menschen das Bedürfnis nach Selbstverwirklichung und innerem Wachstum.

Maslows These wird von der Beobachtung bestätigt, dass in der ganzen Welt den traditionell hoch geachteten Säulen der Gesellschaft heute erwiesenermaßen weniger Respekt gezollt wird als früher. Regierungen, Kirchen, Polizei und Streitkräfte, in Großbritannien die Monarchie, in den USA der Präsident – sie alle haben bewiesen, dass sie mit den gleichen menschlichen Schwächen behaftet sind wie wir selbst auch.

Andererseits haben bestimmte Unternehmen und Marken deutlich wahrnehmbar das Vertrauen der Öffentlichkeit gewonnen. Dafür gibt es konkrete Beweise.

Die Menschen vertrauen ihr Geld zunehmend Banken und Investmentfonds mit ethisch verantwortlicher Geschäftspolitik an, die keine Anteile an umweltfeindlichen Firmen anbieten – deren Profite auf Schädigung der Gesundheit ihrer Kunden beruhen – oder an Firmen, die Lieferanten aus der Dritten Welt ausbeuten.

Anleger sind bereit, dafür geringere Zinsgewinne in Kauf zu nehmen. Und auf den Wirtschaftsseiten der Zeitungen wird heute bereits eine beträchtliche Zahl ethisch orientierter Investmentfonds aufgeführt.

Die britische Co-operative Bank zum Beispiel hat einen deutlich niedrigeren Wechsel an Konteninhabern als andere Banken und ist heute der größte Anbieter von Gold Visa Cards in ganz Europa.

Im Mode- und Kosmetiksegment beruht der Erfolg der Firmen Liz Claiborne und The Body Shop auf ethischen Prinzipien. Und zahlreiche kommerzielle Unternehmen sind im Begriff zu entdecken, dass immer mehr Verbraucher zwischen relativ gleichwertigen Produkten die auswählen, deren Hersteller sich damit auch für einen nicht-kommerziellen Zweck engagieren.

Im angelsächsischen Sprachraum heißt die Vermarktung der mit ideellen, guten Zwecken verknüpften Produkte Cause-Related Marketing.

Procter & Gamble, Australien, ist zum Beispiel mit dem Save the Children Fund verbunden und arbeitet sogar in einem neu aufstrebenden Markt wie Indien bereits mit der UNESCO zusammen, um Kinderarbeiter aus Fabriken und Werkstätten in die Schulen zu holen.

Die britische Supermarktkette Tesco fördert das Programm Computer für Schulen.

In den USA arbeitet Harley-Davidson mit der Muscular Dystrophy Association (Muskelschwund-Selbsthilfeverein).

American Express führt die Kampagne Charge Against Hunger (Krieg dem Hunger) durch.

Zur weiteren Lektüre über Cause-Related Marketing empfehle ich das ausgezeichnete Buch *Brand Spirit* von Hamish Pringle & Marjorie Thompson (John Wiley & Sons, GB, 1999). Ganz allgemein ausgedrückt kommen die Autoren zu dem Schluss, dass die Verbraucher Produkte von Unternehmen, welche die soziale Komponente vernachlässigen, zunehmend links liegen lassen werden, dass aber auch nicht alle sozialen Aufgaben Sponsoren aus Wirtschaft und Industrie anlocken werden.

Ich habe zahlreiche Mitarbeiter der Agentur gefragt, warum sie ihre Arbeit beruflich so interessant und menschlich so lohnend finden. Die meisten sympathisieren mit dem guten Zweck, den sie bewerben sollen, oder stehen sogar mit vollster Überzeugung dahinter, und die positive Zielsetzung allein lohnt schon die Mühe.

Die meisten sozialen Fragen bieten ihre eigene Dramatik und müssen deshalb nicht zusätzlich dramatisiert werden.

Die gemeinnützigen Kunden haben meistens einen klaren Auftrag, ein leidenschaftliches Engagement ihn anderen zu vermitteln, und sind tapfer bereit, einiges dafür zu riskieren. Die ihnen zur Verfügung stehenden knappen Mittel verpflichten sie, sich für packende Ideen mit weitreichender unmittelbarer Wirkung einzusetzen.

Das heißt noch lange nicht, dass sie ihre Ziele ohne Rücksicht auf Verluste durchsetzen wollen. Ihre Kampagnen fordern klar messbare Resultate, messbar anhand von öffentlichem Echo, von Regierungsstatistiken oder Spendeneingängen nach der Werbung, anhand von Anzahl und Länge der Gesellschafts-, Politik- und Mediendebatte zum jeweiligen Thema.

Messbare Ergebnisse fordern natürlich auch kommerzielle Kunden.

Beide operieren in hart umkämpften Märkten.

Beide müssen Hemmschwellen überschreiten und Widerstände gegen das überwinden, was sie zu sagen haben.

Beide müssen Wege und Mittel finden, um die „Radarfallen" eines skeptischen Publikums zu umgehen.

Beide sind darauf angewiesen, dass sie zum allgemeinen Gesprächsthema werden.

Beide müssen provozieren, um zu möglichst geringen Kosten die größtmögliche Werbewirkung zu erzielen.

Beide müssen dabei aber die Integrität ihrer Produkte wahren.

Beide – so scheint es – brauchen die Wirkungskraft einfacher Ideen, die sich in einfache Entscheidungen umsetzen lassen.

Beide brauchen Ideen, die das Leben der Menschen verändern können.

Ideen wie die in diesem Buch gezeigten.

Saatchi & Saatchi a la publicité d'intérêt général inscrite dans ses gènes.

Elle a toujours constitué un fil conducteur dans le travail de l'agence.

A tel point que, il y a quelques années, Paolo Ettorre et son équipe de chez Saatchi & Saatchi Italie ont organisé une exposition rassemblant les idées liées aux causes sociales.

Il existe maintenant une nouvelle exposition ambulante, Saatchi & Saatchi & Social, et ce livre l'accompagne.

Les nombreuses grandes campagnes humanitaires présentées dans le livre et dans l'exposition démontrent clairement l'intérêt de l'agence pour les idées qui font avancer le monde.

Un des aspects fascinants des travaux présentés dans cet ouvrage est la manière dont ils racontent l'histoire de la société, enregistrant les changements de préoccupation du public au fil des ans.

Par exemple, en matière de sexualité abordée dans un cadre de santé publique, il est moins question de contraception et davantage de Sida.

En matière de sécurité routière, on parle moins de blessures et plus de douleur.

Sur le plan de la réalisation, on recourt moins au bidimensionnel et plus à l'événementiel et aux installations, en d'autres termes, à des « idées plus grandes que la publicité ».

Pour ce qui est du style, on cherche désormais moins à choquer qu'à provoquer des inférences durables.

Les images choc sont désormais considérées comme une arme à manier avec « précaution », de peur d'épuiser la capacité du public à compatir. En effet, les images trop douloureuses n'attirent pas la sympathie du public.

Toutefois, cette tactique est parfois inévitable.

La campagne italienne de Greenpeace Women and Children First, (Les femmes et les enfants d'abord, 1996, p. 24) a été produite par Stefano Maria Palombi et Luca Albanese. Elle devait coïncider avec les essais nucléaires dans le Pacifique.

Elle montre un bébé atteint d'hydrocéphalie, son crâne monstrueusement déformé après que sa mère ait été exposée à des retombées radioactives « inoffensives » à la suite d'essais nucléaires soviétiques au Kazakhstan.

L'image est si horriblement bizarre que le texte doit préciser d'emblée qu'il s'agit d'un document réel et non d'une image de synthèse.

Ce qui est intéressant ici, c'est qu'on constate qu'en dépit de certaines différences culturelles, un travail de ce genre est universellement intelligible, quel que soit le pays qui l'a produit.

La publicité est devenue la *lingua franca* du monde.

C'est pourquoi, partout, on peut de plus en plus traiter un sujet par des implications subtiles plutôt qu'en l'abordant de front.

Dans la campagne britannique de la N.S.P.C.C. (Société pour la protection de l'enfance), Can't Look (Je ne peux pas regarder, 1999, p. 26), on ne voit ni adultes violents ni enfants maltraités.

Evitant consciemment toute image choquante, l'équipe de créatifs de Kes Gray et Dennis Willison a décidé d'utiliser l'outil le plus puissant qui soit :

L'imagination du spectateur.

L'équipe s'est donc fixé une règle : Ne rien montrer. Tout laisser entendre.

Il n'y a aucun être vivant dans le film publicitaire.

Uniquement des images figées d'idoles des enfants – les Spice Girls, le footballeur Alan Shearer, le nounours Rupert et Action Man – se masquant les yeux devant des événements douloureux que l'on entend hors champ. C'est ce qu'on ne voit pas qui est le plus angoissant.

Le romancier américain John Updike a inventé une expression amusante en parlant du « concept oxymoroniais de la vérité dans la publicité ». Toutefois, il s'agit là d'un vieux préjugé.

En réalité, en parcourant ce livre, on ne peut qu'être frappé en constatant à quel point ces travaux recourent au pouvoir de la vérité.

Quiconque a jamais écrit une publicité sait que, face au mur de suspicion et de scepticisme érigé par le lecteur ou le spectateur moyen, les mensonges et les demi vérités sont parfaitement inefficaces.

Parallèlement, beaucoup de ceux qui ont travaillé sur des campagnes sociales vous diront que les récits véridiques qu'on leur fait sont souvent si horribles qu'ils ne peuvent être publiés.

De plus en plus d'annonceurs commerciaux comprennent également que le meilleur moyen de s'attirer la confiance, le respect et la loyauté du public est encore de dire la vérité.

Naturellement, pour que cela devienne une stratégie commerciale efficace, il faut un produit dont la vérité, si elle est énoncée, soit convaincante.

Mais pourquoi fabriquerait-on un produit dont ce n'est pas le cas ?

Lors d'une campagne de sensibilisation, il est impossible de mentir.

Dans tout sujet prêtant à controverse (c'est à dire à peu près tous), la plus petite inexactitude peut être utilisée par les adversaires pour discréditer l'ensemble de l'argument. Pour parer à cette éventualité, toute affirmation doit être minutieusement vérifiée.

Pour cette raison, les publicités accompagnées de longs textes présentées dans ce livre informent aussi bien que la plupart des articles de presse les mieux documentés sur le même sujet. A dire vrai, elles sont souvent mieux écrites.

Prenons, par exemple, la campagne de la N.S.P.C.C. Raped as a 3 Year Old (Violé à l'âge de trois ans, 1992,

p. 58), avec la photo d'un homme d'âge mûr que l'on prend d'abord pour le violeur.

Cette affiche est un excellent exemple de la manière dont un langage froid et neutre, toute trace d'indignation et de colère ayant été délibérément et rigoureusement exclue par l'équipe de créatifs de Mike Boles et de Jerry Hollens, peut avoir une force considérable.

Elle ne dit pas au lecteur ce qu'il doit penser. En termes simples, presque laconiques, pratiquement dépourvus d'adjectifs, elle rapporte des faits.

La colère que le sujet suscite à juste titre vient uniquement des conclusions qu'en tire le lecteur.

Richard Myers, directeur artistique, se souvient que lorsque l'affiche fut placardée dans les stations de métro londoniennes, son titre frappant et son texte de presque 500 mots firent s'arrêter un tel nombre de voyageurs, beaucoup ratant leur rame pour finir de la lire, qu'elle dut être enlevée des quais pour des raisons de sécurité.

La cause en question n'aurait pas été mieux servie si un usager était tombé sous une rame en tentant de lire un texte, aussi éloquent soit-il.

Une autre publicité pour le même annonceur, intitulée We Both Have The Same Father (Nous avons le même père, 1995, p. 30) et montrant une adolescente enceinte contemplant son ventre proéminent, semble, au premier abord, énigmatique... jusqu'à ce que l'on saisisse l'implication d'inceste.

Ce n'est là qu'un exemple illustrant que la publicité et les outils de communication n'ont pas d'idéologie inhérente.

Ils reflètent la culture, ils ne l'inventent pas.

Or, nous vivons dans une culture où les causes sociales, à l'instar des produits commerciaux, requièrent une communication efficace.

Car tous les annonceurs sociaux ne sont pas exclus de commerce.

La sécurité routière, la lutte contre le racisme ou la drogue, le recrutement des infirmières ou des enseignants et les campagnes publiques soutenues par des annonceurs commerciaux mettent généralement différentes agences de publicité en compétition et payent comme les autres.

Plus important, toutefois : les campagnes publiques se concentrent sur des idées qui, dans une mesure plus ou moins grande, font changer les perceptions et les comportements sur des questions d'intérêt public graves et importantes.

De grandes idées qui transforment de petits budgets en de puissantes campagnes.

Il est sans doute difficile de faire changer les attitudes du jour au lendemain mais, au moins, une idée dérangeante et spectaculaire peut faire prendre conscience qu'un problème existe.

Il existe de nombreux exemples d'idées provocantes et audacieuses qui, financées par un budget minime,

ont suscité une couverture médiatique gratuite d'une valeur bien supérieure au coût initial de la campagne.

Parmi eux, la série d'affiches de la C.R.E. britannique (Commission pour l'égalité entre les races).

Pour les titres de ces dernières, Chris Kirk et Giles Montgomery ont délibérément choisi des jeux de mots dégageant un humour noir et macabre afin qu'on ne puisse les accuser d'être trop moralisateurs.

Avec l'affiche Worst Marks (jeu de mots entre les pires marques et les plus mauvaises notes, 1997, p. 50), ils ont également pu faire allusion à la question des performances scolaires des minorités ethniques.

Dans le cas des élèves asiatiques, elles sont en fait au-dessus de la moyenne.

Dans la même série, l'affiche Junk Mail (1997, p.171), bénéficie également d'une expérience personnelle, comme c'est souvent le cas. Son directeur artistique, Ajab Samrai Singh, a vu lui-même, alors qu'il avait six ans et vivait dans les West Midlands d'Angleterre, la boîte aux lettres de ses parents imbibée d'essence et incendiée.

Ce genre de campagne fonctionne comme un flot continu de faits et d'opinions apparaissant dans tous les types de média et, de fait, dans tous les types de lieux de travail ou de réunion sociale.

Comme c'est le cas de nombreuses campagnes de sensibilisation, en dépit d'un budget publicitaire relativement petit, le contenu frappant des messages leur a permis d'avoir un effet maximum en générant une grande quantité de débats dans la presse et au sein de l'opinion publique.

Le public a pris conscience de l'existence du C.R.E., dont les objectifs sont passés de 35 à 50% en l'espace de deux ans.

Une bonne idée, ça se vénère pour sa finesse, son mordant, son originalité, parce qu'elle fait mouche ou qu'elle restera dans les mémoires.

C'est ce qui stimule les publicitaires à se lever le matin, ce qui suscite les débats les plus animés au bureau ou les conversations qui se poursuivent tard dans la nuit autour d'un verre entre collègues, ce qui génère le plus d'enthousiasme, de jubilation et d'émotion.

Pour ceux qui consacrent tous leurs talents, leur ambition personnelle et leur professionnalisme à la recherche de moyens de faire évoluer les mentalités et d'influencer les comportements, découvrir l'idée qui transformera le monde est leur quête du Saint Graal.

Qui a dit : « Nous sommes le plus fidèles à nous-mêmes en louant les autres ? »

J'ai rarement rencontré des publicistes qui n'admiraient pas la campagne contre l'alcool au volant, Glasses (1993, p. 140), créée pour Singapour par Dean Turney et Francis Wee.

L'idée est d'une simplicité époustouflante, au point que la première réaction de pratiquement tout

rédacteur ou directeur artistique est : « Comment personne n'y avait-il pensé plus tôt ? »

Puis, la seconde : « Pourquoi n'y ai-je pas pensé le premier ? »

Depuis l'intérieur d'une voiture roulant en ville, on voit une succession de verres de bière vides placés au centre de l'écran, chacun obscurcissant un peu plus la vue.

Au bout du quatrième verre, on voit vraiment flou et la voiture s'écrase contre l'arrière d'un bus.

Si économique, dans tous les sens du terme, et si brillant.

On trouve la même clarté de l'argument dans l'affiche britannique du Mouvement contre la prolifération des armes à feu (Gun Control Network) Less Dead (1997, p.68).

A la suite du massacre d'une classe d'écoliers à Dunblane, en Ecosse, le gouvernement britannique s'apprêtait à présenter un projet de loi pour interdire certaines armes à feu.

Mais cette loi excluait les calibres 22.

Scandalisée et furieuse, une équipe de créatifs de Londres, Bill Gallacher, Robin Murtough et Keith Terry, n'ayant ni argent ni temps, estimèrent qu'ils devaient réagir avant que le parlement ne ratifie cette loi incomplète.

Ayant découvert que Robert Kennedy avait été assassiné avec un calibre 22, ils utilisèrent une image d'archives et improvisèrent avec un Mac une grande affiche qu'ils placèrent sur un camion devant le parlement le jour des débats.

Elle disait : « Si un 22 est moins mortel, pourquoi n'est-il pas moins mort ? »

L'effet saisissant de ces quelques mots contribua à ce que les calibres 22 soient inclus dans la liste des armes proscrites.

Comme le dit Tom Cordner, directeur artistique à Los Angeles : « Une publicité a beau être excellente, on la voit et on l'oublie. Elle est éphémère. En revanche, une excellente idée se fraie un chemin jusque dans notre âme. Elle reste avec nous. »

En arrière-plan de cette observation, il faut savoir que Saatchi & Saatchi estime que, partout dans le monde, la capacité d'attention se réduit rapidement.

Or, comme le dit Bob Isherwood, directeur artistique de l'agence pour le monde entier, dans un tel monde « les idées sont la devise du futur ».

Si c'est vrai, ce n'est pas dans les médias qu'il faut investir massivement mais dans les idées.

L'American Advertising Agencies' Association déclare que le citoyen américain est exposé quotidiennement à 3 000 messages commerciaux, sous une forme ou une autre.

Spots télévisés, affiches, annonces dans la presse, logos, flancs des bus, autocollants sur les sols des supermarchés, emballages de produits... ils sont partout.

De tous ces messages, les consommateurs affirment qu'ils ne réagissent, d'une manière ou d'une autre, qu'à... douze.

Lorsque le fatras d'inepties et de trivialités est si envahissant et le bruit de fond de notre culture de la communication si assourdissant, comment un message peut-il se faire entendre ?

Qu'il s'agisse d'un annonceur commercial ou d'une campagne de sensibilisation, il s'agit clairement là d'un défi.

Ça l'est encore plus pour la campagne de sensibilisation dans la mesure où son budget média est toujours une fraction de celui d'un annonceur commercial.

Par conséquent, si les idées créées pour des campagnes de sensibilisation parviennent à passer par-dessus le vacarme ambiant, malgré tous leurs handicaps, n'ont-elles pas quelques solutions à fournir aux problèmes de communication d'un éventail plus large d'annonceurs ?

Chez Saatchi & Saatchi, on pense pouvoir démontrer que l'agence a créé un certain nombre d'idées qui sont parvenues à influer sur divers problèmes de sociétés.

Un exemple du pur plaisir que l'on peut avoir à se laisser convaincre de réfléchir à un problème social grave nous vient de Nouvelle-Zélande.

En matière de sécurité routière, faire rire est plutôt inhabituel et très difficile, mais Glen Wood et Peter Force, avec leur spot télévisé Grunge Angels (1995, p. 70), y sont parvenus avec une facilité apparente.

La cible, les jeunes, les plus à risque, sont représentés par deux jeunes hommes.

Au son d'un chœur angélique, ils se retrouvent dans les nuages. Les haut-parleurs célestes annoncent : « Pour votre plaisir en cet Au-delà, voici les plus belles chansons d'amour de Whitney Houston... » Manifestement (on peut les comprendre), les deux jeunes considèrent qu'une éternité de ce genre de musique est pire que la mort.

La voix off souligne que « la mort, ça craint » et suggère qu'il serait plus judicieux de mettre sa ceinture.

On trouve encore un sujet grave traité avec un humour basé sur l'absurde dans la campagne italienne de la Guerre contre la Faim pour la FAO, l'Organisation des Nations unies pour l'Alimentation et l'Agriculture (War on Hunger, 1998, p. 134).

Cela commence par un extrait de documentaire monochrome sur une armée en guerre.

Mais on s'aperçoit rapidement que les roquettes sont des épis de maïs et les hélicoptères des tomates.

Les soldats rampent sous les broussailles en brandissant des bananes en guise de mitraillettes.

Un barrage au mortier est tiré avec des artichauts.

C'est un monde de fous.

L'observation est pertinente quand on sait que, dépensé différemment, le budget militaire planétaire résoudrait la plupart des problèmes de la faim dans le monde.

Il vaut sans doute la peine de préciser que la plupart des campagnes présentées dans ce livre ont été primées pour leur créativité dans les plus grands festivals du monde, à Cannes, Londres, New York et ailleurs.

Les prix ne sont peut-être qu'une manie très prisée des publicitaires mais le fait d'être considéré comme le meilleur par ses pairs n'a rien de négligeable.

Même s'ils sont très au fait des genres en compétition, la réaction des juges face à un message éloquent est la même que celle de tout être humain.

Cela ne fait qu'illustrer le fait que ces idées et leur mise en image possèdent une dynamique narrative, qu'elles sont excitantes et puissantes, et nécessitent souvent de surmonter des difficultés inédites.

Parmi ceux qui suivent de près les compétitions de créativité du secteur de la publicité, certains défendent le mythe selon lequel les campagnes de sensibilisation ou caritatives seraient un moyen facile de décrocher des prix.

En fait, c'est tout le contraire, ces catégories étant généralement celles où il y a le plus de candidats.

Toutes les campagnes en compétition bénéficient à parts égales du même type de sujet émotionnel.

Contrairement à ce qu'on croit souvent, il est très difficile de trouver la bonne formule et très facile de se tromper.

A bien des égards, les campagnes de sensibilisation et les publicités commerciales présentent les mêmes problèmes.

Mais elles diffèrent sur un point.

Un des principaux défis qui rend les campagnes de sensibilisation si difficiles mais si gratifiantes quand elles sont réussies est qu'elles visent à transformer d'abord la perception, puis le comportement, d'un public face à un sujet auquel il préférerait ne pas penser.

Contrairement à la publicité commerciale conventionnelle, il ne sert à rien de caresser dans le sens du poil un public qui accepte votre argument.

S'il est vrai que, comme l'a dit le docteur Johnson : « L'âme d'une publicité est la promesse, une grande promesse », alors quelle est la « promesse » dans une campagne de sensibilisation ?

Quand on est avachi devant ses croissants et son café du dimanche matin, on n'a pas envie de penser au Sida, aux mines antipersonnelles ou aux enfants battus.

Nous ne voulons pas nous considérer comme faisant partie du problème du racisme, des accidents de la route ou de la destruction de l'environnement.

Nous ne voulons certainement pas penser au fait que notre simple inertie contribue au sort d'enfants affamés, de réfugiés ou de minorités opprimées.

« Nous sommes tous coupables », qu'ils disent.

Il faut vraiment qu'on en discute maintenant ?

Et bien, oui, si nous voulons que le monde devienne un endroit un peu plus vivable.

Dans le domaine social, les publicitaires doivent découvrir comment susciter la sympathie du public sans faire appel à ses pulsions acquisitives ou au besoin de satisfaire son propre intérêt.

Dans cette recherche, il peut être utile de revenir sur un paradigme élaboré au début des années 40 par un universitaire américain, A.H. Maslow. Il permet d'expliquer pourquoi les consommateurs, notamment dans les sociétés les plus riches, se détournent de plus en plus des incitations trop ouvertement matérialistes à satisfaire leurs propres intérêts.

L'hypothèse de Maslow veut que tous les hommes aient une « hiérarchie de besoins », qu'il illustre généralement par une pyramide à la base de laquelle il place les besoins physiologiques comme la faim et la soif.

Ensuite viennent les besoins de sécurité et de protection.

Suivent les besoins sociaux : le sentiment d'appartenance et l'amour. Puis les besoins d'estime : reconnaissance, amour-propre et statut.

Enfin, au sommet de la pyramide, les besoins d'actualisation : développement personnel et accomplissement.

Cette hypothèse est cohérente avec l'observation fréquente selon laquelle, partout dans le monde, les piliers traditionnels de la société ont aujourd'hui nettement perdu de leur éclat auprès de l'opinion publique.

Les gouvernements, les Eglises, la police, l'armée, la monarchie en Grande-Bretagne et la présidence aux Etats-Unis ont tous démontré qu'ils partageaient les mêmes défauts humains que nous.

D'un autre côté, certaines compagnies et marques ont vu leur degré de confiance et d'estime grandir auprès du public.

On en a des preuves tangibles.

Les gens se tournent de plus en plus vers les banques et les fonds d'investissement qui affichent clairement leur politique éthique en évitant les participations dans les sociétés qui ne respectent pas l'environnement, des corporations dont la prospérité repose sur les dommages causés à la santé de leurs clients, ou des firmes qui exploitent leurs fournisseurs du Tiers-Monde.

Les investisseurs sont prêts à les suivre même s'ils savent que cela réduira probablement le taux de retour sur leur épargne.

Les pages financières des quotidiens publient aujourd'hui des listes de plus en plus longues de fonds d'investissements éthiques.

En Grand Bretagne, la Co-operative Bank a une rotation de détenteurs de comptes nettement inférieure à celle d'autres banques et c'est aujourd'hui le plus grand émetteur de cartes Visa Gold d'Europe.

Dans le secteur de la mode et des cosmétiques, Liz Claiborne et The Body Shop ont tous deux prospéré sur une démarche éthique.

En outre, de nombreuses organisations commerciales découvrent que, au moment de choisir entre des produits et des services plus ou moins identiques, les consommateurs privilégient de plus en plus ceux qui s'identifient à des causes pertinentes non commerciales.

Ce phénomène a été baptisé le « Marketing associé à une cause ».

Procter & Gamble, par exemple, s'est associé en Australie au Save the Children Fund. Même dans un marché économique émergent comme l'Inde, Procter & Gamble travaille avec l'UNESCO pour faire retourner les enfants ouvriers à l'école.

En Grande-Bretagne, la chaîne de supermarchés Tesco soutient « Des ordinateurs à l'école ».

Aux Etats-Unis, Harley-Davidson travaille avec la Muscular Dystrophy Association (Association contre la myopathie).

American Express dirige la campagne contre la faim Charge Against Hunger.

Pour une discussion plus approfondie sur le Marketing associé à une cause, je recommande l'ouvrage actuellement le plus abouti sur le sujet, l'excellent *Brand Spirit*, de Hamish Pringle & Marjorie Thompson (John Wiley & Sons, Royaume Uni, 1999).

Pour résumer, ce livre conclut que les corporations qui négligent la dimension sociale dans leurs communications seront de plus en plus écartées par les consommateurs, même s'il faut reconnaître que toutes les questions de société n'attireront pas forcément le soutien du public.

En préparant ce texte, j'ai parlé à bon nombre de ceux qui ont réalisé les campagnes présentées ici et leur ai demandé pourquoi ils les trouvaient si intéressantes sur le plan professionnel et gratifiantes sur le plan personnel.

La plupart sympathisent, voire s'identifient, avec leur sujet qui, généralement, a un objectif qui mérite clairement qu'on le défende.

La plupart de ces causes sont dramatiques en elles-mêmes, si bien qu'il n'est pas nécessaire d'aller chercher l'intérêt ailleurs.

Les clients ont généralement un projet clair, le communiquent avec passion et sont prêts à faire preuve de courage pour le réaliser.

Leur budget limité les contraint à accepter des projets audacieux ayant un impact immédiat et très puissant.

Ceci dit, les commanditaires de ces campagnes ne sont pas non plus des casse-cou.

Leurs campagnes exigent des résultats clairement quantifiables, par la réaction de l'opinion publique, les statistiques gouvernementales, les retours financiers sous forme de dons ou le volume du débat public, politique ou médiatique suscité.

Ce qui est à peu près ce qu'exigent les annonceurs commerciaux. Il n'y a rien d'étonnant à cela.

Tous deux opèrent sur des marchés où de nombreuses marques sont en concurrence.

Tous deux doivent surmonter des obstacles et des résistances à leurs messages.

Tous deux doivent trouver le moyen de se glisser sous le radar d'un public sceptique.

Tous deux ont besoin qu'on parle d'eux.

Tous deux doivent se montrer provocants afin d'obtenir une réaction au moindre frais.

Pourtant, tous deux doivent préserver l'intégrité de leur marque.

Tous deux, semble-t-il, ont besoin du pouvoir d'idées simples qui se traduisent par des choix simples.

Tous deux on besoin d'idées capables de transformer la vie des gens.

Des idées comme celles présentées dans ce livre.

La publicidad social de Saatchi & Saatchi
por Ed Jones

La publicidad social está en los genes de Saatchi & Saatchi.

Siempre ha sido una constante en el trabajo de la agencia.

Hasta tal punto que, hace algunos años, Paolo Ettorre y todo su equipo de Saatchi & Saatchi de Italia organizaron una exposición sobre sus trabajos relacionados con las causas sociales.

Ahora se ha organizado una exposición itinerante, Saatchi & Saatchi & Social, para la que este libro puede servirles de guía.

Las destacadas campañas sobre temas humanos de importancia que reúnen el libro y la exposición reflejan claramente el interés de la agencia en producir ideas que transformen el mundo.

Un aspecto fascinante del trabajo que se ve en este libro es que actúa como una forma de historia social, reflejando los cambios en las inquietudes públicas a través de los años.

Por ejemplo, en relación con el sexo como tema de salud pública, ahora se oye hablar menos de la contracepción y más sobre el SIDA.

En cuanto a la seguridad vial, se habla menos de daños físicos y más de dolor.

Por lo que respecta a la producción, se usan menos las dos dimensiones y más los actos e instalaciones, o lo que llamamos «ideas mas grandes que anuncios».

En cuanto al estilo, hoy hay menos impacto súbito y más insinuaciones de efecto prolongado.

El impacto se considera ahora un enfoque que debe usarse con cautela por miedo al «cansancio de la compasión».

El motivo de ello es que las imágenes demasiado dolorosas no cuentan con la simpatía de la audiencia.

Pero a veces esta táctica parece inevitable.

El anuncio de Greenpeace Italia, Women and Children First, 1996 (Niños y Mujeres Primero, p. 24), realizado por Stefano Maria Palombi y Luca Albanese, se hizo coincidir con las pruebas nucleares en el Pacífico.

Muestra a un bebé con hidrocefalia, con la cabeza terriblemente deformada a consecuencia de la «inofensiva» lluvia radiactiva a la que se vio sometida su madre en las pruebas anteriores en el soviético Kazakstán.

La imagen es tan extrañamente horrorosa que es necesario dejar claro desde la primera línea del texto que es una fotografía documental real, no una distorsión creada por ordenador.

Se trata de un ejemplo interesante para ilustrar que, a pesar de algunas diferencias culturales, la campaña tiene aquí, por lo general, una inteligibilidad universa , sea cual sea el país que la haya creado.

La publicidad se ha convertido en la lengua internacional.

Éste es el motivo por el cual, ahora en todas partes, es cada vez más fácil abordar un tema con insinuaciones sutiles que frontalmente.

En la campaña británica para la Sociedad Nacional de Prevención de la Crueldad con los Niños (NSPCC), Can't Look, 1999 (p. 26), no aparecen adultos violentos o niños maltratados.

Evitando deliberadamente las imágenes impactantes, el equipo creativo formado por Kes Gray y Dennis Willison decidió usar el instrumento más poderoso.

La imaginación del espectador.

Así que se impusieron una regla: no mostrar nada, insinuarlo todo.

Por eso, no hay personas reales en el anuncio, sólo representaciones estáticas de iconos infantiles —las Spice Girls, el futbolista Alan Shearer, el oso Rupert y Action Man— tapándose los ojos ante los dolorosos sucesos que podemos oír.

Menos es escalofriantemente más.

El novelista norteamericano John Updike ha inventado una divertida expresión al hablar del «concepto oximorónico de la verdad en la publicidad», pero en realidad se trata de un concepto erróneo pasado de moda.

De hecho, un aspecto muy asombroso de los trabajos que se presentan en este libro es el grado remarcable en que usan el poder de la verdad.

Toda persona que haya escrito un anuncio alguna vez sabe que, en vista del altísimo nivel de suspicacia y de escepticismo del lector o espectador medio, las mentiras y las medias verdades son en realidad increíblemente ineficaces.

Al mismo tiempo, las personas que han trabajado en campañas sociales os dirán que a menudo les han contado historias verdaderas tan horribles que no podían salir a la luz.

Del mismo modo, cada vez más anunciantes comerciales se dan cuenta de que el modo de ganarse la confianza, la lealtad, el respeto y el afecto de su audiencia es sencillamente contando la verdad.

Por supuesto, para que esto sea una estrategia comercial efectiva, hace falta tener un producto cuya verdad, si se cuenta, sea persuasiva.

¿Pero por qué presentar otro tipo de producto?

En la publicidad social, es imposible mentir.

En cualquier tema polémico (lo son casi todos), la más mínima inexactitud será aprovechada por los adversarios y usada para desacreditar todos los argumentos.

Para adelantarse a estas posibles críticas, se examinan detenidamente todas las afirmaciones.

Como resultado, los anuncios con texto largo que hay en este libro son tan informativos como la mayoría de los artículos editoriales más rigurosamente documentados sobre el mismo tema.

Y, por cierto, están mejor escritos.

Como ejemplo, tomemos el Raped as a 3 Year Old de la NSPCC de 1992 (p. 58), con la fotografía de un hombre de mediana edad que se supone inicialmente que es el autor de la violación.

Este anuncio es un magnífico ejemplo de cómo el lenguaje sereno y realista, con todo rastro de indignación y cólera excluido de manera deliberada y rigurosa por el equipo creativo de Mike Boles y Jerry Hollens, puede ser enormemente poderoso.

No dice al lector cómo debe pensar.

En los términos más simples, casi lacónicos, prácticamente carentes de adjetivos, informa sobre los hechos. La ira que el tema sin duda merece es provocada enteramente por las conclusiones que saca el lector.

El director creativo Richard Myers recuerda que durante el tiempo en que este cartel estuvo presente en todas las estaciones de metro de Londres, su llamativo texto de casi 500 palabras hacía detenerse a tantas personas —muchos perdían el tren para acabar de leer el texto— que tuvo que apartarse de los andenes por una cuestión de seguridad.

El anuncio no le hubiera parecido bueno al público si alguien hubiera sido arrollado por un tren por leerlo, por más elegantemente escrito que estuviera.

Otro anuncio para el mismo cliente, en el que aparece una chica embarazada que contempla su gran barriga y el titular We Both Have The Same Father (Tenemos el mismo padre, p. 30) de 1995, parece por un momento totalmente inocuo, hasta que se cae en la cuenta de sus implicaciones incestuosas.

Esto es tan sólo un ejemplo de que las estrategias publicitarias y comunicativas no contienen una ideología en sí mismas.

Reflejan su cultura, no la inventan.

Y vivimos en una cultura donde las causas sociales, tanto como los productos comerciales, requieren una comunicación eficaz.

Pues también hay clientes sociales comerciales.

Las campañas de seguridad vial, contra el racismo y las drogas, de reclutamiento de enfermeras y profesores, y la publicidad social financiada por los clientes comerciales se obtienen normalmente en competencia con otras agencias y se pagan del modo habitual.

Aunque más importante es el hecho de que la publicidad social se centra en ideas que logran algún tipo de transformación en las percepciones y actitudes sobre temas de gran importancia e interés públicos.

Grandes ideas que convierten presupuestos pequeños en campañas poderosas.

El comportamiento real puede ser difícil de cambiar inmediatamente, pero, como mínimo, una idea atrevida y dramática puede ser el impulso inicial para concienciar sobre la existencia del problema.

Hay numerosos casos en que una idea provocativa y atrevida, sostenida por un presupuesto en medios mínimo, ha generado muchas veces más su valor, con ríos de tinta de cobertura gratuita por parte de los medios de comunicación.

Un ejemplo es la serie de anuncios para la Comisión para la Igualdad Racial del Reino Unido.

Aquí el juego de palabras del titular de Chris Kirk y Giles Montgomery transmite un humor sombrío y negro deliberadamente diseñado para evitar que se les acuse de echar sermones.

En el cartel Worst Marks (p. 50) de 1997, esto también permitió al anuncio hacer alusión al tema del rendimiento académico de las minorías étnicas.

En el caso de los estudiantes asiáticos, éste se sitúa, de hecho, por encima de la media.

El conocimiento personal, como ocurre tan a menudo, iluminó la realización del anuncio sobre el Junk Mail (correo basura, p. 171) de 1997, perteneciente a la serie que contó con la dirección artística de Ajab Samrai Singh, quien, como niño de seis años criado en una zona pobre de las West Midlands inglesas, pasó por la experiencia de que vertieran gasolina en el buzón de la casa de sus padres.

Una campaña como ésta aparece como parte de una avalancha continua de datos y opiniones en todos los medios y, en realidad, en toda clase de lugares de trabajo y reuniones sociales.

Pero, como ocurre con muchas campañas sociales, a pesar de un presupuesto en medios relativamente pequeño, el sorprendente contenido de los anuncios maximizó su difusión generando grandes cantidades de noticias y debate.

Esto llevó a que el conocimiento de la Comisión para la Igualdad Racial y de sus objetivos aumentara de un 35 a un 50 % en un espacio de dos años.

Una gran idea es venerada por su ingenio, su mordacidad y originalidad, su impacto o vibrante memorabilidad.

Una gran idea es lo que hace levantar a los publicistas por la mañana, lo que provoca el debate más apasionado en el despacho, o el mayor entusiasmo, regocijo y afecto por la noche, cuando se van de copas.

Para aquellos cuyo talento, ambición personal e inquietudes profesionales se centran cada día en encontrar modos de cambiar opiniones y transformar comportamientos, el Santo Grial es descubrir ideas que transformen el mundo.

¿Quién dijo «Somos más fieles a nosotros mismos cuando elogiamos a otros»?

He conocido a pocos publicitarios que no admiren el anuncio contra la conducción en estado ebrio, Glasses, 1993 (p. 140) de Singapur, creado por Dean Turney y Francis Wee.

La idea es una demostración tan increíblemente simple que la primera reacción de casi todo redactor publicitario y director de arte es «¿Por qué nadie pensó en ello antes?»

Y después, «¿Por qué no pensé en ello antes?»

Desde dentro de un coche que conduce por la ciudad, vemos sucesivas jarras de cerveza vacías

situadas en el centro de la pantalla, y cada una empeora la vista algo más.

Tras la cuarta jarra, cuando la vista que hay por delante es verdaderamente borrosa, el coche choca contra la parte trasera de un autobús.

Tan económico, en todos los sentidos, y tan brillante.

Esta asombrosa claridad argumental también se encuentra en el cartel para la Red de Control de Armas del Reino Unido, Less Dead de 1997 (p. 68).

Tras la masacre de una clase de escolares en Dunblane, Escocia, el gobierno británico procedió a presentar una ley para prohibir ciertas armas de fuego.

Pero la ley excluyó las pistolas del calibre 22.

Atónito y enojado, el equipo creativo de Londres compuesto por Bill Gallacher, Robin Murtough y Keith Terry no disponía ni de dinero ni de tiempo, pues el debate parlamentario para aprobar la defectuosa ley era inminente.

Tras descubrir que Robert Kennedy había sido asesinado con una pistola del calibre 22, se sirvieron de una foto de archivo, de cierta improvisación y de un Mac para crear una valla publicitaria, exhibida en un camión en el exterior del Parlamento el día del debate.

Decía: «Si una pistola del calibre 22 es menos mortífera, ¿por qué él no está menos muerto?»

El gran impacto de estas sucintas palabras contribuyó a conseguir la prohibición de las pistolas de este calibre en la ley sobre las armas de fuego.

Tal como dice Tom Cordner, director creativo de Los Angeles: «Un anuncio puede llegar a ser magnífico, pero lo ves y desaparece. Es algo efímero. Pero una gran idea encuentra un lugar donde perdurar en el alma. Permanece contigo».

El contexto de esta observación es que Saatchi & Saatchi cree que el mundo está desarrollando con rapidez una economía de la atención.

Y en la economía de la atención, tal como dice el director creativo de la compañía a escala internacional, Bob Isherwood, «las ideas son la moneda del futuro».

Si eso es cierto, se debe invertir más en las ideas que en los medios de comunicación.

La Asociación Americana de las Agencias de Publicidad estima que los estadounidenses reciben unos tres mil mensajes comerciales al día bajo una u otra forma.

Anuncios televisivos, carteles, anuncios de prensa, logos, publicidad en los autobuses, etiquetas en los supermercados, envoltorios de los productos... están por todas partes.

De todos ellos, los consumidores dicen que tienen algún tipo de reacción ante tan sólo... doce.

Cuando la abundancia de basura y banalidad es tan omnipresente, y el contexto de nuestra cultura comunicativa tan ensordecedor, ¿cómo puede hacerse oír un mensaje?

Tanto para un cliente comercial como para un cliente social, esto es claramente una especie de reto.

En realidad, incluso más para un cliente social, pues el presupuesto del que dispone para los medios de comunicación siempre es una mínima parte del de las campañas comerciales.

Por consiguiente, si las ideas creadas para los clientes sociales pueden de algún modo abrirse camino entre el jaleo ambiental, con todas las desventajas apuntadas, ¿acaso no tendrán algunas lecciones que enseñar para los problemas comunicativos de un abanico más amplio de clientes?

Saatchi & Saatchi cree que es posible demostrar que ha creado una serie de ideas que han logrado cambios en diversos temas sociales.

Un ejemplo del gran placer de ser persuadido para considerar un asunto serio procede de Nueva Zelanda.

La hilaridad absoluta es una vía poco usual y difícil de lograr en un anuncio de seguridad vial, pero Glen Wood y Peter Force, en el anuncio televisivo de la Grunge Angels, 1995 (p. 70), lo consiguen con aparente facilidad.

La audiencia que corre más peligro y está representada por dos hombres jóvenes.

Al son de un coro angelical, se hallan en las nubes.

Por el sistema celestial de megafonía se anuncia: «Para que os divirtáis en esta Otra Vida, las mejores canciones de amor de Whitney Houston...»

Comprensiblemente, ven este tipo de eternidad como un destino peor que la muerte.

La voz que suena por megafonía señala que «la muerte es un asco» y que probablemente lo más sensato sea abrocharse el cinturón de seguridad.

El humor con un toque deliciosamente absurdo aligera otro asunto deprimente en el anuncio italiano de Lucha Contra el Hambre para la Organización de Alimentación y Agricultura de las Naciones Unidas, War on Hunger, 1998 (p. 134).

Empieza con secuencias documentales en blanco y negro de un ejército en guerra.

Pero pronto se ve que sus misiles son maíz tierno y sus helicópteros, tomates. Los soldados se arrastran por la maleza armados de bananas en vez de ametralladoras.

Se lanza una descarga de mortero con alcachofas.

Es un mundo desquiciado.

La observación es apropiada cuando un uso diferente del presupuesto militar global solucionaría la mayoría de los problemas mundiales de hambre.

Quizá valga la pena mencionar que muchos de los anuncios que se muestran en este libro han obtenido los premios creativos más importantes de los concursos internacionales de más prestigio, como los de Cannes, Londres y Nueva York.

Puede que los premios sean el más preciado fetiche del negocio publicitario, pero ser el mejor a juicio de los colegas es difícilmente un motivo de disculpa.

Aparte de estar más familiarizados con los géneros competitivos, la respuesta de los jueces ante un llamamiento elocuente no es diferente de la de cualquier otro ser humano.

Sólo ilustra que estas ideas y producciones tienen un dramatismo, emoción y fuerza excepcionales, a menudo logrados al abordar nuevas y difíciles clases de desafíos.

Algunos de los interesados en los concursos creativos de la industria publicitaria sostienen el mito de que los anuncios sociales y benéficos son una especie de opción fácil para ganar premios.

De hecho, es justo lo contrario, pues estas categorías siempre son las que cuentan con una mayor participación.

Todos los inscritos se benefician por igual del mismo tipo de temas emotivos.

Sin embargo, al contrario de lo que se suele pensar, es muy difícil hacerlo bien y muy fácil hacerlo mal.

En gran medida, la publicidad social y comercial presentan problemas parecidos.

Pero difieren en un aspecto.

Un desafío básico que hace la comunicación social tan difícil pero tan gratificante si se lleva a cabo satisfactoriamente es que el objetivo es transformar primero las percepciones y después las actitudes de la audiencia sobre un tema sobre el cual probablemente preferirían no pensar.

A diferencia de la publicidad comercial convencional, hay pocas posibilidades de ofrecer a la audiencia una gran gratificación personal si acepta el argumento del anuncio.

Si es cierto, como dijo el Dr. Johnson, que «el alma de un anuncio es la promesa, la gran promesa», ¿cuál es la «promesa» de la publicidad social?

Cuando nos abandonamos al café y los cruasanes del domingo, realmente no queremos pensar acerca del SIDA o las minas terrestres o los maltratos a los niños.

No queremos vernos a nosotros mismos como quizá parte del problema del racismo, los accidentes de tráfico o la destrucción medioambiental.

Ciertamente no queremos afrontar el hecho de que con la simple inactividad podemos estar contribuyendo a la difícil situación de los niños hambrientos, los refugiados o las minorías oprimidas.

Dicen que «todos somos culpables». ¿Tenemos que hablar de ello en este preciso momento?

Pues la verdad es que sí, si realmente queremos que el mundo sea un lugar algo mejor.

En el campo social los publicitarios tienen que descubrir una vía de acceso a las simpatías de la audiencia cuando hay pocas posibilidades de apelar al impulso del interés propio o el consumismo.

En la búsqueda de esto, un paradigma concebido a principios de los cuarenta por un académico americano, A.H. Maslow, está resultando útil para explicar por qué los consumidores, sobre todo en las sociedades más ricas, están alejándose cada vez más de los llamamientos burdamente materialistas a su interés propio.

La hipótesis de Maslow es que los humanos tienen una «jerarquía de necesidades», normalmente ilustrada por una pirámide en cuya base están las necesidades fisiológicas de superar el hambre y la sed.

Encima de éstas, vienen las necesidades de seguridad y protección.

A continuación, se sitúan las necesidades sociales del sentimiento de pertenencia y de amor.

En un nivel superior están las necesidades relacionadas con la estima, como el reconocimiento, el amor propio y el status.

Finalmente, en el vértice de la pirámide, están las necesidades ligadas al desarrollo y realización personales.

Esta hipótesis es coherente con la observación que se hace a menudo de que, en todo el mundo, pilares de la sociedad tradicionalmente respetados son hoy perceptiblemente menos valorados que antes.

Gobiernos, iglesias, policía, fuerzas armadas, la monarquía en Gran Bretaña y la presidencia en Estados Unidos, han demostrado compartir los mismos defectos humanos que el resto de nosotros.

Por otra parte, algunas compañías y marcas han incrementado sus niveles percibidos de confianza.

Hay pruebas concretas de ello.

Las personas responden cada vez más a los bancos y fondos de inversión que establecen con firmeza una política ética destinada a evitar su participación en compañías que no respetan el medio ambiente o en corporaciones cuya prosperidad depende del perjuicio a la salud de sus clientes o que explotan a los proveedores del Tercer Mundo.

Los inversores están dispuestos a ello, a pesar de que saben que probablemente reducirá la tasa de rendimiento de sus ahorros.

Actualmente, las páginas financieras de los periódicos incluyen un número significativo de fondos de inversión éticos.

El Co-operative Bank de Gran Bretaña tiene un volumen de facturación de los titulares de cuentas notablemente inferior al de otros bancos y es ahora el mayor emisor de tarjetas Visa Oro de toda Europa.

En el mundo de la moda y la cosmética, Liz Claiborne y The Body Shop han prosperado sobre la base de una postura ética.

Además, muchas organizaciones comerciales están descubriendo que, al decidir entre productos o servicios más o menos iguales, los consumidores cada vez favorecen más a los que se identifican con una causa no comercial importante.

Esta práctica se ha vuelto conocida como márketing relacionado con las causas o márketing social.

Por ejemplo, Procter & Gamble está ligada con Save The Children Fund en Australia. Incluso en un mercado económicamente emergente como la India, Procter & Gamble ya está trabajando con la Unesco para hacer que los niños que trabajan regresen a la escuela.

La cadena de supermercados Tesco de Gran Bretaña apoya el programa Computers For Schools.

Harley-Davidson trabaja con la Asociación de Distrofia Muscular en Estados Unidos.

American Express dirige la campaña Charge Against Hunger.

Para un análisis más a fondo del tema del márketing relacionado con las causas, recomiendo el libro con más autoridad sobre el tema en la actualidad, el excelente *Brand Spirit*, de Hamish Pringle & Marjorie Thompson (John Wiley & Sons, Reino Unido, 1999).

En términos generales, la conclusión del libro es que las corporaciones que desdeñan la dimensión social en sus actividades comunicativas tenderán cada vez más a ser rechazadas por los consumidores, aunque debe admitirse que no todo tipo de temas sociales atraerán el patrocinio corporativo.

Durante la preparación de este texto, hablé con muchas de las personas que crearon las campañas publicitarias que se presentan y les pregunté por qué las encontraron profesionalmente tan interesantes y personalmente tan gratificantes.

La mayoría de ellos sienten una fuerte simpatía personal o incluso una identificación con el tema, que normalmente tiene un objetivo que claramente merece la pena.

La mayoría de las causas son de por sí dramáticas, por lo que no hace falta recurrir al interés de elementos externos.

Los clientes normalmente tienen un *briefing* claro, una pasión por comunicarlo y una predisposición a ser valientes en la manera de hacerlo.

Las limitaciones habituales sobre los gastos les obliga a apoyar ideas atrevidas con un enorme impacto inmediato.

Sin embargo, debe subrayarse que los clientes sociales no son irresponsables en lo que aprueban.

Sus campañas a menudo exigen resultados claramente cuantificables, ya sea por la respuesta popular, por las estadísticas gubernamentales, por las cifras monetarias en la recaudación de fondos o por el volumen de debate público, político o mediático generado.

En realidad, exigen más o menos lo mismo que las campañas de los clientes comerciales.

No hay nada de sorprendente en ello.

Ambos operan en mercados donde compiten muchas marcas.

Ambos deben vencer obstáculos y la resistencia a sus mensajes.

Ambos deben encontrar maneras de eludir el radar de las audiencias escépticas.

Ambos necesitan que la gente hable de ellos.

Ambos tienen que ser provocadores para obtener una respuesta con el menor coste posible.

Pero deben hacerlo de maneras que preserven la integridad de sus marcas.

También parece que ambos necesitan el poder de ideas sencillas que se traduzcan en opciones sencillas.

Ambos necesitan ideas que puedan transformar las vidas de las personas.

Ideas como las que aparecen en este libro.

社會廣告是 Saatchi & Saatchi 的基因原質。

它一直是該廣告公司的工作之持續路線，

就因為如此，在意大利 Saatchi & Saatchi 的 Paolo Ettorre 和他的組員在數年前將該公司各個有意義的廣告概念集合成一個展覽會。

現時正舉行一個新的流動展覽「Saatchi & Saatchi 與社會」[Saatchi & Saatchi & Social]，這本書便是配合這展覽而制定的。

兩者皆包括各項應付嚴重人類問題的傑出運動，它們明顯地展示該公司重視製作改變世界的意念。；

有關道路安全，則注重痛楚，而非損傷。

在執行方面，少用平面方式，而較多運用實際事件及裝置設備，或「意念大於廣告」的形式。

至於風格形式，今日的廣告有較少直率的震撼，但有較多延續的推理，

這種震撼衝擊嘩眾取寵的處理方法現時已被小心地運用，以免有「憐憫疲乏」的效果，理由是痛楚的形象未必能博取到觀眾的同情，

但有時這種手法策略是無可避免的。

意大利的綠色和平 [Greenpeace] 廣告「婦女及兒童優先」[Women and Children First] 1996，（第 24 頁）由 Stefano Maria Palombi 和 Luca Albanese 製作，內容包括在太平洋的核子測試。

在該廣告中，有一名患有腦積水的嬰兒，由於他的母親受到蘇維埃哈薩克 [Soviet Kazakhstan] 早期核試所溢出的「無害」輻射所感染，結果令該嬰兒的頭可怕地畸型，

那形象異常駭人，廣告的第一句有必要說明這是真正的記錄圖片，而不是電腦製造的歪曲畸變。

這例子顯示出不論來自那個國家，雖然有不同的文化，對廣告作品的理解能力普遍是全世界普及一致的。

廣告已成為世界通用的混合語，

因此，現時在世界各地也可以逐漸採用精巧微妙的處理手法，而不用靠震撼衝擊來嘩眾取寵。

英國防止虐待兒童協會 [National Society for the Prevention of Cruelty to Children (NSPCC)] 的廣告運動「別看」[Can't Look] 1999（第 26 頁）裡，就看不到粗暴的成年人或受到虐待的兒童。

創作組 Kes Gray 和 Dennis Willison 故意避免使用嘩眾取寵的畫像，並決定盡量運用最有效力的工具：

觀眾的想像力，

於是他們訂定規條：絕不表露任何事物，所有內容都是含蓄暗示的。

因此廣告內完全沒有人，只描畫兒童喜歡的偶像 – 辣妹樂隊 [Spice Girls]、球星 Alan Shearer、小熊魯珀特 [Rupert The Bear] 和玩具 Action Man – 他們都遮著眼睛，不欲看我們都能聽到的悲痛事件。

表露越少更越令人心寒透骨。

美國作家 John Updike 創出一句「廣告將實情矛盾修飾」的有趣話語，但其實這已是過時的錯誤看法，

實際上，這本書非常觸目之處是其應用實況的力量之顯著程度。

任何寫作廣告的人都知道由於普通讀者或觀眾的疑心和懷疑態度日益提升，謊言和半真半假的廣告實在是毫無作用的。

同時，曾經處理過社會廣告的廣告界人士會告訴你，他們經常聽到一些真正實情，其可怕程度是不能公開發表的。

越來越多商業廣告客戶亦了解到如欲爭取觀眾的信任、支持、尊重和愛戴，最好是簡單地描述真相，

當然，要商業策略有效，你所需要一種在實情披露後仍然有勸誘性的作品。

可是，為什麼要製作任何其他種類的作品呢？

社會廣告是不可能說謊的。

假如任何有爭議性的問題 (差不多全部都是) 稍有少許不正確，都會被對立的一方抓著用來質疑整個爭論，

為了先發制人，每個聲明斷言都要經過小心檢查，

因此，這本書內詳細的廣告便像有關同樣題材經過徹底研究的社論文章一般，同樣資料充實，

而且有時會寫得更好。

以防止虐待兒童協會 [NSPCC] 的「三歲小孩被強暴...」[Raped as a 3 Year Old] 1992（第 58 頁）為例，眾人初時皆假定畫像中的中年男人便是施暴者，

這例子明顯地顯示出冷漠和實話實說的語言，以及被創作組 Mike Boles 和 Jerry Hollens 故意和嚴肅地刪除了的所有忿怒和激憤的跡象能夠如何令廣告的效果更加有力。

它並不告訴讀者如何去思考，

它運用最簡單，精簡的術語，實際上全無修飾形容詞去報導事實，

這題材毫無疑問地應得的忿怒全部來自讀者們自己推斷出來的結論。

創作董事 Richard Myers 記得當這張海報在倫敦的地鐵站張貼時，其引人注意的標題和差不多 500 字的廣告內容令很多人駐足閱讀，很多人因為閱讀而錯過火車班次，為了月台安全起見，廣告更要被移往月台較遠處。

如果為了閱讀這一篇優雅的廣告而跌下月台，這廣告便不是為公眾利益而製作的了。

同一個客戶有另一個廣告，展示一名懷孕的少女注視著她鼓脹的肚子，而標題「我們有同一個父親」[We Both Have The Same Father]，1995（第 30 頁）在那一霎間並不怎麼強烈尖銳，直至讀者深深體會到其亂倫含意。

這只是一個說明廣告與溝通這等技巧本身是沒有固有的思想意識形態的例子，

它們反映文化，但並不創造文化，

而我們生活的文化中，則有很多社會因素像商業產品一樣，需要有效的溝通，

但並非所有的社會客戶都是非商業性質的。

道路安全、反種族歧視和防止毒品濫用的廣告、護士及教師招募和其他現有的商業客戶所支持的社會廣告通常都是經過同業競爭而取得的，並照常獲得酬金。

但更重要的是社會廣告集中注意力於一些意念，這些意念能令嚴重和公眾關注的問題之感受和看法有所轉變，

亦是能將資金少的預算計劃變成有力的廣告的大概念。

要立即改變實際行為可能困難，但最低限度一個侵入性和戲劇化的概念能夠啟發公眾對問題存在的醒覺。

這類以少本預算支持和富挑撥刺激性及大膽冒險的概念而產生比其傳媒專欄方寸高出多倍價值的廣告例子有很多。

其中一個例子是一系列在英國的種族平等廣告，

Chris Kirk 和 Giles Montgomery 所設計的標題雙關語故意傳達一股荒涼、淒慘的幽默，以便迴避大聲叫喊的譴責。

在「最差的印記」[Worst Marks] 的海報 1997（第 50 頁），這亦能使廣告暗示少數民族學術成績的論點，

亞裔學生的成績其實是在平均水平以上。

個人經歷認識很多時亦啟發「郵寄宣傳品」[Junk Mail] 廣告 1997（第 171 頁）。美術設計師 Ajab Samrai Singh 執行了一系列這類廣告，他六歲時，在英國西中部貧困地區長大，曾

有人用汽油從他父母家居的信箱倒進屋內。

這類的廣告似乎已成為滔滔不絕的實況和概念的一部份，出現於各種傳媒，因此亦出現於各類辦公地點和社交聚會。

雖然很多社會廣告的資金成本預算比較少，但由於廣告的內容顯著觸目，引起大量的社論和公眾爭議，充分地令廣告獲得注目。

這令公眾對種族平等運動及其宗旨的認識在兩年期間由百份之三十五增加至百份之五十。

一個傑出的構思會因為其機智妙語、其尖銳潑辣和其獨出心裁、其震撼衝擊或令人振奮難忘之處而受到崇敬。

就是它令到廣告製作人能晨早起來，能在辦公室或在深宵時份，在多杯咖啡中激發起
感情；

對那些每天都將才幹、個人熱衷和專業精神集中於尋找改變見解想法及影響行為態度的方法的廣告製作人，聖杯就是找到改造世界的主題。

誰如說「我們稱讚別人時是最老實的」？

我遇到很少廣告從業員是不欣賞由星加坡的 Dean Turney 和 Francis Wee 所創作的反對醉酒駕駛廣告「酒杯」[Glasses] 1993 (第 140 頁)，

它的構思是極之簡單的表達，簡單得令差不多每個廣告創作者和美術設計師的第一反應都是：「為什麼從來沒有人想到這樣做呢？」

然後他們都說：「為什麼我從來沒有想到這樣做呢？」

在正在穿越城市的汽車車廂內，我們看到一個又一個的空啤酒杯被放在擋風玻璃窗前，每一個遮擋更多視野，

到第四個杯子時，眼前的視野實在不清楚，汽車跟著撞向一輛公共汽車的後面。

就各種意識而言，極之節約簡單，也極之英明卓越。

清晰明顯得令人驚訝的爭議也可以在英國的鎗械控制網 [Gun Control Network] 1997 看得到 (第 68 頁)。

在蘇格蘭鄧伯蘭 [Dunblane, Scotland] 發生整班學童遭屠殺後，英國政府制定禁止某些鎗械的法律，

但該法律沒有包括行兇者當時使用的 .22 口徑的手鎗，

當國會即將就這有裂隙的法律舉行辯論通過時，在倫敦的一個創作組 Bill Gallacher, Robin Murtough 和 Keith Terry 感到驚奇和憤怒之餘，又沒有資金和時間，

他們知道羅拔甘迺迪 [Robert Kennedy] 是被兇徒用 .22 口徑手鎗刺殺的，於是他們利用一幅存庫照片和一個 Mac 電腦，即興湊合創作出一個廣告牌，在國會辯論當日展示在一輛停泊在國會外的貨車上。

廣告牌寫著：「如果 .22 口徑手鎗並不那麼致命，為何要了他的命？」

那少許數個字的震驚效力協助令到該禁止鎗械法例包括 .22 口徑手鎗。

正如美國羅省創作董事 Tom Cordner 所說：「一個廣告可能傑出優越，但你看完之後便沒有了，有點兒瞬間消逝的感覺，可是一個強烈傑出的概念主題能扣人心弦，在你心中留下深刻印象。」

這觀察所得的知識背景是 Saatchi & Saatchi 相信整個世界正在迅速地發展一種注目經濟體系，

而在這注目經濟體系中，就如該公司的全球創作董事 Bob Isherwood 所說：「概念主題是將來的貨幣。」

如果這是真的話，最大的投資應該不是在於媒介，而是在於概念主題。

美國廣告公司協會 [American Advertising Agencies' Association] 估計美國人每天接觸到 3,000 個各種形式的商業信息，

電視廣告、海報、報刊廣告、廣告標識象徵語句、公共汽車車身廣告、超級市場標貼、產品包裝，無處不是，

而消費者表示他們對這麼多的廣告有所反應的數目只是…十二。

當粗製濫造的作品和平凡瑣事是那樣地翻騰起伏的遍布廣告，而我們的溝通文化的背景噪音又那麼的吵耳欲聾時，訊息又如何能傳達到觀眾呢？

不論是商業客戶的產品抑或是有關社會問題，這很明顯地是一種挑戰，

其實對社會主題客戶而言，這是更大的挑戰，因為他們可運用的廣告資金通常只等如商業黃告的一部份，

因此，如果為社會主題客戶所創作的概念能夠成功地衝破這些喧騰嘈雜的周圍環境，在所有這些附帶的不利情況下，他們是否未必能夠領略到一些廣泛客戶遇到的溝通問題呢？

Saatchi & Saatchi 認為可以示範為改變各種社會主題而創作的多種概念。

被說服考慮一個嚴重問題能夠帶來真正的樂趣，其中一個例子來自紐西蘭，

用絕對透徹的歡樂妙趣去處理執行道路安全廣告是一個不尋常而且難辦的角度，但在「邋遢天使」[Grunge Angels] 的電視廣告 1995 (第 XXX 頁)，Glen Wood 和 Peter Force 則操縱得明顯自如，

最脆弱的目標觀眾是由兩位年輕男士扮演。

他們在天使合唱聲中發覺自己身處雲霧之間，

天國的公告系統宣布：「作為後世的娛樂，我們為你帶來 Whitney Houston 最著名的情歌…」

他們很理解地認為這種永恆是比死亡還要差的命運，

配音指出「死亡是極可怕的一回事」，並建議扣上安全帶是明智之舉。

看過 Saatchi & Saatchi 的社會主題片段多次，只有鐵石心腸的觀眾才不會哭的，

而在這一個例子則只有鐵石心腸的人才不會捧腹大笑的。

在意大利為聯合國的糧食與農業組織 [UN Food & Agriculture Organisation] 所創製的「與饑餓戰爭」[War on Hunger] 1998 廣告中，輝煌的荒誕主義演員之該諧幽默帶出另一個殘酷的主題，

廣告的開始是軍隊在戰爭中的單色紀錄片段，

但片段很快便顯示他們的火箭是加色的甜玉米，他們的直升機是蕃茄，

士兵在矮樹叢中爬行，以香蕉作為機關鎗，

臼炮發射的彈幕全是洋蔥，

簡直是一個瘋狂世界。

當全球不同的軍事開支預算會解決世界上大多數的饑餓問題時，這評述意見是恰當的。

值得提及的是在本書刊中展示的廣告，很多曾獲得在康城、倫敦、紐約和其他地方舉辦的世界性重要比賽的至高創作獎項。

獎項可能備受廣告業高度崇拜，但若然受到同業裁定是最好的話，這也是無可厚非的。

各評判者除了對競爭類型風格比較熟識外，他們對意味深長的呼籲與任何其他人是沒有分別的，

這只顯示出這些主題及其製作手法具備傑出的戲劇性場面、振奮激昂和威勢力量，而這通常都是在處理新和困難的挑戰時達到的。

一些對廣告創作比賽有興趣的人接受一種荒誕的說法，那就是社會主題和慈善機構的廣告是贏取獎項的捷徑，

其實事實是剛剛相反，有重大意義的類別常常是最多製作參賽的，

所有參賽作品都是處理同種類的表現感情的主題，

但與大眾的觀點相反的是處理這類主題是很難做得對，而且是很容易處理不當的。

社會主題和商業廣告在大多數細節上都有同樣的難處，

但有一方面它們是不同的，

那就是社會主題溝通是那麼的困難，但如果處理得當是那麼的有價值，這基本挑戰之目的是先改變觀眾對一個他們可能完全不會去思考的主題之直覺概念，繼而改變他們對這主題的看法和態度，

這與傳統的商業廣告不同，即使觀眾接受你的議論，廣告能給與他們的自我滿足是有限的。

就好像 Dr. Johnson 所說「廣告的靈魂在於其諾言，一個大諾言」，如果這是對的，那麼社會主題廣告的「諾言」又是甚麼呢？

當我們在週日喝咖啡和吃牛角飽時，我們事實上是不想思考有關愛滋病、或地震、或虐待兒童的問題，

我們不想將自己視為種族歧視、或道路安全、或環境毀壞問題的一部份，

我們若採取簡單的行動，或者能夠為饑餓的兒童、難民或受到欺壓的少數人的苦況盡一點力，但我們無疑是不想去面對這些事實，

他們說：「我們全部都有罪。」

我們現在是否一定要去討論這些呢？

如果我們嘗試稍為改善這個世界，這其實是對的。

在製作社會主題廣告方面，當吸引那些自私自利或貪得無厭的衝動人士之可能性不大時，廣告從業員便要探索一個可以接觸到觀眾的同情心的方向，

為了協助探索這個方向，在 1940 年代初期，一位美國學術界人士 A H Maslow 設計了一個有用的示例，解釋消費者，尤其是在較富裕社會的消費者，為何逐漸遠離物質主義對他們的私心的吸引。

Maslow 的假設是人類有一個「需求等級制度」，通常以一個金字塔型來舉列說明，最低層是抵抗饑渴的生理需求，

在這一層的上面是對保障和防禦的安全需求，

接著便是歸屬感和愛心的社交人際需求，

再上一層是認可、自尊和身份地位的尊重需求，

最後在金字塔頂的是充份實現抱負的需求，是發展自己的才能和實現理想的需求。

世界各地現今對傳統以來備受尊崇的社會棟梁已比以往低，這論點與 Maslow 的假設相符，

各個政府、教會、警方、軍隊、英國的皇室和美國的總統都與我們所有人一樣有同樣的凡人弱點，

從另一方面來說，某些公司和商標一直增加公眾對他們的信任和信心的程度，

這是有明顯實例的。

有些銀行和投資基金堅決聲明採取道德政策，避免投資對環境不利的公司、或靠損壞顧客健康而興隆的公司、或剝削第三世界供應商的公司，越來越多人響應這些銀行和投資基金，

投資者知道如在這方面投資他們的利潤會可能降低，但他們依然這樣做。

現時各報紙的財經版將合乎道德原則的投資基金列出，數目也相當多。

英國的合作銀行 [Co-operative Bank] 的帳戶成交更換率明顯地比其他銀行較低，現時更是全歐發行最多 VISA 金卡的

銀行。

在時裝和化妝品行業，Liz Claiborne 和 Body Shop 都由於其道德立場而興旺。

此外，很多商業機構體會到越來越多消費者在選擇有同樣等級的商品或服務時，會選擇那些標榜其關心非商業主義的公司，

這樣的做法已成為所謂的「有意義的市場銷售業務」[Cause-Related Marketing]。

例如澳洲 Procter & Gamble 是與救濟兒童基金 [Save The Children Fund] 有關連，即使在印度這個經濟開始顯露的國家中，Procter & Gamble 已經與聯合國教育科學及文化組織 [UNESCO] 一起工作，將兒童工人帶會學校。

英國的連鎖超級市場 Tesco 支持「讓學校有電腦」運動。

美國的 Harley-Davidson 與肌肉萎縮症協會 [Muscular Dystrophy Association] 一起工作。

美國運通 [American Express] 則主持「向饑餓進擊」運動。

如欲知更多關於「有意義的市場銷售業務」的討論，我推薦由 Hamish Pringle 和 Marjorie Thompson 所著作的 Brand Spirit，該書是現時有關該主題的確定性書本。(1999 年由英國 John Wiley & Sons 出版)

概括地說，該書的結論是：雖然並非所有社會問題都會吸引到公司贊助支持，但在溝通方面不顧及社會範圍的公司會越來越受到消費者的抵制。

在準備此原文時，我曾與多為參與這些廣告創作的人傾談，並問他們這些創作為何在專業方面令他們覺得那麼有趣味，而在個人方面又那麼有價值，

他們大多數有強烈的同情心，或與問題認同，主題通常都有一個目的，而這目的又是不言而喻的值得做的。

大多數的問題本身基本上是激動人心，扣人心弦，無須向外吸引興趣，

客戶通常有清楚的概要，有一股熱誠去傳達意念，更樂意去勇敢地做他們要做的事。

慣常的支出限制驅使他們採取冒險大膽而又會有極大和直接效力的主意，

但必須說明社會廣告客戶在認可主意時，是不會不顧後果的魯莽贊成。

他們的廣告通常要求在公眾反應方面、或政府統計數字、或在基金籌款方面的收益、或所引起的公眾、政治或傳媒爭議的份量方面，能夠有清楚地衡量得到的結果，

其實這與商業廣告客戶的要求大致相同，

這點並不是意想不到的。

兩種廣告皆在有很多競爭同業商標的市場運作；

兩者都必須克服對他們信息的阻礙和抗拒；

兩種廣告都要尋求避免抱懷疑態度的觀眾猜疑之途徑；

兩者都需要引起大眾議論；

兩者都要具挑撥性，能引起爭議，以便用最低成本而取得回應；

然而兩種廣告的做法都必須維護其商標的健全型像；

兩者似乎都需要能夠演譯成簡單抉擇的主題力量；

兩種廣告皆需要可以改變人類生命的主題，

像這本書內的各種主題。

Read This You Piece of Shit
Client: Anti-Slavery International
Agency: Saatchi & Saatchi, UK
Year: 1995
Copywriter: Michael Campbell
Art Director: Vanessa Rosser
Client Contact: Mark Covey

Pram/Family Planning
Client: The Health Education Council
Agency: Saatchi & Saatchi, UK
Year: 1975
Copywriter: Andrew Rutherford
Art Director: Ron Mather

Clip this Coupon
Client: Médécins Sans Frontières
Agency: Saatchi & Saatchi, Rome, Italy
Year: 1997
Copywriter: Stefano Maria Palombi
Art Director: Luca Albanese
Photography: Ferdinando Scianna,
Magnum
Client Contact: Antonella Giacobbe

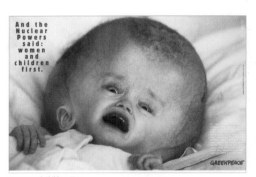

Women and Children First
Client: Greenpeace
Agency: Saatchi & Saatchi, Rome, Italy
Year: 1996
Copywriter: Stefano Maria Palombi
Art Director: Luca Albanese
Photography: Paul Lowe, Network, G neri
Key Account Handler: Alessandro Moresi
Client Contact: Ivan Novelli

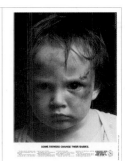

Can't Look
Client: National Society for the
Prevention of Cruelty to Children
(NSPCC)
Agency: Saatchi & Saatchi, UK
Year: 1999
Copywriter: Kes Gray
Art Director: Dennis Willison
Director: Malcolm Venville
Key Account Manager: Norma Clarke
Client Contact: Marian Rose

Pregnant Man
Client: The Health Education Council
Agency: Saatchi & Saatchi, UK
Year: 1970
Copywriter: Jeremy Sinclair
Art Director: Bill Atherton

Some Fathers
Client: NSW Police
Agency: Saatchi & Saatchi, Australia
Year: 1996
Copywriter: Richard Grisdale
Art Director: Fergus Fleming
Key Account Handler: Derick Frere

Same Father
Client: National Society for the
Prevention of Cruelty to Children
(NSPCC)
Agency: Saatchi & Saatchi, UK
Year: 1995
Copywriters: Bill Gallacher, Colin Jones
Art Director: Neil Pavitt
Photographer: Graham Cornthwaite

Astronaut
Client: State of the World Forum
Agency: Saatchi & Saatchi, Wellington,
New Zealand
Year: 1998
Copywriter: John Plimmer
Art Directors: John Fisher, Oliver Maisey,
Gavin Bradley
Typographer: Len Cheeseman
Key Account Handlers: Ian Christie,
Angela Barnett
Client Contact: Tom Rautenberg

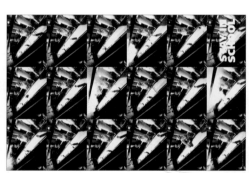

Face
Client: Department of Health/COI
Agency: Saatchi & Saatchi, UK
Year: 1999
Copywriter: Richard Baynham
Art Directors: John Messum,
Ian Gabaldoni
Director: Jonathan Greenhalgh
Key Account Manager: Norma Clarke

Cot
Client: National Society for the
Prevention of Cruelty to Children
(NSPCC)
Agency: Saatchi & Saatchi, UK
Copywriter: Linda O'Sullivan
Art Director: Nick Hine
Director: David Bailey
Voiceover: Alan Rickman

The World Could End This Easily
Client: Greenpeace
Year: 1998
Agency: Saatchi & Saatchi, Auckland,
New Zealand
Copywriter: Andrew Tinning
Art Director: Andrew Tinning
Typographer: Andrew Tinning
Key Account Handler: Andrew Tinning
Client Contact: Paula Gair

Stay In School
Client: Ministry of Education
Agency: Saatchi & Saatchi, Auckland,
New Zealand
Year: 1994
Copywriter: Matt Simpkins
Art Director: James Mok
Producer: Melissa Jansen
Production Company: Silverscreen
Productions
Director: Richard Gibson

Hungry
Client: Second Harvest
Agency: Saatchi & Saatchi, Toronto,
Canada
Year: 1994
Copywriter: Donna McCarthy
Art Director: Jon Mychajlyszyn
Key Account handler: Kim Allen
Client contact: Vicki Sanderson

Day Against Violence
Client: Italian Football Association
Agency: Saatchi & Saatchi, Italy
Year: 1995
Copywriter: Stefano Maria Palombi
Art Director: Fabio Ferri
Agency Producer: Fabrizio Conte
Key Account Handler: Alessandro Moresi
Client Contact: Antonello Valentini
Music: O Sole Mio

Worst Marks
Client: Commission for Racial Equality
Agency: Saatchi & Saatchi, UK
Year: 1997
Copywriter: Chris Kirk
Art Director: Ajab Samrai Singh
Typographer: Nigel Ward
Photographer: John Turner
Key Account Handler: Simone Forster
Client Contact: Marjorie Thompson

Teacher Passing an Examination
Client: Department of Education &
Science
Agency: Saatchi & Saatchi, UK
Year: 1992
Copywriter: Richard Myers
Art Director: Bill Gallacher
Photographer: Graham Cornthwaite

Resolution
Client: Anti-Firecrackers
Agency: Saatchi & Saatchi, Philippines
Year: 1995
Copywriter: Tanke Tankeko
Art Director: Jake Tesoro
Director: Matthew Rosen
Producer: Carrie Villamor

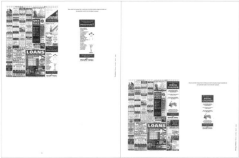

Prostitute
Client: Manos Unidas
Agency: Saatchi & Saatchi, Madrid, Spain
Year: 1999
Copywriter: Mercedes Ruiz
Art Director: Mar Frutos
Producer: Javier Fernandez
Key Account Handler: Alex de Reguero
Client Contact: Charo Marmol

Mining Children
Client: Manos Unidas
Agency: Saatchi & Saatchi, Madrid, Spain
Year: 1999
Copywriter: Mercedes Ruiz
Art Director: Mar Frutos
Producer: Javier Fernandez
Key Account Handler: Alex de Reguero
Client Contact: Charo Marmol

Child Abuse
Client: The Italian Centre for
International Adoption (CIAI)
Agency: Saatchi & Saatchi, Italy
Year: 1997
Copywriter: Guido Cornara
Art Director: Agostino Toscana
Director: Ricky Tognazzi
Key Account Managers: Rachele Dottori,
Matteo Consonni
Client Contact: Gabriella Merguici

Raped as a 3 Year Old
Client: National Society for the
Prevention of Cruelty to Children
(NSPCC)
Agency: Saatchi & Saatchi, UK
Year: 1992
Copywriter: Mike Boles
Art Director: Jerry Hollens
Photographer: Graham Cornthwaite

Dr Jekyll, Mr Hyde
Client: The Italian Centre for
International Adoption (CIAI)
Agency: Saatchi & Saatchi, Milan, Ita y
Year: 1997
Copywriter: Guido Cornara
Art Director: Agostino Toscana
Key Account Handler: Matteo Consonni
Client Contact: Gabriella Merguici

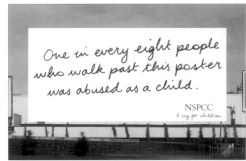

1 in every 8
Client: National Society for the
Prevention of Cruelty to Children
(NSPCC)
Agency: Saatchi & Saatchi, UK
Year: 1994
Copywriter: Paul Bringloe
Art Director: Dominic Corp

Ban Guns
Client: Coalition for Gun Control
Agency: Saatchi & Saatchi, Australia
Year: 1996
Copywriter: Tim Brown
Art Director: Matthew Johnstone
Key Account Handler: Tim Bullock
Client Contact: Rebecca Peters

Bullet
Client: Iniciativa Comunitaria AIDS/
Condoms
Agency: Badillo Nazca Saatchi & Saatchi,
Puerto Rico
Year: 1999
Copywriters: Marcus Grajales,
Ricardo Marti
Illustrator/Photographer:
Malcolm Walker
Key Account Handler: Malcolm Walker

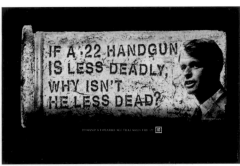

Less Dead
Client: Hand Gun Control Network
Agency: Saatchi & Saatchi, UK
Year: 1997
Copywriter: Robin Murtough
Art Directors: Bill Gallacher, Keith Terry
Typographer: Brian Hackney
Key Account Handler: Emily Stoner
Client Contact: Gill Marshall Andrews

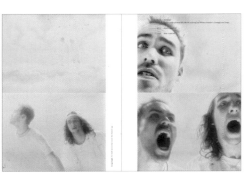

Grunge Angels
Client: The Health Sponsorship Council
Agency: Saatchi & Saatchi, Wellington,
New Zealand
Year: 1995
Copywriters: Glen Wood, Peter Force
Art Directors: Peter Force, Glen Wood
Producer: Angela Cameron
Production Company: Black Stump
Director: Josh Frizzell
Key Account Handler: Neil Cameron
Client Contact: Sophie Hensley

Rubber Woman
Client: Action for AIDS
Agency: Saatchi & Saatchi, Singapore
Year: 1992
Copywriter: Natalie Sinclair
Art Directors: Terence Tan, Ewan Pidgeon

Rubber Man
Client: Action for AIDS
Agency: Saatchi & Saatchi, Singapore
Year: 1992
Copywriter: Natalie Sinclair
Art Directors: Terence Tan, Ewan Pidgeon

Tongue
Client: Hong Kong Language Learning
Centre
Agency: Saatchi & Saatchi, Hong Kong
Year: 1995
Client Contact: Ms Color Tsang

Mother
Client: Ministry of Transport
Agency: Saatchi & Saatchi, Wellington,
New Zealand
Year: 1990
Producer: Jane Byrne
Production Company: Flying Fish
Copywriter: Kim Thorp
Art Director: Gavin Bradley
Director: Gregor Nicholas
Key Account Handler: Nick Farland
Client Contact: Chris Morrison

Job Satisfaction
Client: Department of Health/COI
Agency: Saatchi & Saatchi, UK
Year: 1998
Copywriter: Mike McKenna
Art Director: Colin Jones
Typographer: Roger Kennedy
Key Account Handler: Norma Clarke
Client Contact: Romola Christopherson

A Country Story
Client: Land Transport Safety
Authority/NZ Police
Agency: Saatchi & Saatchi, Wellington,
New Zealand
Year: 1999
Copywriter: Len Potts
Art Director: Gavin Bradley
Director: Tony Williams
Agency Producer: Juliet Dreaver
Account Managers: Wendy Schrijvers,
Helen Tweedie
Client Contact: Wilma Falconer

The Height of It
Client: UNICEF
Agency: Saatchi & Saatchi, Australia
Year: 1999
Copywriter: David Shirlaw
Art Director: Belinda Johnstone
Key Account Handler: Michelle
Greenhalgh

Taxi Confessions
Client: Land Transport Safety Authority/
NZ Police
Agency: Saatchi & Saatchi, Wellington,
New Zealand
Year: 1996
Copywriter: Maggie Mouat
Art Director: Chris Bleackley
Producer: Brigid Howard
Key Account Handlers: Wendy Schrijvers,
Helen Tweedie
Client Contact: Wilma Falconer

Disaster
Client: New Zealand Red Cross
Agency: Saatchi & Saatchi, Wellington,
New Zealand
Year: 1996
Copywriters: Ken Double, Steve Cooper
Art Directors: Len Cheeseman,
Evan Purdie
Typographers: Len Cheeseman,
Carl Kennard
Illustrator: Evan Purdie
Key Account Handlers: Linda Jones,
Bridgette Yates
Client Contact: Martin Robinson

Fight
Client: New Zealand Red Cross
Agency: Saatchi & Saatchi, Wellington,
New Zealand
Year: 1996
Copywriters: Ken Double, Steve Cooper
Art Directors: Len Cheeseman,
Evan Purdie
Typographers: Len Cheeseman,
Carl Kennard
Illustrator: Evan Purdie
Key Account Handlers: Linda Jones,
Bridgette Yates
Client Contact: Martin Robinson

350 Languages
Client: New Zealand Red Cross
Agency: Saatchi & Saatchi, Wellington,
New Zealand
Year: 1996
Copywriters: Ken Double, Steve Cooper
Art Directors: Len Cheeseman,
Evan Purdie
Typographers: Len Cheeseman,
Carl Kennard
Key Account Handlers: Linda Jones,
Bridgette Yates
Client Contact: Martin Robinson

Don't Forget
Client: Action for AIDS
Agency: Saatchi & Saatchi, Singapore
Year: 1993
Copywriter: Dean Turney
Art Director: Francis Wee

Prevent Sickness
Client: Action for AIDS
Agency: Saatchi & Saatchi, Singapore
Year: 1993
Copywriter: Dean Turney
Art Director: Francis Wee

Night Cap
Client: Action for AIDS
Agency: Saatchi & Saatchi, Singapore
Year: 1993
Copywriter: Dean Turney
Art Director: Francis Wee

Right Package
Client: Action for AIDS
Agency: Saatchi & Saatchi, Singapore
Year: 1993
Copywriter: Dean Turney
Art Director: Francis Wee

Preservativo
Client: ANLAIDS
Agency: Saatchi & Saatchi, Rome, Italy
Year: 1995
Copywriter: Stefano Maria Palombi
Art Director: Luca Albanese
Director: Fabrizio Mari
Account Manager: Fiorella Pini
Client Contact: Ferdinando Aiuti

Strangers in the Night
Client: AIDS Awareness
Agency: Saatchi & Saatchi, Yugoslavia
Year: 1998
Music: Strangers in the Night/Chopin's
Funeral March

Love Story
Client: Red Cross
Agency: Saatchi & Saatchi, Barcelona,
Spain
Year: 1987
Copywriters: Luis Casadevall,
Cuca Canals
Art Directors: Oscar Pla, Pepe Rosas
Music: Theme from Love Story

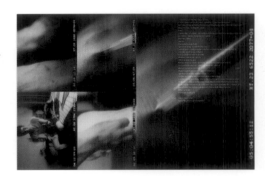

Lenny
Client: Partnership for a Drug-Free
America
Agency: Saatchi & Saatchi, Cliff Freeman,
USA
Director: Tony Kaye
Year: 1995
Music: When I Fall in Love

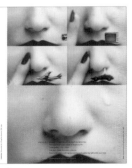

Surfing Monkey
Client: Partnership for a Drug-Free
America
Agency: Saatchi & Saatchi, Team One,
USA
Year: 1999
Copywriter: Greg Collins
Art Directors: Greg Wells, Marne Brobeck
Director: Kyle Bergerser

Celebrities
Client: Partnership for a Drug-Free
America
Agency: Saatchi & Saatchi, New York,
USA
Year: 1994
Art Director: Matthew Schwartz
Copywriter: David George

Nose
Client: Partnership for a Drug-Free
America
Agency: Saatchi & Saatchi, New York, USA
Year: 1988
Copywriter: Jeff Stark
Art Director: Dianne Douglas Graham

Elephant
Client: Environmental Federation of
California
Agency: Saatchi & Saatchi, Team One,
USA
Year: 1992
Copywriter: Court Crandall
Art Director: Angela Dunkle

The Only Fur
Client: International Fund for Animal Welfare
Agency: Saatchi & Saatchi, Rome, Italy
Year: 1996
Copywriter: Bernardo Notargiacomo
Art Director: Fabio Giannotti
Photographer: Marco Delogu
Key Account Handler: Giulio Brunini
Client Contact: Walter Caporale

Hatchet
Client: Fundação S.O.S. Mata Atlântica, Rainforest Conservation
Agency: F Nazca Saatchi & Saatchi, Brazil
Year: 1999
Copywriter: Wilson Mateos
Art Director: Marco Aurélio Monteiro
Photographer: Rodrigo Ribeiro
Key Account Handler: Loy Barjas
Client Contact: P. Kobayashi

Whales
Client: Greenpeace
Agency: Saatchi & Saatchi, Rome, Italy
Year: 1993
Director: Jean Paul Seaulieu
Copywriter: Guido Cornara
Art Director: Luca Albanese
Key Account Handler: Gina De Bellis
Client Contact: Gianni Squitieri

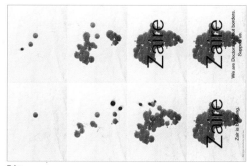

Water Cooler
Client: UNICEF
Agency: Saatchi & Saatchi, Australia
Year: 1999
Copywriter: David Shirlaw
Art Director: Belinda Johnstone
Key Account Handler: Michelle Greenhalgh

Year of the.
Client: World Wildlife Fund
Agency: Saatchi & Saatchi, Vietnam
Year: 1998
Copywriter: Paul Ewen
Art Director: Le Duc Thang
Typographer: Le Duc Thang
Key Account Handler: Michiko Leong
Client Contact: Susie Kukathas

Last Water In Rwanda
Client: UNICEF
Agency: Saatchi & Saatchi, Rome, Italy
Year: 1994
Copywriter: Michela Indiati
Art Director: Grazia Cecconi
Photography: Stan Grossfeld, The Boston Globe
Key Account Handler: Annalisa Donati
Client Contact: Roberto Salvan

Going, Going, Gone
Client: World Wildlife Foundation
Agency: Saatchi & Saatchi, Singapore
Year: 1990
Copywriter: Alex Shipley
Art Director: Ding Yew Moong, Linda Locke

Zaire
Client: Doctors without Borders
Agency: Saatchi & Saatchi, Sweden
Year: 1992

War on Hunger
Client: FAO
Agency: Saatchi & Saatchi, Rome, Italy
Year: 1998
Director: Marco Palanca
Copywriter: Stefano Maria Palombi
Art Directors: Fabio Ferri, Marco Palanca
Key Account Handler: Muriel de Meo
Client Contact: Karin-Lis Svarre

Speed Kills
Client: New Zealand Police
Agency: Saatchi & Saatchi, Wellington, New Zealand
Year: 1994
Copywriter: Marcus Beer
Art Directors: John de Vries, Peter Force
Key Account Handler: Neil Cameron
Client Contact: Jeff Bland

Glasses
Client: Traffic Police
Agency: Saatchi & Saatchi, Singapore
Year: 1993
Copywriter: Dean Turney
Art Director: Francis Wee

Ash
Client: NRMA
Agency: Saatchi & Saatchi, Australia
Year: 1998
Copywriter: Scott Waterhouse
Art Director: Steve Carlin
Key Account Handler: Simone Bartley
Client Contact: Gary Williams

Stripes
Client: Road Safety
Agency: Saatchi & Saatchi, Czech Republic
Year: 1997
Copywriter: Eda Kauba
Art Director: Don Nicolson
Typographer: Roman Zajicek

Just Sit There
Client: Mothers Against Drunk Driving (MADD)
Agency: Saatchi & Saatchi, Toronto, Canada
Year: 1996
Copywriter: Michael Convery
Art Director: Michael Wilson
Typographer: Umbrella Graphics
Key Account Handler: Glenn Hollis
Client Contact: Jim Widemen

The Censor
Client: Index on Censorship
Agency: Saatchi & Saatchi, UK
Year: 1986
Copywriter: Simon Dicketts
Art Director: Fergus Fleming

Free Press
Client: Article 19
Agency: Saatchi & Saatchi, Slovenia
Year: 1997
Copywriter: Milos Ilic
Art Director: Milos Ilic
Key Account Handler: Ana Stanic
Client Contact: Barbara Petric

Spaniel
Client: SPCA
Agency: Saatchi & Saatchi, Singapore
Year: 1997
Copywriter: Jagdish Ramakrishnan
Art Director: Edmund Choe
Typographers: Edmund Choe/
Jagdish Ramakrishnan
Key Account Handler: Bill Timmermann
Client Contact: Deidre Moss

Dog and Gun
Client: Royal Society for the Prevention
of Cruelty to Animals (RSPCA)
Agency: Saatchi & Saatchi, UK
Year: 1986
Director: Bill Long
Producer: Martha Greene

Light Bulb
Client: Barcelona Council/Motorbike
Safety
Agency: Saatchi & Saatchi, Barcelona,
Spain

Don't Piss...
Client: Mothers Against Drunk Driving
(MADD)
Agency: Saatchi & Saatchi, Toronto,
Canada
Year: 1996
Copywriter: Michael Convery
Art Director: Michael Wilson
Typographer: Umbrella Graphics
Key Account Handler: Glenn Hollis
Client Contact: Jim Widemen

Vote No/Vote Yes
Client: World Wildlife Fund
Agency: Saatchi & Saatchi, Milan, Italy
Year: 1990
Copywriter: Stefano Maria Palombi
Art Director: Fabio Ferri
Photography: M Lanin , Panda Foto
Key Account Handler: Pietro Concina
Client Contact: Valerio Neri

Poached Elephant
Client: World Wildlife Foundation
Agency: Saatchi & Saatchi, Singapore
Year: 1993
Copywriter: Simon Kornberg
Art Directors: Linda Locke, Francis Wee

Abbandono
Client: Worldwide Fund for Nature
Agency: Saatchi & Saatchi, Italy
Year: 1987
Copywriter: Maurizio D'Adda
Art Director: Gian Piero Vigorelli
Client: Silvio Berlusconi Editore

Power of One
Client: Earth Communications Office
Agency: Saatchi & Saatchi, Team One,
USA
Year: 1992
Copywriters: Rebecca Rivera,
Michael Everard
Art Director: Graham Katz
Account Manager: Kelley Hill

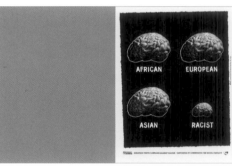

Brains
Client: Commission for Racial Equality
Agency: Saatchi & Saatchi, UK
Year: 1995
Copywriters: Adam Hunt, Ben Nott
Art Directors: Ben Nott, Adam Hunt
Typographer: Mac Macaloon
Key Account Handler: Simone Forster
Client Contact: Marjorie Thompson

Scars
Client: Médécins Sans Frontières
Agency: Saatchi & Saatchi, Rome, Italy
Year: 1997
Copywriter: Stefano Maria Palombi
Art Director: Grazia Cecconi
Photography: James Nachtwey, Magnum
Client Contact: Antonella Giacobbe

Them
Client: Commission for Racial Equality
Agency: Saatchi & Saatchi, UK
Year: 1996
Copywriter: Eugene Ruane
Art Director: Ajab Samrai Singh
Director: John Moore
Account Manager: Simone Forster

Openings
Client: Commission for Racial Equality
Agency: Saatchi & Saatchi, UK
Year: 1994
Copywriter: Giles Montgomery
Art Director: Ajab Samrai Singh
Typographer: Nigel Ward
Key Account Handler: Simone Forster
Client Contact: Marjorie Thompson

Criminal Isn't It?
Client: Commission for Racial Equality
Agency: Saatchi & Saatchi, UK
Year: 1997
Copywriter: Ajab Samrai Singh
Art Director: Ajab Samrai Singh
Typographer: Tim Quest
Photography: Tim O'Sullivan,
Alister Thain
Key Account Handler: Simone Forster
Client Contact: Marjorie Thompson

Junk Mail
Client: Commission for Racial Equality
Agency: Saatchi & Saatchi, UK
Year: 1997
Copywriter: Giles Montgomery
Art Director: Ajab Samrai Singh
Typographer: Nigel Ward
Photographer: John Turner
Key Account Handler: Simone Forster
Client Contact: Marjorie Thompson

Ethnic Cleansing
Client: Médécins Du Monde
Agency: Saatchi & Saatchi, Paris, France
Year: 1994

Next Generation
Client: JIA
Agency: Saatchi & Saatchi, UK
Year: 1995
Copywriter: Maxine Formaggi
Art Director: Nick Schon
Typographer: Roger Kennedy
Key Account Handler: Paul Burns
Client Contact: Antony Wagerman

Saddam
Client: Refugee Council
Agency: Saatchi & Saatchi, UK
Year: 1998
Copywriter: Julian Dyer
Art Director: Ajab Samrai Singh
Typographer: Roger Kennedy
Key Account Handler: Murray Pannell
Client Contact: Rachel Rees

No Flag
Client: Red Cross Kurdish Appeal
Agency: Saatchi & Saatchi, Ireland

Equals
Client: Commission for Racial Equality
Agency: Saatchi & Saatchi, UK
Year: 1997
Copywriter: Kes Gray
Art Director: Dennis Willison
Directors: Nick Sutherland-Dodd & Paul
Arden/Neil Harris, Adam Lyne & Stuart
Douglas, Nick Morris & Jonathan Glazer,
David Kerr & Antony Easton, Ella
Sanderson & Zak Ove, Barbara
Manfredini & Frederico Brugia, Fatima
Andrade & Frances Silor, Ed Sayers &

Jonathan Greenhalgh, Nick Saward &
John O'Donnell, Bruce Williamson &
Martin Brierley, James Studholme & Ivan
Zacharias, Lisa Bryer & Nick Lewin, Sid
Daffran & John Moore, Robert Herman &
Tessa Sheridan
Account Managers: Simone Forester,
Scott Morrison
Music throughout: The Far Too Simple
Beauty, Trembling Blue Stars

Shattered Dreams
Client: NSW Police
Agency: Saatchi & Saatchi Australia
Year: 1997
Creative Director: Michael Newman
Copywriter: Jane Caro
Art Director: Jonathan Teo
Producer: Meredyth Judd
Production Company: Black
Key Account Handler: Derick Frere
Music: Bach's Air on a G-string

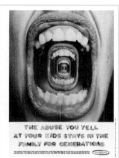

Flowers
Client: Commission Against Assaults
on Women
Agency: Saatchi & Saatchi, Team One,
USA
Year: 1996
Art Director: John Boone
Copywriter: Ron Huey
Key Account Handler: Kelley Hill
Client Contact: Patricia Occhiuzzo
Guggains

Scream
Client: NZ Children & Young Persons
Service
Agency: Saatchi & Saatchi, Wellington,
New Zealand
Year: 1996
Copywriter: John Plimmer
Art Director: John Fisher
Typographer: Len Cheeseman
Key Account Handlers: Wendy Schrijvers
& Helen Tweedie
Client Contact: Susie Hall

Vicious Circle
Client: NZ Children & Young Persons
Service
Agency: Saatchi & Saatchi, Wellington,
New Zealand
Year: 1995
Copywriter: John Plimmer
Art Director: John Fisher
Director: Gregor Nicholas
Producer: Martin Gray
Key Account Handlers: David Hendry,
Wendy Schrijvers
Client Contact: Susie Hall

Fading Fast
Client: Motor Neurone Disease
Association
Agency: Saatchi & Saatchi, UK
Year: 1989
Copywriter: Piers Carter
Art Director: Matt Ryan
Photographer: James Cotier
Key Account Handler: Georgina Matthews

Walkies
Client: The Health Education Council
Agency: Saatchi & Saatchi, UK
Year: 1979

Naledi/Crying Girl
Client: Department of Transport
Agency: Saatchi & Saatchi, South Africa

Scrambled Page
Client: Multiple Sclerosis Society
Agency: Saatchi & Saatchi, UK
Year: 1999
Copywriter: Mike McKenna
Art Director: Greg Martin
Typographer: Tim Quest
Images: The Independent
Key Account Handlers: Harry Corsham,
Carmen Hamdi
Client Contact: Ken Walker

Pin
Client: Multiple Sclerosis Society
Agency: Saatchi & Saatchi, UK
Year: 1997
Copywriters: Bruce Watt, Ian Pearson
Art Director: Greg Milbourne
Typographer: Tim Quest
Key Account Handlers: Edward Drax,
Saul Betmead
Client Contact: Ken Walker

Me No Fry
Client: NSW Health
Agency: Saatchi & Saatchi, Australia
Year: 1991
Copywriter: Paul Fishlock
Art Director: John Isles
Key Account Handler:
Ann Maree Hannan

Eclipse
Client: Action for Blind People
Agency: Saatchi & Saatchi, UK
Year: 1999
Art Directors: Chris Bleackley,
Bill Gallacher
Typographer: Roger Kennedy
Key Account Handler: Jamie Clift

Come and see us
Client: Italian Cancer Society
Agency: Saatchi & Saatchi, Rome, Italy
Year: 1999
Copywriter: Francesco Taddeucci
Art Director: Luca Albanese
Photographer: Valerio De Berardinis

Flies on Food
Client: The Health Education Council
Agency: Saatchi & Saatchi, UK
Year: 1970
Copywriters: Charles Saatchi,
Michael Coughlan
Art Director: John Hegarty

Scrub your Lungs
Client: The Health Education Council
Agency: Saatchi & Saatchi, UK
Year: 1971
Copywriter: Charles Saatchi

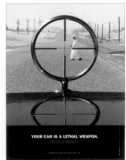

Lethal Weapon
Client: Government of Dubai
Agency: Saatchi & Saatchi, Dubai
Year: 1997
Copywriters: Bob Pedder, Phil Rhodes
Art Director: Mike Sands
Photographer: David Knight
Key Account Handler: Keith Scarratt

Three More Days
Client: Italian Anti-Landmine Association
Agency: Saatchi & Saatchi, Rome, Italy
Year: 1996
Copywriter: Stefano Maria Palombi
Art Director: Grazia Cecconi
Photographer: Marco Biondi
Client Contact: Barbara Laveggio

Landmines in Cambodia
Client: United Nations
Agency: Saatchi & Saatchi, Singapore
Year: 1996
Copywriter: Nicholas Koligiams
Art Director: Lary Ong Yong Hui
Key Account Handler: Bill Timmermann
Client Contact: Joerg Wimmers

Unleaded
Client: Government of Dubai
Agency: Saatchi & Saatchi, Dubai
Year: 1997
Copywriters: Bob Pedder, Phil Rhodes
Art Director: Mike Sands
Photographer: David Knight
Key Account Handler: Keith Scarratt

Pavement
Client: Anti-Dogfouling
Agency: Saatchi & Saatchi, Czech
Republic
Year: 1996
Copywriters: Eda Kauba, Don Nicolson
Art Directors: Don Nicolson, Eda Kauba
Client Contact: Matthew Callachor

Atomic Bomb
Client: State of the World Forum
Agency: Saatchi & Saatchi, Wellington,
New Zealand
Year: 1998
Copywriter: John Plimmer
Art Director: John Fisher
Typographer: Len Cheeseman
Key Account Handlers: Wendy Schrijvers,
Helen Tweedie
Client Contact: Susie Hal

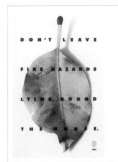

Leaf/Match
Client: NRMA
Agency: Saatchi & Saatchi, Australia
Year: 1997
Copywriter: Mike Newman
Art Director: Jonathan Teo
Key Account Handler: Darren Oliver
Client Contact: Gilly Paxton

Off Duty
Client: CCTV
Agency: Saatchi & Saatchi, China
Year: 1998
Copywriter: Wei Wei Chen
Art Director: Wei Wei Chen
Producer: Tony Leung
Director: Wei Wei Xu

Chain Letter
Client: New Zealand AIDS Foundation
Agency: Saatchi & Saatchi, Wellington,
New Zealand
Year: 1996
Copywriter: Maggie Mouat
Art Director: Chris Bleackley
Typographer: Eric de Vries
Key Account Handlers: Maggie Mouat,
Chris Bleackely
Client Contact: Christopher Barron

Slow Poison
Client: Tata Tea Limited/Anti-Smoking
Agency: Saatchi & Saatchi, India
Year: 1999
Copywriter: Anirban Sen
Art Director: Shrikant Lele
Key Account Handlers: Geetha Krishnan,
Premdeep Gangadharan
Client Contact: Aloke Bangerjee

Clean Up
Client: Islington Council
Agency: Saatchi & Saatchi, UK
Year: 1996
Copywriter: John Pallant
Art Director: Matt Ryan
Key Account Handler: Nick McKelvie
Music: Morning Mood from Grieg's Peer
Gynt Suite

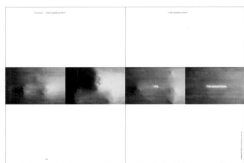

Anybody Out There?
Client: The Samaritans
Agency: Saatchi & Saatchi, UK
Year: 1985
Copywriters: Simon Dicketts,
Mark Williams
Art Director: Fergus Fleming
Director: Barney Edwards

Die and Live
Client: Mary Potter Hospice
Agency: Saatchi & Saatchi, Wellington,
New Zealand
Year: 1996
Copywriter: John Plimmer
Art Directors: Len Cheeseman,
John Fisher
Typographers: Len Cheeseman,
Eric de Vries
Key Account Handler: Helen Tweedie
Client Contact: Rosheen Whelen

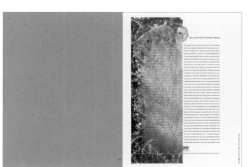

Start Again
Client: Stroke Association
Agency: Saatchi & Saatchi, Wellington,
New Zealand
Year: 1997
Copywriter: John Plimmer
Art Director: John Fisher
Typographer: Len Cheeseman
Key Account Handler: David Hendry
Client Contact: Brian O'Grady

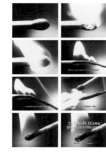

Blind
Client: Tata Tea Limited/Elind Campaign
Agency: Saatchi & Saatchi, India
Year: 1999
Copywriter: Satyadev Barman
Art Director: Viral Pandya
Key Account Handler: Abhijit Das
Client Contact: Upendra Raina,
Ruchi Anrendran

Matches
Client: Antena 3 Television/Organ
Donation
Agency: Saatchi & Saatchi, Spain
Year: 1992
Copywriter: Miguel Roig,
Manuel Salgado, Luis von Kobbe
Art Directors: Miguel Roig,
Manuel Salgado, Luis von Kobbe

Prisoner
Client: Rand AID (Home of the Aged)
Agency: Saatchi & Saatchi, South Africa
Year: 1998
Copywriter: Wyn Crane
Art Director: Simon Minchin, Tony Gillan
Typographer: Simon Minchin
Director: Sergio
Key Account Handlers: Wyn Crane,
Sue Hendrickz
Client Contact: Joan Migdin

Punch These
Client: The Samaritans
Agency: Saatchi & Saatchi, Wellington,
New Zealand
Year: 1995
Copywriter: Glen Wood
Art Director: Peter Force
Typographer: Craig Morganty
Key Account Handler: Neil Cameron
Client Contact: The Samaritans,
Christchurch

Bus
Client: The Samaritans
Agency: Saatchi & Saatchi, Wellington,
New Zealand
Year: 1996
Copywriter: Maggie Mouat
Art Director: Chris Bleackley
Key Account Handler: David Hendry
Client Contact: Samaritans Wellington

Texts and scripts

Read This You Piece of Shit, p. 7
Headline: Read This You Piece Of Shit.
Copy: If you're offended by this advertisement, you should be.
Nobody should be treated like this.

Yet unfortunately, there are millions of people around the word who are. For many, a verbal lashing is the very least they have to worry about. In Brazil for example, Amazonian estate workers face a punishment called 'the trunk'. A man who hasn't felled his quota of trees, is stripped, tied up and left in a hollowed out tree trunk for three days. As if that isn't punishment enough, the trunk is smeared with honey to attract ants and other insects.

In India, children face similar horrors. Kids as young as six are sold to work in carpet factories. When the loom-masters can't find enough children to buy, they kidnap them. The kids are made to work all day. If they slow down at all, they are not allowed to sleep at night. If they make one mistake, they are beaten. One child was doused with paraffin and set ablaze because he asked for time off. Six others were so viciously beaten for just playing, one of them died.

In Nepal, slavery is just as widespread. Ten year old girls are abducted and sold into prostitution in India.

First they have to go through a 'grooming' period. Stripped naked, they are locked in a tiny room for days at a time without food. They are burnt with cigarettes, beaten and raped until eventually they become totally submissive. Only then will they fetch the highest prices from Bombay's brothel keepers.

Just as prostitution can be a form of slavery, so can marriage.

In many parts of the world parents still control who their daughters wed. Who they choose very much depends on what the groom's family offers in exchange. The bride's welfare matters little.

Consequently, there are many women forced to marry against their will. Some even as young as nine. One twelve-year-old Nigerian girl hated her husband so much she kept trying to run away from him.

To stop her he hacked off both her legs. As you can see, slavery isn't a thing of the past.

Nor is it just a problem for the Third World.

In Britain alone, there have been 1700 cases of abused domestic servants reported since 1987. Most of them are young girls from poor backgrounds overseas. They see working in Britain as an answer to their problems. But when they get here, they are often treated no better than animals. Many are made to sleep on the floor and just fed scraps. They have to work an 18 hour day. If they complain, they're beaten or caned. Some aren't even a lowed out. Some are raped.

The list of atrocities goes on and on.

There are still over 100 million slaves in the world. Each one probably has a story as pain-filled as these.

Anti-Slavery International campaigns for the abolition of slavery. We know that it's only by making the facts of these people's lives known and by bringing slavery out into the open that we'll ever destroy it.

Indeed, by lobbying and by raising world awareness of these issues, we've persuaded governments and the UN to tackle the problem.

In some countries like Thailand, India and Pakistan we've even pushed them into changing the law. None of this would have been possible without the help of our supporters. They have sent letters and asked questions of individuals, companies and governments all around the world.

To keep the pressure on them, we need your help in our forthcoming campaigns.

If you'd like to be involved, fill out the coupon below and become a member. In time, we'll make sure no one knows what it feels like to be treated as a slave.
Anti-Slavery International, Stableyard, Broomgrove Road, London SW9 9TL.
Tel: 0171 924 9555 Fax: 0171 738 4110.

Pram/Family Planning, p. 18
Mother: You don't wanna be bothered with all that family plannin' stuff love – Scott! Leave off, will ya? – I mean, what can all them doctors and clinics tell ya that anyone with a bit of common couldn't work out for themselves? Or ask a friend. That's what I did – Anna! Leave that baby alone! 'ow many times I gotta tell ya? If you don't wanna get pregnant, you should... y'know what I mean... be careful an' that. Just use your 'ead.
Man's Voiceover: Don't listen to old wives' tales about family planning.
Your doctor or clinic will welcome you, married or single, with friendly and accurate advice.
Look in the phone book under Family Planning.
Mother: Anyway... with this lot, 'ow could I afford contraceptives?
Man's Voiceover: It'll cost you nothing.

Clip this Coupon, p. 22
Copy: Cut Out This Coupon. It Will Be Like Putting Your Picture Here.

Women and Children First, p. 24
Headline: And The Nuclear Powers Said: Women And Children First.
Copy: No, this is not a graphic elaboration. It's a child from Kazakhstan, born with hydrocephalus. This deformity is a result of the radiation the child's mother was exposed to. Now, don't get angry with us for showing it to you, get angry with those who hid it from you, maintaining that nuclear tests are not risky.

Can't Look, p. 26
Sound: Baby crying.
Scene 1
Woman: Shut up. I'm going to smack your face against that door if you don't stop that screaming now.

Scene 2
Man: Come and sit over here.

Scene 3
Man: You're brainless. You're stupid.
You're no child of mine.

Scene 4
Child: Mummy, where are you?
I don't like being on my own.

Scene 5
Man: Not a word to anyone. This is going to be our little secret.

Woman's Voiceover & Title: Sometimes we can't bear to look either.
Cruelty to children can be stopped and with your help it can be stopped forever.
Woman's Voiceover: Please support the NSPCC's Full Stop campaign.
Title: NSPCC. Cruelty to children must stop. Full Stop.

Pregnant Man, p. 28
Headline: Would You Be More Careful If It Was You That Got Pregnant?
Copy: Anyone married or single can get advice on contraception from the Family Planning Association, Margaret Pyke House, 27–35 Mortimer Street, London W1N 8BQ. Tel 01 636 9135.

Some Fathers, p. 29
Headline: Some Fathers Change Their Babies.
Copy: You can see the damage that's been done to the child's head. Or can you?

The fact is that while the physical wounds will heal in time, the mental scars will last a lifetime.

Changing a happy, well-balanced child into a nervous wreck.

Thousands of children are abused in this way each year. By their fathers and their mothers alike.

But if you suspect that a child is being abused by anyone, you're the one who's responsible.

Because after all, if you're not reporting child abuse you might as well be doing it.

If you have any information about the abuse of children, please call us on Wednesday, September 4th.
1 800 011 233. Report it and stop it. NSW Police Service.

Same Father, p. 30
Headline: We Both Have The Same Father
Copy: This is Sally's story.

'My mum died when I was twelve. One night when I had a bad dream my dad said I could sleep in his bed.

To start with he just cuddled me, but then he started doing other things. I wanted him to stop but he wouldn't. I hated it, it really hurt. He said it meant he loved me.

The next day when I was leaving for school he said I mustn't tell anyone about what happened. After that he wanted me to sleep with him every night. He called it our little secret.

Later, when my periods stopped my dad kept me off school. He told them I was ill.

Sometimes I can feel the baby moving inside me, it feels horrible.'

Luckily Sally's school reported her absence and now she's getting all the support she needs.

Of course, there's more to her abuse than becoming pregnant.

She'll need long term counselling to tackle the emotional damage, such as feelings of guilt and an inability to form relationships.

In fact, all forms of abuse can cause emotional harm. Not just the more obvious forms involving sexual assault and physical brutality.

For example, withdrawal of any signs of affection, ignoring children, constantly criticising or shouting at them can lead to emotional scars which last a lifetime. Sometimes, children can even be driven to commit suicide.

Because of all this, the NSPCC is launching 'A Cry for Children'. It's a cry to everyone to stop and think about their behaviour towards children.

To recognise the impact that any form of cruelty can have on a child. And to realise that the way children are treated affects their whole lives.

Please answer the cry.

If you, or someone you know is suffering abuse, call the NSPCC Child Protection Helpline on 0800 800 500.

Or, if after reading this, you would find more information helpful, please call us on 071 825 2775.

NSPCC. A Cry for Children.

Astronaut, p. 31
Headline: Does the World Have Its Priorities Right?
Copy: The State of the World Forum is bringing together many of the world's most influential people to debate vital issues facing humanity... nuclear disarmament... ending conflict... the role of women and child development. It's about getting our future priorities right. Join the debate via our website between 27 October and 1 November. It's your chance to change the world.

Face, p. 32
Title: This girl wants a chat.
Title: Lost your patience?
Title: Staff Nurse Robinson knows it will soon be a two way conversation
Nurse: Hi Rachel, you've got me again. Another girl's night in, eh?
Title: The new NHS needs more nurses.
Woman's Voiceover: Nurses make a difference. For information on nursing or returning to nursing, with improved pay and conditions, call 0845 60 60 655.

Cot, p. 36
Man's Voiceover: It's here where one in ten of all killings take place.
There are one to two deaths every week.
In a year there are over 5000 beatings, and over 1700 sexual assaults.
Title: In Britain, 36,000 children live with the threat of being abused every day.
Title: NSPCC. A Cry For Children.

The World Could End This Easily, p. 40
Copy: The world could end this easily.
Speak out against nuclear testing.
Greenpeace. 0800 22 33 44.

Stay In School, p. 42
Title: Stay In School.

Hungry, p. 44
Boy's Voiceover: If I said the word 'fuck' it would probably bother you.
If I told you I was hungry, it probably wouldn't.
Fuck, I'm hungry.
Title: Good food should never go to waste.

Day Against Violence, p.46
Titles: It seemed impossible.
It happened on the 12th February, 1995.
One billion seven hundred million people saw it all over the world.
For the first time ever.
The Italian football teams entered the field wearing the other teams shirts.
And they read a message that football must unite, not divide.
Today, that idea belongs to everyone.
Nothing is impossible.

Worst Marks, p. 50
Headline: Children From Ethnic Minorities Often Get The Worst Marks At School.

Teacher Passing an Examination, p. 51
Copy: He'd been struggling with multiplication. He simply couldn't see how it worked until his teacher came up with a different way of explaining it.
Headline: A Teacher Passing An Examination.
Copy: The moment when a pupil grasps a concept which has been proving difficult is probably one of the best things about teaching. It means that the teacher has found a way through that makes sense. It couldn't be more significant.

Getting the penny to drop is at the very heart of teaching. It's the connection between knowledge being imparted and understood. For the teacher and the pupil it's a shared achievement.

It's the very thing that may draw you towards a career in teaching. If it does, you'll be pleased to learn that the other rewards are worthwhile too.

From December, there's a starting salary of around £14,000 for primary and secondary school teachers with a good honours degree in inner London (including inner London allowance and supplement).

The Head teacher of a large inner London secondary school could expect to earn up to £48,000.

It isn't easy money, of course. After all, teaching isn't a mechanical process. It can't be.

Each class is made up of pupils with a wide range of abilities, interests, attitudes and backgrounds.

As a teacher you have to learn about these differences, remember them and respond to them.

For instance, the speed at which children learn varies between individuals and between topics, yet the teacher has to reach them all.

Blank faces may call for an entirely novel way of explaining something, and an inventive approach can work wonders for classroom morale generally.

In a sense, a teacher sits an examination every day. And has to pass.

A daunting prospect or an invigorating challenge?

If you think it's the latter, training can take your urge to teach and hone your natural skills to prepare you for the daily examination. And for a career that's doubly rewarding.

You can learn about becoming a teacher by ringing 0345 300121 quoting Dept. code IS/4/A or sending the coupon below.

Teaching brings out the best in people.

Resolution, p. 52
Title: In the Philippines, thousands of children spend New Year's Day in hospitals with fingers missing and hands blown off due to cheaply manufactured firecrackers. This campaign aims to put an end to the vicious cycle.
Teacher: Class, what is your New Year's Resolution?
Child: Ma'am, I won't play with firecrackers anymore.
Title: This New Year hands off Firecrackers.

Prostitute, p. 54
Headline: Would You Like To Work In Europe As A Prostitute?
Copy: There are millions of women who have no choice.

Like immigrant women who are deceived by international sex dealing organisations. They are victims of exploitation, and cannot make decisions regarding their own lives.

You will be surprised to learn about the methods used nowadays to diminish the human being.

Manos Unidas wants to end these ways of abuse. Help us abolish slavery.

Note: As you can see from the page insert on the left, you could find this execution amongst the classified ads (job opportunities section) in the main Spanish newspapers.

Mining Children, p. 55
Headline: Metallurgical Company Needs Mining Children.
Copy: There are millions of children that do not need to look for a job – they have it imposed.

Like the children who are employed as cheap manpower.

They are victims of exploitation and cannot make decisions regarding their own lives.

You will be surprised to learn about the methods used nowadays to diminish the human being.

Manos Unidas wants to end these ways of abuse. Help us to abolish slavery.

Note: The page on the left shows how these executions ran in the classified ads (job opportunities section) in the main Spanish newspapers.

Child Abuse, p. 56
Man 1: Beautiful girl, eh?
Man 2: Is she a virgin?
Man 1: Sure, she's my daughter.
Man 2: How much?
Man 1: Only $100.
Man 2: What can she do?
Man 1: Everything – but don't kill her.
... come along sweetheart.
Voiceover: If it happened to your daughter, you'd be frightened, wouldn't you?
When you are abroad, remember it.
A child is a child all over the world.
Title: Centro Italiano per L'adozione Internationale (The Italian Centre for International Adoption).
Per donazioni c/c n. 10837 presso la Cariplo, agenzia 15 di Milano.

Raped as a 3 Year Old, p. 58
Headline: What's It Like To Be Raped As A 3 Year Old?
A Victim Explains.
Copy: I first remember being sexually abused by my father when I was about 3. It may have happened before, I don't know.

I can see it now, me lying in bed, with that big face coming towards me. He'd kiss me goodnight, but he didn't stop at kissing.

He used to tell me it was our secret. And if I ever told anyone about it I'd be sent away.

But even as a child I knew something wasn't right. It was those words, 'I'll protect you.' How could he be protecting me? He was bloody hurting me.

It's strange really, he was my enemy, but at the same time my only friend in the world. He made me depend on him. He controlled me. My body was his toy for more than 9 years.

At school I found it hard to mix. I felt different. I'd never let anyone get close to me. In the changing rooms after PE I hated people seeing my naked body. I was so ashamed, I thought they might be able to tell what had been happening to me and call me a poofter.

Even when I managed to find a girlfriend I still wasn't sure if I was heterosexual. I was terribly rough with her. I suppose I wanted to be in control of someone, like my father was with me.

Sex terrified me. Having an orgasm just made me think of what my father did inside of me. And that big smiling face.

I met someone else eventually. We got married. After 2 years she left me. She said I was cold and didn't understand her.

But that's how I was. I just wasn't aware of causing or feeling mental or physical pain. Something inside me had been switched off long ago. There were times when I could actually cut myself with a knife and not feel a thing.

After the divorce, I turned to drink. It was a way of escaping. But I still suffered deep depressions.

Last year, my father finally died. I think that's what made me contact the NSPCC. I was 53 years old, and it was the first time I'd ever told anyone about my childhood.

Once a week for 6 months a Child Protection Officer worked with me. He got me to tell him everything about my experience. Talking about it was very painful. For over 40 years I guess I'd been trying not to think about it.

Eventually though, it started to work. He made me realise that what happened wasn't my fault.

For the first time I can ever remember I actually began to feel good about myself. It was just like being let out of a dark and lonely cell.

I'll never forget what happened to me. But at least I can start to live my life.

For further information on the work of the NSPCC, or to make a donation, please write to: NSPCC, 67 Saffron Hill, London EC1N 8RS or call 071 242 1626.

To report a suspect case of abuse call the NSPCC Child Protection Helpline on 0800 800 500.

Dr Jekyll, Mr Hyde, p. 59
Headline: Doctor Jekyll, Mister Hyde
Copy: You are a reliable, affectionate and attentive family man. You have a beautiful wife and a lovely nine-year-old daughter. Your family's love is the greatest of all blessings to you. You would defend it against anything and anybody. Then, comes the time when you have to go away on business. You're going to an exotic destination, Bangkok for example, one of those countries where anything is tolerated, where 'they have quite different traditions and customs'. And there, together with shirts and souvenirs in an open-air market, they offer you a little girl. She is a pretty 9-year-old girl who resembles your daughter a little, but actually looks more like a full-grown woman. You think that this is just the way to do things over there, and your quick-change starts: you are turning into a different person. The world paedophilia market, a rich and powerful market of death, is counting on another win. In fact, most of their profits do not come from criminals and perverts. They come from ordinary people, people like yourself. At CIAI (The Italian Centre for International Adoption) they have been fighting to assert a very simple concept for many years, which no one should ever forget, especially when travelling abroad: a child is a child, wherever you are in the world.
Donations can be charged to your credit card by calling on number +39–2–55–01–20–11 or by bank transfer to A/C No.10837 at Cariplo, Branch 15, Milan, Italy.

1 in every 8, p.60
Headline: One in every eight people who walk past this poster was abused as a child.
NSPCC. A cry for children.

Ban Guns, p. 64

Bullet, p. 66
Headline: Penis Without A Condom.
Copy: Get free ones by calling 250-8629.

Less Dead, p. 68
Copy: If A .22 Handgun Is Less Deadly, Why Isn't He Less Dead?
Demand a firearms act that kills the .22.

Grunge Angels, p. 70
Woman's Voiceover: Greetings! For your entertainment this afterlife we bring you Whitney Houston's greatest love songs.
Sound: Screams.
Title: Death Sucks.
Wear A Seatbelt.

Rubber Woman, p. 74
Headline: Rubber. The Latest In Bedroom Wear.

Rubber Man, p. 75
Headline: Boys Always Look Better In Rubber.

Tongue, p. 76
Headline: She Wants To Put Her Tongue In Your Mouth.
Copy: Make learning Cantonese or Mandarin easy. Call Hong Kong Language Learning Centre. 2385 5331.

Mother, p. 78
Title: Warning. The following scene may disturb some viewers.
Man's Voiceover: What you're about to see will shock you; it's the result of a seven-year-old girl in the back seat of a car travelling at 50 kilometres an hour without wearing a seat belt. Please look closely at the wounds.
No seat is safe without a seat belt.
Wear one always.
Title: The Road Toll Must Come Down.

Job Satisfaction, p. 81
Headline: How Do You Get Job Satisfaction From Sending Someone Home To Die?
Copy: By the time he got to hospital, Eric's chronic illness had nearly finished him. Breathing and swallowing were difficult and painful.
Anything more vigorous could be excruciating.
Despite this, Eric, who was 83, was determined to end his days at home. But he wasn't going anywhere until his nurse had made him strong enough.
Oxygen, medication and artificial feeding gradually made Eric feel more comfortable.
The nurse always managed to find time for Eric and his family: to advise, reassure, or simply to listen.
After three weeks his symptoms had stabilised enough for him to go home.
When Eric and his nurse finally said goodbye, they parted as friends.
Nursing older people is rarely easy, you need to be resilient, compassionate, with lots of initiative.
But just think of the rewards. Imagine the job satisfaction you get from fulfilling a dying man's last wish.
No other career comes close.
Call 0345646464 Quoting 2J. Anytime.
Nursing. Have you got what it takes?

A Country Story, p. 82
Episode 1
Title: On August 24, Danny will marry Tessa.
Mum: Breakfast!
Pete: Yum! Bacon!
Can Tessa cook?
Mum: Of course she can cook.
Dad: That's funny – her mother can't.
Mum: Bruce!
Man's Voiceover: If you were going to write this family a letter you'd address it to the Carters, care of Central Hawkes Bay.
Man's Voiceover: This farm's been in the Carter family for over 80 years. Danny is next in line. And soon after the wedding he and Tessa will share this house. And another generation will be trained to work this land. And so it will go on.
Danny: Dad, I'll, um, pick up those hinges before footy training tonight if you like.
Dad: Yeah, that'd be good.
Danny: We'll leave about 4pm Pete.
Pete: Fine.
Mum: And don't be there all night
Title: More later.

Episode 2
Title: In five weeks, Danny will marry Tessa.
Man's Voiceover: As they have done over the last few years, Danny and Pete call into the drinkery on their way home from footy training.
Blue: Hey – here comes Mr Four Weeks. Gidday Pete.
Pete: How are you this evening Blue?
Blue: Look who's back.
Danny: Hey Matthew. Where've you been?
Matthew: Oh went down Palmy man, look at that A & P show.
Pete: See anything good?
Matthew: Prize bull – fella from Waikato with a prize bull... charge $5 for a look.
Danny: Did you get to see it?
Matthew: I said what about a concession man, for a family? He said to me 'How many of you's?' And I told him... just me and the missus and our 13 kids. He said to me 'Man, you stay right there. I'll get that bull to have a gawk at you!'
Man's Voiceover: It's become a bit of a welcome habit this. Matthew has always returned from somewhere. And he's always got a story to tell. They reckon it's called The Owl because old Blue doesn't give a hoot if you stay there all night. But, probably there's another reason.
Title: More later.

Episode 3
Title: In four weeks, Danny will marry Tessa.
Pete: A penny for your thoughts Danny.
Danny: Well little brother, I was just thinking how damn lucky we are. Not a care in the world. No rat race. No grasping for money.
Pete: That's very deep.
Danny: Forget that, brother – where's this penny you owe me?
Pete: Here!
Man's Voiceover: They have always got on this well. Had to really. And now, in a few more weeks Pete will be best man at the wedding.
Danny: Give up?
Pete: Depends.
Danny: Depends on what?
Pete: Well, I'm best man, right?
Danny: Right.
Pete: I make a speech right?
Danny: Right.
Pete: How much do you want me to say about that bird you met at Massey a few years ago?
Danny: Want a hand? Nice shirt.
Pete: What was her name again? Irene!?
Danny: Forget the penny!
Pete: (sings) Irene good night Irene, Irene good night...
Title: More later.

Episode 4
Title: In three weeks, Danny will marry Tessa.
Coach: Okay boys, there's no way we're going to let those townies thrash us again. We have got to hit them hard by first whistle. You got to let them know who's boss.
Speaking of which, there's a few beers on tonight on account of Danny and Tessa and all that. Okay that's it.
Captain: ...Yeah hang on a sec blokes, I would just like to say we wish you a lot of success... and... anyway here's to Danny and Pete...
Clubmate: Danny and Tess.
Captain: Oh yeah... Danny and Tess... good luck.
Danny: Gidday!
Matthew: How long to go mate?
Danny: Couple of weeks.
Matthew: My old uncle got married again the other day...
Danny: How old is he?
Matthew: 91.
Danny: 91! Why'd he want to get married at that age?
Matthew: He didn't want to – he had to!
Title: More later.

Episode 5
Title: In two weeks, Danny will marry Tessa.
Danny: Hi mum!
Mum: You're late. Try these... Tessa made them.
Tessa: Pete?
Danny: Nice cakes, Tessa.
Tessa: Muffins.
Danny: Nice cakes, muffins.
Dad: We had a visitor this morning boys.
Pete: Anyone important?
Dad: Yes, a very important young man, from the Farm Labourers' Union.
He wanted to know about wages and conditions of everyone.
So I told him about the head shepherd, you know, couple of hundred a week and free house and that.
Then there is the roustie, hundred and sixty and free house and that.
Then he says: Any others? I said well then there's the half-wit – he does most of the work on the place and he gets about $40 a week. So he says: forty dollars a week! That's the one I want to talk to. And I said you are! And he left.
Title: More later.

Episode 6
Title: This week, Danny will marry Tessa.
Man's Voiceover: This week Danny and Tessa will become the new Mr and Mrs Carter... and once again the family farm will move on to younger, stronger hands.
Blue: Hey Danny...
Hang on Matt...
Hey Danny, listen to this...
Go on Matt...
Matthew: I am just telling these fellas here about that day that townie bloke, you know that lifestyle bloke was asking Skinny. He said to him 'Excuse me Skinny, when that horse of yours was crook with the cough and that, what'd you give him?' And Skinny says 'I gave him the phenyl'. Anyway a couple of days later the townie bloke's back, and he bottles up Skinny and he says 'Hey Skinny I gave that horse of mine phenyl and he died!' And Skinny says 'Yeah... mine too.'
Blue: Hey Danny, message; Tessa is at your folk's place an... some detail about the big event.
Danny: Oh yeah, okay, thanks, we'd better go. Come on Pete, want a lift?
Matthew: One more and then we're off.
Title: More soon.

Episode 7
Title: Danny will marry Tessa this week.
Blue: Hello, hold it boys... this could be the war office...
Hello. Owl... Gidday Bruce... no they were here all right.
Dad: Thank you Blue, thanks.
Dad: That's that... trouble with the Ute... I'll have to go out and get 'em.
Mum: Trouble with the Ute?... Why didn't they phone?
Dad: Oh Mother, Oh Mother.
Title: Country people die on country roads.
Title: More later.

Episode 8
Title: Danny is dead.
Man's Voiceover: Both Matthew and young Danny died in the crash that night. Country people do die on country roads. Pete will never be the same. He's in Christchurch. At the spinal clinic. He can't walk. And he never will.
Tessa: Have they come up with any offers on the farm yet mum?
Mum: I think so.
Dad: One or two people interested.
Mum: Tell Bruce.
Tessa: I'm going away. Not forever. Just for a while. But I'll keep in touch.
Dad: Whereabouts away?
Tessa: Stay up north with my Aunt in Piha.
Dad: Really.
Mum: She's going away Dad, she's having Danny's baby.
Dad: It never stops Mum, does it? It just never stops.
Super and Man's Voiceover: No more ever.
Country people die on country roads.

The Height of It, p. 93

Taxi Confessions, p. 94
Driver: You have to tell me what street, because otherwise, if you go to sleep, I don't know where to take you.
Man: Oi. Taxi!
Man: Yeah, you go to all these pubs and you never find them. Yeah you just...
Woman: And he holds up his arm and he's got this handcuff on it. Handcuff!
Man: I'm not going home.
Man: This is where you want to go.
Man: Woooo, we're here!
Man: You order a bacon burger and all they give you is bloody rind. You know? It's always the same.
Man: One second he was behind me and the next he was gone.
Man: Herne Bay thanks.
Driver: Herne Bay, whereabouts?
Couple: Is there the White Lady or something down here? It is.
Yeah, just down there.
You're looking really good tonight.
Man: He goes to these overseas pubs and he always get lost.
Man: No, no, no, because it's not there.
It's not where we're going.
It's where we came from.
Man's Voiceover and Title: If you drink and then get a taxi, you're a bloody genius.

Disaster, p. 96
Headline: Wherever We Go It's A Disaster.
Copy: Avoiding disaster is not something we care to think about. We need to be prepared for catastrophes that can suddenly happen anywhere at any time, be it a war in Rwanda or a plane going down in the Ruahines. For millions the Red Cross emblem has become a familiar and reassuring sight in the aftermath of a disaster. We prepare ourselves for an instant response, and through our first aid and rescue courses, we also prepare you. Although we may ask for your help now and then, one day you might need ours.

Fight, p. 98
Headline: We Teach Them How To Fight.
Copy: All's fair in love and war? No it isn't. Even in battle there are rules. In the course of humanitarian work in war zones all over the world the Red Cross encounters soldiers who have no idea what their obligations are to prisoners, to civilians or to the enemy.
If we can teach those soldiers about the conduct required of them by the Geneva Conventions, then we can save lives. You may be surprised by some of the work Red Cross does, but whatever it is and wherever it takes us we still need your help to do it.

350 Languages, p. 99
Headline: How To Say 'Don't Shoot Me' In 350 Languages.
Copy: The idea for the Red Cross emblem was born on a battlefield in Solferino in 1859. Today it still separates medics from soldiers, life from death. It is protected by Geneva Convention and to misuse it is a crime under law. It doesn't belong on a first aid kit. It can't be used by vets or medical centres. It is a symbol of protection, neutrality and humanity. The New Zealand Red Cross has a duty to protect it, because without it we can't protect you.

Don't Forget, p. 100
Headline: Don't Forget How To Have Sex After Drinking.
Copy: Things slip your mind after drinking. Protect yourself from AIDS. Use a condom. Just remember where you put it.

Prevent Sickness, p. 101
Headline: Take As Required To Prevent Sickness After Drinking.
Copy: Drinking can lead to unsafe sex. Protect yourself with a condom. Because AIDS will make you sick. Permanently.

Night Cap, p. 103
Headline: No Matter How Much You Drink Remember To Have A Nightcap.
Copy: The more you drink, the more you forget. Reduce the risk of getting AIDS. Remember. Wear a condom to bed.

Right Package, p. 102
Headline: If You Want Your Employees To Stay Longer, Give Them The Right Package.
Copy: What your employees get up to in bed is none of your business. But it could have a disturbing impact on your company's business.
Suppose a member of your staff contracts the HIV virus.
Eventually, if they develop the AIDS illness, you' l have to replace them.
In the meantime, you and your other employees might worry about whether it's safe to have HIV-infected people working in your midst. Fortunately it is safe.
You'll also want to know the legal implications. And whether the worker will be covered by insurance, or if your company is responsible.
It's important to find out the answers to these questions now. Because if your business isn't already affected by AIDS, it soon could be.
By the year 2000, the epidemic will be a bigger problem in Asia than it is in the currently worst-affected area, Africa. And by then, over 40% of new infections will be occurring here – unless you take action now to help prevent the spread of this disease.
Start by getting in touch with your local AIDS action group and government health authority. They should be able to answer your questions.
They'll also advise you on taking the necessary steps to help prevent AIDS from spreading in your company. Such measures as having a health expert talk to your employees. Putting up posters about AIDS prevention on your notice boards. And even installing condom dispensing machines in your washrooms. You can locate your nearest AIDS action group by inquiring at your local United Nations Development Programme office or at the UNDP in New Delhi (see address below).
Take action now. You'll boost staff morale showing that you care.
And you'll avoid losing valuable employees to AIDS.

Preservativo, p. 105
Woman's Voiceover: Condom, condom, condom, condom, condom, condom, condom.
Title: We'll never get tired of repeating it. The condom is the most reliable weapon against AIDS.
Convince your partner to use it
ANLAIDS.
The presenter is a famous Italian TV personality Alba Parrietti.
The commercial caused a scandal, the Catholic Church being opposed to the use of condoms, and the word 'condom' being forbidden on state-owned Italian TV channels.

Strangers in the Night, p. 106
The music on this commerical is Strangers in the Night. During the commercial the track changes from the smooth upbeat of the original, to a more fragmented, sadder version, reflecting the transformation of the musical notes into crucifixes.
Title: Stop Aids With Love.

Love Story p. 108
Music: Theme from Love Story
Man's Voiceover: Lots of people like these two will make love on the beach this summer.
Red Cross.
Make love!
Title: Red Cross Volunteers.

Lenny, p. 113
Lenny: ...You know, I just felt, I ke, real good man
Y'know, I wasn't like racing, I wasn't speeding, y'know, I was like mellow.
And I like threw up the first time and everything and after when I threw up, man, I said Wow! This shit is fucking like – good.
Right...
Y'know, okay ...oh y'know ...oh you know when you used to go on a ride and, y'know, your adrenaline ...pumps. Know what I'm saying?
That's the feeling.
Like that.
I had cellulitis in my thigh.
I got a scar so big. It's unbelievable man.
I almost got er... I had er gangrene on my foot, and that they almost took my foot off.
I consider myself pretty intelligent.
I can do whatever I want to do, man.
Whatever I want to do, I can do.
I threw up man, my guts.
And as I threw up, I'm like, Damn boy, this is fucking what I want, y'know?
I just want to be nice man – that's all I wanna do – that's it. Why can't people just do that? Maybe everybody should shoot up and mellow out.
I got these tracks man, all over my body.
The pus was just coming out of the little hole here, like nothing.
I used to do a lot more things, y'know, like,
I used to go to movies more and go out to lots of restaurants, I used to go to Broadway shows, I like Broadway shows they're nice, man.
By the time 97 rolls around, 96 at this time right, 1996 August 17th, 18th – whatever it is – you will come here with your cameras and I'll be a totally different person.
I'll be successful.
And I'll bet my life on it.
Title: Heroin. Want some?
Partnership for a Drug-Free America.

Surfing Monkey, p. 117
Woman's Voiceover: Once again folks item J343 is the Surfing Monkey coin bank.
It's great for graduation, wedding gifts and I believe we sold out on this one last time so please don't let this one pass you by.
Now let's go to caller Scott in Nashville.
Now Scott, I understand that you have just bought fifteen of our surfing monkey banks. Is that true?
Scott:... yeah!
(background noise & laughter)
Scott: Shh, man!... I'm on TV...
Title: Marijuana. A very expensive habit.
Partnership for a Drug-Free America.

Celebrities, p. 118
Headline: In Advertising, They Say One Of The Surest Ways To Get Your Message Across Is To Put Celebrities In Your Ad.
Partnership for a Drug-Free America.

Nose, p. 119
Woman's Voiceover: One gram of cocaine costs as much as a boom box.
Three grams of cocaine costs as much as a TV.
Seven grams, a trip to Paris.
One gram a week for a year, a new car.
If you're on coke, everything you work for is disappearing right under your nose.
Title: Partnership for a Drug-Free America.

Elephant, p. 121
Sound: (thoughout) Elephant footsteps.
Man's Voiceover: One of these women showed her respect for nature by donating part of her pay cheque to the Environmental Federation of California.
The other did not.
Now, you may not know which one gave to the environment but an elephant never forgets.
Support nature at the office by donating to the payroll deduction plan for the environment.
Title: Environmental Federation of California.
For information call 1–800–368–1819.

The Only Fur, p. 124
Headline: The Only Fur I'm Not Ashamed To Wear.
Copy: International Fund for Animal Welfare.
The model is the Marquise Marina Ripa di Meana. When this poster appeared, she was the Italian Ambassador for the International Fund for Animal Welfare.

Hatchet, p. 125

Whales, p.126
Voiceover: What whales want is just what we want. To be free to live in peace, to reproduce without problems. But today more than ever, their existence is in danger. Greenpeace has always fought to save them from extinction. Help Greenpeace. 06/57.82.484

Water Cooler, p. 128
Headline: Save 100 Hurricane Mitch Victims From Dehydration For Just $12.
Copy: Help UNICEF help children in emergency situations. Call 1800 025 192.

Year of the.., p. 129
Headline: Year Of The.
Copy: The tiger is being erased. Total extinction is now a very real danger. WWF, the World Wide Fund For Nature, is working vigorously to help protect tigers everywhere from deforestation and the illegal body part trade. In this, the Year of the Tiger, please do what you can to help us keep the tiger cause alive and back in the headlines.
For further details, please call 703 3772.

Last Water in Rwanda, p. 130
Headline: The Only Water Left In Rwanda.
Copy: Millions of Rwandan refugees badly need potable water, as they need food, medicine and air to breathe.

Going, Going, Gone, p. 131
Sound: African music and drums with elephant noises.
Title: Going.
Sound: The drums turn to gun shots.
Title: Going.
Title: Gone.
Title: Extinction is forever. Don't let it happen.

Zaire, p. 132
Sound (throughout): Blood drips.
Voiceover: Zaire. Zaire is bleeding.
We are Doctors without Borders: Support us.

War on Hunger, p. 134
Sound: Battle sounds.
Title: War on Hunger.
Telefood '98.

Speed Kills, p. 138
Copy: Speed Kills.

Glasses, p. 140
Sound: Glasses being placed one by one on table top.
Title: Each drink you have before driving impairs your judgement.
Sound: Skidding.
Title: Don't Drink & Drive.

Ash, p. 142
Headline: The Ash From Just One Cigarette.
Copy: Don't treat the roadside like an ashtray.

Stripes, p. 144
Headline: Only An Ox Does Not Give Way To A Zebra.
Copy: Thoughtless driving kills.
(Being called 'an ox' in Czech is equivalent to being called an asshole.)

Just Sit There, p. 145
Headline: Sit There All Day Every Day.
That's What Jail's Like.
Mothers Against Drunk Driving.

The Censor, p. 146
Title: The Censor
Man: Stop!
Show me that piece again.
Go on... hurry up.
No, no, no, leave that out.
You must not do that.
No, no, no. That is not allowed.
Stop that.
Omit that.
Omit it.
That's not allowed, you know that.
Omit that.
That... that... and that!
Well, go on... go on, dance.
Stop! Why aren't you dancing?
You call that a dance?
Stop that! I will not have any innuendo.
Man's Voiceover: This short play by the Czech writer Ivan Kraus, censored in his own country, was published in Index On Censorship, a magazine which exposes the suppression of artists around the world and offers them a platform.
Index is for the censored artist, and for you.
Title: Index on Censorship.

Free Press, p. 148
Headline: Free Press.
Article 19.

Spaniel, p. 149
Copy: I will not lift my leg to your Mercedes Benz.
I will not bite the pizza delivery man.
I will not hide my bone under your pillow.
I will not dig under the pillow in the middle of the night to look for bones.
I will not lick your face immediately after licking my private parts.
Adopt a pedigree pet from the SPCA.
Call 287 5355.

Dog and Gun, p. 150
Sound: A little girl singing throughout:
How much is that doggie in the window, the one with the waggly tail. How much is that doggie in the window, I do hope that doggie's for sale...
Title: 92p a day.
£6.44 a week.
£27.50 a month.
£330 a year.
£3,630 a lifetime.
Man's Voiceover: Before you give someone a dog this Christmas, please count the costs.
Title: RSPCA.

Light Bulb, p. 151
Man's Voiceover: This can happen when you ride a bike and don't wear a helmet.
But if you wear a helmet it won't happen.
Wear a helmet. Keep your head.
Title: Barcelona Council.
Barcelona – more than ever.

Don't Piss..., p. 152
Headline: Don't Piss Your Life Away.
Mothers Against Drunk Driving.

Vote No, p. 153
Headline: The No Sky.
Copy: Look at it. This is the sky of those who kill thousands of animals each year, for sport. The sky of those who are trying to block the Referendum on hunting. But it is also the sky of all the lazy or indifferent people who do not vote on June 3. So take a good look at it. If a No vote wins today, this lifeless sky will be your sky tomorrow.

Vote Yes, p. 153
Headline: The Yes sky.

Copy: Vote Yes, on June 3, to ban hunting. You will read the results in the sky.
Look at it. This is the sky of those who work each day to defend nature. The sky of those who understand that a ban on hunting in Italy means the opening of a wonderful new season. Give wings to the values you believe in: vote Yes on June 3. You will read the results in the sky.

Poached Elephant, p. 154
Sound: Classical music.
Title: Poached fish.
Title: Poached egg.
Title: Poached elephant.
Sound: Music stops.
Sound: Gun shot.
Title: Ivory.
Title: Don't let the slaughter start again.
Title: Don't buy it. Don't sell it. Don't wear it. Don't use it.

Abbandono, p. 156
Man's Voiceover: What if it were them who abandoned us?
If it were them to condemn us to a summer fit only for a dog?
Title: Whoever abandons animals is an animal!

Power of One, p. 155
Title: Not so long ago a woman from Alabama wanted to sit at the front of the bus.
Title: And a gentleman from India wanted to raise consciousness without raising his voice.
Title: In East Germany, a man wanted to break free.
Title: And a woman travelled the world, giving hope to those who had none.
Title: This is the power of one.
Title: To protect your home in the Amazon.
Title: To prevent poaching of the African mountain gorilla.
Title: To rescue harp seals in Finland.
Title: Or to care for the environment in our own backyard.
Title: The power of one is to do something.
Title: Anything.
Title: Earth Communications Office

Brains, p. 163
Copy:
African
European
Asian
Racist
European Youth Campaign Against Racism – supported by Commission for Racial Equality.

Scars, p. 164
Headline:
In Asia
In Africa
In America
In Europe
Copy: Where there are wars, epidemics and natural disasters, we're there too. Every day, for 25 years, stitching-up the world's wounds.
Medici Senza Frontiere, via Ostiense 6/E tel. 06 573 00900 fax 06/573 00902 Roma c.c.p 874 86007.

Them, p. 166
Man 1: Sorry!
Man 2: That's alright mate.
I reckon we should just send them all back, don't you?
Woman's Voiceover: Just this once we're going to grant him his wish.
Man 2: Pakis, Jews, Italians...
Woman's Voiceover: And see what happens to Britain. Thousands of 'them' leave our hospitals.
Thousands of 'them' leave the transport system.
Hundreds of 'them' leave journalism.
Thousands of 'them' leave construction.
Thousands of 'them' stop teaching.
Thousands of 'them' close down their shops.
Hundreds of 'them' close factories putting thousands on the dole.
Hundreds of 'them' stop competing for Britain.
Thousands of 'them' leave the finance industry.
And the sacrifices made by millions of 'them' will be forgotten.
Man 2: Send them back home – that would be good, that, wouldn't it?
Man 2: Fancy a curry?
Title: Them? They're us.

Openings, p. 168
Headline: Who Says Ethnic Minorities Can't Get Jobs?
There Are Openings Everywhere.
Copy: Lavatory attendant. Office cleaner. Somebody has to do all the low-paid, menial jobs, but why is it so often people from ethnic minorities? Prejudice, racial discrimination and harassment are denying people the choice of job they deserve. It's unjust and unfair. More than that, it's a terrible waste of British talent.
Getting into a skilled profession is hard enough for young people these days.
But it's even harder for ethnic minorities.
For a start, qualifications count, but most ethnic minorities are still more likely to be unemployed than white people.
They have to apply for more jobs before they get one. In a recent investigation, one in three companies who were tested refused interviews to Black and Asian applicants.
But they did offer interviews to white applicants with the same qualifications.
If they do find a job, ethnic minorities often find promotion harder to achieve than their white colleagues.
There's a disproportionately low number of ethnic minorities at managerial level.
For example, in one large transportation company 30% of the whole workforce are from ethnic minorities, but they account for only 3% of the management.
On top of all this ethnic minorities face racial harassment in the workplace.
If they complain about it they are often told to accept harassment as part of the job.
Sadly, most people do accept it.
Those who don't may have to take their employer to an industrial tribunal where hard evidence must be provided to support their complaint.
Whether or not they win their case they may well have to start the trying process of searching for a job all over again.
No wonder ethnic minorities have found it so difficult to make progress in Britain.
However, bad as the situation seems, some aspects have changed for the better.
A West Indian who came here in the fifties to work for British Rail remembers.
'It was hell. For the first ten years nobody would sit next to me in the lunch break. They gave you the worst job, paid you less, gave you no training.
They insulted you. There were 'No nigger' notices everywhere. It was very different then. There was no law against it.'
Thankfully, the law has changed.
In 1976 the Race Relations Act was passed, making it unlawful for employers to discriminate on the grounds of colour, race, ethnic or national origin.
Those who discriminate face hefty bills for compensation and legal costs, as well as having their guilt aired in public.
The Act certainly put an end to blatant discrimination like the 'No nigger' notices.
But it didn't put an end to the more subtle discrimination that still exists today.
Such as when an employer says 'Sorry there is someone more qualified for the job', when there isn't.
Or when a manager 'forgets' to mention a promotion to someone.
This is discrimination.
It's subtle, perhaps even unintentional, but it can be very demoralising.
Imagine being told over and over again that you are not qualified for a job when you know very well that you are.
What could you do about it?
If your case is strong enough you could talk to the Commission for Racial Equality.
We are the independent body funded by the Home Office whose job it is to eliminate every kind of racial discrimination.
To this end we give support to victims of discrimination in industrial tribunals. (It's not always ethnic minorities. We've dealt with cases of white workers being treated unfairly by Black or Asian bosses.)
We're also working with trade unions to help them fight racial discrimination and harassment, within their own organisations as much as in the workplace.
Many trade unions now have especially designated officers who can give practical support and advice to people who have been discriminated against.
You'll find similarly qualified officers at your local Racial Equality Council and Citizens Advice Bureau.
What's more, with our help companies are adopting equal opportunity policies. These prevent discrimination before it can happen, giving everyone a fair chance.
If you'd like to talk to someone about implementing such a policy in your company, please write to us at the address below.
This is how we'll defeat racism.
Not by violence, but by accepting each other as equals. By opening our minds.
For the sake of ourselves and of the generation who are growing up now, this would be the most promising opening possible.

Criminal Isn't It?, p. 170
Headline: Criminal Isn't it?
Copy: Car theft 9 months.
Car theft 1 1/2 years.

Junk Mail, p. 171
Headline: And You Get Annoyed About Junk Mail.

Ethnic Cleansing, p. 172
Headline: Discussions About Ethnic Cleansing, Doesn't That Seem Familiar To You?
Copy: Put an end to Serbian nationalist crimes against humanity.

Next Generation, p. 173
Headline: You May Not Care Whether Jewish Life Survives Into The Next Generation. But He Does.
Copy: Jewish life has survived for thousands of years. Fascism has survived for seventy. But in all that time it has been devastating. The warning signs are still here and every one of them carries the same message: don't become complacent. That's why the JIA has such a vital role to play. We need to be able to respond to the persecution of Jews anywhere in the world, at any time. We need to be alert to any threat. We respond to those threats by providing funds for the Jewish Agency, helping it to rescue Jews wherever they are, and to bring them to the safety of Israel.
When they arrive, we help them to build new lives with new opportunities. Israel holds the key to all our futures. Help us to teach the next generation the importance of Israel and the need for us to preserve Jewish life all over the world.
Show your commitment to the JIA by telephoning us on 0345 585 004 today and we'll talk about how you can help.
You might not think that you're needed. But we do.

Saddam, p. 174
Headline: If You Don't Want Kurdish Refugees In Your Country Send Them Back To Me.
Copy: Saddam Hussein, Slobodan Milosevic, Pol Pot, Adolf Hitler.
The names change. Their crimes against humanity don't. The 1951 UN Convention on Refugees was drawn up in direct response to the Holocaust. Within its pages the international community acknowledged a joint obligation to provide a safe haven for those fleeing torture, persecution and death. Britain was one of the first countries to sign up. Honouring a document that's nearly 50 years old might seem like an out-dated idea. Unfortunately poisonous gas, concentration camps and ethnic cleansing aren't.
www.refugeecouncil.org.uk or 0171 820 3055.

No Flag, p. 175
Headline: Not Even A Flag To Wrap Themselves In.
Copy: Red Cross Kurdish Appeal.
Phone (01) 766877 or (01) 765135 with your pledges.

Equals, p. 169
This is the product of 14 commercial directors each volunteering to be given a single word brief such as 'eating', 'work', 'religion', 'sleep' etc. They were asked to film in eight seconds, in black and white, their idea of what this word meant when applied to 'equality'.
Title: Commission for Racial Equality.
Title: 1997 European Year Against Racism supported by the Home Office.

Shattered Dreams, p. 180
Title: You can do something about domestic violence.
Call the Police.

Flowers, p. 182
Copy: David brings me flowers.
And tells me he loves me.
And I want to believe him.
My friends say I'm stupid.
But they don't know David.
David brings me flowers.
And tells me he's sorry.
When he loses his temper.
And accidentally hits me.
My friends say I'm stupid.
But they don't know David.
David hit me last night.
It all seems like a blur.
And my friends they were right.
But David brings me flowers.
If you're a teen in an abusive relationship.
There's someone you can talk to. Just call 213–626–3393. We're the Los Angeles Commission on Assaults Against Women and we can help.

Scream, p. 183
Headline: The Abuse You Yell At Your Kids Stays In The Family For Generations.
Copy: You're useless. You're dumb. I wish you'd never been born. Shout verbal abuse like this at your kids and you don't just hurt them, you teach them to be abusive parents too. Break the cycle. Call 0800 222 999 for a free parenting booklet that will help.

Vicious Circle, p. 184
Scene 1
Man: Do you think I go out with my mates just to make your life a misery?
Woman: Shut up.
Man: Do you?
Woman: Shut up.
Man: When was the last time you put your arms around me?
Woman: Leave me alone.
Man: Have I got a sign round my face that says I'm fucking invisible?
Woman: No.
No.
No.
Man: Have I?
Woman: Leave me alone.
Man: Am I invisible?
Woman: Shut up.
Woman: Just shut up, just leave me alone.
Man: Listen I'm going on the piss tonight.

Scene 2
Man: Do you think I go out with my mates just to make your life a misery?
Woman: Shut up.
Man: Do you?
Woman: Shut up.
Man: When was the last time you put your arms around me?
Woman: Leave me alone.
M: Have I got a sign round my face that says I'm fucking invisible?
Woman: No.
No.
No.
Man: Am I invisible?
Woman: Shut up.

Scene 3
Man: Do you think I go out with my mates just to make your life a misery?
Woman: Shut up.
Man: Do you?
Title: It's up to you to break the cycle.
For more information 0800 222 999.

Fading Fast, p. 190
Headline: My Picture Is Fading Fast.
So Am I.
Copy: Every day I am more helpless as my muscles waste away. There is no cure for my disease and no hope for me but I want there to be hope for others. Please send a donation to help people to live with MND and to pay for research.
Motor Neurone Disease Association.
PO Box 246, Northampton NN1 1TR.

Walkies, p. 194
Woman: Come along darling, walkies!
Come on!
Come along, Roger.
Man's Voiceover: It may come as a nasty shock, but people need exercising just as much as dogs.
If you just went for a few good walks, that would be a start.
The chances are you'll actually like it.
Woman: Here Roger, fetch!
Man's Voiceover: Once you really get going, your heart, your lungs and muscles all get stronger. You'll shake off depression, you'll feel a new man, or a new woman.
Woman: Away you go.
Man's Voiceover: You'll put more effort in to everything you do.
And get a lot more out of it.
Woman: Roger, come back at once!
Man's Voiceover: A few minutes' exercise every day could add so much more to your life. Look after yourself.
Title: Look after yourself!

Naledi/Crying Girl, p. 196
Headline: Scarred For Life By A Car That Missed Her By Miles.
Copy: Naledi was safe in bed while her daddy was walking home drunk from the shebeen. He never knew what hit him, but she'll suffer for the rest of her life.
Watch Your Step.

Scrambled Page, p. 197
Headline: MS Scrambles Messages Between The Brain And The Body.
Copy: It can disrupt every part of the body, every aspect of your life. At any time.
During MS Week, we are aiming to raise awareness (and hopefully some money) to help us to fight this unpredictable disease.
To find out more about Multiple Sclerosis, freefone the MS Helpline on 0808 800 8000.
The MS Society. Providing the Strength to Fight MS.

Pin, p. 198
Headline: What's MS Like?
Close Your Eyes And Stick A Pin In This Page Every Day For The Rest Of Your Life.
Copy: Today your whole body hurts
Today you can't feel your fingers.
Today you have muscle spasms.
Today you can't move your left leg.
Today you can't drive.
Today you can't climb the stairs.
Today you feel ok.
Today you're impotent.
Today your vision is blurred.
Today you have no balance.
Today you can't move your right leg.
Today you can't feel your fingers.
Today you can't concentrate.
Today your whole body hurts.
Today you feel great.
Today you feel like you have fish swimming around inside your body.
Today your hearing is muffled.
Today you can't move.
Today you can't stop shaking.
Today you can't talk.
Today you can't feel your toes.
Today you can't move your right arm.
Today you're incontinent.
Today you're deaf.
Today you can't feel your feet.
Today you feel fine.
Today you can't move.
Today you can't stop shaking.
Today you can't talk.
Today you can't feel your fingers.
Today you feel tired.
Today you can't climb the stairs.
MS is a disease that attacks the central nervous system. You never know from one day to the next which part of your body it will affect, and how severely. Anyone can get MS and we want you to find out more about it. For more information or to make a donation please call us 24 hours on 0800 100 133.
The MS Society. Providing the Strength to Fight MS.

Me No Fry, p. 200
Headline: Me No Fry.
Copy: NSW Health. For a state of better health.

Eclipse, p. 201
Headline: It's A Once In A Lifetime Opportunity. Miss It.

Come and see us, p. 202
Headline: Come And See Us.
Copy: The cure for breast cancer is prevention.

Flies on Food, p. 204
Copy: This is what happens when a fly lands on your food.
Flies can't eat solid food, so to soften it up they vomit on it. Then they stamp the vomit in until it's liquid, usually stamping in a few germs for good measure.
Then when it's good and runny they suck it all back again, probably dropping some excrement at the same time.
And then, when they've finished eating, it's your turn.
Cover food. Cover eating and drinking utensils. Cover dustbins.

Scrub your Lungs, p. 205
Headline: You Can't Scrub Your Lungs Clean.
Copy: Lung cancer kills thirteen times more smokers than non-smokers.

Lethal Weapon, p. 206
Headline: Your Car Is A Lethal Weapon.
Copy: Drive carefully.
Published in the interests of the environment in the UAE.

Three More Days, p. 207
Headline: Only Three Days Left Until 'Anti-Landmines Day'.
Copy: Statistics of despair: 110 million landmines set in 64 countries around the world; a victim every 20 minutes; from 5 to 10 million mines produced each year; 100 million more ready in the world's arsenal; 90% of casualties to women and children.
Numbers for hope: Postal account No. 189241, Mani Tese, Italian Campaign Against Landmines, via Cavengahi 4, 20149 Milan.
On Saturday, April 13, come to Piazza Santi Apostoli to sign our petition and make your contribution.

Landmines in Cambodia, p. 208
Headline: Can A $3 Landmine Cripple A Whole Economy?
Copy: It can when farmers are too afraid to plough their fields; when children are too scared to walk to school; when the simplest daily activities become a game of Russian roulette. Yet, in addition to the 110 million landmines still lying buried in the Third World, another 2 million are being planted each year. Help abolish landmines. It's the only way the Third World can make a step forward. To find out how you can help, please write to your local government or to the Mine Clearance and Policy Unit, Department of Humanitarian Affairs, United Nations, New York, NY 10017.

Unleaded, p. 209
Headline: Don't Pump Our Children Full Of Lead.
Copy: Use unleaded petrol.
Published in the interests of the environment in the UAE.

Pavement, p. 210
Headline: It's Even More Disgusting On The Pavement.
Copy: If your dog shits in the street, please clean it up.

Atomic Bomb, p. 211
Copy: International cooperation has done a remarkable job of threatening us all with annihilation. Now perhaps it can defuse the situation. If you ever wanted to change the world this is your chance. Join the debate via our website between 27 October and 1 November. www.worldforum.org

Leaf/Match, p. 212
Headline: Don't Leave Fire Hazards Lying Round The House.

Off Duty, p. 213
Husband: We have been married for 18 years.
Wife: It has generally been a peaceful life.
Husband: We're busy with our own things.
Wife: Day after day, it's work, home, kids. Nothing out of the ordinary. When he was laid off...
Husband: It happened so suddenly. My mind went blank.
Wife: He looked so scared. Tears were welling in his eyes.
Husband: The first thing to go was my self-esteem. I could only think of drowning my misery with alcohol.
Wife: He needs my support.
Husband: She's been so encouraging.
Wife: Don't worry. It will turn out well.
Husband: Being laid off has been the best thing to happen to us for a while.
Wife: We've never been closer.
Husband: On my birthday...
Wife: I bought him a pair of shoes.
Husband: New shoes.
Wife: For you to explore a whole new world of possibilities.
Husband: I was moved to tears. This new job is better. Well, at least better than sitting around the house. As long as our hearts are one, nothing else really matters.
Title: Your support is his strength.

Chain Letter, p. 216
Copy:
Dear Eric,
There is a virus spreading through our community, which is claiming a life every week. It is spread through contaminated blood or sexual contact. I'm sure you know what I'm talking about. HIV and ultimately AIDS.
The only way we can stop it spreading is to spread the word faster than the virus.
And the word is condoms. Practise safe sex and use them. It's that simple.
Now take this letter and copy it 6 times. Send them to people who you consider make the world a better place. Don't be embarrassed, we could all do with a reminder.
If you send the letter on to six people this week, and each of these people do the same, by the end of the month 7,776 people will be better informed. If you choose to do nothing, by the end of the year several million people will have missed our message.
We owe it to everyone to spread the word and beat the virus.
Signed: Someone who cares.
PS. If you could afford to send a donation to the Aids Foundation they would very much appreciate it.
Their address is:
NZ AIDS Foundation, PO Box 7287, Wellington, New Zealand.

Slow Poison, p. 217
Headline: Slow Poison.
Copy: Issued in the public interest by Tata Tea Limited.

Clean Up, p. 220
Music: Morning Mood from Grieg's Peer Gynt Suite.
Man: Morning!
Turned out nice again...
Sound: Squelching and sliding noises.
Title: You wouldn't.
Title: Don't let your dog.

Anybody Out There?, p. 222
Man's Voiceover: Is there anybody out there?
Is there anybody out there?
Is there anybody... out there?
Is there anybody out there?
Title: Yes.
The Samaritans.

Die and Live, p. 224
Headline: Ron Was All Set To Die. Then Came The Worst News Of All. 'You're Going To Live.'
Talk about gutted, well you would be wouldn't you. There you are, assured of having terminal cancer when, like a bolt from the blue, your doctor delivers the killer blow. 'The treatment has worked. The cancer has been eradicated. You're going to live.' Devastation hits. The outlook simply could not be worse.
Now you have to remember that Ron's story is fairly unique. Most people wouldn't react the way he did. But the thing about dying (or in Ron's case not dying) is that no two people react the same way.
When he was first diagnosed with cancer, Ron, quite naturally, was shocked. It was the worst thing he'd ever heard. But over time his outlook changed. He accepted his fate. He even started to plan for it, his whole life becoming geared up to dying. And that's where the problems started. So prepared for death was Ron that he reached a stage of contentment. Normally in our field this is the best possible outcome. In fact it is good when a terminally ill patient reaches this phase, because it is so unusual. At Mary Potter Hospice we feel as if we've done our job to the best of our ability if we can help a patient reach this point.
'You're going to live Ron.' Hold the wreaths. Cancel that hearse. Surely it's the best news he could ever get, right? Wrong. You see his life was so geared to dying that in a funny sort of way, it had become his reason for living. He'd started saying his goodbyes, everything was leading nicely towards a well plotted out conclusion, he was outta here.
And then in one cruel blow, that reason for living was taken away from him. Death's door was slammed in his face. Suddenly all the preparations and mental anguish he'd been through had been for nothing. Floundering around in his new lease on life Ron started to imagine illnesses. He had got a heart condition. He was convinced of it. He didn't of course, in truth it was a head condition and the mind being the most powerful organ of all did the rest for him. Ron became a man hell bent on finding an excuse for wallowing in imminent death. That was where he now felt the most comfortable. He'd come to rely on all the new found support services available to the dying. He'd adapted too well to all the attention and sympathy. That's not to say he enjoyed them, but he needed them. And it was in this state that he lived out his days.
Ron's tragic fate was largely self imposed. And although he was never a patient at Mary Potter Hospice, it is a true story from our head doctor (Ron was one of his patients when he worked in England) that highlights the sort of problems we regularly encounter.
And it has important ramifications for Mary Potter Hospice when it comes to how we handle patients. Because sometimes even when everything takes a turn for the best, the situations actually become much worse. That is how unpredictable our working day is. That's why we're constantly looking to learn from the Rons of this world so that situations like his don't repeat themselves.
It's been said that only two things in life are certain: death and taxes. While taxes are frighteningly predictable, death isn't. Ron's story is testament to that, and so is Nell's. But her story is right at the opposite end of the spectrum. Possibly the perfect death. Petronella, Nell to her friends, came from Kapiti way. She was an inpatient at Mary Potter Hospice but only very briefly. Nell was in her early 60s when she was referred to us in May 1994. She had growths on her liver, kidney, pancreas and stomach. This wasn't her first brush with cancer, back in 1989 she'd had to have a kidney removed. But when she was diagnosed this time, she was told she had just two months to live. Nell came into the Hospice in tremendous pain and vomiting constantly. We too were convinced that she was not long for this world, we wouldn't put a time limit on it though. If it's one thing we've learned it's that putting an expiry date on a person can be one of the worst things to do. For a start it is virtually impossible to be accurate. But more importantly, it can lead to situations like Ron's.
At first we thought Nell's cancer was raging out of control, but she didn't. She

was sure she'd just pulled a muscle and that was causing the pain. She was wrong. But she also felt the drugs she was on could be causing the problems, and this time she was right. In the two weeks that she was in the Hospice we were able to get her onto a course of pain control which didn't cause her to vomit. She went home pain free and ready to get on with life. She still had cancer, it was still incurable, but she had a lot of living to do.

More and more these days we're finding that our patients are happier to be treated away from the hospice building itself. They still come in, and our beds are still full, but they tend to come in periodically for treatment and pain control assessments, then they head back home, where they're most comfortable. We encourage this as much as possible. It's a risk that if patients check into the Hospice too soon, they may resign themselves to dying too soon. But at home, they tend to get on with life, as Nell did.

Two months went by, then three then six. Nell just kept lusting for life. She regularly consulted with her GP, and our Hospice doctor would visit her up the coast every couple of months. She used naturopathic remedies too. But it was her outlook that did the most good of all. If she'd believed her initial death sentence, if she'd decided to stay at Mary Potter, she could well have just stopped living. Thankfully she didn't. She wanted to stay at home with her husband.

She wanted to leave home with her husband too. Which they did often. They'd hook up the caravan and go for long trips all around New Zealand. Far from being like Ron, far from becoming consumed by death, Nell became even more consumed by life. At the end of 1995 complications set in. Nell had a bowel blockage. But even this didn't stop her. She had an operation which fixed it, and led to an excellent recovery. She was still a box of birds some sixteen months after she was meant to die. By May 1996 though, her disease finally began to catch up with her. She became tired and pain again reared its head. Nell herself realised that her time was ending. She could no longer swallow her pills so pain relief had to be administered through a needle under her skin. Only at this point, some two years after her first diagnosis, did Nell decide to return to the Hospice to die.

As we said before, we try not to say when people are going to die. What often happens though, is that the patients themselves tell us. Something deep inside them lets them know it is about to happen. That's how it was with Nell. On the morning of the day she died she knew it would be her last. She called in all of her family one by one to say her goodbyes and once that was completed they all gathered around her, and she died peacefully.

Nell was an amazing woman, forever smiling and always positive, even though the threat of cancer hung over her for seven years. The memory of her still lingers strong in the minds of the staff at the Hospice, and with other terminally ill people that she gave support and encouragement to. In a strange way, far from finding her illness frightening, she found it liberating. She didn't know how long she had to live, but she was absolutely determined to make the most of it. As one of our staff remarked afterwards, she adopted the Frank Sinatra approach to dying. She did it her way.

At Mary Potter Hospice we have a mantra; making the most of life. As Nell showed, often this can be achieved away from the hospice building itself. That's why we're extending our services into the community. It's also why, with tremendous local support, we have just built an outpatient unit in the Kapiti region. And with your support during our street appeal this year we'll be able to do even more to help the dying (and those who find out they're not actually dying after all) to make the most of life.

Start Again, p. 227
Headline: A Stroke Isn't The End You Just Have To Start Again.
Copy: You have a one in eight chance of suffering a stroke. Of course, if you are a smoker, your risk increases five times. High blood pressure increases your chance four times. And if you are a smoker with high blood pressure then you've hit the jackpot. Your chance of suffering a stroke is 18 times greater.

A stroke results from a sudden interruption of the blood supply to part of your brain and it causes brain damage. You will suffer some or even all of the following symptoms. Death (the worst outcome, so we thought we would get it out of the way first). Loss of consciousness. Paralysis or weakness in your face, arm or leg on one side. You could well be unable to communicate. Perhaps you'll have difficulty swallowing or eating. You might have a loss of bladder or bowel control. Impairment to vision is on the cards. Loss of memory and loss of emotional control feature. Your earning potential could well go out the window. And depression, it goes without saying, is very common. Often you are left with a body that has two totally different halves.

One side can be pretty much as it was before. But you'll need to teach the other side how to move, co-ordinate, speak, eat, and walk from scratch. After all that, it's hardly surprising that the common perception is that if you're lucky enough to survive a stroke you're actually not very

lucky at all. It's with some pleasure that we can tell you this isn't so. There's a good chance that you'll be able to make a partial, even a full recovery. Intensive therapy, skilled nursing, and time can help you regain full control of the body. Another positive side of stroke is that as we learn more about the causes we can significantly lower the chances that you will suffer one. Excessive alcohol, smoking, high stress level, lack of exercise, high blood cholesterol, heart disease, diabetes and obesity all play a part. Many of these can be controlled through medication, changes to diet or work habits, or in the case of excessive alcohol for example, a healthy dose of self control (don't worry, we're not being total wowsers, just encouraging a bit of moderation). The Stroke Foundation is New Zealand's only body committed solely to helping the victims of stroke, their family and friends. But, surprise, surprise, we are not a rich organisation. In order to continue our work, our research, our support services and our preventative education programmes we need your help. You can make a donation to the Stroke Foundation, PO Box 2320 Wellington, or phone your donation to 0800 Stroke (0800 787 653). Any amount you can spare will help us to spread the word about preventing stroke, and ensure that more people realise it's not a one-sided story.

Enquiries may be directed to the Stroke Foundation of New Zealand Inc. PO Box 2320, Wellington. Telephone (04) 472 8099, Fax (04) 472 7019.

Blind, p. 228
Headline: blind/blaind/adj., v., n. & adv – adj. 1 lacking the power of sight.
Blind/blaind/adj., v., n., & adv. – adj. 2 (often foll. by to) unwilling or unable to appreciate (a factor, circumstance, etc.)
Copy: Spend a day with the blind It'll make you see things differently.
Issued in the public interest by Tata Tea Limited. Making a difference... daily.

Matches, p. 229
Man's Voiceover: When one life is extinguished, something inside it can light up another one.
Life calls you. Donate your organs.
Man's Voiceover and Title: Life calls you. Donate your organs.
Man's Voiceover: This is a public service message from Antena 3 TV.
Created by Saatchi & Saatchi Advertising.

Prisoner, p. 230
Man's Voiceover: Some prisoners have electricity and three meals a day
Some prisoners have hot running water and colour television.
Other prisoners don't...
And their only crime was to outlive their income.
So please, help Rand Aid make the difference.
011–882 2510.

Punch These, p. 232
Headline: Angry, Frustrated, Confused? Punch these.
Copy: The Samaritans. Ph. 366 5676.

Bus, p. 286
Copy: Samaritans Ph. 4 739 739.

Texte und Drehbücher

Read This You Piece of Shit, S. 7
Überschrift: Lies das hier, du Arschloch!
Text: Wenn diese Überschrift Sie beleidigt, empfinden Sie ganz richtig. Niemand sollte so behandelt werden.
Leider werden aber Millionen von Menschen in aller Welt so behandelt.
Für viele sind allerdings verbale Angriffe die geringste Sorge. In Brasilien werden die Holzplantagenarbeiter im Amazonasgebiet zum Beispiel mit dem „Baumstamm" bestraft: Ein Mann, der seine Fällquote nicht geschafft hat, wird drei Tage lang gefesselt in einem ausgehöhlten Baumstamm liegen gelassen. Und wenn das noch nicht reicht, wird der Baumstamm mit Honig eingeschmiert, damit er Ameisen und andere Insekten anlockt.
In Indien werden Kinder auf ähnlich grausame Weise gestraft, indem man sie im Alter von nur sechs Jahren als Arbeiter an Teppichfabriken verkauft. Wenn die Webmeister nicht genug Kinder zu kaufen finden, kidnappen sie welche. Die Kinder müssen den ganzen Tag arbeiten. Wenn sie zu langsam arbeiten, dürfen sie nicht schlafen gehen. Wenn sie einen Fehler machen, werden sie verprügelt. Ein Kind wurde mit Paraffin übergossen und angezündet, weil es um etwas Urlaub gebeten hatte. Sechs andere wurden – weil sie gespielt hatten! – so brutal zusammengeschlagen, dass eines starb.
Auch in Nepal ist der Sklavenhandel noch weit verbreitet. Zehnjährige Mädchen werden entführt und als Prostituierte in Indien verkauft. Dort werden sie als Erstes auf ihre Aufgabe „vorbereitet", d. h. ohne Nahrung tagelang in einen winzigen Raum eingesperrt. Sie werden mit glühenden Zigaretten verbrannt, geschlagen und vergewaltigt, bis sie absolut gefügig sind. Erst dann erzielt man mit ihnen die höchsten Preise bei Bombays Bordellbesitzern.
Nicht nur die Prostitution ist eine Art Sklaverei, die Ehe kann es auch sein. In vielen Teilen der Welt bestimmen immer noch die Eltern, wen die Tochter heiratet. Ihre Wahl hängt in hohem Maße von dem Brautpreis ab, den die Familie des jungen Mannes zahlt. Das Wohl der Braut spielt überhaupt keine Rolle. So werden viele Frauen gegen ihren Willen zur Ehe gezwungen. Einige sind erst neun. Eine zwölfjährige Nigerianerin hasste ihren Ehemann so sehr, dass sie ihm immer wieder davonlief. Um sie endgültig daran zu hindern, hackte er ihr beide Beine ab.
Sie sehen also, dass Sklaverei keineswegs der Vergangenheit angehört. Sie ist auch nicht nur in Ländern der Dritten Welt ein Problem. Allein in Großbritannien sind (seit 1987) 1.700 Fälle misshandelter Hausangestellter bekannt geworden. Die meisten kommen aus armen Ausländerfamilien. Sie dachten, wenn sie hier arbeiten könnten, wären alle ihre Probleme gelöst. Stattdessen werden sie in Großbritannien oft nicht besser behandelt als die Haustiere. Sie haben einen 18-Stunden-Tag, und wenn sie sich beschweren, setzt es Hiebe, oft mit dem Stock. Manche von ihnen haben nie Ausgang. Einige werden vergewaltigt.
Die Liste der Grausamkeiten ist endlos.
Es gibt immer noch 100 Millionen Sklaven überall auf der Welt. Jeder kann über ebenso leidvolle Erfahrungen berichten wie die hier Zitierten.
Anti-Slavery International kämpft für die Abschaffung der Sklaverei. Wir wissen, dass unsere einzige Erfolgschance darin besteht, diese menschlichen Tragödien und die Tatsache, dass Sklaverei noch immer existiert, ins öffentliche Bewusstsein zu rücken. Durch Druck auf Politiker und durch publizistische Tätigkeit haben wir viele Regierungen und die Vereinten Nationen dazu gebracht, sich mit dem Problem zu befassen.
In einigen Ländern wie Thailand, Indien und Pakistan haben wir die Regierungen sogar dazu bewegt, ihre Gesetze zu ändern. Das wäre ohne unsere freiwilligen Helfer nicht möglich gewesen. Sie schrieben Briefe an einzelne Persönlichkeiten, an Firmen und Regierungen in aller Welt und stellten den Empfängern unangenehme, drängende Fragen.
Um diesen Druck aufrechtzuerhalten, brauchen wir Ihre Hilfe bei zukünftigen Kampagnen.
Wenn Sie mitmachen wollen, füllen Sie den Coupon aus und werden Sie Mitglied. Gemeinsam werden wir mit der Zeit dafür sorgen, dass niemand mehr zu spüren bekommt, was es heißt, wie ein Sklave behandelt zu werden.
Anti-Slavery International
Stableyard, Broomgrove Road,
London SW9 9TL.
Tel: 0171 924 9555. Fax: 0171 738 4110.

Pram/Family Planning (Kinderwagen/Familienplanung), S. 18
Mutter: Man sollte sich gar nicht um all den Familienplanungskram kümmern. Scott, lass das!
Ich meine man bloß, was die Doktors und alle einem sagen, da kommt jeder mit'm bisschen Grips ja wohl alleine drauf. Freundinnen fragen, das isses.
Hannah, wirst du wohl das Baby in Ruhe lassen?! Wie oft soll ich dir das noch sagen!!
Wenn du nicht schwanger werden willst, solltest du – na, du weißt schon – aufpassen und so.
Einfach deinen Grips gebrauchen.
Sprecher: Hören Sie nicht auf Altweibermärchen über Familienplanung. Ihr Arzt oder Ihre Beratungsstelle wird Sie freundlich beraten und präzise informieren, egal, ob Sie verheiratet oder allein stehend sind.
Schauen Sie im Telefonbuch unter Familienplanung nach.
Einblendung: Schauen Sie im Telefonbuch unter Familienplanung nach.
Mutter: ... Bei allem, was die Gören kosten, bleibt für die Pille ja auch gar nichts übrig.
Sprecher: Es kostet Sie auch gar nichts.

Clip this Coupon, S. 22
Überschrift: Schneiden Sie diesen Coupon aus.
Text: Schneiden Sie diesen Coupon aus. So, als wäre hier Ihr Gesicht abgebildet.

Women and Children First, S. 24
Überschrift: Und die Atommächte sagten: Erst die Frauen und Kinder!
Text: Nein, dies ist keine Grafik, sondern das Foto eines Kindes aus Kasachstan, das mit einem Wasserkopf zur Welt kam. Diese Missbildung ist das Ergebnis radioaktiver Strahlung, der die Mutter ausgesetzt war. Seien Sie nicht uns böse, dass wir es Ihnen zeigen. Seien Sie denen böse, die es Ihnen nicht gezeigt haben und behaupten, Atomtests wären unschädlich.

Can't Look, S. 26
Toneffekte: Baby schreit
1. Szene: Frau: Sei still! Ich hau' dei nen Kopf an die Tür, wenn du nicht sofort mit dem Gekreische aufhörst!
2. Szene: Mann: Komm und setz dich hierher.
3. Szene: Mann: Du bist dumm. Du bist blöd. Du bist nicht mein Kind.
4. Szene: Kind: Mami, wo bist du? Ich hab' Angst, wenn ich so allein bin.
5. Szene: Mann: Du darfst niemandem davon erzählen. Das ist unser kleines Geheimnis.
Sprecherin und Einblendung: Manchmal ertragen auch wir es nicht hinzuschauen. Grausamkeit gegenüber Kindern kann gestoppt werden. Mit Ihrer Hilfe für immer.
Sprecherin: Bitte unterstützen Sie die neue Schluss-Punkt-Kampagne der NSPCC.
Einblendung: NSPCC. Grausamkeit gegenüber Kindern muss aufhören. Schluss und Punkt.

Pregnant Man, S. 28
Überschrift: Wären Sie vorsichtiger, wenn Sie schwanger werden könnten?
Text: Eheleute oder Alleinstehende erhalten Beratung und Information zur Empfängnisverhütung von der Family Planning Association, Margaret Pyke House, 27–35 Mortimer Street, London W1N 8BQ. Tel. 0171 636 9135.

Some Fathers, S. 29
Überschrift: Einige Väter verändern ihre Kinder.
Text: Wir sehen die Wunden am Kopf des Kindes. Oder vielleicht nicht?
Tatsache ist, dass die äußeren Wunden bald verheilen, die Narben in der Seele aber ein Leben lang schmerzen und ein glückliches, ausgeglichenes Kind in ein seelisches Wrack verwandeln.
Tausende von Kindern werden jedes Jahr misshandelt. Von Vätern wie Müttern. Wenn Sie vermuten, dass ein Kind von anderen misshandelt wird, sind Sie dafür verantwortlich.
Denn wenn Sie nicht melden, dass ein Kind misshandelt wird, könnten Sie es ebensogut selbst besorgen.
Wenn Ihnen irgendwelche Fälle von Kindesmisshandlung bekannt sind, rufen Sie uns bitte am Mittwoch, den 4. September, an. 1 800 011 233. Melden und stoppen. NSW Police Service.

Same Father, S. 30
Überschrift: Wir haben beide denselben Vater.
Text: Das ist Sallys Geschichte:
„Meine Mutter ist gestorben, als ich zwölf war. Eines Nachts hatte ich schlecht geträumt, und mein Vater sagte, ich könnte zu ihm ins Bett kommen. Zuerst hat er mich nur gestreichelt, aber dann hat er noch was anderes gemacht. Ich wollte, dass er damit aufhört, aber er hat weitergemacht. Es war schrecklich, es tat richtig weh. Er hat gesagt, das ist, weil er mich liebt.
Als ich am nächsten Tag zur Schule gehen wollte, hat er gesagt, ich soll niemandem davon erzählen. Danach wollte er, dass ich jede Nacht bei ihm schlafe. Er nannte das unser kleines Geheimnis.
Später, als meine Tage plötzlich aufhörten, ließ mein Vater mich nicht mehr in die Schule und meldete mich krank.
Manchmal bewegt sich das Baby in meinem Bauch. Das fühlt sich ganz schrecklich an."
Zum Glück meldete Sallys Schule ihr Fehlen an anderer Stelle, und heute bekommt sie alle Unterstützung, die sie braucht.
Natürlich ist die Schwangerschaft nicht die einzige Auswirkung des Missbrauchs. Sally wird noch lange Zeit psychologische Hilfe benötigen, um ihre Schuldgefühle zu überwinden und beziehungsfähig zu werden.
Alle Formen des Missbrauchs – und nicht nur die offensichtlichen Formen wie sexuelle Übergriffe oder brutale Schläge – können seelische Schäden verursachen. Es gibt subtilere Formen wie Liebesentzug, Nichtbeachtung, ständiges Kritisieren oder Anbrüllen. All das kann seelische Wunden schlagen, die ein Leben lang nicht ausheilen. Manchmal werden Kinder sogar zum Selbstmord getrieben.
Deswegen leitet die NSPCC ihre Kampagne „Wir schreien für die Kinder" – ein Aufruf an alle, innezuhalten und über ihr Verhalten Kindern gegenüber nachzudenken. Sich bewusst zu machen, was jede Form von Grausamkeit in den Kindern bewirkt. Und zu erkennen, dass sie ihr ganzes Leben lang davon geprägt sein werden, wie wir sie behandelt haben.
Bitte reagieren Sie auf unseren Schrei.
Wenn Sie selbst missbraucht wurden oder jemanden kennen, der darunter zu leiden hat, rufen Sie die NSPCC Kinderschutz-Hotline an: 0800 800 500.
Wenn Sie nach dem Lesen dieses Textes weitere Informationen hilfreich finden würden, rufen Sie uns unter 071 825 2775 an.
NSPCC. Wir schreien für die Kinder.

Astronaut, S. 31
Überschrift: Hat die Welt die richtigen Prioritäten gesetzt?
Text: Das Forum über den Zustand der Welt bringt viele der international einflussreichsten Persönlichkeiten zusammen, die hier wichtige, die ganze Menschheit betreffende Fragen diskutieren: Atomwaffen-Abrüstung, Konfliktlösung, die Rolle der Frau und Entwicklungsförderung für Kinder. Dabei geht es darum, die richtigen Prioritäten für die Zukunft zu setzen. Tragen Sie durch den Besuch unserer Website (vom 27. Oktober bis 1. November) und Ihren Kommentar zu dieser Debatte bei! www.worldforum.org.

Face, S. 32
Einblendung: Dieses Mädchen möchte einfach mit jemandem reden.
Einblendung: Haben Sie die Geduld verloren?
Einblendung: Schwester Robinson weiß, es wird bald zum Gespräch kommen.
Krankenschwester: Hallo, Rachel, jetzt hast du wieder mich erwischt.
Wieder mal 'ne Nacht hier?
Einblendung: Der neue NHS (Nationaler Gesundheitsdienst) braucht mehr Krankenpflegepersonal.
Sprecherin: Krankenschwestern und -pfleger können etwas verändern. Wenn Sie sich für diesen Beruf oder den Wiedereinstieg in die Krankenpflege interessieren (bei höherem Gehalt und besseren Arbeitsbedingungen), rufen Sie uns an unter 0845 60 60 655.

Cot (Wiege), S. 36
Sprecher: Hier passiert einer von zehn Morden.
Jede Woche ein bis zwei.
In einem Jahr gibt es über 5.000 Misshandlungen durch Prügel und über 1.700 sexuelle Übergriffe.
Einblendung: In Großbritannien müssen 36.000 Kinder täglich damit rechnen, sexuell missbraucht zu werden.
Einblendung: NSPCC. Wir schreien für die Kinder.

The World Could End This Easily, S. 40
Text: Die Welt könnte so leicht untergehen. Protestieren Sie gegen Atomtests! Greenpeace 0800 22 33 44.

Stay in School, S. 42
Einblendung: Bleib lieber in der Schule!

Hungry, S. 44
Sprecher: Wenn ich „Fuck" sage, stört dich das wahrscheinlich.
Wenn ich „ich habe Hunger" sage, stört dich das wahrscheinlich nicht.
Fuck, ich habe Hunger.
Einblendung: Gutes Essen sollte niemals vergeudet werden.

Day Against Violence, S. 46
Einblendung: Es schien unmöglich.
Einblendung: Es geschah am 12. Februar 1995.
Einblendung: Über 1,7 Milliarden Menschen sahen es überall auf der Welt.
Zum ersten Mal.
Die beiden italienischen Fußballmannschaften betraten das Feld – jede in den Trikots der gegnerischen Mannschaft.
Und verlasen eine Botschaft, dass der Fußball verbinden und nicht spalten sollte.
Heute denken alle so.
Das verdanken sie auch uns.
Saatchi & Saatchi
Nichts ist unmöglich.

Worst Marks, S. 50
Überschrift: Die Kinder ethnischer Minderheiten kriegen in der Schule oft die schlimmsten Verletzungen.
(engl. Wortspiel: worst marks: schlechteste Schulnoten + schlimmste Wundmale/Striemen)

Teacher Passing an Examination, S. 51
Bildlegende: Er hatte sich mit dem Multiplizieren abgemüht. Er begriff einfach nicht, wie das funktionierte, bis seinem Lehrer einfiel, wie er es ihm auf eine ganz andere Art und Weise erklären konnte.
Überschrift: Ein Lehrer in der Prüfung.
Text: Der Augenblick, wenn ein Schüler einen schwierigen Sachverhalt begreift, gehört wahrscheinlich zu den besten Momenten des Lehrerdaseins. Er bedeutet, dass es dem Lehrer gelungen ist, seinen Stoff so zu vermitteln, dass dem Schüler ein Licht aufgeht. Nichts könnte von größerer Bedeutung sein.
Das wesentliche Ziel des Unterrichtens ist es, den Groschen so anzustoßen, dass er fällt. Und wenn er fällt, ist das der Punkt, an dem Lehren und Lernen sich treffen und Lehrer und Schüler einen gemeinsamen Erfolg verbuchen können.
Genau das bewegt Sie vielleicht dazu Lehrer zu werden. In diesem Fall wird es sie freuen zu erfahren, dass der Beruf auch in anderer Hinsicht lohnend ist.
Ab Dezember gibt es ein Anfangs-Jahresgehalt von rund £ 14.000 für Primar- und Sekundarschullehrer mit gutem Abschluss, die in Inner London arbeiten (und in den Genuss der damit verbundenen Aufwandsentschädigung und Gehaltszulage kommen) möchten.
Der Direktor/Die Direktorin einer großen Sekundarschule in Inner London kann ein Jahresgehalt von bis zu £ 48.000 erwarten. Das ist natürlich kein leicht verdientes Geld. Schließlich ist Unterrichten keine mechanische Tätigkeit. Kann es gar nicht sein.
In jeder Klasse sitzen Schüler mit vielen verschiedenen Fähigkeiten, Interessen und Einstellungen aus ganz unterschiedlichen Familien. Als Lehrer müssen Sie diese Unterschiede erkennen, im Gedächtnis behalten und darauf eingehen. Zum Beispiel lernen nicht alle Menschen gleich schnell bzw. nicht gleichmäßig gut in allen Fächern, der Lehrer muss den Stoff jedoch allen vermitteln.
Ausdruckslose Gesichter sind vielleicht ein Ansporn dazu, etwas ganz anders als üblich zu erklären. Ein fantasievoll gestalteter Unterricht kann in Bezug auf die Arbeitsmoral der Klasse Wunder wirken.
In gewisser Weise muss ein Lehrer jeden Tag eine Prüfung ablegen – und bestehen! Entmutigt Sie das? Oder fühlen Sie sich herausgefordert? Wenn Sie auf diese zweite Frage mit Ja antworten, könnten Sie durch die Lehrerausbildung Ihr pädagogisches Talent entfalten und sich auf eine in doppelter Hinsicht lohnende Tätigkeit vorbereiten.
Wenn Sie mehr über die Ausbildung wissen möchten, rufen Sie 0345 300121 an (Bezug: Dept.code IS/4/A) oder schicken Sie uns den ausgefüllten Coupon.
Unterricht geben heißt das Beste aus den Menschen hervorzulocken.

Resolution (Gute Vorsätze), S. 52
Einblendung: Auf den Philippinen verbringen Tausende von Kindern den Neujahrstag in Krankenhäusern. Billige Feuerwerkskörper haben ihnen Finger oder Hände weggerissen.
Diese Kampagne will dem Teufelskreis ein Ende machen.
Lehrer: Kinder, welchen guten Vorsatz habt ihr für das neue Jahr gefasst?
Kind: Ich werde nie wieder mit Feuerwerk spielen.
Einblendung: Dieses Neujahr Hände weg von Feuerwerkskörpern!

Prostitute, S. 54
Überschrift: Möchtest du in Europa als Prostituierte arbeiten?
Text: Millionen von Frauen haben gar keine Wahl. Zum Beispiel Ausländerinnen, die von internationalen Zuhälterringen getäuscht werden. Sie werden ausgebeutet und können über ihr Leben nicht selbst entscheiden.
Sie werden staunen, mit welchen Methoden noch heute Menschen erniedrigt werden.
Manos Unidas will dieser Ausbeutung ein Ende machen. Helfen Sie uns, die Sklaverei abzuschaffen.
Anmerkung: Wie aus der linken Seite ersichtlich, erschien diese Anzeige im Kleinanzeigenteil unter Stellenangebote.

Mining Children, S. 55
Überschrift: Metallurgische Firma sucht Kinder für den Bergbau.
Text: Millionen von Kindern müssen sich keinen Job suchen, er wird ihnen aufgezwungen.
Kinder werden als billige Arbeitskräfte benutzt.
Sie werden ausgebeutet und können über ihr Leben nicht selbst entscheiden.
Sie werden staunen, mit welchen Methoden noch heute Menschen erniedrigt werden.
Manos Unidas will diesem Missbrauch ein Ende setzen. Helfen Sie uns, die Sklaverei abzuschaffen.
Anmerkung: Wie aus der linken Seite ersichtlich, wurde diese Anzeige im Kleinanzeigenteil der größten spanischen Tageszeitungen unter Stellenangebote platziert.

Child Abuse (Kindesmissbrauch), S. 56
1. Mann: Hübsche Braut, was?
2. Mann: Noch Jungfrau?
1. Mann: Na klar, ist meine Tochter.
2. Mann: Wie viel?
1. Mann: Nur 100 Dollar.
2. Mann: Und was kann sie?
1. Mann: Alles – aber lass sie leben.
... Komm mit, mein Schatz.
Stimme aus dem Off: Wenn das Ihre Tochter wäre, hätten Sie doch sicher Angst um sie – oder?
Und wenn Sie ins Ausland fahren, vergessen Sie es nicht:
Ein Kind ist überall auf der Welt ein Kind.
Einblendung: Centro Italiano per L'adozione Internazionale (Italienisches Zentrum für Internationale Adoption). Per donazioni c/c n. 10837 presso la Cariplo, agenzia 15 di Milano.

Raped as a 3 Year Old, S. 58
Überschrift: Wie ein Dreijähriger die Vergewaltigung erlebte. Ein Opfer berichtet.
Text: Ich weiß noch, ich war drei Jahre alt, als mein Vater mich zum ersten Mal

missbrauchte. Vielleicht hatte er es schon vorher getan, und ich kann mich bloß nicht daran erinnern. Ich sehe mich noch jetzt im Bett liegen und sein großes Gesicht, das mir immer näher kommt. Er gab mir einen Gutenachtkuss. Bloß – beim Küssen blieb es nicht.

Er sagte immer zu mir: „Das ist unser kleines Geheimnis." Und wehe ich erzähle jemandem davon, ich würde von zu Hause wegmüssen. Schon als kleines Kind wusste ich, dass da etwas nicht stimmte. Er sagte immer: „Ich beschütze dich." Wie konnte das sein? Wo er mir doch so verdammt wehtat!

Es ist merkwürdig. Eigentlich war er ja mein Feind und trotzdem der einzige Freund, den ich hatte. Er machte mich von ihm abhängig. Er beherrschte mich. Mein Körper gehörte über neun Jahre lang ihm.

Ich hatte Kontaktschwierigkeiten in der Schule. Ich empfand mich als anders, ließ niemanden an mich ran. Ich hasste es, mich nach dem Sport im Umkleideraum nackt zu zeigen. Ich schämte mich ganz entsetzlich und hatte Angst, die anderen könnten sehen, was mein Vater mit mir gemacht hatte, und mich 'ne Tunte nennen.

Selbst als ich schließlich eine Freundin hatte, wusste ich immer noch nicht, ob ich wirklich heterosexuell war. Ich war furchtbar grob zu ihr. Ich nehme an, dass ich nun derjenige sein wollte, der jemand anderen beherrschte, wie mein Vater mich beherrscht hatte.

Sex machte mir schreckliche Angst. Beim Orgasmus dachte ich immer daran, wie es mein Vater in mir getan hatte, und an sein großes, befriedigt lächelndes Gesicht. Schließlich traf ich eine andere Frau. Wir haben geheiratet. Zwei Jahre später hat sie mich verlassen. Sie sagte, ich sei gefühlskalt und hätte kein Verständnis für sie.

Genau so war es. Ich merkte es gar nicht, wenn ich anderen, oder sogar mir selbst, seelischen oder körperlichen Schmerz zufügte. In meinem Innersten war etwas seit langem erloschen. Es gab Zeiten, in denen ich mich in den Finger schneiden konnte, ohne Schmerz zu empfinden. Nach der Scheidung fing ich an zu trinken. Es war eine Art Flucht. Ich hatte aber immer noch tiefe Depressionen.

Letztes Jahr ist mein Vater gestorben. Das gab mir wohl den Anstoß, mich an die NSPCC zu wenden. Ich war 53 Jahre alt, und zum ersten Mal in meinem Leben erzählte ich jemandem von den Erlebnissen meiner Kindheit. Ein Kinderschutzbeauftragter arbeitete mit mir sechs Monate lang einmal die Woche. Er brachte mich dazu, ihm alles zu erzählen. Das war unheimlich schwer und schmerzhaft. Über vierzig Jahre lang hatte ich versucht, gar nicht darüber nachzudenken.

Schließlich setzte die Wirkung ein. Er half mir zu erkennen, dass es nicht meine Schuld war. Soweit ich mich erinnern kann, fühlte ich mich zum ersten Mal in meinem Leben wohl in meiner Haut. Es war, als wäre ich aus einer dunklen Einzelhaftzelle entlassen worden.

Ich werde nie vergessen, was mir passiert ist, aber wenigstens kann ich jetzt anfangen mein Leben zu leben.

Wenn Sie mehr über die Arbeit der NSPCC wissen oder spenden möchten, schreiben Sie an: NSPCC, 67 Saffron Hill, London EC1N 8RS, oder rufen Sie uns an: 071 242 1626. Wenn Sie einen Fall von Kindesmissbrauch melden möchten, rufen Sie bitte die NSPCC Kinderschutz-Hotline an unter 0800 800 500.

Dr Jekyll, Mr Hyde, S. 59
Überschrift: Doktor Jekyll, Mister Hyde
Text: Sie sind ein zuverlässiger, zärtlicher und aufmerksamer Familienvater. Sie haben eine hübsche Frau und eine niedliche neunjährige Tochter. Die Liebe Ihrer Frau und Tochter ist Ihr größtes Glück. Sie würden es gegen alles und jeden verteidigen. – Und dann müssen Sie manchmal geschäftlich verreisen, an exotische Bestimmungsorte wie Bangkok zum Beispiel, in eines dieser Länder, wo alles toleriert wird, wo sie „ganz andere Traditionen und Bräuche haben". Dort bietet man Ihnen auf einem Markt neben Hemden und Souvenirs auch ein kleines Mädchen an, eine niedliche Neunjährige, die Ihrer eigenen Tochter sogar ein bisschen ähnlich sieht, aber eigentlich wie eine erwachsene Frau wirkt. Sie denken, so macht man das eben hier, und verändern sich blitzschnell. Plötzlich sind Sie ein ganz anderer Mensch, und der internationale Markt der Pädophilie – ein reicher und einflussreicher Markt des Todes – kann einen neuen Gewinn verbuchen. Tatsächlich macht er die dicksten Profite nicht durch Geschäfte mit Kriminellen und Perversen, sondern mit normalen Männern – Männer wie Sie. Das CIAI (Italienisches Zentrum für Internationale Adoption) kämpft seit vielen Jahren für etwas, das niemand vergessen sollte, besonders auf Auslandsreisen: Ein Kind ist ein Kind, überall auf der Welt.

Spenden können von Ihrem Kreditkartenkonto abgebucht werden, wenn Sie die Nummer 0039 2 55 01 20 11 anrufen, oder Sie überweisen Ihre Spende auf das Konto Nr. 10837 bei Cariplo, Zweigstelle 15, Mailand, Italien.

1 in every 8, S. 60
Text: Einer von acht Menschen, die an diesem Plakat vorübergehen, wurde als Kind missbraucht.
NSPCC. Wir schreien für die Kinder.

Ban Guns, S. 64

Bullets, S. 66
Überschrift: Penis ohne Kondom.
Text: Gratisproben unter 250 8629.

Less Dead, S. 68
Text: Wenn ein 22er weniger tödlich ist, warum ist ER dann nicht weniger tot? Fordern Sie ein Feuerwaffengesetz, das den 22er-Revolver zur Strecke bringt!

Grunge Angels, S. 70
Sprecherin: Ich begrüße Sie! Zu Ihrer Unterhaltung bringen wir in diesem Nach-Leben Whitney Houstons schönste Liebeslieder.
Toneffekte: Entsetzensschreie
Einblendung: Tod ist Scheiße.
Schnallen Sie sich an.

Rubber Woman, S. 74
Überschrift: Der letzte Schrei als Bettwäsche.

Rubber Man, S. 75
Überschrift: Männer sehen in Gummi immer besser aus.

Tongue, S. 76
Überschrift: Sie will ihre Zunge/Sprache in Ihren Mund legen.
Text: Kantonesisch- oder Mandarinlernen leicht gemacht.
Rufen Sie das Hong Kong Language Learning Centre an unter 2385 5331.

Mother, S. 78
Einblendung: Achtung! Die folgende Szene könnte einige Zuschauer stark erschüttern.
Sprecher: Was Sie jetzt sehen werden, wird Sie erschüttern: Das kommt dabei heraus, wenn ein siebenjähriges Mädchen unangeschnallt auf dem Rücksitz eines Wagens sitzt, der bei einer Geschwindigkeit von nur 50 Stundenkilometern verunglückt. Bitte schauen Sie sich die Verletzungen genau an.
Kein Sitz ist sicher ohne Sicherheitsgurt. Schnallen Sie sich immer an.
Einblendung: Die Zahl der Verkehrsopfer muss gesenkt werden.

Job Satisfaction, S. 81
Überschrift: Wie finden Sie Befriedigung im Beruf, wenn Sie jemanden zum Sterben nach Hause schicken?
Text: Als er schließlich im Krankenhaus landete, hatte Erics chronische Krankheit ihn schon fast besiegt. Er konnte nur noch mühsam atmen und schlucken. Jede weitere noch so kleine Anstrengung war zu viel.

Dennoch war der 83-jährige Eric fest entschlossen, seine Tage zu Hause zu beschließen. Allerdings nicht, bevor seine Krankenschwester ihn wieder zu Kräften gebracht hatte.

Sauerstoff, Medikamente und künstliche Ernährung linderten allmählich seine Beschwerden. Die Krankenschwester schaffte es immer, Zeit für Eric und seine Familie zu finden um zu beraten, zu beruhigen oder einfach zuzuhören.

Nach drei Wochen war sein Zustand so stabil, dass er nach Hause entlassen werden konnte. Als Eric und seine Krankenschwester einander auf Wiedersehen sagten, schieden sie als Freunde.

Die Pflege alter, kranker Menschen ist selten eine leichte Aufgabe. Man braucht viel Kraft, Mitgefühl und Initiative. Aber denken Sie nur an den menschlichen Lohn. Wie befriedigend muss es sein, wenn man einem Sterbenden den letzten Wunsch erfüllen kann?

Kein anderer Beruf bietet diese Erfüllung.
Rufen Sie an: 0345646464.
Bezug: 2J. Jederzeit.
Krankenpflege. Haben Sie das Zeug dazu?

A Country Story, S. 82
1. Episode
Überschrift: Am 24. August wird Danny Tessa heiraten.
Mutter: Frühstück ist fertig!
Pete: Hmm, lecker! Schinken!
Mutter: Natürlich kann sie kochen
Vater: Komisch, ihre Mutter kann's nicht.
Mutter (entrüstet): Bruce!
Sprecher aus dem Off: Wenn Sie dieser Familie einen Brief schicken wollten, müssten Sie ihn an die Carters, bei Central Hawkes Bay, adressieren. Die Farm ist seit über 80 Jahren im Besitz der Familie. Danny soll sie als Nächster übernehmen. Bald nach der Hochzeit werden er und Tessa in das alte Farmhaus einziehen. So wird die nächste Generation das Land bebauen. Und immer so fort.
Danny: Papa, ich – äh – wenn du willst, hol' ich heut' Abend vor'm Fußbal training die Scharniere ab.
Vater: Ja, tu das.
Danny: Wir fahren um vier, Pete.
Pete: Okay.
Mutter: Und bleib' nicht die ganze Nacht da!
Einblendung: Fortsetzung folgt.

2. Episode
Überschrift: In fünf Wochen wird Danny Tessa heiraten.
Sprecher aus dem Off: Wie in den letzten Jahren auch gehen Danny und Pete nach dem Fußballtraining in die Kneipe
Blue: He, hier kommt Mr.-Vier-Wochen!
Tag, Pete.
Pete: Wie geht's, Blue?
Blue: Guck mal, wer da ist.
Danny: He, Matthew, wo hast du gesteckt?
Matthew: Och, in Palmy, zur A&P-Show.
Pete: Haste was Gutes gesehen?
Matthew: 'nen Preisbullen. 'nen Typ aus Waikato mit 'nem Preisbullen. Wollte gleich fünf Dollar für einmal Angucken.
Danny: Und, hast du'n gesehen?
Matthew: Ich fragte den Typen, ob er 'nen Familienrabatt gibt, und er fragte, wie viele wir sind. Als ich sagte, nur ich und meine Olle und unsere 13 Kinder, da sagt der doch: Warte hier, ich hol' den Bullen, damit der dich angaffen kann!
Sprecher aus dem Off: Das ist so etwas wie eine willkommene Gewohnheit geworden: Matthew kommt immer irgendwoher und hat dann tolle Geschichten zu erzählen. Die Leute sagen, die Kneipe heißt deshalb „Die Eule", weil es Blue egal ist, wenn die Leute die ganze Nacht dort bleiben, aber wahrscheinlich gibt's noch einen anderen Grund.
Einblendung: Fortsetzung folgt.

3. Episode
Überschrift: In vier Wochen wird Danny Tessa heiraten.
Pete: Einen Penny für das, was du gerade denkst, Danny.
Danny: Na ja, kleiner Bruder. Ich dachte gerade, dass wir bis jetzt verdammt viel Glück gehabt haben. Keine Sorgen. Kein Abstrampeln. Keine Geldgier.
Pete: Wieso auf einmal so tiefsinnig?
Danny: Vergiss es, Pete. He, und wo ist der Penny, den du mir schuldest?
Pete: Hier.
Sprecher: Sie haben sich schon immer so gut vertragen. Mussten sie auch. Und in wenigen Wochen ist Pete Brautführer bei Dannys Hochzeit.
Danny: Gib her!
Pete: Hängt davon ab.
Danny: Hängt wovon ab?
Pete: Na ja, ich bin Brautführer, nicht?
Danny: Genau.
Pete: Ich halte eine Rede, nicht?
Danny: Genau.
Pete: Und was soll ich dann über die Kleine sagen, die du vor'n paar Jahren bei Massey aufgerissen hast?
Danny: Gleich kleb' ich dir eine.
Nette Kleine.
Pete: Wie hieß sie doch gleich? Irene!?
Danny: Vergiss den Penny.
Pete (singt): Irene good night, Irene, Irene, good night ...
Einblendung: Fortsetzung folgt.

4. Episode
Überschrift: In drei Wochen wird Danny Tessa heiraten.
Trainer: O.K., Jungs. Wir werden uns von den Townies nicht noch mal schlagen lassen. Müssen hart rangehn, vom ersten Anpfiff an. Müsst ihnen zeigen, wer hier der Boss ist. Apropos Boss: Ich geb' heute Abend ein paar Bier aus, wegen Danny und Tessa und so. O.K., das wär's.
Kapitän: ... Moment mal, Jungs. Ich wollt' nur sagen, wir wünschen euch alles Gute, und ... also, ein Hoch auf Danny und Pete ...
Fußballer: Danny und Tess.
Kapitän: Ach ja, Danny und Tess ...
Viel Glück!
Danny: Guten Tag!
Matthew: Wie lang hast du noch?
Danny: Drei Wochen.
Matthew: Mein alter Onkel hat neulich wieder geheiratet.
Danny: Wie alt ist er denn?
Matthew: 91.
Danny: 91!? Warum wollte er denn in dem Alter noch heiraten?
Matthew: Was heißt wollen? Er musste!
Einblendung: Fortsetzung folgt.

5. Episode
Überschrift: In zwei Wochen wird Danny Tessa heiraten.
Danny: Hallo, Mama!
Mutter: Du bist spät dran. Probier mal .. hat Tessa gebacken.
Tessa: Pete?
Danny: Leckere Brötchen, Tessa!
Tessa: Das sind Muffins.
Danny: Na schön, sind trotzdem lecker.
Sprecher: Diese Woche schon werden Danny und Tessa das neue Ehepaar Carter sein, und die Familienfarm wird in die jüngeren, stärkeren Hände der nächsten Generation übergehen.
Vater: Wir hatten heute Morgen Besuch, Jungs.
Pete: Irgendjemand Wichtiges?
Vater: Ja, sehr wichtig, von der Farmarbeitergewerkschaft. Er wollte alles wissen über unsere Löhne und Arbeitsbedingungen und so. Ich hab' ihm gesagt, wie viel der erste Schafhirte verdient, 'n paar hundert pro Woche und freie Wohnung und so. Und dann, wie viel der Hilfsarbeiter kriegt, hundertsechzig und freies Wohnen und so. Dann fragte er, ob wir noch andere beschäftigen. Da hab' ich gesagt: Na ja, dann hab'n wir da noch den Blöden, der die meiste Arbeit macht und etwa 40 Dollar die Woche kriegt. Da sagt er: 40 Dollar die Woche? Mit dem will ich reden. Und ich sagte, der Blöde, das bist du. Da ging er dann endlich.
Einblendung: Fortsetzung folgt.

6. Episode
Überschrift: Nächste Woche wird Danny Tessa heiraten.
Sprecher: Diese Woche werden Danny und Tessa das neue Ehepaar Carter ... und wieder einmal geht die Farm der Familie in jüngere, stärkere Hände über.
Blue: He, Danny ...
Halt dich fest, Matt ...
He, Danny, hör dir das an ...
Schieß los, Matt ...
Matthew: Ich erzähle den Jungs gerade von dem Kerl – weißt du noch –, dem Großstadttyp, der mit Skinny quatschte: He, Skinny, als dein Pferd Husten hatte und so – was hast du ihm gegeben? Und Skinny sagt: Ich gab ihm Phenyl. Jedenfalls kommt der Typ 'n paar Tage später wieder und knöpft sich Skinny vor: He, Skinny, ich hab' meinem Pferd Phenyl gegeben, und jetzt ist es tot! Und Skinny sagt: Yeah, meins auch.
Blue: He, Danny ... soll dir was ausrichten. Tessa ist bei dir zu Hause ... Irgendwas wegen des großen Tages.
Danny: O.K., danke. Gehn wir. Los komm, Pete, soll ich dich mitnehmen?
Matthew: Noch eins, dann geht's los.
Einblendung: Fortsetzung folgt.

7. Episode
Überschrift: Danny wird Tessa diese Woche heiraten.
Blue: He, hört auf, Jungs, das ist hier keine Boxkampfarena. Tag, Eule. Tag, Bruce ... ne, sie waren hier, ja sicher.
Vater: Danke, Blue, danke.
Vater: Das war's ... Probleme mit dem Pick-up. Ich muss hin und sie abholen.
Mutter: Probleme mit dem Pick-up?
Warum haben sie nicht angerufen?
Vater: Oh, Mutter, Mutter!
Einblendung: Leute vom Lande sterben auf Landstraßen.
Einblendung: Fortsetzung folgt.

8. Episode
Überschrift: Danny ist tot.
Sprecher: Matthew und der junge Danny fielen in dieser Nacht einem Autounfall zum Opfer. Leute vom Lande sterben auf Landstraßen. Pete wird auch nicht mehr der Alte sein: Er ist jetzt in Christchurch. In der Spezialklinik für Querschnittsgelähmte. Er kann nicht laufen. Und wird's nie wieder können.
Tessa: Hat's schon Kaufgebote für die Farm gegeben, Mama?
Mutter: Ich glaub' ja.
Vater: Ein oder zwei Interessenten ...
Mutter: Sag es Bruce.
Tessa: Ich gehe fort. Nicht für immer. Nur für 'ne Weile. Aber ich melde mich.
Vater: Wohin gehst du denn?
Tessa: Nach Piha, zu meiner Tante.
Vater: Soso.
Mutter: Sie geht fort, Vater. Sie bekommt Dannys Baby.
Vater: Es hört nie auf, nicht, Mutter? Es hört einfach nie auf.
Einblendung und Sprecher: Nie mehr. Nie wieder. Nie wieder.
Nie wieder.
Leute vom Lande sterben auf Landstraßen.

The Height of It, S. 93

Taxi Confessions, S. 94
Fahrer: Sie müssen mir schon die Straße sagen, denn wenn Sie einschlafen, weiß ich nicht, wohin ich Sie bringen soll.
Mann: He, hallo! Taxi!
Mann: Ja, man geht in all diese Kneipen, und man findet sie einfach nicht. Ja, man ...
Frau: Und er hält den Arm hoch, und da hat er Handschellen dran. Handschellen!!
Mann: Ich geh' nach Hause.
Mann: Hier, da müssen Sie hin.
Mann: Wow, wir sind da!
Mann: Man bestellt einen Schinkenburger, und was kriegt man? 'ne Scheiß-Speckschwarte. Immer dasselbe!
Mann: Erst war er hinter mir – und im nächsten Moment ... weg war er!
Mann: Herne Bay, bitte.
Fahrer: Wo in Herne Bay?
Paar: Ist da das Lokal White Lady?
Ja genau.
Ja, genau da unten.
Mann: Er geht in diese ausländischen Schuppen – und da versackt er immer.
Mann: Nein, nein, nein, das ist es nicht. Dahin wollen wir nicht. Da kommen wir ja gerade her.
Sprecher und Einblendung: Wenn Sie sich betrinken und dann ein Taxi nehmen, müssen Sie ein absolutes Genie sein.

Disaster, S. 96
Überschrift: Wo immer wir hingehen, ist es eine Katastrophe.
Text: Wir denken nicht darüber nach, wie wir einer Katastrophe entgehen können. Wir müssen jederzeit auf eine Katastrophe vorbereitet sein – ob es ein Krieg in Ruanda oder ein Flugzeugabsturz in den Ruahines* ist. Für Millionen ist das Zeichen des Roten Kreuzes zu einem vertrauten und beruhigenden Zeichen von Katastrophenhilfe geworden. Wir bereiten uns darauf vor, sofort zu reagieren, und mit Erste-Hilfe- und Bergungskursen bereiten wir auch Sie vor. Sicher bitten wir Sie hin und wieder um Hilfe, aber eines Tages könnten auch Sie unsere Hilfe brauchen.
(*Bergkette auf der Nordinsel Neuseelands)

Fight, S. 98
Überschrift: Wir bringen Ihnen das Kämpfen bei.
Text: In der Liebe wie im Krieg ist alles erlaubt? Ist es nicht! Selbst der Krieg hat seine Regeln. Bei seinen humanitären Hilfsaktionen in Kriegsgebieten in aller Welt begegnet das Rote Kreuz Soldaten, die keine Ahnung von ihren Verpflichtungen gegenüber Gefangenen, Zivilisten und sogar ihren Gegnern im Kampf haben.
Wenn wir diesen Soldaten beibringen, die Genfer Konventionen einzuhalten, können wir Leben retten.
Einige Aktivitäten des Roten Kreuzes mögen Sie verwundern, aber was immer wir tun und wo immer wir hingehen, um zu helfen – wir sind bei allem auf Ihre Hilfe angewiesen.

350 Languages, S. 99
Überschrift: Wie sagt man „Erschieß mich nicht" in 350 Sprachen?
Text: Das rote Kreuz des Roten Kreuzes wurde 1859 zuerst auf einem Schlachtfeld in Solferino benutzt. Heute trennt es noch immer medizinische Helfer von Soldaten, Leben vom Tod.
Dieses Zeichen steht unter dem Schutz der Genfer Konvention, und sein Missbrauch wird als Gesetzesverstoß geahndet.
Es gehört nicht auf einen Erste-Hilfe-Koffer und darf nicht von Tierärzten oder Polikliniken verwendet werden.
Es steht für Schutz, Neutralität und Menschlichkeit.
Das neuseeländische Rote Kreuz ist dazu verpflichtet es zu schützen, denn ohne dieses Symbol könnten wir Sie nicht schützen.

Don't Forget, S. 100
Überschrift: Denk nach dem Trinken daran, wie man am sichersten verkehrt.
Text: Alkohol macht vergess ich. Schütze dich vor AIDS. Trage ein Kondom. Vergiss nicht, wo du es hingelegt hast.

Prevent Sickness, S. 101
Überschrift: Nach Alkoholgenuss bei Bedarf zur Vorbeugung von Krankheit anzuwenden.
Text: Zu viel Alkohol kann zu ungeschütztem Verkehr animieren. Schütze dich mit einem Kondom. Denn AIDS macht dich krank. Für immer.

Right Package, S. 102
Überschrift: Wenn Sie Ihre Angestellten länger behalten möchten, geben Sie Ihnen das richtige Paket.
Text: Was Ihre Angestellten im Bett anstellen, geht Sie nichts an. Es könnte jedoch die Arbeit Ihrer Firma stören.
Angenommen, einer Ihrer Mitarbeiter infiziert sich mit dem HIV-Virus?
Wenn schließlich bei ihm AIDS ausbricht, müssen Sie sich einen neuen Mitarbeiter suchen.
Bis dahin machen Sie und seine Kollegen sich vielleicht Sorgen darüber, ob es ungefährlich ist, HIV-Infizierte in der Firma zu haben. Glücklicherweise besteht auf diesem Wege keine Ansteckungsgefahr.
Sie möchten sicher auch über die rechtlichen Aspekte Bescheid wissen. Ob der Mitarbeiter durch die Versicherung gedeckt ist oder ob Ihre Firma dafür geradestehen muss.
Es ist wichtig, dass Sie die Antworten auf diese Fragen kennen. Denn wenn Ihr Unternehmen nicht sowieso schon in irgendeiner Weise von AIDS betroffen ist, dann könnte das bald geschehen.
Im Jahr 2000 wird die Epidemie in Asien ein größeres Problem sein als im derzeit am schlimmsten betroffenen Gebiet: Afrika. Bis zum Jahr 2000 werden über 40 Prozent der Neuinfizierungen hier geschehen – es sei denn, Sie unternehmen etwas, um die Verbreitung dieser Krankheit zu stoppen.
Beginnen Sie damit, dass Sie sich mit der örtlichen AIDS-Hilfe und dem Gesundheitsamt in Verbindung setzen. Sie sind sicher in der Lage, Ihre Fragen zu beantworten, und beraten Sie über die notwendigen Schritte zur AIDS-Verhütung in Ihrer Firma. Zum Beispiel könnte ein Spezialist zu Ihren Angestellten sprechen. Sie könnten Plakate über AIDS-Verhütung am Schwarzen Brett aufhängen. Sie können die Adresse einer AIDS-Aktionsgruppe in Ihrer Nähe vom örtlichen Büro des UN-Entwicklungsprogramms oder von der UNDP-Zentrale in Neu Delhi erfragen (Adressen s.u.).
Unternehmen Sie jetzt etwas. Sie werden Ihrer Belegschaft Auftrieb geben, wenn Sie sich um Ihre Mitarbeiter kümmern.
Und Sie werden keine wertvollen Mitarbeiter an AIDS verlieren.

Night Cap, S. 103
Überschrift: Egal, wie viel du trinkst, vergiss keine Nachtmütze nicht!
Text: Je mehr du trinkst, desto vergesslicher wirst du. Mindere dein AIDS-Risiko. Vergiss es nicht: Dein kleiner Mann braucht eine Nachtmütze, wenn er ins Bett geht!

Preservativo, S. 105
Stimme aus dem Off:
Kondom, Kondom, Kondom, Kondom, Kondom, Kondom, Kondom
Einblendung: Wir sagen es noch einmal und noch einmal und immer wieder.
Das Kondom ist die zuverlässigste Waffe im Kampf gegen AIDS.
Überzeuge deinen Partner davon, damit er es auch benutzt.
ANLAIDS.

Strangers in the Night, S. 106
Die Hintergrundmusik für diesen Werbespot ist der Song „Strangers in the Night". Im Verlauf des Spots ändert sich der Rhythmus zu einer zerrissenen, traurigeren Version – die musikalische Entsprechung zu den Noten, die sich auf dem Bildschirm in Kruzifixe verwandeln.
Einblendung: Stoppen Sie AIDS mit Liebe!

Love Story, S. 108
Musik: Love Story
Sprecher: Viele werden es diesen beiden diesen Sommer nachmachen.
Rotes Kreuz
Macht Liebe!
Einblendung:
Freiwillige Helfer – Rotes Kreuz.

Lenny, S. 113
Lenny: Ich fühlte mich einfach – wie – voll gut, Mann.
Weißte, das war nicht wie beim Rennfahren, ich war nicht high, wa, ich war wie – total relaxed. Na ja, beim ersten Mal hab' ich bloß gereihert, alles rausgekotzt, verstehste, und danach – Mann eh, – wow, hab' ich gesagt, der Stoff ist obergeil!
Genau.
Weißte, okay, du verstehst schon, wa, wenn du 'ne schnelle Schüssel unterm Arsch hast, wa – deine Adrenalinpumpen – verstehste?
Das isses. Genau so.
Ich hatte Zellulite im Oberschenkel. Hab' soo 'ne lange Narbe. Echt wahnsinnig, Mann.
Ich hatte fast ... mein Fuß ist fast abgefault, fast hätten sie mir den abgehackt.
Ich fand mich ziemlich intelligent.
Ich kann tun und lassen, was ich will, Mann.
Egal was – ich kann's tun.
Hab' mir fast alles aus dem Bauch gekotzt, da bin ich wie – verdammter Kerl – das will ich, verstehste.
Ich will nur 'n netter Typ sein, weiter nichts, nichts weiter. Warum können die Leute das nicht einfach tun!? Vielleicht sollten sie sich alle mal einen setzen und relaxen.
Ich hab' die Kratzer am ganzen Körper, Mann. Die Katze kam aus dem kleinen Loch da geschossen wie nix.
Früher hab' ich mehr gemacht, verstehste ... ins Kino, Essen gegangen, Broadway-Shows angeguckt. Ich mag Broadway-Shows, die sind cool, Mann.
1997 – wir hab'n jetzt 1996, okay? – 17. oder 18. August 1996 oder so – kommt ihr mit euren Kameras wieder her, und ich werd' ein ganz neuer Mensch sein.
Erfolgreich.
Dafür verwett' ich mein Leben!
Einblendung: Heroin.
Auf den Geschmack gekommen?
Partnership for a Drug-Free America
(Partnerschaft für ein drogenfreies Amerika).

Surfing Monkey, S. 117
Sprecherin: Und wieder bieten wir Ihnen den Artikel J343: die Sparbüchse „Surfing Monkey". (Monkey steht für Injektion/Schuss und Surfen für das Erlebnis des Drogenrauschs.)
Ein wunderschönes Geschenk zur Graduierung, zur Hochzeit lieber Freunde. Soweit ich weiß, war sie das letzte Mal völlig ausverkauft. Deshalb versäumen Sie diesmal nicht, sich eine zu sichern. Wir sind jetzt mit Scott aus Nashville verbunden.
Hallo, Scott, wie ich höre, haben Sie gerade fünfzehn unserer Surfing-Monkey-Sparbüchsen gekauft? Stimmt das?
Scott: ... Genaau!
(Im Hintergrund Stimmengewirr und Gelächter)
Scott: Ruhig, Leute! Ich bin im Fernsehen.
Einblendung: Marihuana. Eine sehr teure Angewohnheit.
Partnership for a Drug-Free America.

Celebrities, S. 118
Überschrift: In der Werbeszene heißt es, der sicherste Weg zum Erfolg einer Anzeige/eines Spots führt über Berühmtheiten.
Partnership for a Drug-Free America.

Nose, S. 119
Sprecherin: Ein Gramm Kokain kostet so viel wie ein Kofferradio mit CD-Player.
Drei Gramm Kokain kosten so viel wie ein guter Fernseher.
Für sieben kriegt man einen Flug nach Paris.
Für ein Gramm pro Woche ein ganzes Jahr ein neues Auto.
Wenn du an Kokain hängst, verschwindet alles, wofür du arbeitest, direkt vor deiner Nase.
Einblendung: Partnership for a Drug-Free America.

Elephant, S. 121
Tonuntermalung des gesamten Spots: Elefantentritte
Sprecher: Eine von diesen beiden Frauen bewies ihre Achtung vor der Natur, indem sie dem kalifornischen Umweltschutzbund einen Teil ihres Gehalts spendete.
Die andere tat nichts dergleichen.
Sie wissen vielleicht nicht, welche von beiden für den Umweltschutz spendete, aber Elefanten vergessen nie etwas.
Unterstützen Sie die Natur im Büro, indem Sie am Gehaltsabzugsprogramm zugunsten der Umwelt teilnehmen.
Einblendung: Environmental Federation of California.
Informationen unter 1 800 368 1819.

The Only Fur, S. 124
Überschrift: Der einzige Pelz, den ich trage, ohne mich zu schämen.
Text: International Fund for Animal Welfare (Internationaler Tierschutzbund).

Hatchet, S. 125

Whales, S. 126
Stimme aus dem Off:
Die Wale wollen das Gleiche wie wir: in Freiheit und Frieden leben, sich ohne Probleme vermehren. Heute ist ihr Überleben jedoch mehr denn je gefährdet. Greenpeace hat sich von Anfang an dafür eingesetzt, sie vor dem Aussterben zu bewahren.
Helfen Sie Greenpeace.
06 57 82 484.

Water Cooler, S. 128
Überschrift: Bewahren Sie die Opfer von Hurrikan Mitch vor Austrocknung – mit nur 12 Dollar.
Text: Helfen Sie UNICEF in Notfällen helfen. Rufen Sie 1800 025 192 an.

Year of the., S. 129
Überschrift: Jahr des ...
Text: Der Tiger ist im Begriff vernichtet zu werden. Sein völliges Aussterben ist eine ganz reale Möglichkeit. WWF, der World Wide Fund for Nature, setzt sich mit aller Kraft dafür ein, den Tiger in allen seinen Lebensbereichen zu schützen, und kämpft daher auch gegen Entwaldung und den illegalen Handel mit seinen Körperteilen. Helfen Sie uns in diesem Jahr des Tigers nach Kräften, den Tiger am Leben zu erhalten und wieder in die Schlagzeilen zu bringen.
Weitere Informationen unter Tel. 703 3772.

Last Water in Rwanda, S. 139
Überschrift: Der letzte Tropfen Wasser in Ruanda.
Text: Millionen von Flüchtlingen aus Ruanda brauchen dringend Trinkwasser – ebenso dringend wie Essen, Medizin und Luft zum Atmen.

Going, Going, Gone, S. 131
Toneffekte: Afrikanische Musik und Trommeln. Trompetenstöße von Elefanten.
Einblendung: Eins
Toneffekte: Aus dem Getrommel werden Schüsse.
Einblendung: Zwei
Einblendung: Drei und du bist weg!
Einblendung: Auslöschung ist für immer. Lass es nicht dazu kommen.

Zaire, S. 132
Toneffekte: Geräusch fallender Blutstropfen (konstant)
Sprecher: Zaire. Zaire blutet. Wir sind Ärzte ohne Grenzen. Helfen Sie uns!

War on Hunger, S. 134
Toneffekte: Schlachtengetümmel.
Einblendung: Krieg dem Hunger.
Telefood '98.

Speed Kills, S. 138
Text: Raserei tötet.

Glasses, S. 140
Toneffekte: Stück für Stück werden Gläser auf einen Tisch gestellt.
Einblendung: Jedes Glas, das Sie leeren, bevor Sie sich ans Steuer setzen, beeinträchtigt Ihr Reaktionsvermögen.
Toneffekte: Bremsgeräusche, quietschende Reifen und Krach eines Zusammenstoßes
Einblendung: Kein Alkohol am Steuer!

Ash, S. 142
Überschrift: Die Asche von nur einer Zigarette.
Text: Der Straßenrand ist kein Aschenbecher!

Stripes, S. 144
Überschrift: Nur ein Hornochse lässt einem Zebra nicht den Vortritt.
Text: Fahrlässiges Fahren tötet.

Just Sit There, S. 145
Überschrift: Jeden Tag und alle Tage da sitzen?
So sieht's aus – im Gefängnis.
Mütter gegen Alkohol am Steuer.

The Censor, S. 146
Einblendung: Der Zensor
Mann: Halt!
Zeigen Sie mir das Stück noch mal.
Los, los ... beeilen Sie sich!
Nein, nein, nein, nein, lassen Sie das weg.
Das dürfen Sie nicht tun.
Nein, nein, nein. Das ist nicht gestattet.
Hören Sie damit auf!
Lassen Sie das weg!
Lassen Sie's!
Das ist nicht erlaubt, das wissen Sie.
Lassen Sie das weg!
Das – das – und das auch.
Nun, machen Sie weiter, weiter-weiter.
Tanzen Sie.
Halt! Warum tanzen Sie nicht?
Nennen Sie das einen Tanz?
Hören Sie auf, Anspielungen dulde ich nicht.
Sprecher: Dieses Ministück des tschechischen Autors Ivan Kraus wurde in seinem eigenen Land von der Zensur verboten und im Index on Censorship veröffentlicht, einer Zeitschrift, die diesen Künstlern ein Forum bietet und die Unterdrückung aufdeckt, unter der Künstler in aller Welt zu leiden haben. Index ist für den zensierten Künstler – und für Sie.
Einblendung: Index on Censorship.

Free Press, S. 148
Überschrift: Freie Presse
Text: Artikel 19

Spaniel, S. 149
Text: Ich werde deinen Mercedes nicht anpinkeln.
Ich werde den Pizzaboten nicht ins Bein beißen.
Ich werde meinen Knochen nicht unter deinem Kopfkissen verstecken.
Ich werde nicht mitten in der Nacht unter dem Kissen nach Knochen suchen.
Ich werde dir nicht ins Gesicht sabbern, nachdem ich meinen Allerwertesten abgeschleckt habe.
Adoptieren Sie ein gut erzogenes Haustier vom SPCA (Tierschutzverein)!
Tel. 287 53 55.

Dog and Gun, S. 150
Toneffekte: Während des ganzen Spots singt eine Kinderstimme: How much is that doggie in the window, the one with the waggly tail. How much is that doggie in the window, I do hope that doggie's for sale. (Wie viel kostet der Hund im Schaufenster, der mit dem wedelnden Schwanz ... Ich hoffe, man kann ihn kaufen.)
Einblendung: 92 Pence pro Tag
£6,44 pro Woche
£27,50 pro Monat
£330 pro Jahr
£3.630 ein Leben lang
Sprecher: Bevor Sie jemandem einen Hund zu Weihnachten schenken, machen Sie die Rechnung auf.
Einblendung: RSPCA (Britischer Tierschutzbund).

Light Bulb (Glühbirne), S. 151
Sprecher: Das kann passieren, wenn Sie ohne Helm Fahrrad fahren.
Wenn Sie einen Helm tragen, kann das nicht passieren.
Tragen Sie einen Schutzhelm und behalten Sie Ihren Kopf!
Einblendung: Barcelona Stadtrat
Barcelona – mehr denn je zuvor.

Don't Piss..., S. 152
Überschrift: Wirf dein Leben nicht weg!
Mütter gegen Alkohol am Steuer.

Vote No, S. 153
Überschrift: Der Nein-Himmel.
Text: Schauen Sie her! Das ist der Himmel derer, die jährlich Tausende von Vögeln töten – als Sport. Der Himmel derer, die versuchen das Referendum zum Jagdverbot zu stoppen. Aber auch der Himmel all der Trägen oder Gleichgültigen, die am 3. Juni nicht wählen gehen. Schauen Sie genau hin, denn dieser leblose Himmel wird morgen auch Ihr Himmel sein.

Vote Yes, S. 153
Überschrift: Der Ja-Himmel.
Text: Stimmen Sie am 3. Juni mit Ja, um die Vogeljagd zu verbieten. Die Ergebnisse können Sie dann am Himmel ablesen. Schauen Sie genau hin: Dies ist der Himmel derer, die sich jeden Tag zum Schutz der Natur einsetzen. Der Himmel derjenigen, die wissen, dass das Jagdverbot in Italien die Eröffnung einer ganz neuen wunderbaren Saison bedeutet. Verleihen Sie den Werten, an die Sie glauben, Flügel: Stimmen Sie am 3. Juni mit Ja. Die Ergebnisse können Sie dann am Himmel ablesen.

Poached Elephant (Von Wilderern erschossener Elefant), S. 154
Toneffekte: Klassische Musik
Einblendung: Pochierter Fisch
Einblendung: Verlorenes Ei
Einblendung: Verlorener Elefant
Toneffekte: Musik hört auf
Toneffekte: Gewehrschuss
Einblendung: Elfenbein
Einblendung: Lassen Sie nicht zu, dass sie von neuem abgeschlachtet werden.
Einblendung: Kaufen Sie es nicht. Verkaufen Sie es nicht. Tragen Sie es nicht. Verwenden Sie es nicht.

Abbandono (Ausgesetzt), S. 156
Sprecher: Was wäre, wenn die UNS aussetzen würden?
Wenn sie es wären, die UNS zu einem Sommer verdammen würden, den man keinem Hund zumuten kann?
Einblendung: Wer Tiere aussetzt, ist eine Bestie!

Power of One, S. 155
Einblendung: Es ist noch gar nicht so lange her, da wollte eine Frau aus Alabama vorne im Bus sitzen.
Einblendung: Und ein sanfter Mann aus Indien wollte das öffentliche Bewusstsein wecken, ohne die Stimme zu erheben.
Einblendung: In Ostdeutschland wollte ein Mann frei sein.
Einblendung: Und eine Frau reiste durch die ganze Welt und gab denen Hoffnung, die keine mehr hatten.
Einblendung: Das ist eine Einerpotenz.
Einblendung: Um ihr Zuhause im Amazonasgebiet zu schützen.
Einblendung: Um die afrikanischen Berggorillas vor Wilderern zu schützen.
Einblendung: Um Sattelrobben im finnischen Nordmeer zu retten.
Einblendung: Oder sich um die Umwelt vor der eigenen Haustür zu kümmern.
Einblendung: Einerpotenz – Es liegt in der Macht jedes Einzelnen, etwas zu tun.
Einblendung: Alles Mögliche.
Einblendung: Earth Communications Office.

Brains, S. 163
Text: Afrikaner
Europäer
Asiate
Rassist
Europäische Jugendkampagne gegen Rassismus – unterstützt von der Kommission für Rassengleichheit.

Scars, S. 164
Überschriften: In Asien
In Afrika
In Amerika
In Europa
Text: Wir sind da, wo es Kriege, Epidemien und Naturkatastrophen gibt. Seit 25 Jahren vernähen wir jeden Tag die Wunden der Welt.
Medici senza frontiere (Ärzte ohne Grenzen), via Ostiense 6/E,
Tel. 06 573 00 900, Fax 06 573 00 902,
Rom c.c.p. 874 86007.

Them (Die da), S. 166
1. Mann: Sorry.
2. Mann: Ist schon o.k., Mann.
Ich finde, man sollte die da alle wieder dahin zurückschicken, wo sie hergekommen sind, wa?
Sprecherin: Ausnahmsweise wollen wir ihm seinen Wunsch erfüllen ...
2. Mann: Pakistanis, Juden, Italiener ...
Sprecherin: ... und mal sehen, was in Großbritannien passiert, wenn ... Tausende von „denen da" die Krankenhäuser verlassen.
Tausende von „denen da" die Redaktionen verlassen.
Tausende von „denen da" die Baustellen verlassen.
Tausende von „denen da" die Schulen verlassen.
Tausende von „denen da" ihre Läden schließen.
Hunderte von „denen da" ihre Fabriken schließen und Tausende arbeitslos machen.
Hunderte von „denen da" aufhören, als Sportler für Großbritannien zu kämpfen.
Tausende von „denen da" die Finanzwelt verlassen.
... und die Opfer, die Millionen von ihnen gebracht haben, vergessen sind.
2. Mann: Schick sie alle nach Hause. Das wär doch geil, wa!?
2. Mann: Ich hätt' jetzt Lust auf 'nen Curry, du auch?
Einblendung: Die da? Die da sind wir alle.

Openings, S. 168
Überschrift: Wer sagt, Angehörige ethnischer Minderheiten kriegen keine Jobs? Möglichkeiten gibt's überall.
Text: Toilettenfrau. Büroreinigungskraft. Irgendjemand muss ja all die schlecht bezahlte, „niedrige" Arbeit tun, warum sind das aber so oft die Angehörigen anderer Volksgruppen? Vorurteile, Rassendiskriminierung und Mobbing verbauen ihnen die Wahl des Berufs, den sie verdient haben. Das ist ungerecht und unfair. Mehr noch, das bedeutet eine ungeheure Verschwendung an britischen Talenten.

Es ist heutzutage sowieso schwer, einen Ausbildungsplatz und dann eine qualifizierte Arbeit zu bekommen.

Für Angehörige ethnischer Minderheiten ist es noch schwerer.

Obwohl die Qualifikationen zählen, sind häufig mehr Angehörige ethnischer Minderheiten arbeitslos als Weiße. Sie müssen sich öfter bewerben, bis sie eine Stelle finden. Eine Umfrage ergab kürzlich, dass eine von drei befragten Firmen schwarzen oder asiatischen Bewerbern ein Vorstellungsgespräch verweigerten, während sie weiße Bewerber mit den gleichen Qualifikationen dazu einluden.

Wenn sie doch eine Stelle finden, haben Angehörige ethnischer Minderheiten es oft schwerer befördert zu werden als ihre weißen Kollegen. Die Zahl britischer Manager mit dunklerer Hautfarbe ist unverhältnismäßig klein. In einem großen Verkehrsunternehmen sind zum Beispiel 30 Prozent der Beschäftigten ausländischer Herkunft, aber nur drei Prozent der leitenden Angestellten.

Noch dazu sind diese ethnischen Minderheiten am Arbeitsplatz rassistischen Belästigungen ausgesetzt. Wenn sie sich darüber beschweren, bekommen sie oft zu hören, sie müssten das als Teil ihrer Arbeit hinnehmen. Traurigerweise akzeptieren es die meisten.

Alle, die es nicht hinnehmen, müssen ihren Arbeitgeber vielleicht sogar vor Gericht verklagen, wo sie harte Fakten als Beweis für ihre Klage beizubringen haben. Ob sie nun ihren Fall gewinnen oder nicht, auf jeden Fall müssen sie wohl mit der schwierigen Jobsuche ganz von vorn anfangen. Kein Wunder, dass Angehörige ethnischer Minderheiten solche Mühe gehabt haben, in Großbritannien vorwärts zu kommen.

So schlimm die Situation auch scheinen mag, einiges hat sich zum Guten verändert. Eine Frau, die in den fünfziger Jahren aus Westindien einwanderte, um für British Rail zu arbeiten, erinnert sich: „Es war die Hölle. In den ersten zehn Jahren hat sich keiner während der Frühstückspause neben mich gesetzt. Man bekam den schlimmsten Job, kriegte weniger Geld und keinerlei Ausbildung. Man wurde beleidigt. Überall hingen Schilder mit ‚No Nigger'. So war das damals, als es noch kein Gesetz dagegen gab."

Zum Glück sind die Gesetze geändert worden. 1976 trat das Gesetz über Rassenbeziehungen (Race Relations Act) in Kraft, das es einem Arbeitgeber verbietet, Bewerber/Angestellte aufgrund von Hautfarbe, Rassenzugehörigkeit, ethnischer oder nationaler Herkunft zu diskriminieren.

Das Gesetz machte sicherlich der ganz offenkundigen Diskriminierung ein Ende (etwa den ‚No Nigger'-Schildern). Es hat jedoch nicht die unterschwellige Diskriminierung gestoppt, die zum Beispiel so aussieht, dass der Arbeitgeber sagt: „Tut uns Leid, wir haben schon jemanden, der für den Job besser qualifiziert ist." – selbst wenn er niemanden hat. Oder wenn ein Abteilungsleiter der Geschäftsführung gegenüber zu erwähnen „vergisst", dass jemand eigentlich befördert werden müsste.

Das ist Diskriminierung. Sie ist subtil, vielleicht nicht einmal bewusst beabsichtigt, und wirkt doch sehr entmutigend. Stellen Sie sich einmal vor, dass Ihnen immer wieder gesagt wird, Sie seien für diese Stelle nicht genügend qualifiziert, wenn Sie genau wissen, dass Sie es sind!

Was können Sie dagegen tun? In einem besonders klaren, krassen Fall wenden Sie sich an die Kommission für Rassengleichheit. Wir sind eine vom Innenministerium finanzierte unabhängige Körperschaft, deren Aufgabe es ist, jede Art von Rassendiskriminierung zu beseitigen. Wir helfen Opfern von Diskriminierung durch Industriegerichte. (Und zwar nicht nur denen mit anderer Hautfarbe. Wir hatten auch mit Fällen zu tun, in denen weiße Arbeiter von ihren schwarzen oder asiatischen Arbeitgebern diskriminiert wurden.)

Wir arbeiten auch mit den Gewerkschaften zusammen in ihrem Kampf gegen Rassendiskriminierung und Belästigung in ihren eigenen Reihen und am Arbeitsplatz.

Ebenso qualifizierte Berater finden Sie in Ihrem Racial Equality Council vor Ort und in Ihrer Bürgerberatungsstelle.

Wir helfen vielen Firmen dabei, eine Politik gleicher Chancen für alle zu verfolgen, die jeder Diskriminierung von vornherein das Wasser abgräbt.

Wenn Sie mit jemandem darüber reden wollen, wie diese Politik auch in Ihrer Firma umgesetzt werden könnte, schreiben Sie uns an die unten angegebene Adresse.

Auf diese Weise werden wir den Rassismus besiegen. Nicht durch Gewalt, sondern indem wir einander als gleichwertig achten. Indem wir offen werden. Für uns selbst und für die jetzt heranwachsende Generation wäre das die größte Chance überhaupt.

Criminal Isn't It?, S. 170
Überschrift: Kriminell, oder?
Text: Autodiebstahl, 9 Monate
Autodiebstahl, 18 Monate.

Junk Mail, S. 171
Überschrift: Und Sie ärgern sich über Werbewurfsendungen!

Ethnic Cleansing, S. 172
Überschrift: Diskussionen über ethnische Säuberungen. Klingt das nicht irgendwie bekannt?
Text: Machen Sie den Verbrechen serbischer Nationalisten gegen die Menschheit ein Ende!

Next Generation, S. 173
Überschrift: Ihnen ist es vielleicht gleichgültig, ob jüdisches Leben sich auch noch in der nächsten Generation fortsetzt. Ihm nicht!
Text: Das Judentum besteht seit Tausenden von Jahren. Der Faschismus überstand nur siebzig, in denen er allerdings großes Unheil anrichtete. Die Alarmglocken läuten noch immer und sie alle warnen: Werden Sie nicht gleichgültig! Deshalb spielt die JIA eine so wichtige Rolle. Wir müssen jederzeit und überall auf der Welt der Verfolgung von Juden entgegentreten. Wir müssen auf jede Bedrohung gefasst sein. Wir tun das, indem wir der Jewish Agency Mittel zur Verfügung stellen, damit sie überall Juden retten und nach Israel in Sicherheit bringen kann.

Wenn sie dort ankommen, helfen wir ihnen, ein neues Leben mit neuen Möglichkeiten aufzubauen. Israel besitzt den Schlüssel zu unser aller Zukunft. Helfen Sie uns dabei, der nächsten Generation beizubringen, wie wichtig Israel ist und wie wichtig es ist, dass wir jüdisches Leben überall auf der Welt bewahren.

Unterstützen Sie die JIA, indem Sie uns noch heute unter 0345 585 004 anrufen und mit uns besprechen, wie Sie helfen können. Vielleicht glauben Sie gar nicht, dass man Sie braucht. Wir schon.

Saddam, p. 174
Überschrift: Wenn Sie keine Kurden als Flüchtlinge in Ihrem Land wollen, schicken Sie sie zu mir zurück!
Text: Saddam Hussein, Slobodan Milosevic, Pol Pot, Adolf Hitler.
Die Namen ändern sich – die Verbrechen gegen die Menschheit bleiben gleich.

Die UN Flüchtlingskonvention von 1951 war eine direkte Reaktion auf den Holocaust. Damit bekannte sich die weltweite Staatengemeinschaft zu ihrer Verpflichtung, allen Zuflucht zu gewähren, die in ihrer Heimat der Folter und Verfolgung oder dem sicheren Tod preisgegeben wären.

Großbritannien gehörte zu den ersten Unterzeichnerländern. Es ist vielleicht altmodisch, wenn man sich an eine 50 Jahre alte Vereinbarung hält. Leider kommen Giftgas, Konzentrationslager und ethnische Säuberungen nie aus der Mode.
www.refugeecouncil.org.uk oder
Tel. 0171 820 3055.

No Flag, S. 175
Überschrift: Nicht mal 'ne Fahne als Zudecke
Text: Rotes Kreuz Kurdenhilfe
Rufen Sie (01) 76 68 77 oder (01) 76 51 35 an, um zu spenden.

Equals, S. 177
Dieser Spot ist das Ergebnis der Bemühungen von 14 Werbefilmern, die sich erboten, zu einem einzigen Wort wie „essen", „arbeiten", „Religion", „Schlaf" etc. einen 8-Sekunden-Film in Schwarz-weiß zu drehen, in dem sie die Bedeutung dieses Wortes in Bezug auf „Gleichheit" interpretierten.
Einblendung: Commission for Racial Equality (Kommission für Rassengleichheit).
Einblendung: 1997 Europäisches Jahr gegen Rassismus, gefördert vom britischen Innenministerium.

Shattered Dreams, S. 180
Einblendung: Sie können etwas gegen Gewalt in der Familie tun.
Rufen Sie die Polizei!

Flowers, S. 183
Text: David bringt mir Blumen
und sagt mir, dass er mich liebt.
Ich will ihm glauben.
Meine Freunde sagen, ich bin blöd.
Aber sie kennen David nicht.
David bringt mir Blumen
und sagt mir, es tut ihm Leid,
wenn er die Beherrschung verliert
und mich aus Versehen trifft.
Meine Freunde sagen, ich bin blöd.
Aber sie kennen David nicht.
Letzte Nacht schlug er mich.
Alles ist ganz verschwommen.
Und meine Freunde hatten Recht.
Aber David bringt mir Blumen.
Wenn Sie in Ihrer Beziehung unter Gewalt zu leiden haben, können Sie mit uns sprechen. Rufen Sie einfach an unter: 213 626 33 93.
Wir – das ist die Los Angeles Commission on Assaults Against Women, und wir können helfen.

Scream, S. 183
Überschrift: Die Schimpfworte, mit denen Sie Ihre Kinder anschreien, bleiben in Ihrer Familie bis ins dritte und vierte Glied.
Text: Du bist nicht zu gebrauchen. Du bist dumm. Ich wünschte, du wärest nie auf die Welt gekommen.

Wenn Sie Ihre Kinder so beschimpfen, tun Sie ihnen nicht nur weh, sondern bringen Ihnen auch bei, später ihre eigenen Kinder so zu behandeln. Brechen Sie aus diesem Teufelskreis aus! Rufen Sie 0800 22 29 99 an, wenn Sie eine Gratisbroschüre für Eltern haben möchten, die Ihnen weiterhelfen wird.

Vicious Circle, S. 184
1. Szene
Mann: Denkst du etwa, ich geh' nur mit meinen Kumpels aus, um dir das Leben zur Hölle zu machen?
Frau: Halt die Klappe!
Mann: Denkst du das, hä?
Frau: Halt die Klappe!
Mann: Wann hast du mich das letzte Mal umarmt?
Frau: Lass mich in Ruhe.
Mann: Steht irgendwo auf meinem Gesicht, dass ich scheiß-unsichtbar bin, was?
Frau: Nein. Nein. Nein.
Mann: Unsichtbar, hä?
Frau: Lass mich in Ruhe!
Mann: Bin ich etwa unsichtbar?
Frau: Halt's Maul und lass mich in Ruhe!
Mann: Hör zu, ich hau' jetzt ab, werd' einen abhotten.

2. Szene
Mann: Denkst du etwa, ich geh' nur mit meinen Kumpels aus, um dir das Leben zur Hölle zu machen?
Frau: Halt die Klappe!
Mann: Denkst du das, hä?
Frau: Halt die Klappe!
Mann: Wann hast du mich das letzte Mal umarmt?
Frau: Lass mich in Ruhe.
Mann: Steht irgendwo auf meinem Gesicht, dass ich scheiß-unsichtbar bin, was?
Frau: Nein. Nein. Nein.
Mann: Unsichtbar, hä?
Frau: Halt's Maul!

3. Szene
Mann: Denkst du etwa, ich geh' nur mit meinen Kumpels aus, um dir das Leben zur Hölle zu machen?
Frau: Halt die Klappe!
Mann: Denkst du das, hä?
Einblendung: Es liegt an Ihnen, den Teufelskreis zu durchbrechen. Mehr Information gibt's unter 0800 222 999.

Fading Fast, S. 190
Überschrift: Mein Bild verblasst rasch. Genau wie ich auch.
Text: Von Tag zu Tag bin ich hilfloser, weil meine Muskeln schwinden. Meine Krankheit ist unheilbar, und für mich gibt es keine Hoffnung mehr. Ich möchte aber, dass es noch Hoffnung für andere gibt. Deshalb bitte ich Sie: Geben Sie eine Spende, damit andere Menschen mit MNS leben und wieder andere die Krankheit erforschen können.
Motor Neurone Disease Association, P.O. Box 246, Northampton NN1 1TR.
Eingetragener Verein Nr. 294354.

Walkies (Gassi gehen), S. 194
Frau: Komm, mein Schatz. Gassi gehen! Komm, komm!
Nun komm schon, Roger!
Sprecher: Das ist vielleicht eine böse Überraschung für Sie, aber Menschen brauchen ebenso viel Bewegung wie Hunde.
Wenn Sie nur einige längere Spaziergänge machen würden, wäre das schon ein Anfang.
Höchstwahrscheinlich wird es Ihnen sogar gefallen.
Frau: Hier, Roger, fass!
Sprecher: Wenn Sie erst einmal angefangen haben, werden Ihr Herz, Ihre Lungen und Muskeln leistungsfähiger. Ihre depressive Stimmung verschwindet, und Sie fühlen sich wie neu geboren.
Frau: Lauf-lauf-lauf!
Sprecher: Sie packen alles mit mehr Energie an. Und es kommt mehr dabei heraus.
Frau: Hierher, Roger, bei Fuss!
Sprecher: Ein paar Minuten Bewegung jeden Tag – und Ihr Leben wird lebendiger. Tun Sie etwas für Ihre Gesundheit!
Einblendung: Tun Sie etwas für Ihre Gesundheit!

Naledi/Crying Girl, S. 196
Überschrift: Für's Leben gezeichnet – und das von einem Auto, das sie um Meilen verfehlt hat!
Text: Naledi lag sicher in ihrem Bettchen, als ihr Papa betrunken von der Schnapsbude nach Hause torkelte. Er hat gar nichts mehr gespürt, aber sie wird den Rest ihres Lebens darunter leiden. Achten Sie auf Ihre Schritte!

Scrambled Page, S. 197
Überschrift: MS bringt die Botschaften durcheinander, die das Gehirn an den Körper sendet.
Text: MS kann jeden Teil Ihres Körpers durcheinander bringen, jeden Aspekt Ihres Lebens. Jederzeit.
Mit unserer MS-Woche wollen wir die Krankheit bekannter machen und (hoffentlich) Spenden sammeln, damit wir diese unberechenbare Krankheit besser bekämpfen können.
Für mehr Informationen über Multiple Sklerose rufen Sie kostenlos die MS-Hotline an: 0808 800 8000.
Die MS-Gesellschaft gibt Kraft zum Kampf gegen MS.

Pin, S. 198
Überschrift: Was ist Multiple Sklerose? Schließen Sie die Augen und stechen Sie für den Rest Ihres Lebens jeden Tag eine Reißzwecke in diese Seite!
Text: Heute haben Sie am ganzen Körper Schmerzen.
Heute haben Sie kein Gefühl in den Fingern.
Heute haben Sie Muskelspasmen.
Heute können Sie Ihr linkes Bein nicht bewegen.
Heute können Sie nicht Auto fahren.
Heute können Sie nicht Treppen steigen.
Heute fühlen Sie sich wohl.
Heute sind Sie impotent.
Heute können Sie nicht richtig sehen.
Heute haben Sie Gleichgewichtsstörungen.
Heute können Sie Ihr rechtes Bein nicht bewegen.
Heute haben Sie kein Gefühl in den Fingern.
Heute können Sie sich nicht konzentrieren.
Heute haben Sie am ganzen Körper Schmerzen.
Heute fühlen Sie sich pudelwohl.
Heute haben Sie ein Gefühl, als ob Fische in Ihrem ganzen Körper herumschwimmen.
Heute können Sie nur gedämpft hören.
Heute können Sie sich gar nicht bewegen.
Heute können Sie das Zittern nicht unterdrücken.
Heute können Sie nicht sprechen.
Heute können Sie Ihre Zehen nicht spüren.
Heute können Sie Ihren rechten Arm nicht bewegen.
Heute sind Sie inkontinent.
Heute sind Sie taub.
Heute können Sie Ihre Füße nicht spüren.
Heute fühlen Sie sich wohl.
Heute können Sie sich gar nicht bewegen.
Heute können Sie das Zittern nicht unterdrücken.
Heute können Sie nicht sprechen.
Heute haben Sie kein Gefühl in den Fingern.
Heute sind Sie müde.
Heute können Sie nicht Treppen steigen.
Multiple Sklerose (MS) ist eine Krankheit, die das Zentrale Nervensystem angreift. Von einem Tag zum andern weiß man nie, welcher Körperteil wie stark davon betroffen ist. Jeder kann an MS erkranken, und wir möchten, dass Sie mehr darüber wissen. Wenn Sie das auch möchten oder spenden wollen, rufen Sie uns rund um die Uhr unter 0800 100 133 an.
Die MS-Gesellschaft gibt Kraft zum Kampf gegen MS.

Me No Fry, S. 200
Überschrift: Ich nix Braten.
NSW Health. Für mehr Gesundheit.

Eclipse (Totale Sonnenfinsternis), S. 201
Überschrift: Es ist die Gelegenheit, die du nie wieder bekommst. Verpasse sie!

Come and see us, S. 202
Überschrift: Besuchen Sie uns doch mal!
Text: Die Heilung für Brustkrebs heißt Vorsorge.

Flies on Food, S. 204
Text: Folgendes geschieht, wenn eine Fliege auf Ihrem Essen landet:
Fliegen können keine feste Nahrung aufnehmen, deshalb kotzen sie erst einmal drauf und stampfen ihre Kotze (und meistens auch ein paar Bazillen) so lange ein, bis das Feste sich verflüssigt hat. Wenn es dann so richtig schön schleimig ist, schlürfen sie es weg, wobei sie höchstwahrscheinlich hinten einen kleinen Fliegenschiss fallen lassen. Und wenn die Fliegen aufgegessen haben, sind Sie dran!
Decken Sie Ihre Nahrungsmittel ab.
Decken Sie Geschirr und Essbesteck ab.
Decken Sie Mülltonnen ab.

Scrub your Lungs, S. 205
Überschrift: Sie können Ihre Lungen nicht sauber schrubben.
Text: Lungenkrebs tötet dreizehnmal mehr Raucher als Nichtraucher.

Lethal Weapon, S. 206
Überschrift: Ihr Auto ist eine tödliche Waffe.
Text: Fahren Sie vorsichtig!
Im Interesse der Umwelt im UAE veröffentlicht.

3 More Days, S. 207
Überschrift: Nur noch drei Tage bis zum „Anti-Landminen-Tag".
Text: Statistik der Verzweiflung:
110 Millionen Landminen in 64 Ländern der Welt – 1 Opfer alle 20 Minuten von 5 bis 10 Millionen produzierten Landminen pro Jahr – 100 Millionen weitere Landminen lagern in den Waffenkammern der Welt – 90 Prozent der Opfer sind Frauen und Kinder.

Zahlen der Hoffnung: Konto Nr. 189241, Postbank Mani Tese, Italienische Kampagne gegen Landminen, via Cavengahi 4, I–20149 Mailand.

Kommen Sie am Samstag, 13. April, zur Piazza Santi Apostoli, um unsere Petition zu unterzeichnen und Ihren Beitrag zu leisten.

Landmines in Cambodia, S. 128
Überschrift: Kann eine Landmine für nur 3 Dollar eine ganze Wirtschaft lahm legen?
Text: Sie kann es, wenn die Bauern zu viel Angst vor ihr haben, um ihr Feld zu pflügen – wenn Kinder zu viel Angst haben, um zur Schule zu gehen – wenn die einfachsten täglichen Verrichtungen zum russischen Roulette werden. Zusätzlich zu den bereits verlegten 110 Millionen Landminen in der Dritten Welt werden jedes Jahr weitere 2 Millionen vergraben. Helfen Sie mit bei der Abschaffung von Landminen. Nur so kommt die Dritte Welt einen Schritt weiter. Wenn Sie wissen möchten, wie Sie helfen können, schreiben Sie an Ihre Landesregierung oder die Abteilung Mine Clearance and Policy, Dept. of Humanitarian Affairs, United Nations, New York, N.Y. 10017.

Unleaded, S. 209
Überschrift: Pumpen Sie unsere Kinder nicht mit Blei voll!
Text: Tanken Sie bleifrei!
Im Interesse der Umwelt im UAE veröffentlicht.

Pavement, S. 210
Überschrift: Auf dem Bürgersteig ist es noch ekliger!
Text: Wenn Ihr Hund sein Geschäft auf der Straße erledigt, bringen Sie das bitte wieder in Ordnung!

Atomic Bomb, S. 211
Text: Internationale Zusammenarbeit hat Erstaunliches geleistet, um uns alle mit der totalen Vernichtung zu bedrohen. Heute kann sie vielleicht die Situation entschärfen. Wenn Sie sich jemals gewünscht haben, Sie könnten die Welt verbessern, ist das Ihre Chance: Leisten Sie einen Beitrag zum Thema auf unserer Website, 27. Oktober bis 1. November, www.worldforum.org.

Leaf/Match, S. 212
Überschrift: Lassen Sie keine feuergefährlichen Dinge herumliegen!

Off Duty (Arbeitsfrei), S. 213
Mann: Wir sind seit 18 Jahren verheiratet.
Frau: Im Allgemeinen war unser Leben schön und friedlich.
Mann: Wir waren mit unseren eigenen Dingen beschäftigt.
Frau: Jeden Tag arbeiten, nach Hause kommen, Kinder erziehen. Nichts Besonderes. Als er arbeitslos wurde ...
Mann: Das kam so plötzlich. Ich war wie gelähmt.
Frau: Die Angst stand ihm im Gesicht. Er hatte Tränen in den Augen.
Mann: Als Erstes ging meine Selbstachtung flöten. Das Einzige, was mir einfiel, war mein Elend in Alkohol zu ertränken.
Frau: Er braucht meine Hilfe.
Mann: Sie hat mich immer ermutigt.
Frau: Mach dir keine Sorgen. Es wird alles wieder gut.
Mann: Arbeitslosigkeit war das Beste, was uns passieren konnte.
Frau: Wir waren uns noch nie so nahe wie jetzt.
Mann: An meinem Geburtstag ...
Frau: ... kaufte ich ihm ein Paar Schuhe, ...
Mann: Neue Schuhe!
Frau: ... damit du in eine ganz neue Welt voller Möglichkeiten eintreten konntest. Er war sehr gerührt.
Mann: Ich war zu Tränen gerührt. Die neue Arbeit ist besser. Na ja, jedenfalls besser als gar keine Arbeit. Solange wir ein Herz und eine Seele sind, ist alles andere unwichtig.
Einblendung: Ihre Unterstützung ist seine Stärke.

Chain Letter, S. 216
Text:
Lieber Eric,
bei uns ist ein Virus ausgebrochen, an dem jede Woche ein Mensch stirbt. Es wird durch verseuchtes Blut oder sexuellen Kontakt übertragen. Sicher weißt du, wovon ich spreche. HIV und schließlich AIDS.

Das können wir nur stoppen, indem wir die gute Nachricht verbreiten, und zwar noch schneller, als das Virus sich ausbreitet.

Die gute Nachricht ist das Kondom. Benutze es, und du bist beim Sex sicher. So einfach ist das.

Kopiere diesen Brief sechsmal und schick ihn an alle, von denen du annimmst, dass sie die Welt ein bisschen heller machen könnten. Es muss dir nicht peinlich sein. Wir alle könnten eine Erinnerung gut gebrauchen.

Wenn du diesen Brief noch diese Woche an sechs Leute schickst und jeder von diesen sechs wieder an sechs weitere, werden Ende des Monats 7.776 Menschen besser informiert sein. Wenn du aber nichts tust, werden Ende des Jahres mehrere Millionen Menschen unsere Nachricht verpasst haben.

Wir schulden es allen Menschen, diese gute Nachricht weiterzusagen und so das Virus zu besiegen.

Unterschrieben von einem, dem es nicht egal ist.

PS: Wenn du es dir leisten kannst, der AIDS-Stiftung eine Spende zu schicken, wäre das sehr willkommen. Ihre Adresse lautet:
NZ AIDS Foundation
PO Box 7287
Wellington
Neuseeland

Slow Poison, S. 217
Titre : Poison lent.
Texte : Publié dans l'intérêt public par Tata Tea Limited.

Clean Up, S. 220
Aus dem Off: Morgen!
Schönes Wetter heute ...
Toneffekte: plätschernde, rutschende Laute
Schildinschrift: Sie würden so etwas nie tun.
Schildinschrift: Dann verbieten Sie es auch Ihrem Hund!

Anybody Out There?, S. 222
Sprecher: Ist da jemand?
Ist da jemand?
Ist da ... irgend ... jemand?
Ist da jemand?
Einblendung: JA.
Die Samariter.

Die and Live, S. 224
Überschrift: Ron war schon auf seinen Tod gefasst. Dann bekam er die schlimmste Nachricht von allen: „Sie werden leben."

Wie am Boden zerstört – das würde Ihnen sicher nicht passieren, was? Da sitzen Sie nun und wissen, dass Sie Krebs im Endstadium haben, und dann erschlagen die Ärzte Sie wie ein Blitz aus heiterem Himmel mit der Nachricht: „Die Behandlung hat angeschlagen, der Krebs ist ausgemerzt. Sie werden leben." Das war wie ein Todesstoß. Es hätte keine schlimmere Prognose geben können.

Man muss wissen, dass Rons Geschichte ziemlich einzigartig ist. Die meisten würden anders reagieren als er. Es gibt jedoch keine zwei Menschen, die genau gleich auf die Aussicht reagieren, dass sie sterben werden (in Rons Fall: leben werden).

Als bei Ron zum ersten Mal Krebs festgestellt wurde, war er natürlich zutiefst erschüttert. Es war die schlimmste Nachricht, die er jemals erhalten hatte. Mit der Zeit änderte sich seine Einstellung jedoch. Er akzeptierte sein Schicksal und begann sogar die eigene Beerdigung zu planen. Sein ganzes Leben war nur noch auf den Tod ausgerichtet. Und genau darin lag das Problem. Ron hatte sich nämlich so vollkommen auf sein Ableben eingestellt, dass er direkt damit zufrieden war.

Normalerweise ist diese Zufriedenheit das optimale Ergebnis unserer Arbeit. Es ist sehr gut, wenn ein sterbenskranker Patient diesen Zustand erreicht, was nicht oft vorkommt. Wir vom Mary Potter Hospiz haben das Gefühl, dass wir unser Bestes gegeben haben, wenn einer unserer Patienten diesen Punkt seiner inneren Entwicklung erreicht.

„Sie werden leben, Ron." Behalten Sie Ihre Kränze. Bestellen Sie den Leichenwagen ab. Das war doch bestimmt die beste aller Nachrichten für Ron, oder? Im Gegenteil! Er hatte sich so darauf konzentriert bald zu sterben, dass der Tod in gewisser Weise zu seinem Lebensgrund geworden war. Er hatte sich schon von vielen Menschen verabschiedet, sein Leben lief nur auf das wohl durchdachte Ende hinaus. Bald würde er „da oben" sein.

Und dann, mit einem einzigen grausamen Schlag, nahm man ihm das, wofür er lebte. Der Tod schlug ihm die Tür vor der Nase zu. Plötzlich waren alle Vorbereitungen und durchgestandenen Ängste umsonst gewesen. Ron hatte in seinem neu geschenkten Leben den Boden unter den Füßen verloren und wurde hypochondrisch. Er hatte es am Herzen, davon war er fest überzeugt. Natürlich hatte er nichts am Herzen, sondern im Kopf, und sein Gehirn (das wichtigste aller Organe) tat ein Übriges. Ron war ganz versessen darauf, sich Gründe dafür einzubilden, warum er bald sterben müsse. Mit dem Gedanken an den Tod fühlte er sich inzwischen am wohlsten. Er verließ sich auf all die neuen Hilfsdienste, die den Sterbenden zur Verfügung stehen. Er hatte sich an all die Zuwendung und Sympathie gewöhnt. Nicht, dass sie ihm Spaß machten, aber er brauchte sie. Und in diesem Zustand verbrachte er sein ganzes weiteres Leben.

Rons tragisches Schicksal war zum größten Teil selbst gemacht. Er kam zwar nie ins Mary Potter Hospiz, aber wir erfuhren seine (wahre) Geschichte von unserem Chefarzt (der ihn während seines Aufenthaltes in England betreut hatte), und sie ist beispielhaft für die Probleme, mit denen wir regelmäßig zu tun haben.

Außerdem können wir von Rons Fall auch lernen, wie wir Patienten behandeln oder nicht behandeln sollten. Manchmal kann sich nämlich eine Situation trotz einer Wendung zum Besseren wesentlich verschlimmern. So unberechenbar sind unsere Arbeitstage. Deshalb bemühen wir uns ständig, von den Rons dieser Welt zu lernen, damit sich Situationen wie seine nicht wiederholen.

Man sagt, es gebe nur zwei Dinge im Leben, die unausweichlich sind: der Tod und die Steuern. Während die Steuern leider nur zu genau im Voraus abgeschätzt werden können, ist der Tod nicht voraussagbar. Das belegt außer Rons Fall auch Nells Geschichte, allerdings am anderen Ende des Spektrums. Möglicherweise der vollkommene Tod. Petronella – Nell für ihre Freunde – kam aus der Gegend von Kapiti. Sie lag nur kurz im Mary Potter Hospiz. Als sie im Mai 1994 eingewiesen wurde, war sie Anfang 60 und hatte Krebstumore in Leber, Niere, Bauchspeicheldrüse und Magen. Schon 1989 hatte man ihr wegen Krebs eine Niere entfernt. Diesmal wurde ihr mitgeteilt, sie habe nur noch zwei Monate zu leben. Nell kam zu uns, weil sie unter starken Schmerzen und ständigem Erbrechen litt. Auch wir waren der Meinung, sie hätte nicht mehr lange zu leben, hüteten uns aber, uns zeitlich irgendwie festzulegen. Wenn wir eines gelernt haben, dann dies: Bei der Bestimmung der „Mindesthaltbarkeit" eines Menschen sollte man äußerst vorsichtig sein. Erstens ist es praktisch unmöglich, den Tod genau vorherzusagen, und zweitens könnte eine solche Prognose Reaktionen wie die von Ron hervorrufen.

Zunächst dachten wir, Nells Krebs wüte dermaßen, dass praktisch nichts mehr zu machen sei. Sie dachte das gar nicht, war sicher, ihre Schmerzen stammten von einer Muskelzerrung. Das stimmte natürlich nicht. Aber sie hatte auch das Gefühl, dass die ihr bislang verschriebenen Medikamente ihr nicht bekamen und sie daher so viel erbrechen musste, und das stimmte tatsächlich. Innerhalb von zwei Wochen konnten wir sie auf eine Schmerzmedikation einstellen, die kein Erbrechen verursachte. Sie wurde schmerzfrei nach Hause entlassen, wo viele Aufgaben auf sie warteten. Sie hatte immer noch Krebs, war immer noch unheilbar krank, hatte aber noch viel vor mit ihrem Leben.

Zunehmend erleben wir, dass unsere Patienten sich lieber ambulant behandeln lassen. Unsere Betten sind zwar immer noch voll belegt, weil die Patienten immer wieder stationär zu uns kommen, allerdings für kürzere Zeiten, um sich behandeln und neu auf Schmerzmedikation einstellen zu lassen. Danach kehren sie wieder nach Hause zurück, wo sie sich am wohlsten fühlen. Dazu ermutigen wir unsere Patienten, so oft es geht. Wenn sie nämlich zu früh ins Hospiz kommen, geben sie innerlich vielleicht auch früher auf und sterben eher. Zu Hause dagegen leben sie weiter wie zuvor und leben länger – genau wie Nell.

Es vergingen zwei Monate, dann drei, dann sechs. Nell hatte immer noch Spaß am Leben. Sie ging regelmäßig zu ihrem Hausarzt, und außerdem besuchte unser Hospizarzt sie alle paar Monate. Sie nahm auch pflanzliche Medikamente ein. Das beste Mittel war jedoch ihre positive Lebenseinstellung. Wenn sie ihr erstes Todesurteil akzeptiert und sich entschlossen hätte, im Mary Potter Hospiz zu bleiben, wäre sie möglicherweise schon bald gestorben. Zum Glück blieb sie nicht. Sie wollte zu Hause bei ihrem Mann bleiben.

Sie wollte auch zusammen mit ihrem Mann das Haus verlassen, und genau das taten sie oft, hängten den Wohnwagen an ihr Auto und bereisten ganz Neuseeland. Ganz anders als Ron ging Nell nicht in ihrem Tod auf, sondern in ihrem Leben. Ende 1995 tauchten Komplikationen auf: Nell hatte einen Darmverschluss. Selbst das konnte sie nicht aufhalten. Der Darmverschluss wurde operativ beseitigt, und Nell erholte sich rasch davon. Sechzehn Monate nach ihrem prognostizierten, aber nicht eingetretenen Tod war sie immer noch quicklebendig. Im Mai 1996 schließlich holte die Krankheit sie ein, mit Müdigkeit und Schmerzen. Diesmal erkannte Nell selber, dass sie nur noch wenig Zeit hatte. Sie konnte keine Tabletten mehr schlucken, sodass man ihr Schmerzmittel subkutan spritzen musste. Erst jetzt – zwei Jahre nach der ersten Todesprognose – fasste Nell den Entschluss, zum Sterben in unser Hospiz zurückzukehren.

Wir vermeiden es, wie gesagt, den Patienten mitzuteilen, wann sie unserer Meinung nach sterben werden. Es kommt häufig vor, dass die Patienten es uns selber sagen. Etwas tief in ihrem Innern sagt ihnen, wann es so weit ist. So war es auch bei Nell. Am Morgen ihres Todestages wusste sie, dass es ihr letzter Tag sein würde. Sie ließ ihre ganze Familie rufen und verabschiedete sich von jedem Einzelnen. Dann saßen alle um ihr Bett, und sie schlief friedlich ein.

Nell war eine bemerkenswerte Frau, immer freundlich und positiv, obwohl sie sieben Jahre lang mit dem Krebs leben musste. Alle Hospiz-Angestellten und Patienten, denen sie Mut zusprach, erinnern sich lebhaft an sie.

Seltsamerweise empfand sie ihre Krankheit nicht als beängstigend, sondern als befreiend. Sie wusste nicht, wie lange sie noch zu leben hatte, war aber fest entschlossen, das Beste aus jedem Tag zu machen. Einer von uns hat später bemerkt, sie habe dem Tod gegenüber die Frank-Sinatra-Haltung eingenommen: She did it her way – sie tat es auf ihre Weise.

Im Mary Potter Hospiz haben wir ein Mantra: Mach das Beste aus dem Leben. Nell hat uns gezeigt, dass das häufig nur außerhalb unserer Mauern möglich ist, weshalb wir auch an anderen Orten tätig sind. Mit großer Unterstützung durch die Lokalbevölkerung haben wir gerade eine Poliklinik im Gebiet von Kapiti gebaut. Und mit Ihrer Hilfe wird die diesjährige Straßensammlung es uns ermöglichen, noch mehr zu tun, um den Sterbenden (und allen, die dann doch nicht so schnell sterben) zu helfen, das Beste aus ihrem Leben zu machen.

Start Again, S. 227
Überschrift: Ein Schlaganfall ist nicht das Ende, nur alles noch mal auf Anfang.
Text: Es steht eins zu acht, dass Sie einmal einen Schlaganfall haben werden. Wenn Sie Raucher/-in sind, erhöht das Ihr Risiko natürlich um ein Fünffaches. Hoher Blutdruck tut's um das Vierfache. Und wenn Sie Raucher/-in mit hohem Blutdruck sind, gewinnen Sie den Jackpot: Ihr Risiko ist 13-mal so groß.

Bei einem Schlaganfall wird die Blutversorgung eines Gehirnteils unterbrochen, was zu dauerhaften Hirnschäden führt. Sie werden dann unter einigen oder allen der folgenden Symptome leiden: Tod (im schlimmsten Fall, deshalb wollten wir diesen Punkt gleich abhaken). Koma. Einseitige Gesichts-, Arm- oder Beinlähmung oder Muskelschwächung. Sprachverlust ist auch möglich. Vielleicht fällt das Schlucken oder Kauen schwer. Möglicherweise leiden Sie an Blasen- und/oder Darmschwäche/Inkontinenz. Geschwächtes Sehvermögen gehört auch zum Risikopaket. Gut möglich, dass Sie nicht mehr erwerbstätig sein können. Und selbstverständlich sind Depressionen eine häufige Begleiterscheinung. Oft haben Sie dann einen Körper aus zwei völlig verschiedenen Hälften.

Eine Seite ist gegenüber früher wahrscheinlich nicht viel anders. Aber der anderen Seite müssen sie ganz von vorne beibringen, sich koordiniert zu bewegen, zu sprechen, zu essen und zu laufen. Wen wundert's also, dass man nach allgemeiner Einschätzung gar nicht so viel Glück hatte, wenn man das Glück hatte, einen Schlaganfall zu überleben. Es freut uns Ihnen sagen zu können, dass das nicht stimmt. Sie haben gute Chancen, sich zum größten Teil, vielleicht sogar ganz, zu rehabilitieren. Intensive Behandlung, kompetente Pflege und Krankengymnastik können Ihnen mit der Zeit die vollständige Kontrolle über Ihren Körper wiedergeben. Ein Schlaganfall kann auch insofern positive Auswirkungen haben, als wir – je mehr wir über seine Ursachen wissen – Ihr eigenes Schlaganfall-Risiko erheblich senken können. Zu viel Alkohol, Rauchen, zu viel Stress, zu wenig körperliche Bewegung (Sport etc.), hohe Cholesterinwerte, Herzkrankheiten, Diabetes und Übergewicht – all das spielt eine Rolle. Vieles kann man medikamentös, mit Umstellung der Ess- und Arbeitsgewohnheiten oder, im Fall von zu viel Alkohol, einer gehörigen Portion Selbstbeherrschung in den Griff kriegen. (Keine Angst, wir sind keine absoluten Abstinenzler, wollen nur zu ein wenig Mäßigung ermutigen!) Die Schlaganfall-Stiftung ist die einzige Körperschaft in Neuseeland, die den Opfern von Schlaganfällen, deren Familien und Freunden beisteht. Aber, welch eine Überraschung: Wir sind keine reiche Organisation. Damit wir unsere Arbeit, Forschung, Dienste und Informations- und Präventivkampagnen weiter durchführen können, brauchen wir Ihre Hilfe. Sie können mit einer Spende an die Stroke Foundation, PO Box 2320, Wellington, helfen und diese auch per Telefon ankündigen: 0800 787 653. Jeder Betrag, den Sie erübrigen können, wird es uns ermöglichen, die gute Nachricht über die Prävention von Schlaganfällen weiterzusagen und sicherzustellen, dass viele Leute erfahren:
Es ist keine einseitige Angelegenheit.

Anfragen bitte an die Stroke Foundation of New Zealand Inc., PO Box 2320, Wellington. Tel. (04) 472 8099, Fax (04) 472 7019.

Blind, S. 228
Überschrift: blind, adj. + adv. 1. ohne Sehvermögen
blind, adj.+ adv 2. übertr. zum Ausdruck eingeschränkter Urteilskraft
Text: Verbringen Sie einen Tag mit den Blinden, und Sie werden die Dinge anders sehen.
Im Interesse der Öffentlichkeit von Tata Tea Ltd. veröffentlicht. Making a difference ... daily (Ändert täglich etwas).

Matches (Streichhölzer), S. 229
Sprecher: Wenn das Leben eines Menschen ausgelöscht wird, kann etwas aus seinem Innern übrig bleiben und ein anderes Leben retten.
Das Leben ruft dich auf: Spende deine Organe!
Sprecher und Überschrift: Das Leben ruft dich auf: Spende deine Organe!
Sprecher: Dies ist ein gemeinnütziger Aufruf von Antenne 3 TV.
Gestaltet von Saatchi & Saatchi Advertising.

Prisoner, S. 230
Sprecher: Einige Strafgefangene haben Elektrizität und kriegen drei Mahlzeiten pro Tag.
Einige Gefangene haben fließend Warmwasser und Farbfernsehen.
Andere haben das alles nicht ...
Ihr einziges Verbrechen war, dass sie über ihre Verhältnisse lebten.
Deshalb helfen Sie bitte Rand Aid, damit das anders wird: 011 882 2510.

Punch These, S. 232
Überschrift: Wütend? Frustriert? Verwirrt? Hau in diese Tasten!
Text: The Samaritans, Tel. 366 66 76.

Bus, S. 286
Text: Samariter, Tel. 4 739 739.

Read This You Piece of Shit, p. 7

Titre : Lis ça, tas de merde.

Texte : Ce message vous choque ?

Il y a de quoi.

Personne ne mérite d'être traité de cette manière.

Pourtant, hélas, c'est le cas de millions de gens partout dans le monde. Pour la plupart, les violences verbales sont le moindre de leurs soucis. Au Brésil, par exemple, des ouvriers amazoniens sont exposés à un châtiment appelé « le tronc ». Celui qui n'a pas abattu son quota d'arbres est déshabillé, ligoté et laissé dans un tronc d'arbre évidé pendant trois jours. Comme si cela ne suffisait pas, le tronc est badigeonné de miel pour attirer les fourmis et d'autres insectes.

En Inde, des enfants subissent des horreurs similaires. Certains sont vendus dès l'âge de six ans à des fabriques de tapis. Lorsque les chefs d'ateliers manquent d'enfants à acheter, ils en kidnappent. Les enfants doivent travailler toute la journée. S'ils ne vont pas assez vite, on les empêche de dormir la nuit. S'ils commettent une erreur, on les bat. Un enfant a été aspergé de paraffine et brûlé vif parce qu'il demandait à faire une pause. Six autres ont été si violemment battus que l'un d'entre eux en est mort.

Au Népal, l'esclavage est aussi répandu. Des fillettes de dix ans sont enlevées et vendues à des réseaux de prostitution en Inde.

D'abord, elles doivent subir une période de « dressage ». Elles sont enfermées nues dans une minuscule cellule pendant des jours sans nourriture. Elles sont brûlées avec des cigarettes, battues et violées jusqu'à ce qu'elles deviennent totalement soumises. Après quoi, on se les arrache à prix d'or dans les bordels de Bombay.

Si la prostitution peut être une forme d'esclavage, le mariage peut l'être aussi. Dans de nombreuses régions du monde, les parents décident encore qui leurs filles épouseront. Leur choix dépend pour beaucoup de ce que la famille du gendre a à offrir. Le bien-être de la jeune fille ne compte pratiquement pas. De nombreuses femmes sont ainsi mariées contre leur gré. Certaines dès l'âge de neuf ans. Une Nigérienne âgée de douze ans détestait tant son mari qu'elle essayait sans cesse de s'enfuir.

Pour l'en empêcher, il lui a coupé les deux jambes à la hache. Comme vous pouvez le constater, l'esclavage n'appartient pas au passé. Ce n'est pas non plus uniquement un problème du Tiers-Monde. En Grande-Bretagne, 1 700 cas de violences sur des domestiques ont été enregistrés depuis 1987. Il s'agissait pour la plupart de jeunes étrangères issues de milieux pauvres. Elles croyaient que venir travailler en Grande-Bretagne résoudrait leurs problèmes. Une fois sur place, elles sont souvent traitées comme des animaux. Beaucoup doivent dormir à même le sol et sont nourries avec des restes. Elles travaillent 18 heures par jour. Si elles se plaignent, elles sont battues ou fouettées. Certaines n'ont pas le droit de sortir. Certaines sont violées. La liste des atrocités ne s'arrête pas là.

Il existe encore plus de 100 millions d'esclaves dans le monde. Chacun a probablement une histoire aussi douloureuse à raconter.

Anti-Slavery International se bat pour l'abolition de l'esclavage. Nous savons que ce n'est qu'en rendant public le sort de ces personnes et en dénonçant l'esclavage que nous parviendrons à le faire disparaître.

De fait, en exerçant des pressions auprès des politiques et en sensibilisant les opinions publiques à ces questions, nous avons déjà convaincu des gouvernements et les Nations unies de se pencher sur le problème. Dans certains pays comme la Thaïlande, l'Inde et le Pakistan, nous les avons même poussés à modifier les lois. Rien de ceci n'aurait été possible sans l'aide de ceux qui nous soutiennent. Ils ont écrit et interrogé des individus, des compagnies et des gouvernements partout dans le monde. Pour ne pas relâcher la pression, nous avons besoin de votre aide pour nos campagnes à venir.

Si vous souhaitez vous engager à nos côtés, remplissez le coupon ci-dessous et devenez membre. Avec le temps, nous nous assurerons que plus personne ne sait ce que signifie d'être traité comme un esclave.

Anti-Slavery International, Stableyard, Broomgrive Road, Londres SW9 9TL.

Téléphone : 0171 924 9555.

Télécopie : 0171 738 4110.

Pram/Family Planning, p. 18

Mère : Qu'est-ce que tu vas t'embêter avec cette histoire de planning familial, ma chérie ?

Scott, laisse ça, veux-tu ?

Je veux dire, qu'est-ce que tous ces médecins et ces cliniques peuvent bien te raconter qu'une personne dotée d'un minimum de jugeote ne peut pas deviner par elle-même ?

Tu n'as qu'à demander à tes amies. C'est ce que j'ai fait, moi.

Hannah, laisse le bébé tranquille. Combien de fois faut-il que je te le dise ?

Si tu ne veux pas tomber enceinte, tu n'as qu'à... tu vois ce que je veux dire... être prudente et tout ça.

Sers-toi de ta tête.

Voix off masculine : En matière de planning familial, n'écoutez pas les remèdes de bonnes femmes. Que vous soyez célibataire ou mariée, votre médecin ou votre clinique vous donneront des conseils amicaux et précis.

Cherchez dans l'annuaire sous Planning Familial.

Mère : De toutes manières, je n'ai pas les moyens d'acheter des contraceptifs... avec toute cette marmaille.

Voix off masculine : Cela ne vous coûtera rien.

Clip this Coupon, p. 22

Texte : Découpez cette vignette. Ce sera comme de mettre votre photo ici.

Women and Children First, p. 24

Titre : Et les puissances nucléaires déclarèrent : les femmes et les enfants d'abord.

Texte : Non, il ne s'agit pas d'un montage photo. C'est un enfant du Kazakhstan atteint d'hydrocéphalie. Cette malformation est due aux radiations auxquelles sa mère a été exposée. Non, ne nous en voulez pas de vous le montrez, prenez-vous en à ceux qui vous l'ont caché, prétendant que les essais nucléaires ne présentaient aucun danger.

Can't Look, p. 26

Son : Pleurs de bébé.

Scène 1 : Femme : Tais-toi ! Je vais te fracasser le crâne contre cette porte si tu n'arrêtes pas de crier comme ça !

Scène 2 : Homme : Viens t'asseoir ici.

Scène 3 : Homme : Tu n'as rien dans la tête. Tu n'es qu'un idiot. Tu n'es pas mon fils.

Scène 4 : Enfant : Maman, où tu es ? J'aime pas être tout seul.

Scène 5 : Homme : Pas un mot à qui que ce soit. Ce sera notre petit secret.

Voix off féminine & texte superposé : Parfois, nous non plus nous ne supportons pas de regarder.

La cruauté envers les enfants peut cesser. Avec votre aide, elle peut cesser pour toujours.

Voix off féminine : Soutenez la nouvelle campagne 'Point final' de la N.S.P.C.C.

Titre : N.S.P.C.C. La cruauté envers les enfants doit cesser. Point Final.

Pregnant Man, p. 28

Titre : Seriez-vous plus prudent si c'était vous qui tombiez enceinte ?

Texte : Mariés ou célibataires, vous pouvez obtenir des renseignements sur la contraception auprès de l'Association de Planning Familial, Margaret Pyke House, 27–35 Mortimer Street, Londres W1N 8QB. Tel. 01 636 9135.

Some Fathers, p. 29

Titre : Certains pères changent leurs bébés.

Texte : On peut voir les blessures que l'enfant a à la tête. Ou... les voit-on vraiment ?

Ses plaies physiques finiront par cicatriser, mais ses blessures psychologiques, elles, lui resteront toute sa vie. C'est ainsi qu'on change un enfant heureux et équilibré en malade des nerfs.

Des milliers d'enfants comme lui sont maltraités chaque année. Par leur père comme par leur mère. Mais si vous soupçonnez qu'un enfant est victime de violences, c'est vous le responsable. Parce qu'après tout, si vous ne dénoncez pas les mauvais traitements infligés à un enfant, c'est comme si vous les lui infligiez vous-même.

Si vous avez des informations concernant des violences contre un enfant, appelez-nous le mercredi 4 septembre. 1 800 011 233. Appelez et mettez un terme à ces violences. Département de police du N.S.W. (New South Wales).

Same Father, p. 30

Titre : Nous avons tous les deux le même père.

Texte : Voici l'histoire de Sally.

Ma mère est morte quand j'avais douze ans. Une nuit, après que j'avais fait un cauchemar, mon père m'a dit que je pouvais dormir dans son lit.

Au début, il m'a juste serrée contre lui, puis il a commencé à faire d'autres choses. C'était horrible, ça me faisait mal. Il a dit que c'était parce qu'il m'aimait.

Le lendemain, avant que je parte à l'école, il m'a fait jurer de n'en parler à personne. Après ça, il a voulu que je dorme avec lui toutes les nuits. Il appelait ça notre petit secret.

Plus tard, quand j'ai cessé d'avoir mes règles, mon père m'a gardee à la maison. Il a raconté à l'école que j'étais malade.

Parfois, je sens le bébé qui bouge dans mon ventre. C'est une sensation horrible.

Heureusement, l'école s'est inquiétée de son absence et Sally reçoit à présent tout le soutien dont elle a besoin.

Naturellement, sa grossesse n'est pas la seule conséquence de son viol.

Il lui faudra suivre un soutien psychologique à long terme afin de soigner ses troubles affectifs, tels que les sentiments de culpabilité et l'incapacité à nouer des liens avec les autres.

De fait, toutes les formes de violence peuvent entraîner des troubles psychologiques. Pas uniquement les actes les plus visibles tels que les viols et les brutalités physiques.

Par exemple, priver soudainement un enfant de tous signes d'affection, le négliger, le critiquer ou lui crier après constamment peuvent entraîner des blessures affectives qui durent toute une vie. Parfois, cela conduit même des enfants au suicide.

Pour ces raisons, la N.S.P.C.C. lance « Un cri au secours pour les enfants ». Un cri pour que tout le monde s'arrête un instant et réfléchisse à la manière dont on se comporte avec les enfants, pour que chacun reconnaisse les effets de toute forme de cruauté sur un enfant, pour comprendre que la manière dont un enfant est traité affecte toute sa vie. S'il vous plaît, répondez à ce cri.

Si vous ou une personne de votre connaissance souffrez de violences, appelez la ligne de Protection de l'enfance de la N.S.P.C.C. au 0800 800 500.

Ou si, après avoir lu ceci, vous aimeriez avoir plus d'informations, appelez-nous au 071 825 2775.

N.S.P.C.C. Un cri à l'aide pour les enfants.

Astronaut, p. 31

Titre : Le monde a-t-il bien choisi ses priorités ?

Texte : Le Forum sur l'état du monde rassemble un grand nombre des personnalités les plus influentes de la planète pour débattre de questions virtuelles concernant l'humanité... le désarmement nucléaire... la fin des conflits... le rôle de la femme et le développement de l'enfant. Il s'agit de bien choisir nos priorités pour l'avenir. Participez au débat via notre site internet entre le 27 octobre et le 1er novembre. C'est l'occasion ou jamais pour changer le monde.

Face, p. 32

Texte superposé : Cette jeune fille veut discuter.

Texte superposé : Vous avez perdu patience ?

Texte superposé : L'infirmière Robinson sait que ce sera bientôt une conversation à deux sens.

Infirmière : Salut Rachel, tu m'as encore eue.

Encore une nuit passée à faire la fête entre copines, hein ?

Texte superposé : Le nouveau département de la santé a besoin d'infirmières.

Voix off féminine : Les infirmières font la différence. Pour vous informer sur la carrière d'infirmière ou reprendre une carrière interrompue, avec un salaire plus élevé et de meilleures conditions de travail, appelez le 0845 60 60 655.

Cot, p. 36

Voix off masculine : C'est là qu'un meurtre sur dix a lieu.

Qu'on compte entre un et deux morts par semaine.

Chaque année, on enregistre plus de 5 000 coups et blessures, et plus de 1 700 agressions sexuelles.

Texte superposé : En Grande-Bretagne, 36 000 enfants vivent tous les jours sous la menace de mauvais traitements.

Texte superposé : N.S.P.C.C.

Un cri à l'aide pour les enfants.

The World Could End This Easily, p. 40

Texte : Le monde pourrait s'arrêter aussi facilement que ça.

Prononcez-vous contre les essais nucléaires.

Greenpeace 0800 22 33 44

Stay In School, p. 42

Texte superposé : Ne quittez pas l'école.

Hungry, p. 44

Voix off de garçon : Si je prononce le mot « merde », ça vous dérangera sans doute.

Si je vous disais que j'ai faim, ça ne vous fera rien.

Merde, j'ai faim.

Texte superposé : On ne devrait jamais gaspiller la bonne nourriture.

Day Against Violence, p. 46

Texte superposé : Cela paraissait impossible.

Pourtant, c'est arrivé le 12 février 1995.

Un milliard sept cent millions de gens dans le monde l'ont vu.

Pour la première fois.

L'équipe italienne de football est entrée sur le terrain en portant les maillots de l'équipe adverse.

Elle a lu un message disant que le football devait réunir et non diviser.

Aujourd'hui, cette idée appartient à tout le monde.

C'est aussi grâce à nous.

Saatchi & Saatchi.

Rien n'est impossible.

Worst Marks, p. 50

Titre : Les enfants de minorités ethniques sont souvent les plus marqués par l'école.

Teacher Passing an Examination, p. 51

Illustration : Il se débattait avec les tables de multiplication. Il ne comprenait pas comment ça marchait, jusqu'à ce que son professeur trouve une autre manière de le lui expliquer.

Enseignant passant un examen

Texte : Le moment où un élève saisit un concept qui lui a posé des difficultés est sans doute une des plus grandes joies de l'enseignement. Cela signifie que l'enseignant a trouvé une explication qui fait tilt. Rien n'est plus important. Trouver l'explication juste est au cœur même de l'enseignement. C'est le lien entre la connaissance transmise et celle assimilée. Pour l'enseignant comme pour l'élève, c'est un accomplissement partagé.

C'est précisément ce qui peut donner envie de faire carrière dans l'enseignement. Si c'est le cas pour vous, vous serez sans doute ravi d'apprendre qu'il y a également d'autres gratifications qui en valent la peine.

A compter de décembre, le salaire de départ à Londres pour des enseignants de primaire et de secondaire ayant réussi leur diplôme avec mention bien tourne autour de £14 000 (incluant une allocation et une prime pour Londres intramuros).

Le directeur d'une grande école secondaire dans Londres peut espérer gagner jusqu'à £48 000.

Certes, ce n'est pas de l'argent facile. Après tout, enseigner n'est pas un processus mécanique. Ce serait impossible.

Chaque classe est constituée d'élèves présentant une grande variété d'aptitudes, d'intérêts, de comportements et d'histoires personnelles. En tant qu'enseignant, vous devez apprendre à connaître ces différences, à vous en souvenir et à y répondre. Par exemple, la vitesse d'apprentissage varie selon les enfants et les disciplines, pourtant l'enseignant doit tous les mener au même niveau.

Des visages perplexes signifient parfois qu'il faut trouver une nouvelle manière d'expliquer quelque chose et une approche innovatrice peut parfois faire des merveilles sur le moral d'une classe. Dans un sens, l'enseignant passe un examen chaque jour.

Et il doit réussir.

Une perspective décourageante ou un défi excitant ? Si pour vous, cela représente la seconde option, une formation peut peaufiner vos compétences naturelles et vous préparer à cet examen quotidien. Ainsi qu'à une carrière gratifiante à plus d'un titre.

Pour vous Informer sur la formation des enseignants, appelez le 0345 300121 en mentionnant la référence IS/4/A ou renvoyez le coupon ci-dessous.

Enseigner fait ressortir ce qu'il y a de mieux en chacun de nous.

Resolution, p. 52

Texte superposé : Aux Philippines, des milliers d'enfants passent le 1er de l'an à l'hôpital avec des doigts en moins ou des mains arrachées à cause de pétards bon marché.

Cette campagne a pour but de mettre un terme à ce cercle vicieux.

Maîtresse : Les enfants, quelle sera votre résolution pour la nouvelle année ?

Enfant : Je ne jouerai plus avec des pétards, Madame.

Texte superposé : Cette année, pas touche aux pétards !

Prostitute, p. 54

Titre : Ça vous dirait de travailler comme prostituée en Europe ?

Texte : Des millions de femmes n'ont pas ce choix, comme les immigrées dupées par des organisations internationales spécialisées dans le marché du sexe. Exploitées, elles n'ont aucun pouvoir de décision sur leur vie.

Vous seriez surpris d'apprendre les méthodes utilisées aujourd'hui pour asservir l'être humain.

Manos Unidas veut mettre un terme à ces violences. Aidez-nous à abolir l'esclavage.

Note : Comme vous pouvez le constater dans l'encadré à gauche, on trouve parfois ce genre de message dans les petites annonces (rubrique emplois) des plus grands quotidiens espagnols.

Mining Children, p. 55

Titre : Société métallurgique cherche enfants mineurs.

Texte : Des millions d'enfants n'ont pas besoin de chercher un emploi, il le leur est imposé. Ils sont employés comme main-d'œuvre bon marché. Exploités, ils n'ont aucun pouvoir de décision sur leur vie.

Vous seriez surpris d'apprendre les méthodes utilisées aujourd'hui pour asservir l'être humain.

Manos Unidas veut mettre un terme à ces violences. Aidez-nous à abolir l'esclavage.

Note : Le message page de gauche est un exemple de ce qu'on trouve dans les petites annonces (rubrique emplois) des plus grands quotidiens espagnols.

Child Abuse, p. 56

Homme 1 : Elle est belle, hein ?

Homme 2 : Elle est vierge ?

Homme 1 : Bien sûr, c'est ma fille.

Homme 2 : Combien ?

Homme 1 : $100 seulement.

Homme 2 : Qu'est-ce qu'elle fait ?

Homme1 : Tout... mais ne la tuez pas.

...Viens, ma chérie.

Voix off : Si cela arrivait à votre fille, vous auriez peur, non ?

Quand vous voyagez à l'étranger, n'oubliez pas : un enfant est un enfant, partout dans le monde.

Texte superposé : Centro Italiano per l'Adozione Internazionale (Centre italien pour l'adoption internationale)

Pour vos dons c/c N° 10837.

La Cariplo, agence 15, Milan.

Raped as a 3 Year Old, p. 58

Titre : Qu'est-ce que ça fait d'être violé à l'âge de trois ans ? Une victime explique.

Texte : Mon premier souvenir d'avoir été violé par mon père remonte à quand j'avais environ 3 ans. Cela s'était peut-être déjà produit auparavant, je ne m'en rappelle pas.

Je me revois, couché dans mon lit, ce grand visage descendant vers moi.

Il venait m'embrasser avant que je m'endorme, mais il ne s'arrêtait pas là. Il me disait que c'était notre secret.

Que si jamais je le disais à quelqu'un, il me renverrait de la maison.

Mais, même à cet âge, je savais que quelque chose n'était pas bien. Il me disait : « Je te protégerai ». Comment pouvait-il me protéger ? Il me faisait mal.

C'est étrange. C'était mon ennemi mais, en même temps, mon seul ami. Il me faisait dépendre de lui. Il me contrôlait. Mon corps a été son jouet pendant plus de 9 ans.

A l'école, j'avais du mal à me mêler aux autres. Je me sentais différent. Dans les vestiaires après la gym, je ne supportais pas que les autres voient mon corps nu. J'avais tellement honte, je croyais qu'ils seraient capables de voir ce qui se passait et qu'ils me traiteraient de tapette.

Même quand j'ai réussi à avoir une petite amie, je n'étais toujours pas certain d'être hétérosexuel. J'étais très dur avec elle. Je suppose que je voulais contrôler quelqu'un, comme mon père faisait avec moi. Le sexe me terrifiait. Avoir un orgasme me rappelait ce que mon père faisait en moi. Et ce grand visage souriant.

J'ai fini par rencontrer quelqu'un. On s'est marié. Elle m'a quitté au bout de deux ans. Elle disait que j'étais froid et que je ne la comprenais pas.

Mais j'étais comme ça. Je n'étais pas conscient de provoquer ou de ressentir de la douleur psychologique ou physique. Quelque chose en moi s'était eteint depuis longtemps. Il m'arrivait même de me couper avec un couteau sans rien sentir. Après le divorce, je me suis mis à boire. C'était une échappatoire. Mais je traversais encore des périodes de graves dépressions. L'année dernière, mon père a fini par mourir. Je crois que c'est ça qui m'a poussé à contacter la N.S.P.C.C. (Association pour la protection de l'enfance). J'avais 53 ans et c'était la première fois que je parlais à quelqu'un de mon enfance.

Pendant 6 mois, une fois par semaine, un officier de la Protection de l'enfance a travaillé avec moi. Il m'a fait tout lui raconter. Lui parler fut très douloureux. Pendant 40 ans, j'avais essayé de ne pas y penser.

Au bout d'un moment, ça a fini par marcher. Il m'a fait comprendre que ce qui m'était arrivé n'était pas de ma faute.

Pour la première fois, je me souviens de m'être senti bien avec moi-même. C'était comme de sortir d'une cellule sombre où j'étais resté enfermé tout ce temps.

Je n'oublierai jamais ce qui m'est arrivé mais, au moins, je peux commencer à vivre ma vie.

Pour plus d'informations sur le travail de la N.S.P.C.C., ou pour faire un don, écrivez à : N.S.P.C.C., 67 Saffron Hill, Londres EC1N 8RS ou appelez le 071 242 1626.

Pour dénoncer un cas éventuel de violences contre un enfant, appelez la ligne de la protection de l'enfance de la N.S.P.C.C. au 0800 800 500.

Dr Jekyll, Mr Hyde, p. 59
Le docteur Jekyll et Monsieur Hyde.
Texte : Vous êtes un père de famille fiable, affectueux et attentionné. Vous avez une épouse ravissante et une adorable petite fille de neuf ans. Votre petite famille est ce que vous avez de plus cher. Vous êtes prêt à la défendre corps et âme. Puis, un beau jour, vous partez en voyage d'affaires. Vous mettez le cap vers une destination exotique, Bangkok par exemple, dans un de ces pays où tout est toléré, où « les us et coutumes sont très différents de chez nous ». Là, entre des chemises et des souvenirs dans un marché ouvert, on vous propose une petite fille. C'est une charmante gamine de neuf ans qui ressemble un peu à la vôtre mais a déjà tous les attributs d'une jeune femme. Vous vous dites que c'est ainsi que se font les choses par ici et votre pouls s'accélère. Vous vous métamorphosez en une autre personne.
Le marché mondial de la pédophilie, un marché de mort riche et puissant, vient de remporter une nouvelle victoire. De fait, ce ne sont pas les criminels et les pervers qui lui apportent ses plus grands bénéfices, mais des gens ordinaires, des gens comme vous. Au CIAI (Centre italien pour l'adoption internationale), on se bat depuis des années pour faire respecter un concept très simple, que personne ne devrait jamais oublier, surtout quand on voyage à l'étranger : un enfant est un enfant, où que vous soyez.
Vous pouvez effectuer vos dons par carte de crédit en appelant le +39 2 55 01 20 11 ou par virement bancaire sur le compte A/C N.10837 à Cariplo, branche 15, Milan, Italie.

1 in every 8, p. 60
Titre : Une personne sur huit qui passent devant cette affiche a été victime de violences pendant son enfance.
N.S.P.C.C.
Un cri à l'aide pour les enfants.

Ban Guns, p. 64

Bullet, p. 66
Titre : Pénis sans préservatif.
Texte : Procurez-vous en gratuitement en appelant le 250 8629.

Less Dead, p. 68
Texte : Si un calibre 22 est moins mortel, pourquoi n'est-il pas moins mort ? Exigez une loi contre les armes à feu qui élimine les calibres 22.

Grunge Angels, p. 70
Voix off : Bienvenue ! Pour votre plaisir en cet Au-delà, voici les plus belles chansons d'amour de Whitney Houston.
Effets sonores : Hurlements...
Texte superposé : La mort, ça craint !
Attachez vos ceintures.

Rubber Woman, p. 74
Titre : Latex. Le dernier cri en matière de lingerie fine.

Rubber Man, p. 75
Titre : Les hommes sont tellement plus sexy en latex.

Tongue, p. 76
Titre : Elle veut mettre sa langue dans votre bouche.
Texte : Apprenez facilement le cantonais et le mandarin. Appelez le centre d'apprentissage des langues de Hong Kong au 2385 5331.

Mother, p. 78
Texte superposé : Attention. La scène qui va suivre peut heurter les âmes sensibles.
Voix off masculine : Ce que vous allez voir va vous choquer, c'est ce qui arrive à une fillette de sept ans assise sans ceinture sur le siège arrière d'une voiture roulant à cinquante kilomètres heure. Examinez attentivement ses blessures.
Aucun siège n'est sûr sans ceinture, attachez-la, toujours.
Texte superposé : La mortalité sur les routes doit baisser.

Job Satisfaction, p. 81
Titre : Comment être satisfait de son travail en renvoyant quelqu'un mourir chez lui ?
Texte : Lorsqu'Eric est arrivé à l'hôpital, sa maladie chronique l'avait pratiquement achevé. Respirer et digérer lui étaient devenu difficiles et douloureux.
Le moindre effort lui était une véritable torture. Malgré cela, Eric, âgé de 83 ans, était résolu à finir ses jours chez lui. Mais il ne pouvait aller nulle part tant que son infirmière ne l'aurait pas suffisamment remis sur pied.
L'oxygène, les médicaments et l'alimentation artificielle lui ont progressivement rendu un peu de ses forces. Son infirmière était toujours parvenue à trouver du temps pour lui et ses proches : afin de les conseiller, les rassurer ou simplement de les écouter.
Au bout de trois semaines, ses symptômes s'étaient suffisamment stabilisés pour qu'il rentre chez lui.
Le jour de son départ, Eric et son infirmière étaient devenus des amis.
Soigner des personnes âgées est rarement facile. Il faut être résistant, avoir de la compassion et le sens de l'initiative. Mais pensez à la gratification. Songez à la satisfaction professionnelle que vous avez en exauçant le dernier vœu d'un mourant.
Il n'y a pas d'autre métier pareil.
Appelez le 0345 64 64 64, citant la référence 2J. A n'importe quelle heure de la journée. Infirmière. L'avez-vous en vous ?

A Country Story, p. 82
Episode 1
Titre : Le 24 août, Danny épousera Tessa.
Maman : Le petit déjeuner est servi !
Pete : Miam ! Du bacon ! Tessa sait cuisiner ?
Maman : Bien sûr qu'elle sait cuisiner !
Pete : C'est étrange. Sa mère, elle, n'a jamais appris.
Maman : Bruce !
Voix off masculine : Si vous deviez écrire une lettre à cette famille, vous l'adresseriez aux Carter, bureau de poste central de Hawkes Bay.
Voix off masculine :Cette ferme appartient à la famille Carter depuis plus de 80 ans. Danny en héritera un jour. Peu après eur mariage, Tessa et lui s'installeront dans cette maison. Une nouvelle génération de Carter apprendra à travailler cette terre et tout continuera comme avant.
Danny : Papa, si tu veux, je passerai prendre ces gonds avant mon entraînement à la course ce soir.
Père : Ouais, bonne idée.
Danny : Il faut partir vers 4 heures de l'après-midi, Pete.
Pete : D'accord.
Maman : Et n'y passez pas toute la nuit !
Titre : A suivre.

Episode 2
Titre : Dans cinq semaines, Danny épousera Tessa.
Voix off masculine : Comme ils le font toujours depuis plusieurs années, Danny et Pete s'arrêtent au café avant de rentrer chez eux après l'entraînement.
Blue : Tiens ! Voilà monsieur «plus que quatre semaines» ! Salut Pete !
Pete : Comment ça va ce soir, Blue ?
Blue : Regarde qui est de retour !
Danny : Hé, Matthew ! Où étais-tu passé ?
Matthew : Je suis descendu à Palmy pour voir la foire agricole.
Pete : Tu y as vu des choses intéressantes ?
Matthew : Un taureau champion. Il appartenait à ce type de Waikato... il demandait $5, rien que pour le voir.
Danny : Et tu l'as vu ?
Matthew : Je lui ai demandé : «Tu ne ferais pas des réductions pour famille nombreuse, par hasard ?». Il m'a répondu : «Vous êtes combien ? ». Je lui ai dit : «Rien que moi, ma bourgeoise et nos 13 mômes.» Alors, il a dit : «Ne bouge pas de là, je vais chercher la bête. Il faut qu'elle voit ça !»
Voix off masculine : C'est devenu une sorte de routine que tout le monde apprécie. Matthew revient toujours de quelque part. Et il a toujours une bonne histoire à raconter. Les garçons ont surnommé le café «L'oiseau de nuit» parce que Blue se fiche pas mal que vous restiez toute la nuit. Mais il y a sans doute une autre raison.
Titre : A suivre.

Episode 3
Titre : Dans quatre semaines, Danny épousera Tessa.
Pete : Je te donne un penny si tu me dis à quoi tu penses, Danny.
Danny : Tu sais, frérot, je me disais qu'on avait vraiment de la chance. On a aucun souci. On n'est pas pris à la gorge par la concurrence. On n'est pas sur la paille.
Pete : Très profond.
Danny : Laisse tomber, frérot. Alors, il est où mon penny ?
Pete : Tiens !
Voix off masculine : Ils se sont toujours entendus comme cul et chemise. Dans quelques semaines, Pete sera son témoin au mariage.
Danny : Tu capitules ?
Pete : Ça dépend.
Danny : Dépend de quoi ?
Pete : Je vais être ton témoin, non ?
Danny : Oui.
Pete : Je vais devoir faire un discours, non ?
Danny : Oui.
Pete : Tu me donnes combien pour ne pas parler de cette fille que tu as rencontrée à Massey il y a quelques années ?
Danny : Tu veux un coup de main ?
Jolie chemise.
Pete : Comment elle s'appelait, déjà ? Irène ?
Danny : Laisse tomber le penny.
Pete : (chante) Irène bonne nuit, Irène. Irène, bonne nuit...
Texte superposé : A suivre.

Episode 4
Titre : Dans trois semaines, Danny épousera Tessa.
Entraîneur : OK, les garçons, pas question de se laisser ridiculiser une fois de plus par ces gars de la ville. Il faut les écraser dès le coup d'envoi. Montrez-leur qui sont les chefs.
En parlant de chefs, il y aura un pot ce soir en l'honneur de Danny et Tessa et tout ça...
Voilà, c'est tout.
Capitaine : ... Oui, minute, les gars. Je voulais juste dire que je vous souhaitais beaucoup de réussite et que... enfin... à la santé de Danny et de Pete...
Membre du club : Danny et Tessa.
Capitaine : Ah oui... Danny et Tessa... bonne chance.
Danny : Salut !
Matthew : C'est dans combien de temps ?
Danny : Deux semaines.
Matthew : Mon vieil oncle s'est remarié l'autre jour.
Danny : Il a quel âge ?
Matthew : 91.
Danny : 91 ! Pourquoi voulait-il se marier à cet âge ?
Matthew : C'est pas qu'il voulait, il était obligé.
Texte superposé : A suivre.

Episode 5
Titre : Dans deux semaines, Danny épousera Tessa.
Danny : Bonjour Maman !
Mère : Tu es en retard. Goûte ça... c'est Tessa qui les a faits.
Tessa : Pete ?
Danny : Délicieux tes gâteaux, Tessa !
Tessa : Muffins.
Danny : Délicieux tes gâteaux, Muffins.
Père : On a eu de la visite ce matin, les garçons.
Pete : Quelqu'un d'important ?
Père : Oui, un jeune homme très important, du syndicat agricole.
Il voulait connaître le salaire de tout le monde.
Alors je lui ai parlé du berger en chef, tu sais, environ $200 par semaine, un logement de fonction et tout.
Puis je lui ai parlé du manœuvre, qui gagne $150 par semaine, avec un logement de fonction et tout ça.
Puis il a demandé : « Il n'y a personne d'autre ? » J'ai dit : « Et bien, il y a l'idiot de service. Il fait la plupart du boulot et gagne environ $40 par semaine ».
« $40 par semaine ! Alors c'est à lui que je veux parler » qu'il dit. « C'est ce que vous êtes en train de faire » que je lui réponds. Du coup, il est parti.
Texte superposé : A suivre.

Episode 6
Titre : Danny épousera Tessa cette semaine.
Voix off masculine : Cette semaine, Danny et Tessa deviendront les nouveaux M. et Mme Carter et, une fois de plus, la ferme passera entre des mains plus jeunes, plus vigoureuses.
Blue : Hé, Danny...
Une minute Matt...
Hé, Danny, écoute ça...
Vas-y, Matt...
Matthew : Je leur racontais l'histoire de ce type de la ville, tu sais ce snob qui a demandé à Skinny : « Dis donc, Skinny, quand ton cheval est tombé malade, avec la toux et tout, qu'est-ce que tu lui as donné ? » Skinny lui a répondu : « Du phénol ». Quelques jours plus tard, le type revient et dit à Skinny : « Hé ! Skinny, j'ai donné du phénol à mon cheval et il est mort ». Alors Skinny répond : « Je sais... le mien aussi »
Blue: Hé ! Danny, tu as un message. Tessa est chez tes parents et... quelque chose à propos du grand jour.
Danny : OK, merci, on ferait mieux d'y aller. Viens Pete. On te dépose quelque part ?
Matthew : Encore un verre et on y va.
Texte superposé : A suivre.

Episode 7
Titre : Danny épousera Tessa cette semaine.
Blue : Salut. Une minute, les gars... c'est peut-être une urgence. Bonjour... Bonjour Bruce. Non, ils étaient bien ici tout à l'heure.
Père : Merci Blue, merci.
Père : Ils ont dû avoir un problème avec la voiture. Va falloir que j'aille les chercher.
Mère : Un problème avec la voiture ?
Pourquoi ils n'ont pas téléphoné ?
Père : Oh, Maman, Oh Maman...
Texte superposé : Les gens de la campagne meurent sur les routes de campagne.
Texte superposé : A suivre.

Episode 8
Titre : Danny est mort.
Voix off masculine : Matthew et le jeune Danny ont tous deux trouvé la mort dans l'accident de voiture. Les gens de la campagne meurent sur des routes de campagne. Pete ne sera plus jamais le même. Il est à Christchurch, dans le service des hémiplégies. Il ne peut plus marcher et ne marchera plus jamais.
Tessa : Il y a déjà eu des offres pour la ferme, Maman ?
Mère : Je crois.
Père : Une ou deux personnes sont intéressées.
Mère : Dis-le à Bruce.
Tessa : Je m'en vais. Pas définitivement. Juste pour un temps. Mais je vous tiendrai au courant.
Père : Où tu vas ?
Tessa : Dans le nord, chez ma tante à Piha.
Père : Vraiment ?
Mère : Elle s'en va Papa. Elle va avoir le bébé de Danny.
Père : Ça ne s'arrête jamais, Maman, pas vrai ? Ça ne finit jamais.
Texte superposé & voix off masculine : L'histoire s'arrête ici. Définitivement. Les gens de la campagne meurent sur des routes de campagne.

The Height of It, p. 93

Taxi Confessions, p. 94
Chauffeur : Faut que vous me disiez dans quelle rue on va, autrement, si vous vous endormez, je ne saurai pas où vous conduire.
Homme : Hé, Taxi !
Homme : Ouais, on va dans tous ces bars et on ne les trouve jamais. Ouais, on ne fait que...
Femme : Puis il tend son bras et je vois une paire de menottes accrochées. Des menottes !
Homme : Je ne veux pas rentrer chez moi.
Homme : Je vous conseille cet endroit.
Homme : Woooo, on est arrivé !
Homme : Tu commandes un burger au bacon et on t'apporte une couenne dégueulasse ! Tu comprends, c'est toujours pareil.
Homme : Un instant, il était derrière moi, et l'instant suivant, il avait disparu.
Homme : A Herne Bay, merci.
Chauffeur: Où ça à Herne Bay ?
Couple : Il n'y a pas la Dame Blanche ou quelque chose du genre là-bas ?
Oui, juste là-bas en bas.
Tu es superbe, ce soir.
Homme : Il traîne dans tous ces bars à l'étranger et, chaque fois, il se perd.
Homme : Non, non, non. Parce que ce n'est pas là. Ce n'est pas là qu'on va. C'est de là qu'on vient.
Voix off masculine & texte superposé : Si vous buvez et que vous prenez un taxi, vous êtes sacrement malin.

Disaster, p. 96
Titre : Partout où nous allons, c'est la catastrophe.
Texte : Nous ne cherchons pas à éviter les catastrophes. Nous devons nous tenir prêts à intervenir partout où elles surviennent, qu'il s'agisse d'une guerre au Ruanda ou d'un avion qui s'écrase dans les Ruahines. Pour des millions de gens sinistrés, l'emblème de la Croix-Rouge est devenu une vision familière et rassurante. Nous nous tenons prêts à réagir sur-le-champ et, avec nos cours de premiers soins et de secourisme, nous vous préparons vous aussi. On vous demandera peut-être votre aide de temps à autre mais, un jour, il se peut que vous ayez besoin de la nôtre.

Fight, p. 98
Titre : Nous leur apprenons a se battre.
Texte : En amour comme en guerre, tout est permis ? Non. Même au combat, il y a des règles. Au cours de ses activités humanitaires partout dans le monde, la Croix-Rouge rencontre des soldats qui ignorent qu'ils ont des obligations vis-à-vis de leurs prisonniers, des populations civiles et de l'ennemi.
Si nous pouvons enseigner à ces soldats la conduite exigée d'eux par la Convention de Genève, nous pourrons sauver des vies. Vous seriez sans doute surpris par certaines des missions de la Croix-Rouge, mais quelles qu'elles soient et où qu'elles nous entraînent, nous avons toujours besoin de votre aide pour les mener à bien.

350 Languages, p. 99
Titre : Comment dire « ne m'abattez pas » en 350 langues ?
Texte : L'idée de l'emblème de la Croix-Rouge est née sur un champ de bataille, à Solférino, en 1859. Aujourd'hui, il distingue encore les infirmiers des soldats, la vie de la mort. Il est protégé par la Convention de Genève et en abuser est un crime puni par la loi. Il ne peut figurer sur un kit de premiers soins. Les vétérinaires et les centres médicaux n'ont pas le droit de s'en servir. C'est un symbole de protection, de neutralité et d'humanité. La Croix-Rouge néo-zélandaise a le devoir de le protéger, parce que, sans lui, nous ne pouvons pas vous protéger.

Don't Forget, p. 100
Titre : N'oubliez pas comment faire l'amour après avoir bu.
Texte : Après quelques verres de trop, on est souvent distrait. Protégez-vous contre le Sida. Utilisez un préservatif. Mais n'oubliez pas où il faut le mettre.

Prevent Sickness, p. 101
Titre : Prendre autant que nécessaire pour éviter la maladie après abus d'alcool.
Texte : L'abus d'alcool peut entraîner des pratiques sexuelles à risque. Protégez-vous avec un préservatif. Parce que le Sida vous rendra malade. Définitivement.

Right Package, p. 102
Titre : Si vous voulez garder vos employés plus longtemps, équipez-les comme il faut.
Texte : Ce que font vos employés au lit ne vous regarde pas. Mais cela pourrait avoir des effets néfastes sur votre entreprise.
Imaginez qu'un membre de votre personnel contracte le virus VIH.
S'il développe un Sida, vous finirez par devoir le remplacer.
En attendant, vous et ses collègues vous demanderez s'il est prudent de travailler avec des personnes contaminées par le VIH. Heureusement, il n'y aucun danger.
Vous voudrez également connaître les implications légales, si l'employé sera couvert par son assurance ou s'il est à la charge de votre entreprise.
Il est important d'obtenir des réponses à ces questions dès à présent. Parce que, si votre entreprise n'est pas encore contaminée par le Sida, elle pourrait l'être très bientôt.
D'ici l'an 2000, l'épidémie sera un problème plus grave encore en Asie qu'elle l'est actuellement dans la région la plus touchée, l'Afrique. D'ici là, plus de 40% des nouvelles infections se produiront ici – à moins que vous ne réagissiez dès maintenant en aidant à prévenir la propagation de cette maladie.
Commencez par contacter une association locale de lutte contre le Sida et les autorités sanitaires gouvernementales. Elles devraient pouvoir répondre à vos questions.
Elles vous conseilleront également sur les mesures à prendre pour éviter que le Sida ne se propage dans votre entreprise. Ces mesures peuvent inclure de faire venir un spécialiste de la santé pour parler à vos employés, ce placer des affiches de prévention sur les panneaux d'affichages, voire même d'installer un distributeur de préservatifs dans les toilettes. Vous trouverez l'association de lutte contre le Sida la plus proche de vous en contactant le bureau local du Programme de Développement des Nations Unies ou au PNUDD de New Delhi (voir adresse ci-dessous).
Agissez maintenant. Vous remonterez le moral de votre personnel en lui montrant que vous tenez à lui.
Et vous éviterez que le Sida ne vous enlève de précieux employés.

Night Cap, p. 103
Titre : Même quand vous buvez trop, n'oubliez pas votre bonnet de nuit.
Texte : Plus vous buvez, plus vous oubliez. Limitez les risques d'attraper le Sida. N'oubliez pas. Portez un préservatif au lit.

Preservativo, p. 105
Voix off : Préservatif, préservatif, préservatif, préservatif, préservatif, préservatif, préservatif.
Texte superposé : On ne se lassera jamais de le répéter.
Le préservatif est l'arme la plus fiable contre le Sida. Persuadez votre partenaire d'en utiliser un.
ANLAIDS.

Strangers in the Night, p. 106
Tout au long de cette publicité, on entend « Strangers in the night ». Peu à peu, on passe de la version suave originale à une version plus saccadée et triste, reflétant la transformation des notes de musique en crucifix.
Titre: Arrêtez le Sida avec l'amour.

Love Story, p. 108
Musique : Love Story.
Voix off masculine : Beaucoup de gens comme ces deux-là feront l'amour sur la plage cet été. Croix-Rouge.
Faites l'amour !
Texte superposé : Les volontaires de la Croix-Rouge.

Lenny, p. 113
Lenny : Tu sais, je me sentais vachement bien, mec. Tu sais, j'avais pas de palpitations, je n'étais pas speed, ni rien. J'étais comme dans du coton.
La première fois, j'ai gerbé, mais vraiment tout gerbé, tu sais. Et après, je me suis dit : Woaw ! Cette merde, c'est vraiment de la bonne, mec.
Tu vois ?
Tu sais... tu sais, tu te souviens quand tu roulais en trombes et que tu sentais les décharges d'adrénaline, tu vois ce que je veux dire...
C'est la même sensation.
C'est exactement ça.
J'avais de la cellulite sur la cuisse.
J'ai une cicatrice grosse comme ça.
Incroyable, mec.
J'ai failli... J'ai eu une gangrène au pied, ils ont bien failli m'amputer.
Je me considérais plutôt intelligent comme mec.
Je peux faire tout ce que je veux, mec.
Tout ce que j'ai envie de faire, je peux le faire.
J'ai vidé mes tripes, mec, et pendant que je gerbais, je me suis dit, putain, voilà ce que je veux, tu sais.
Je veux juste être un type bien, c'est tout ce que je veux, c'est tout.
Pourquoi que tout le monde peut pas être comme ça ? Peut-être que tout le monde devrait se shooter et flotter dans du coton.
J'ai eu des croûtes partout sur le corps.
T'avais qu'à appuyer un peu et du pus sortait de partout.
Avant, je faisais beaucoup plus de choses, tu sais. J'allais au cinoche plus souvent, au resto, ou voir des shows à Broadway.
J'aime bien les shows de Broadway, c'est super, mec.
Avant la fin de 1997, on est en 96, non ?
Le 17 ou 18 août 1996 ou quelque chose comme ça. Enfin, quand tu reviendras avec tes caméras, je serai quelqu'un de complètement différent.
J'aurai réussi dans la vie.
Je te parie ce que tu veux.
Texte superposé : L'héroïne.
Vous en voulez ?
Partenariat pour une Amérique sans drogue.

Surfing Monkey, p. 117
Voix off féminine : Une fois de plus, mesdames et messieurs, l'article J343 : la tirelire du Singe Surfeur. Idéale pour les cadeaux de diplômes de fin d'année ou de mariage. D'ailleurs, je crois bien que la dernière fois que nous avons présenté cet article, il a fait un malheur.
Nous avons quelqu'un en ligne. Scott, de Nashville.
Allô, Scott ! Si je ne me trompe pas, vous venez d'acheter quinze de nos Singes Surfeurs, c'est bien ça ?
Scott : ... Ouais !
(Bruits de fond et rires)
Scott : Chut... Je passe à la télé.
Texte superposé : Marijuana. Une habitude qui coûte très cher.
Partenariat pour une Amérique sans drogue.

Celebrities, p. 118
Titre : En publicité, on dit que le meilleur moyen de faire passer un message est de mettre des célébrités dans son annonce.
Partenariat pour une Amérique sans drogue.

Nose, p. 119
Voix off féminine : Un gramme de cocaïne coûte autant qu'un radiocassette.
Trois grammes de cocaïne coûtent autant qu'un poste de télévision.
Sept grammes, qu'un voyage à Paris.
Un gramme par semaine pendant un an, qu'une nouvelle voiture.
Quand vous êtes accro à la coke, tout ce que vous gagnez vous passe sous le nez.
Texte superposé : Partenariat pour une Amérique sans drogue.

Elephant, p. 121
Effets spéciaux (toute la durée du message) : Pas d'éléphants.
Voix off masculine : L'une de ces femmes a montré son respect pour l'environnement en reversant une partie de son salaire à la Fédération californienne pour l'Environnement.
L'autre pas.
Vous ne devinerez peut-être pas laquelle des deux a donné pour l'environnement mais l'éléphant, lui, n'oublie jamais.
Défendez la nature en souscrivant au plan de déductions sur salaires pour l'environnement.
Fin Texte superposé : Fédération californienne pour l'Environnement.
Pour plus d'informations, appelez le 1 800 368 1819.

The Only Fur, p. 124
La seule fourrure que je n'ai pas honte de porter.
Texte : Fonds international pour la sauvegarde des animaux.

Hatchet, p. 125

Whales, p. 126
Voix off : Les baleines n'en demandent pas plus que nous. Elles veulent être libres de vivre en paix, se reproduire sans problèmes. Mais aujourd'hui plus que jamais, leur existence est en danger. Greenpeace s'est toujours battue pour les sauver de l'extinction.
Aidez Greenpeace. 06 57 82 484.

Water Cooler, p. 128
Titre : Sauvez 100 victimes de l'ouragan Mitch de la déshydratation avec $12 seulement.
Texte : Aidez l'UNICEF à aider les enfants en situations d'urgence.
Appelez le 1 800 025 192.

3 More Days, p. 207
Titre : Plus que trois jours avant la journée contre les mines antipersonnel.
Texte : Statistiques du désespoir :
110 millions de mines antipersonnel posées dans 64 pays dans le monde ; une nouvelle victime toutes les 20 minutes ;
5 à 10 millions de nouvelles mines fabriquées chaque année ; 100 millions de mines attendant d'être posées dans l'arsenal mondial ; 90% de femmes et d'enfants parmi les victimes.
Chiffres de l'espoir : compte postal n° 189241. Mani Tese, Campagne italienne contre les mines antipersonnel, via Cavengahi 4, I–20149 Milan.
Le samedi 13 avril, rendez-vous sur la Piazza Santi Apostoli pour signer notre pétition et apporter votre contribution.

Landmines in Cambodia, p. 208
Titre : Une mine antipersonnel d'une valeur de $3 peut-elle mutiler toute une économie ?
Texte : Oui, quand les paysans ont trop peur de labourer leurs champs, quand les enfants sont trop terrifiés pour aller à l'école à pied, quand les activités quotidiennes les plus banales deviennent un jeu de roulette russe. Pourtant, outre les 110 millions de mines antipersonnel toujours enfouies dans le Tiers-Monde, deux autres millions de mines sont posées chaque année. Aidez à abolir les mines antipersonnel. C'est le seul moyen pour que le Tiers-Monde puisse faire un pas en avant. Pour savoir comment vous pouvez aider, écrivez à votre gouvernement local ou au Service des politiques anti-mines et de déminage, département des affaires humanitaires, Nations unies, New York, N. Y. 10017.

Unleaded, p. 209
Titre : Ne plombez pas nos enfants. Utilisez de l'essence sans plomb.
Texte : Publié dans l'intérêt de l'environnement dans les Emirats Arabes Unis.

Pavement, p. 210
Titre : C'est encore plus dégoûtant sur le trottoir.
Texte : Si votre chien fait dans la rue, soyez gentil de ramasser.

Atomic Bomb, p. 211
Texte : La coopération internationale a merveilleusement réussi à nous menacer tous d'annihilation. A présent, elle peut peut-être désamorcer la situation. Si vous avez jamais voulu changer le monde, c'est le moment ou jamais. Participez au débat via notre site web entre le 27 octobre et le 1er novembre. www.worldforum.org.

Leaf/Match, p. 212
Titre : Ne laissez rien traîner dans la maison qui risque de déclencher un incendie.

Off Duty, p. 213
Mari : On est marié depuis 18 ans.
Femme : Nous avons mené une vie plutôt tranquille.
Mari : On suit notre petit chemin sans embêter personne.
Femme : Jour après jour, le boulot, la maison, les enfants. Rien d'extraordinaire. Puis il a été licencié...
Mari : Ça s'est passé si vite. Je n'ai pas compris ce qui m'arrivait
Femme : Il avait l'air si angoissé. Il avait les larmes aux yeux.
Mari : La première chose que j'ai perdu, c'est mon amour-propre. Je n'avais qu'une envie, noyer ma honte dans l'alcool.
Femme : Il a besoin de mon soutien.
Mari : Elle m'a beaucoup encouragé.
Femme : Ne t'inquiète pas. Tout va s'arranger.
Mari : Mon licenciement a été ce qui pouvait nous arriver de mieux l'espace d'un moment.
Femme : Nous n'avons jamais été aussi proches l'un de l'autre.
Mari : Pour mon anniversaire ..
Femme : Je lui ai offert une paire de chaussures.
Mari : Des chaussures neuves.
Femme : Pour que tu explores un nouveau monde plein de possibilités.
Mari : J'ai été ému aux larmes. Mon nouveau job est mieux. En tous cas, c'est mieux que de traîner à ne rien faire à la maison. Tant qu'on est tous les deux ensemble, rien d'autre n'a d'importance.
Texte superposé : Votre soutien fait sa force.

Chain Letter, p. 216
Texte : Cher Eric,
Un virus mortel se répand dans notre communauté, faisant une nouvelle victime chaque semaine. Il se propage à travers le sang contaminé et les rapports sexuels. Je suis sûr que tu sais de quoi je parle : du VIH et du Sida.
Le seul moyen de l'éradiquer est de transmettre ce message plus rapidement que le virus.
Et le message est : préservatifs. Pratiquez le sexe sans risque et utilisez-les. C'est aussi simple que ça.
Recopie cette lettre 6 fois et envoie-la à ceux qui, selon toi, contribue à faire de ce monde en endroit meilleur. Ne sois pas gêné, on a tous besoin d'un petit rappel de temps à autre.
Si tu envoies cette lettre à six personnes cette semaine et que chacune de ces personnes fait de même, à la fin du mois 7 776 personnes seront mieux informées. Si tu préfères ne rien faire, à la fin de cette année plusieurs millions de gens n'auront pas eu notre message.
Nous devons à tous de transmettre le message et de battre le virus de vitesse.
Signé : Quelqu'un qui te veut du bien.
P.S. Si tu peux envoyer un don à la Aids Foundation, ils t'en seront très reconnaissants. Voici leur adresse :
NZ Aids Foundation
BP 7287, Wellington,
Nouvelle-Zélande.

Slow Poison, p. 217
Titre : Poison lent.
Texte : Réalisé dans l'intérêt public par Tata Tead limited.

Clean Up, p. 220
Musique : Morning has broken...
Homme : Bonjour !
Encore une belle journée ...
Effets spéciaux : Bruits d'effort et de glissement.
Texte superposé : Vous ne feriez pas ça.
Texte superposé : Ne laissez pas votre chien le faire.

Anybody Out There ? p. 222
Voix off masculine : Il y a quelqu'un ?
Il y a quelqu'un ?
Il y a... quelqu'un ?
Il y a quelqu'un ?
Texte superposé : Oui.
The Samaritans (équivalent de SOS Amitié).

Die and Live, p. 224
Ron était prêt à mourir. Puis est arrivée la pire des nouvelles : « Tu vas vivre. »
Texte : Vous parlez d'un sale coup ! Vous aussi vous feriez une drôle de tête, non ? Vous étiez là, bien tranquillement avec votre cancer en phase terminale quand, sans crier gare, votre médecin vous assène le coup fatal : « Le traitement a marché. Le cancer a été éradiqué. Vous allez vivre. » Vous êtes dévasté. Vos perspectives ne pourraient être plus sombres.
Il faut dire que l'histoire de Ron est plutôt unique. La plupart des gens ne réagiraient pas comme lui. Mais justement, face à une mort annoncée (ou dans le cas de Ron, la survie) personne ne réagit de la même manière.
Lorsqu'on lui a annoncé qu'il avait un cancer, naturellement, Ron a reçu un choc. C'était la pire nouvelle qu'on lui ait jamais annoncée. Mais, avec le temps, il a vu les choses d'un autre œil. Il a accepte son sort, commençant même à planifier son départ, concentrant toute sa vie sur lui. C'est là que les problèmes ont commencé. Ron était si prêt à mourir qu'il avait atteint un état d'apaisement. Normalement, dans notre domaine, c'est ce qu'on peut espérer de mieux. Il est bon qu'un patient en phase terminale atteigne cette phase, même si c'est très rare. Au Mary Potter Hospice, nous considérons que nous avons fait notre travail au mieux quand un de nos patients en arrive là.
« Tu vas vivre, Ron. » Remballez vos couronnes. Décommandez le corbillard. On ne peut rêver meilleure nouvelle, pas vrai ? Faux. C'est que sa vie était tellement axée sur sa mort que, d'une manière étrange, c'était devenu sa raison de vivre. Il avait commencé à faire ses adieux et s'acheminait tranquillement vers une conclusion bien planifiée. Il en avait terminé.
Soudain, par un cruel coup du sort, cette raison d'être s'envolait en fumée. On lui claquait au nez la porte de la mort. Tous ses préparatifs et ses angoisses avaient été vains. Se traînant comme une âme en peine dans ce nouveau report de vie, Ron s'imagina des maladies. Il devint persuadé d'être cardiaque. Il n'en était rien, bien sûr. Il souffrait surtout d'un trouble psychologique et son cerveau, le plus puissant des organes, se chargea du reste Ron s'échinait à se trouver des prétextes afin de se complaire dans une mort imminente. C'était ainsi qu'il se sentait le mieux. Il était devenu dépendant de tous les services de soutien disponibles pour les mourants. Il s'était trop bien adapté aux attentions et à la compassion des autres. Cela ne veux pas dire qu'il les aimait, mais il en avait besoin. C'est dans cet état qu'il vécut jusqu'à la fin de sa vie.
Ron s'est en grande partie imposé à lui-même son destin tragique. Ce n'était pas un patient du Mary Potter Hospice, mais son histoire nous a été rapportée par notre médecin chef (Ron fut l'un de ses patients en Angleterre) car elle illustre bien le genre de problèmes auxquels nous sommes régulièrement confrontés.
Cette histoire a également d'importantes implications dans la manière dont nous traitons nos patients au Mary Potter Hospice. Parce qu'il arrive que des événements prenant une tournure positive aggravent considérablement une situation. C'est dire si nos journées de travail à l'hospice sont imprévisibles. C'est pourquoi nous cherchons constamment à tirer des enseignements des Ron de ce monde afin que ce genre de situations ne se reproduise pas.
On dit qu'il n'y a que deux choses dans la vie qui soient inévitables : les impôts et la mort. Si les impôts sont d'une prévisibilité redoutable, ce n'est pas le cas de la mort. L'histoire de Ron en témoigne, tout comme celle de Nell. Mais son histoire à elle se situe aux antipodes. C'est sans doute celle de la mort parfaite. Petronella, Nell pour ses amis, venait de Kapiti Way. Elle ne fut hospitalisée au Mary Potter Hospice que très brièvement. Elle avait tout juste soixante ans lorsqu'on nous l'a envoyée en mai 1994. Elle avait des tumeurs au foie, aux reins, au pancréas et à l'estomac. Ce n'était pas la première fois qu'elle avait affaire au cancer. En 1989, elle avait subi l'ablation d'un rein. Cette fois, lorsque le diagnostic tomba, on lui annonça qu'il ne lui restait que deux mois à vivre. Nell arriva à l'Hospice en proie à une douleur terrible et vomissant constamment. Nous aussi, nous étions convaincus qu'elle n'en n'avait plus pour longtemps, mais nous n'avons pas cherché à estimer combien de temps au juste. Si nous avons appris une chose, c'est qu'il n'y a rien de pire que de plaquer une date d'expiration sur un malade. D'une part, c'est virtuellement impossible. Mais plus important encore, cela peut entraîner des situations comme celle de Ron.
D'abord, nous avons cru que le cancer de Nell avait atteint un stade incontrôlable, ce n'était pas le cas. Elle était persuadée que sa douleur était simplement due à l'étirement d'un muscle. Elle se trompait. Elle pensait aussi que les médicaments qu'on lui avait prescrits provoquaient ses troubles et là, elle avait raison. Au cours des deux semaines qu'elle a passées à l'Hospice, nous l'avons remise sur un traitement de contrôle de la douleur qui ne la faisait plus vomir. Elle rentra chez elle sans souffrir et prête à reprendre le cours de sa vie. Elle avait toujours le cancer, et il était toujours incurable, mais elle avait encore beaucoup de choses à vivre.
Ces derniers temps, nous découvrons que nos patients sont plus heureux quand ils sont traités ailleurs que dans les bâtiments de l'Hospice. Ils continuent de venir et nos lits sont toujours pleins, mais ils ne viennent que périodiquement pour qu'on ajuste leurs traitements et évalue l'efficacité des remèdes contre la douleur. Ensuite, ils rentrent chez eux, où ils sont plus à leur aise. Nous l'encourageons le plus possible. Lorsque les patients sont hospitalisés trop tôt, ils risquent de se résigner trop vite à la mort. En revanche, chez eux, ils continuent à mener une vie normale, comme Nell.
Deux mois passèrent, puis trois, puis six. Nell avait toujours le même appétit de vivre. Elle voyait régulièrement son médecin traitant et notre médecin de l'Hospice lui rendait visite sur la côte tous les deux mois. Elle utilisait également des remèdes naturels. Mais c'est surtout son moral qui lui faisait le plus de bien. Si elle avait cru à sa première sentence de mort et avait choisi de rester à Mary Potter, elle aurait peut-être capitulé. Heureusement, il n'en fut rien. Elle voulait être chez elle avec son mari.
Elle voulait aussi être avec son mari ailleurs que chez elle. Ce qu'ils faisaient souvent. Ils accrochaient leur caravane à l'arrière de leur voiture et partaient pour de longs voyages dans toute la Nouvelle-Zélande. Contrairement à Ron, qui était entièrement absorbé par la mort, elle était absorbée par la vie. Fin 1995, des complications survinrent.
Nell eut une obstruction intestinale. Cela ne l'arrêta pas. Elle subit une intervention puis eut une excellente convalescence. Seize mois après sa mort annoncée, elle débordait encore de vie. Toutefois, en mai 1996, sa maladie finit par reprendre le dessus. Elle devint fatiguée et la douleur réapparut. Nell comprit que la fin était proche. Elle ne pouvait plus avaler ses pilules et les analgésiques devaient lui être administrés par perfusion. Ce n'est qu'alors, deux ans après son premier diagnostic, qu'elle décida de revenir à l'Hospice pour y mourir.
Comme nous l'avons déjà dit, nous ne cherchons pas à savoir quand les gens vont mourir. Souvent, ce sont les patients eux-mêmes qui nous l'annoncent. Quelque chose au fond d'eux-mêmes le devine. Ce fut le cas pour Nell. Le matin de sa mort, elle savait que ce serait son dernier. Elle a appelé un par un les membres de sa famille pour leur faire ses adieux, puis ils se sont tous rassemblés autour de son lit et elle est morte paisiblement.
Nell était une femme extraordinaire, toujours souriante, toujours positive, malgré la menace du cancer qui a pesé sur elle pendant sept ans. Son souvenir est encore très présent dans l'esprit du personnel de l'Hospice et celui des autres malades en phase terminale qu'elle a soutenus et encouragés. D'une étrange manière, au lieu d'être terrifiée par sa maladie, elle l'a trouvée libératoire. Elle ignorait combien de temps il lui restait à vivre, mais elle était résolue à en profiter jusqu'au bout. Elle a choisi la manière de Frank Sinatra : elle est morte à sa façon.
Au Mary Potter Hospice, nous avons une devise : profiter de la vie jusqu'au bout. Comme l'a montré Nell, cela peut souvent se faire en dehors de l'Hospice. C'est pourquoi nous étendons nos services au sein de la communauté. C'est aussi pourquoi, grâce à un formidable soutien local, nous venons de construire un service de consultation dans la région de Kapiti. Grâce à votre soutien lors de notre campagne de rue cette année, nous pourrons en faire encore plus pour aider les mourants (et ceux qui découvrent que, finalement, ils ne sont pas en train de mourir) à profiter de la vie jusqu'au bout.

Start Again, p. 227
Titre : Une congestion cérébrale n'est pas la fin, c'est un nouveau début.
Texte : Vous avez une chance sur huit de faire une congestion cérébrale. Naturellement, si vous fumez, vous multipliez ce risque par cinq. L'hypertension le multiplie par quatre. Si vous êtes fumeur et faites de l'hypertension, vous avez alors gagné le gros lot ! Le risque de congestion cérébrale est 18 fois plus grand. La congestion cérébrale est due à une interruption de l'approvisionnement en sang d'une partie du cerveau et peut provoquer des lésions cérébrales. Vous présenterez alors une partie ou tous les symptômes suivants : mort (dans le pire des cas, c'est pourquoi autant commencer par là) ; perte de connaissance; paralysie ou faiblesse dans un côté du visage, un bras ou une jambe. Incapacité à communiquer. Vous risquez d'avoir des difficultés à déglutir et à manger. Vous ne maîtriserez plus votre vessie ou vos intestins. Des troubles oculaires sont également au programme, ainsi que des pertes de mémoire et du contrôle des émotions. Vous pouvez tirer un trait sur votre pouvoir d'achat. Bien sûr, la dépression est très fréquente. Souvent, vous vous retrouvez avec un corps constitué de deux moitiés complètement différentes.
Un côté continue de fonctionner plus ou moins comme avant. Mais il faut réapprendre à l'autre côté à bouger, à coordonner ses mouvements, à parler, à manger et à marcher. Au bout du compte, il n'y a rien d'étonnant à ce qu'on considère souvent que, si on a la chance d'avoir survécu à une congestion cérébrale, c'est qu'on n'est pas aussi chanceux que ça. C'est avec un certain plaisir qu'on peut vous annoncer que ce n'est pas le cas. Il y a de bonnes chances pour que vous retrouviez une partie de vos facultés, voire même toutes. Une thérapie intensive, un accompagnement qualifié et le temps vous aideront à retrouver le contrôle de votre corps. Autre point positif : à mesure que nous en apprenons davantage sur les causes de la congestion cérébrale, nous pouvons faire baisser considérablement votre risque d'en subir une. L'abus d'alcool, la tabagie, le stress, le manque d'exercice, les forts taux de cholestérolémie, les maladies cardio-vasculaires, le diabète et l'obésité y contribuent tous. Un grand nombre de ces troubles peuvent être traités avec des médicaments, un changement des habitudes alimentaires et professionnelles ou, dans le cas de l'abus d'alcool, une bonne dose de volonté (ne vous inquiétez pas, on ne cherche pas à vous gâcher la vie, juste à vous inciter à un peu de modération). La Stroke Fondation de Nouvelle-Zélande est la seule organisation à se consacrer uniquement aux victimes de congestion cérébrale, à leur famille et à leurs proches. Mais – surprise ! – nous ne sommes pas riches. Afin de poursuivre notre travail, nos recherches, nos services de soutien et nos programmes d'éducation préventive, nous avons besoin de votre aide. Envoyez un don à la Stroke Foundation. BP 2320 Wellington, ou téléphonez au 0800 Stroke (0800 787 653). N'importe quelle somme que vous pourrez donner nous aidera à informer plus de gens et à leur faire comprendre que la congestion cérébrale n'est pas une fatalité.
Pour plus d'informations, contactez la Stroke Foundation of New Zeland Inc.
BP 2320, Wellington.
Téléphone (04) 472 80 99.
Télécopie (04) 472 70 19.

Blind, p. 228
Aveugle [avœgl] adj. et n. fin XIe lat. ab oculis 1. Qui est privé du sens de la vue.
Aveugle [avœgl] adj. et n. fin XIe lat. ab oculis 2. Dont la raison, le jugement, est incapable de rien discerner (un facteur, des circonstances, etc.).
Texte : Passez une journée avec un aveugle. Vous verrez les choses sous un autre œil. Publié dans l'intérêt public par Tata Tea Limited. Sachons faire la différence... tous les jours.

Matches, p. 229
Voix off masculine : Lorsqu'une vie s'éteint, quelque chose en elle peut en allumer une autre.
La vie vous appelle. Donnez vos organes.
Voix off masculine et titre : La vie vous appelle. Donnez vos organes.
Voix off masculine : Ceci est un message d'intérêt public d'Antena 3 TV.
Créé par Saatchi & Saatchi Advertising.

Prisoner, p. 230
Voix off masculine : Certains prisonniers ont l'électricité et trois repas par jour.
Certains prisonniers ont l'eau chaude et la télévision en couleurs.
D'autres n'ont pas cette chance. .
Leur seul crime est d'avoir survécu à leurs revenus.
Aidez Rand Aid à faire la différence.
011 822 25 10.

Punch These, p. 232
Titre : En colère, frustré, perdu ?
Tapez là-dessus.
Texte : The Samaritans (SOS Amitié) :
Tel. 0800 22 33 44.

Bus, p. 286
Texte : SOS Amitié. Tel. 4 73 97 39.

Read This You Piece of Shit, p. 7

Titular: Lee esto, tío mierda.

Texto: Si este anuncio no te ofende, debería hacerlo.

Nadie debería ser tratado así.

Pero, desgraciadamente, en todo el mundo hay millones de personas que sufren este trato. Para muchos, un ataque verbal es la menor de sus preocupaciones. En Brasil, por ejemplo, los trabajadores de las haciendas amazónicas se enfrentan a un castigo denominado «el tronco». A cualquier hombre que no haya talado su cuota de árboles, lo desnudan, lo atan y lo abandonan en un tronco de árbol vaciado durante tres días. Por si fuera poco, untan el tronco con miel para atraer a hormigas y otros insectos.

En la India, los niños padecen horrores semejantes. Criaturas de apenas seis años son vendidas para trabajar en las fábricas de alfombras. Cuando los dueños de los telares no consiguen suficientes niños para comprar, los secuestran. Les obligan a trabajar todo el día. Si bajan un poco el ritmo, no les dejan dormir por la noche. Si cometen un error, les golpean. A un niño lo rociaron con parafina y le prendieron fuego por haber pedido un rato libre. Otros seis recibieron unas palizas tan fuertes por jugar que uno de ellos murió.

En Nepal, la esclavitud está igualmente generalizada. Chicas de diez años de edad son raptadas y vendidas para trabajar como prostitutas en la India.

Primero pasan por un período de «preparación». Las encierran desnudas en habitaciones diminutas durante días, sin comida. Las queman con cigarrillos, les propinan palizas y las violan hasta que, finalmente, su sumisión es total. Sólo entonces los dueños de los burdeles de Bombay pagan los mejores precios por ellas.

Y si la prostitución puede convertirse en una forma de esclavitud, también puede serlo el matrimonio.

En muchas partes del mundo, los padres todavía tienen el poder de elegir esposo para sus hijas. La elección depende en gran parte de lo que la familia del novio ofrece a cambio. El bienestar de la novia importa poco.

Así pues, muchas mujeres se ven forzadas a casarse contra su voluntad. Algunas incluso a la temprana edad de nueve años. Una niña nigeriana sentía tanto odio por su marido que constantemente intentaba escapar.

Para detenerla, el esposo le cortó ambas piernas. Ya habrás podido comprobar que la esclavitud no pertenece al pasado.

Ni tampoco es un problema exclusivo del Tercer Mundo.

Sólo en Gran Bretaña se han producido 1.700 casos de abusos de sirvientas domésticas desde el año 1987. La mayoría de ellas son chicas procedentes de entornos pobres en países lejanos. Creen que trabajar en Gran Bretaña será la respuesta a sus problemas. Pero cuando llegan aquí, a menudo son tratadas como animales. Muchas deben dormir en el suelo y alimentarse de las sobras. Están obligadas a trabajar 18 horas al día. Y si se quejan, reciben palizas o azotes. A algunas ni siquiera se les permite salir. Algunas son violadas.

La lista de atrocidades es interminable.

Todavía hay más de 100 millones de esclavos en todo el mundo. Y todos ellos probablemente tengan una historia tan dolorosa como estas.

La Anti Slavery International (Asociación Internacional contra la Esclavitud) lucha por la abolición de la esclavitud. Sabemos que únicamente podremos destruirla dando a conocer los detalles de las vidas de estas personas y sacándola a la luz pública.

Con nuestra presión y concienciando a todo el mundo sobre estos temas hemos convencido a los gobiernos y a las Naciones Unidas para que aborden el problema.

En algunos países como Tailandia, la India y Pakistán, incluso hemos conseguido que cambien las leyes. Nada de esto hubiera sido posible sin la ayuda de nuestros colaboradores, que han enviado cartas e investigado a personas, empresas y gobiernos en todo el mundo.

Necesitamos tu ayuda para nuestras futuras campañas para continuar ejerciendo esta presión.

Si quieres colaborar, rellena el cupón adjunto y hazte socio. Con el tiempo lograremos que nadie sepa lo que significa ser tratado como un esclavo.

Anti-Slavery International, Stableyard, Broomgrove Road, London SW9 9TL.
Tel: 0171 924 9555. Fax: 0171 738 4110.

Pram/Family Planning, p. 18

Madre: Cariño, no te preocupes por todo ese rollo de la planificación familiar.
Scott, deja eso, ¿quieres?
Me refiero a ¿qué pueden decirte todos esos doctores y dispensarios que no sepa alguien con un poco de sentido común?
Pregunta a tus amigas, es lo que hice yo.
Hannah, deja al bebé en paz... ¿cuántas veces tendré que decírtelo?
Si no quieres quedarte embarazada deberías... ya sabes qué quiero decir, deberías tener cuidado y todo eso.
Piensa con la cabeza...

Voz en off masculina: No hagas caso de los cuentos de viejas sobre planificación familiar.
Casada o soltera, tu médico o dispensario te ofrecerá consejo amistoso y preciso.
Consulta el apartado «Planificación familiar» de la guía telefónica.

Sobreimpresión: Consulta el apartado «Planificación familiar» de la guía telefónica.

Madre: ...de todos modos, con tantos hijos, ¿cómo podría permitirme los anticonceptivos?

Voz en off masculina: No te costarán nada.

Clip this Coupon, p. 22

Texto: Recorta este cupón. Será como poner aquí tu fotografía.

Women and Children First, p. 24

Titular: Y las potencias nucleares dijeron: las mujeres y los niños primero.

Texto: No, no se trata de una imagen manipulada. Es un niño de Kazakstán, nacido con hidrocefalia. Esta deformidad es consecuencia de la radiación a la que estuvo expuesta su madre. Ahora bien, no te enfades con nosotros por enseñártelo, enfádate con aquéllos que te lo ocultaron afirmando que las pruebas nucleares no son peligrosas.

Can't Look, p. 26

Sonido: El llanto de un bebé
Escena 1
Mujer: Cállate. ¡Si no paras de chillar, te aplastaré la cabeza contra la puerta!
Escena 2
Hombre: Ven y siéntate aquí.
Escena 3
Hombre: Eres un descerebrado. Un estúpido. Es imposible que seas hijo mío.
Escena 4
Niño: Mamá, ¿dónde estás?
No me gusta estar solo.
Escena 5
Hombre: No le digas nada a nadie.
Va a ser nuestro pequeño secreto.
Voz en off femenina & sobreimpresión: A veces tampoco podemos soportar mirarlo.
La crueldad hacia los niños puede cesar y, con tu ayuda, para siempre.
Voz en off femenina: Colabora con la nueva campaña de la NSPCC. (Sociedad Nacional de Prevención de la Crueldad con los Niños) para ponerle punto final.
Sobreimpresión: NSPCC. La crueldad con los niños debe cesar. Punto final.

Pregnant Man, p. 28

Titular: ¿Irías con más cuidado si fueses tú el que se quedara embarazado?

Texto: Cualquiera que esté casado o soltero puede asesorarse sobre la contracepción en la Family Planning Association (Asociación de Planificación Familiar), Margaret Pyke House, 27–35 Mortimer Street, London W1N 8BQ.
Tel. 01 636 9135.

Some Fathers, p. 29

Titular: Algunos padres transforman a sus hijos.

Texto: Puedes ver los daños causados en la cabeza del niño. ¿Puedes verlo?

La cuestión es que mientras que las heridas físicas se curarán con el tiempo, el pánico psicológico durará toda la vida.

Se ha convertido a un niño feliz y equilibrado en un niño con los nervios destrozados.

Miles de niños son maltratados de este modo cada año. Tanto por sus padres como por sus madres.

Pero si sospechas que un niño es maltratado, tú eres el responsable. Porque, al fin y al cabo, si no das parte de ello, también tienes parte de culpa.

Si tienes información sobre niños maltratados, llámanos el miércoles 4 de septiembre. 1 800 011 233.
Denúncialo y páralo. NSW Police Service (Servicio de Policía de NSW).

Same Father, p. 30

Titular: Los dos tenemos el mismo padre.

Texto: Ésta es la historia de Sally.
Mi madre murió cuando tenía doce años. Una noche en que tuve una pesadilla, mi padre me dijo que podía dormir en su cama.

Al principio tan sólo me acurrucaba, pero después empezó a hacer otras cosas. Quería que parara pero él seguía. Lo odiaba, realmente dolía. Me dijo que eso significaba que me quería.

Al día siguiente, cuando me disponía a ir al colegio, me dijo que no debía contarle a nadie lo que había ocurrido. Después de eso, quería que durmiera con él cada noche. Lo llamaba nuestro pequeño secreto.

Más tarde, cuando dejé de tener la menstruación, mi padre me prohibió ir a la escuela. Les dijo que estaba enferma. Alguna vez puedo sentir cómo se mueve el bebé dentro de mí, es una sensación horrible.

Afortunadamente, la escuela de Sally informó de su ausencia y ahora está recibiendo todo el apoyo que necesita.

Por supuesto, las consecuencias del abuso que padeció van más allá del embarazo.

Necesitará una terapia larga para tratar de resolver el daño emocional, como el sentimiento de culpa y la incapacidad de establecer relaciones.

De hecho, todas las formas de abuso pueden causar daño emocional.

No sólo las más evidentes, como la agresión sexual y la brutalidad física.

Por ejemplo, la ausencia de cualquier muestra de afecto, el hacer caso omiso de los niños, la crítica o los gritos constantes pueden producir cicatrices emocionales para toda la vida.

A veces, los niños pueden incluso ser empujados al suicidio.

Por todo ello, la NSPCC. (Sociedad Nacional de Prevención de la Crueldad con los Niños) está lanzando «Una llamada en favor de los niños». Es una llamada a todos para detenernos a reflexionar sobre el comportamiento hacia los niños.

Para reconocer el efecto que cualquier forma de crueldad puede tener sobre un niño. Y para darnos cuenta de que el modo en que los niños son tratados les afecta de por vida.

Responde a la llamada.

Si tú o alguien que conoces es objeto de abusos, llama a la Línea de Protección a la Infancia de la NSPCC, 0800 800 500.

O, si después de leer esto, crees que necesitas más información, llámanos al 071 825 2775.

NSPCC. Una llamada en favor de los niños.

Astronaut, p. 31

Titular: ¿Tiene el mundo las prioridades adecuadas?

Texto: The State of the World Forum reúne a muchas de las personas más influyentes para debatir asuntos virtuales que afronta la humanidad... el desarmamento nuclear... el fin de los conflictos... el papel del desarrollo de las mujeres y los niños. Se trata de establecer nuestras prioridades futuras. Únete al debate a través de nuestra página web entre el 27 de octubre y el 1 de noviembre. Es tu oportunidad de cambiar el mundo.

Face, p. 32

Sobreimpresión: Esta chica quiere hablar.
Sobreimpresión: ¿Has perdido la paciencia?
Sobreimpresión: La enfermera Robinson sabe que pronto será una conversación a dos.
Enfermera: Hola, Rachel, aquí me tienes otra vez.
¿Otra noche sin salir, chicas?
Sobreimpresión: El nuevo Servicio Nacional de la Salud necesita más enfermeras.
Voz en off femenina: Las enfermeras marcan la diferencia. Para más información sobre los estudios de enfermería o el regreso a la enfermería activa, con un salario y unas condiciones mejores, llama al teléfono 0845 60 60 655.

Cot, p. 36

Voz en off masculina: Uno de cada diez asesinatos tiene lugar aquí.
Cada semana se producen una o dos muertes.
En un año se propinan más de 5.000 palizas y se cometen más de 1.700 abusos sexuales.
Sobreimpresión: En Gran Bretaña, 36.000 niños viven bajo la amenaza de padecer abusos cada día.
Sobreimpresión: NSPCC. (Sociedad Nacional de Prevención de la Crueldad con los Niños). Una llamada en favor de los niños.

The World Could End This Easily, p. 40

Texto: El mundo podría acabarse así de fácilmente.
Pronúnciate en contra de las pruebas nucleares.
Greenpeace 0800 22 33 44.

Stay In School, p. 42

Sobreimpresión: No dejes la escuela.

Hungry, p. 44

Voz en off masculina: Si dijera «joder», probablemente te molestaría.
Si te dijera que tengo hambre, probablemente no.
Joder, tengo hambre.
Sobreimpresión: La comida en buen estado nunca debería desperdiciarse.

Day Against Violence, p. 46

Sobreimpresión: Parecía imposible.
Ocurrió el 12 de febrero de 1995.
Unos 170.000 millones de personas lo vieron en todo el mundo.
Por primera vez.
Los equipos de fútbol italianos salieron al campo vistiendo las camisetas del equipo contrario.
Y leyeron un mensaje: el fútbol debe unir, no dividir.
Ahora, todos compartimos esa idea. Nada es imposible.

Worst Marks, p. 50

Titular: Los niños de las minorías étnicas a menudo obtienen las peores marcas en la escuela.

Teacher Passing an Examination, p. 51

Texto de la ilustración: Se había estado peleando con la multiplicación. No había manera de que entendiera su mecanismo hasta que el profesor se lo explicó de otro modo.

Titular: El profesor a examen.

Texto: El momento en que un alumno capta un concepto que le ha resultado difícil es probablemente una de las mejores cosas de ser profesor. Significa que el profesor ha encontrado una explicación comprensible. No podría ser más significativo.

Hacer comprensible una explicación es lo más importante de la enseñanza.

Es la conexión entre el conocimiento impartido y comprendido. Para el profesor y el alumno es un logro compartido.

Es seguramente el mayor atractivo de ser un profesional de la enseñanza.

Si es así, te alegrará saber que hay otras gratificaciones que también valen la pena.

Desde diciembre, hay un sueldo inicial de unas 14.000 libras para los profesores de primaria y secundaria con una buena licenciatura que trabajen en los barrios del centro de Londres (incluyendo el sobresueldo y el complemento ofrecidos en estos barrios).

El director de una escuela grande del centro de Londres podría ganar hasta 48.000 libras.

No es dinero fácil por supuesto. Al fin y al cabo, enseñar no es un proceso mecánico. No lo puede ser. Cada clase está compuesta de alumnos con una amplia variedad de capacidades, intereses, actitudes y procedencias.

Como profesor tienes que conocer estas diferencias, recordarlas y actuar en consecuencia.

Por ejemplo, la rapidez con que los niños aprenden varía según los individuos y según los temas, pero el profesor tiene que llegar a todos ellos.

Los rostros perplejos puede que pidan una manera completamente nueva de explicar algo, y un enfoque imaginativo puede hacer maravillas para la moral general de la clase.

En cierto sentido, un profesor se presenta a un examen cada día. Y tiene que aprobarlo.

¿Una perspectiva desalentadora o un reto estimulante?

Si crees que es lo último, la formación puede colmar tus ganas de enseñar y poner a punto tus habilidades naturales para prepararte para el examen diario. Y para una profesión que es absolutamente gratificante.

Si quieres ser profesor, puedes informarte llamando al 0345 300121, código de departamento IS/4/A, o enviando el cupón de abajo.

La enseñanza hace que las personas den lo mejor de sí.

Resolution, p. 52

Sobreimpresión: En Filipinas, miles de niños pasan el Fin de Año en hospitales con los dedos amputados o las manos destrozadas por culpa de los petardos de fabricación barata.
Esta campaña tiene por objetivo acabar con este círculo vicioso.
Maestra: ¿Cuál es el buen propósito para este Fin de Año?
Niño: No jugaré más con petardos, señorita.
Sobreimpresión: Este fin de año, no toques los petardos

Prostitute, p. 54

Titular: ¿Te gustaría trabajar en Europa como prostituta?

Texto: Hay millones de mujeres que no tienen otra opción.

Como las mujeres inmigrantes engañadas por las organizaciones internacionales de prostitución. Son víctimas de la explotación, y no pueden decidir sobre sus propias vidas.

Te sorprendería conocer los métodos que se emplean en la actualidad para degradar al ser humano.

Manos Unidas quiere poner fin a estas formas de abuso. Ayúdanos a acabar con la esclavitud.

Nota: Como puedes ver en la página izquierda, puedes encontrar esta forma de esclavitud entre los anuncios clasificados (sección de bolsa de trabajo) de los principales periódicos españoles.

Mining Children, p. 55

Titular: Compañía metalúrgica necesita niños mineros.

Texto: Hay millones de niños que no necesitan buscar un trabajo que se les impone.

Como los niños que son empleados como mano de obra barata.

Son víctimas de la explotación y no pueden decidir sobre sus propias vidas.

Te sorprendería conocer los métodos que se emplean en la actualidad para degradar al ser humano.

Manos Unidas quiere poner fin a estas formas de abuso. Ayúdanos a acabar con la esclavitud.

Nota: La página de la izquierda muestra cómo aparecen estos abusos en los anuncios clasificados (sección de bolsa de trabajo) de los principales periódicos españoles.

Child Abuse, p. 56

Hombre 1: Una niña preciosa, ¿verdad?
Hombre 2: ¿Es virgen?
Hombre 1: Claro, es mi hija.
Hombre 2: ¿Cuánto?
Hombre 1: Sólo 100 dólares.
Hombre 2: ¿Qué puede hacer?
Hombre 1 : De todo, pero no la mates.
...ven aquí, cariño.
Voz en off: Si le ocurriera a tu hija, estarías aterrorizado, ¿no?
Recuérdalo cuando vayas al extranjero.
Un niño sigue siendo un niño en todo el mundo.
Sobreimpresión: Centro Italiano per l'Adozione Internationale (Centro Italiano para la Adopción Internacional).
Per donazioni c/c n. 10837 presso la Cariplo, agenzia 15 di Milano

Raped as a 3 Year Old, p. 58

Titular: ¿Cómo es una violación a los tres años? Una víctima lo explica.

Texto: La primera vez que recuerdo haber sufrido abusos sexuales por parte de mi padre era cuando tenía unos 3 años. Puede que hubiera ocurrido antes, no lo sé.

Es como si ahora mismo lo viera, yo acostado en la cama y su gran cara acercándose a mí. Me daba el beso de buenas noches, pero no paraba de besarme.

Me solía decir que era nuestro secreto y que si alguna vez se lo contaba a alguien me echaría de casa.

Pero incluso siendo un niño sabía que había algo que no estaba bien. Eran esas palabras, «Te protegeré». ¿Cómo podía protegerme si me estaba haciendo un daño terrible?

Es realmente extraño, porque era mi enemigo, pero al mismo tiempo mi único amigo en el mundo. Me hizo depender de él. Me controlaba.

Mi cuerpo fue su juguete durante más de nueve años.

En la escuela tenía problemas para relacionarme. Me sentía diferente.

No dejaba nunca que nadie se acercara a mí. En los vestuarios, tras la clase de gimnasia, odiaba que la gente viera mi cuerpo desnudo. Me sentía tan avergonzado que pensaba que podrían ser capaces de darse cuenta de lo que me pasaba y llamarme maricón.

Incluso cuando llegué a encontrar una novia aún no estaba seguro de ser heterosexual. Era muy brusco con ella. Supongo que quería controlar a alguien, como mi padre hacía conmigo.

El sexo me aterrorizaba. El tener un orgasmo me hizo pensar en lo que mi padre hizo dentro de mí. Y ese gran rostro sonriente.

Finalmente encontré a otra persona. Nos casamos. Tras dos años me dejó. Me dijo que era frío y que no la comprendía.

Pero así es como era. No era consciente de causar o sentir dolor mental o físico. Algo dentro de mí se había apagado desde hacía mucho tiempo. Había momentos en los que de hecho podía cortarme con un cuchillo y no sentir nada.

Tras el divorcio, me di a la bebida. Era un modo de evadirme. Pero aun así sufría profundas depresiones.

El año pasado mi padre por fin murió. Creo que eso fue lo que me hizo ponerme en contacto con la NSPCC. (Sociedad Nacional de Prevención de la Crueldad con los Niños).

Tenía 53 años, y era la primera vez que le hablaba a alguien de mi infancia.

Durante seis meses, una vez a la semana me atendía un funcionario de Protección a la Infancia. Me hizo contarle todo sobre mi experiencia. Hablar de ello era muy doloroso. Supongo que durante más de cuarenta años había tratado de olvidarlo.

Pero finalmente empezó a funcionar. Me hizo darme cuenta de que lo que había ocurrido no era mi culpa.

Es la primera vez en toda mi vida que recuerdo haberme empezado a sentir bien conmigo mismo. Era como si se me permitiera salir de una oscura y solitaria celda.

Nunca olvidaré mi experiencia. Pero, al menos, puedo empezar a vivir mi vida.

Para más información sobre la labor de la NSPCC o para hacer una donación, escribe a: NSPCC, 67 Saffron Hill, London EC1N 8RS, o llama al 071 242 1626.

Para informar sobre un posible caso de abuso sexual, llama a la Línea de Protección a la Infancia de la NSPCC, 0800 800 500.

Dr Jekyll, Mr Hyde, p. 59
Titular: Doctor Jekyll, Mister Hyde
Texto: Eres un hombre familiar de confianza, cariñoso y atento. Tienes una hermosa esposa y una hija adorable de nueve años. El amor de tu familia es tu mayor bendición. Lo defenderías contra todo y contra todos. Entonces, llega el momento en que tienes que hacer un viaje de negocios. Vas a un destino exótico, Bangkok, por ejemplo, uno de esos países en que todo se tolera, donde «tienen tradiciones y costumbres bastante diferentes». Y allí, junto con las camisetas y souvenirs de un mercado al aire libre, te ofrecen una niña. Es una niña preciosa de nueve años que se parece un poco a tu hija, aunque su aspecto es más propio del de una mujer adulta. Piensas que sencillamente es la manera en que allí se hacen las cosas, y empieza tu rápida transformación: te estás convirtiendo en otra persona. El mercado mundial de la pedofilia, un rico y poderoso mercado de la muerte, se anota otra victoria. De hecho, la mayoría de sus beneficios no proceden de criminales y pervertidos. Proceden de la gente corriente, gente como tú. En el CIAI (Centro Italiano para la Adopción Internacional) han luchado durante años para reivindicar un concepto muy simple, que nadie debería olvidar nunca, sobre todo cuando se viaja por el extranjero: un niño sigue siendo un niño, en cualquier parte del mundo.
Se pueden hacer donaciones con tarjeta de crédito llamando al número +39 2 55 01 20 11 o por transferencia bancaria a la c/ n.° 10837 de Cariplo, sucursal 15, Milano, Italia.

1 in every 8, p. 60
Titular: Una de cada ocho personas que pasa por delante de este cartel sufrió abusos en la infancia
NSPCC. Una llamada en favor de los niños.

Ban Guns, p. 64

Bullet, p. 66
Titular: Pene sin condón.
Texto: Consíguelos gratis llamando al 250 8629.

Less Dead, p. 68
Texto: Si una pistola del calibre 22 es menos mortífera, ¿por qué él no está menos muerto?
Exige una ley de armas de fuego que mate la pistola del calibre 22.

Grunge Angels, p. 70
Voz en off femenina: ¡Felicidades! Para que os divirtáis en esta Otra Vida, las mejores canciones de amor de Whitney Houston.
Efectos especiales: Gritos...
Sobreimpresión: La muerte es un asco. Ponte el cinturón de seguridad.

Rubber Woman, p. 74
Titular: Goma. Lo último en ropa de cama.

Rubber Man, p. 75
Texto: Los chicos siempre están mejor con goma.

Tongue, p. 76
Titular: Quiere meter su lengua en tu boca.
Texto: Aprende cantonés o mandarín de un modo fácil. Llama al Hong Kong Language Learning Centre (Centro de Idiomas Hong Kong) 2385 5331.

Mother, p. 78
Sobreimpresión: Advertencia. Esta escena puede herir la sensibilidad de algunos espectadores.
Voz en off masculina: Lo que verá a continuación le dejará atónito. Es lo que queda de una niña de siete años que viajaba en el asiento trasero sin cinturón de seguridad, a 50 quilómetros por hora. Por favor, fíjese bien en las heridas.
No hay asiento seguro sin cinturón de seguridad. Llévelo siempre puesto.
Sobreimpresión: El precio que pagamos en la carretera es demasiado alto

Job Satisfaction, p. 81
Titular: ¿Cómo puedes disfrutar de tu trabajo enviando a alguien a morir a casa?
Texto: Para cuando llegó al hospital, la enfermedad crónica de Eric ya casi había acabado con él. Respirar y tragar le resultaba difícil y doloroso.

Cualquier actividad algo más vigorosa le provocaba un dolor atroz.

A pesar de ello, Eric, de 83 años, estaba decidido a pasar sus últimos días en casa. Pero no iría a ninguna parte hasta que su enfermera hubiera repuesto suficientemente sus fuerzas.

Finalmente, gracias al oxígeno, la medicación y la alimentación artificial, Eric se sintió mejor.

La enfermera siempre se las arreglaba para encontrar tiempo para Eric y su familia: para aconsejarles, animarles o simplemente escucharles.

Al cabo de tres semanas, los síntomas se habían estabilizado lo suficiente para que pudiera volver a casa.

Al despedirse, Eric y su enfermera eran amigos.

Cuidar a ancianos pocas veces resulta fácil. Requiere fortaleza, compasión y mucha iniciativa.

Pero piensa en lo gratificante que puede ser. Imagina la satisfacción que puede proporcionarte tu trabajo cuando te permite hacer realidad el último deseo de una persona moribunda.

Ninguna otra profesión está tan cerca. Llama al teléfono 0345 64 64 64 y pide la clave 2J. A cualquier hora.
Enfermería. ¿Estás a la altura?

A Country Story, p. 82
Secuencia 1
Sobreimpresión: Danny y Tessa se casan el 24 de agosto
Madre: ¡El desayuno está listo!
Pete: ¡Mmm! ¡Bacon! ¿Tessa sabe cocinar?
Madre: Por supuesto que sabe.
Padre: Qué curioso, porque su madre no sabe.
Madre: ¡Bruce!
Voz en off masculina: Si tuvieras que enviarle una carta a esta familia, la dirigirías a los Carter, a Central Hawkes Bay.
Voz en off masculina: Esta granja ha pertenecido a los Carter durante 80 años. Danny la heredará. Y después de casarse, vivirá en ella con Tessa. Y enseñarán a una nueva generación a cultivar la tierra. Y así una generación tras otra.
Danny: Papá, si quieres esta tarde arreglaré esas bisagras antes del entrenamiento.
Papa: Estaría muy bien.
Danny: Pete, nos iremos sobre las 4.
Pete: Muy bien.
Madre: Y no os quedéis ahí toda la noche.
Sobreimpresión: Poco después, más.

Secuencia 2
Sobreimpresión: Danny y Tessa se casan dentro de cinco semanas.
Voz en off masculina: Tal y como han hecho los últimos años, Danny y Pete se pasan por el bar de vuelta a casa tras el entrenamiento.
Blue: Vaya, aquí tenemos al Sr. Cuatro Semanas. ¿Qué hay?
Pete: ¿Cómo estás hoy, Blue?
Blue: Mira quién ha vuelto.
Danny: Hombre, Matthew. ¿Dónde has estado?
Matthew: Me acerqué hasta Palmy, a la feria agrícola.
Pete: ¿Viste algo bueno?
Matthew: Un toro de competición, unos tíos de Waikato con un sementa ... tenías que pagar 5 dólares por mirar.
Danny: ¿Y pudiste verlo?
Matthew: Le dije si no podía hacernos un precio especial por familia numerosa. Me preguntó cuántos éramos y le dije que sólo yo, mi mujer y nuestros 13 hijos. Me dijo «tío, quedaté ahí. Traeré al toro para que te eche un vistazo».
Voz en off masculina: Esto se está convirtiendo en un hábito de bienvenida. Matthew siempre vuelve de algún sitio. Y siempre tiene algo que explicar. Creen que el local se llama El Búho porque al viejo Blue le importa un rábano si te quedas ahí toda la noche. Pero seguramente habrá otro motivo.
Sobreimpresión: Poco después, más.

Secuencia 3
1. Sobreimpresión: Danny y Tessa se casan dentro de cuatro semanas.
Pete: Un penique si me dices en qué piensas, Danny.
Danny: Bueno, hermanito. Sólo pensaba en lo afortunado que soy. Sin ninguna preocupación. Sin presiones. Sin agobios por el dinero.
Pete: Eso es muy profundo.
Danny: Olvídalo... ¿dónde está ese penique?
Pete: Toma.
Voz en off masculina: Siempre se han llevado así de bien. En realidad no les quedaba otro remedio. Y ahora, dentro de unas semanas, Pete será el padrino de la boda.
Danny: ¿Lo dejas?
Pete: Depende.
Danny: ¿De qué depende?
Pete: Bueno, soy el padrino, ¿no?
Danny: Claro.
Pete: Voy a hablar, ¿no?
Danny: Claro.
Pete: ¿Qué quieres que diga sobre aquel bombón que conociste en Massey hace unos años?
Danny: ¿Te echo una mano?
Bonita camisa.
Pete: ¿Cómo se llamaba? ¡Irene!
Danny: Olvida el penique.
Pete: (canta) «Irene goodnight Irene, Irene good night...»
Sobreimpresión: Poco después, más.

Secuencia 4
Sobreimpresión: Danny y Tessa se casan dentro de tres semanas.
Entrenador: Muy bien, chicos, no vamos a dejar que esos de ciudad nos humillen de nuevo. Vamos a machacarles tan pronto suene el silbato. Vamos a dejarles claro quién manda aquí.
Por cierto, aquí van unas cuantas cervezas para esta noche, por Danny y Tessa, ya sabéis.
Muy bien, esto es todo.
Capitán: ... Eh, chicos, esperad un momento, me gustaría deseaross mucha suerte, y... bueno... por Danny y Pete...
Compañero del club: Danny y Tess.
Capitán: Oh, sí, Danny y Tess... buena suerte.
Danny: ¡Buena suerte!
Matthew: ¿Cuánto queda?
Danny: Un par de semanas.
Matthew: Mi tío volvió a casarse el otro día.
Danny: ¿Cuántos años tiene?
Matthew: 91.
Danny: ¡91! ¿Y para qué quiere casarse a esa edad?
Matthew: No quería... tuvo que hacerlo.
Sobreimpresión: Poco después, más.

Secuencia 5
Sobreimpresión: Danny y Tessa se casan dentro de dos semanas.
Danny: ¡Hola, mamá!
Madre: Llegas tarde... pruébalos...
Los ha hecho Tessa.
Tessa: ¿Y Pete?
Danny: Unos pastelillos muy buenos, Tessa.
Tessa: Son magdalenas.
Danny: Muy buenos los pastelillos... magdalenas.
Padre: Hemos tenido visita esta mañana.
Pete: ¿Alguien importante?
Padre: Sí, un joven muy importante, del sindicato de los granjeros.
Quería saber lo que cobraba cada uno y sus condiciones de trabajo.
Así que le conté lo del jefe de ganado, ya sabes, un par de cientos a la semana, alojamiento gratis y tal.
Luego está el chico para todo: ciento sesenta y alojamiento gratis, y tal.
Entonces ha preguntado: ¿alguien más? Bueno está el tonto... hace la mayor parte del trabajo aquí. Cobra unos 40 dólares a la semana. Y entonces dice: ¡40 dólares a la semana!, quiero hablar con él. Y le dije, soy yo. Y se ha ido.
Sobreimpresión: Poco después, más.

Secuencia 6
Sobreimpresión: Danny y Tessa se casan esta semana.
Voz en off masculina: Esta semana Danny y Tessa se convertirán en los nuevos Sr. y Sra. Carter... y de nuevo la granja familiar pasará a manos más jóvenes y fuertes.
Blue: Eh, Danny.
Un momento, Matt...
Eh, Danny, escucha esto...
Adelante, Matt...
Matthew: Estaba diciéndole a estos tipos que ese chico de ciudad, ya sabes, ese tío elegante, le preguntó a Skinny. Le dijo: «Perdona, Skinny, cuando tu caballo tenía tos y tal, ¿qué le diste?», y Skinny va y le dice: «Le di fenil». Bueno, pues al cabo de unos días, el tío de ciudad vuelve, coge a Skinny y le dice: «Eh, Skinny, le di fenil a mi caballo y murió». Y Skinny va y dice: «Sí, el mío también».
Blue: Eh Danny, un mensaje; Tessa está en tu casa... por algún detalle del gran día.
Danny: Oh, sí, gracias, mejor que vayamos.
Pete, ¿te llevamos?
Matthew: Otra y nos vamos.
Sobreimpresión: Poco después, más.

Secuencia 7
Sobreimpresión: Danny y Tessa se casan esta semana.
Blue: Hola, un momento, chicos... esto podría ser el Ministerio de la Guerra.
Hola... buenos días, Bruce... no, han estado aquí hace un momento.
Padre: Gracias, Blue, gracias.
Padre: Ya está... problemas con los Ute... tendré que salir a buscarles.
Madre: ¿Problemas con los Ute?
¿Por qué no han llamado?
Padre: Oh, Dios mío, Dios mío
Sobreimpresión: La gente del campo muere en las carreteras rurales.
Sobreimpresión: Poco después, más.

Secuencia 8
Sobreimpresión: Danny ha muerto.
Voz en off masculina: Aquella noche Matthew y el joven Danny murieron en el accidente. La gente del campo muere en las carreteras rurales. Pete nunca volverá a ser el mismo. Está en Christchurch. En la clínica para enfermedades de la columna. No puede andar y nunca va a poder.
Tessa: ¿Ha habido alguna oferta por la granja, mamá?
Madre: Eso creo.
Padre: Hay uno o dos interesados.
Madre: Díselo a Bruce.
Tessa: Me voy. No es definitivo, sólo una temporada. Pero daré señales de vida.
Padre: ¿Adónde?
Tessa: Al norte, con mi tía de Pina.
Padre: ¿En serio?
Madre: Papá, se va, va a tener el hijo de Danny.
Padre: Nunca va a terminar, ¿verdad, mamá? Nunca va a terminar.
Sobreimpresión & voz en off masculina: Nunca más
Jamás.
La gente de campo muere en las carreteras rurales.

The Height of It, p. 93

Taxi Confessions, p. 94
Taxista: Tendrá que decirme qué calle, porque si se duerme, no sabré adónde llevarle.
Hombre: ¡Eh, taxi!
Hombre: Sí, vas a todos esos pubs y nunca los encuentras, sólo...
Mujer: Y levanta el brazo y lleva unas esposas. Unas esposas.
Hombre: No voy a casa.
Hombre: Debes ir a casa.
Hombre: Uuhh, hemos llegado.
Hombre: Pides una hamburguesa de bacon y te dan una mierda de ternera.
¿Sabes? Siempre igual.
Hombre: Estaba detrás mío y de repente se había ido.
Hombre: Herne Bay, gracias.
Taxista: Herne Bay, ¿dónde exactamente?
Pareja: ¿Está ahí el White Lady o algo así?
Sí.
Sí, aquí mismo. Estás guapísimo hoy.
Hombre: Va a todos esos pubs extranjeros y siempre se pierde.
Hombre: No, no, no, porque no está aquí.
No es el sitio adonde vamos.
Es de donde veníamos.
Voz en off masculina & sobreimpresión: Si bebes y luego tomas un taxi, eres un maldito genio.

Disaster, p. 96
Titular: Allí donde vamos hay un desastre.
Texto: Evitar desastres no es algo que nos molestemos en pensar. Tenemos que estar preparados para las catástrofes repentinas que puedan ocurrir en cualquier sitio a cualquier hora, sea una guerra en Ruanda o un avión que se ha estrellado en las Ruahines. Para millones de personas el emblema de la Cruz Roja se ha convertido en una imagen familiar y tranquilizadora tras un desastre. Nos preparamos para una respuesta inmediata, y mediante nuestros cursos de primeros auxilios y de rescate, también te preparamos a ti. Aunque a veces te pidamos ayuda, puede que algún día seas tú quien necesite la nuestra.

Fight, p. 98
Titular: Les enseñamos cómo luchar.
Texto: ¿Todo vale en el amor y en la guerra? No, no todo vale. Incluso en la guerra hay reglas. En el curso del trabajo humanitario en las zonas en guerra de todo el mundo, la Cruz Roja encuentra soldados que no saben nada sobre sus obligaciones con respecto a los prisioneros, la población civil o el enemigo.

Si podemos enseñar a esos soldados la conducta que les exigen las Convenciones de Ginebra, podemos salvar vidas. Quizá os sorprenda parte del trabajo que realiza la Cruz Roja, pero sea lo que sea y adónde nos lleve, todavía necesitamos tu ayuda para hacerlo.

350 Languages, p. 99
Titular: Cómo decir «no me dispares» en 350 lenguas.
Texto: El emblema de la Cruz Roja nació en un campo de batalla en Solferino, en el año 1859. Hoy todavía separa a los médicos de los soldados, la vida de la muerte. Está protegido por la Convención de Ginebra su uso incorrecto es un delito legal. No pertenece al botiquín de primeros auxilios ni puede ser usado por veterinarios o centros médicos. Es un símbolo de protección, neutralidad y humanidad. La Cruz Roja de Nueva Zelanda tiene el deber de protegerlo, porque sin él no podemos protegerte.

Don't Forget, p. 100
Titular: No te olvides de cómo tener relaciones sexuales después de beber.
Texto: Las cosas se olvidan después de beber. Protégete del SIDA. Usa un condón. Tan sólo recuerda dónde lo pones.

Prevent Sickness, p. 101
Titular: Toma lo necesario para no encontrarte mal después de beber.
Texto: Beber puede llevar al sexo no seguro. Protégete con un condón.
Porque el SIDA hará que te encuentres mal. Para siempre.

Right Package, p. 102
Titular: Si quieres que tus empleados permanezcan más tiempo en la empresa, dales el lote adecuado.
Texto: Lo que tus empleados hacen en la cama no es cosa tuya. Pero podría afectar negativamente a los negocios de tu empresa.

Supón que un miembro de tu equipo de trabajo contrae el virus VIH.

Si con el tiempo desarrolla la enfermedad del SIDA, tendrás que sustituirlo.

Mientras tanto, es probable que tú y el resto de los empleados os preocupéis sobre si es seguro que haya personas infectadas por el VIH trabajando entre vosotros. Afortunadamente, es seguro.

También querrás conocer las implicaciones legales. Y si el seguro cubrirá al trabajador, o si tu compañía es la responsable.

Es importante conocer las respuestas a estas cuestiones ahora. Porque si tu negocio no está todavía afectado por el SIDA, pronto podría estar o.

En el año 2000, la epidemia será un problema mayor en Asia de lo que es actualmente en el área más afectada, África. Y para entonces, más de un 40% de las nuevas infecciones se producirán aquí, a menos que tomes medidas ahora para ayudar a prevenir la propagación de esta enfermedad.

Empieza por ponerte en contacto con tu grupo local de acción del SIDA y con la administración sanitaria. Responderán a tus preguntas.

También te aconsejarán tomar las medidas necesarias para contribuir a prevenir la propagación del SIDA en tu empresa. Medidas como que un experto en sanidad hable con tus empleados. Poner pósters sobre la prevención del SIDA en los tablones de anuncios. E incluso instalar máquinas expendedoras de condones en los servicios. Puedes encontrar el grupo de acción del SIDA más próximo informándote en la oficina local del Programa de Desarrollo de las Naciones Unidas o en el PDNU de Nueva Delhi (ver la dirección abajo).

Toma medidas ya. Levantarás la moral del personal demostrando que te preocupas.

Y evitarás perder empleados valiosos a causa del SIDA.

Night Cap, p. 103
Titular: No importa cuánto bebas.
Acuérdate de llevar un gorro de dormir.
Texto: Cuanto más bebes, más olvidas.
Reduce el riesgo de contraer el SIDA.
Recuerda. Llévate un condón a la cama.

Preservativo, p. 105
Voz en off: Condón, condón, condón, condón, condón, condón condón
Sobreimpresión: No nos cansaremos de repetirlo.
El condón es el arma más fiable contra el sida.
Convence a tu pareja para que lo utilice.
ANLAIDS.

Strangers in the Night, p.106
La música de este anuncio es Strangers in the Night. Durante el anuncio la melodía pasa del suave compás de la canción original a una versión más fragmentada y triste, que refleja la transformación de las notas musicales en crucifijos.
Sobreimpresión: Detén el sida con amor.

Love Story, p. 108
Música: Love Story
Voz en off masculina: Este verano, mucha gente hará el amor en la playa, como esta pareja.
Cruz Roja.
¡Haz el amor!
Sobreimpresión: Voluntarios de la Cruz Roja.

Lenny, p. 113
Lenny: ¿Sabes, tío?, me hizo sentir bien de verdad.
¿Sabes? No era como ir de prisa, como ir al máximo, ¿sabes?, era como relajante. Y bueno, la primera vez vomité, lo vomité todo, ¿sabes? Y después de vomitar, tío, dije ¡Uau! Esta mierda está de puta madre. Bueno.
¿Sabes? Bueno, te acuerdas de cuando íbamos en coche y la adrenalina subía, ¿sabes lo que te digo, no?
Es una sensación así.
Así.
Tenía celulitis en los muslos.
Y ahora tengo una cicatriz así de grande.
Es increíble, tío.
Casi... Tuve gangrena en el pie y casi me lo cortan.
Me considero bastante inteligente.
Puedo hacer lo que quiera, tío.
Lo que quiera, puedo hacer.
Vomité, tío, hasta la última papilla, y mientras vomitaba pensaba, mierda tío, eso es lo que quiero, ¿sabes?
Sólo quiero ser un buen tipo... sólo quiero eso. Sólo eso. ¿Por qué no podemos hacer sólo eso? Quizás todo el mundo debería chutarse y relajarse.
Tío, tengo estas marcas por todo el cuerpo.
Y el pus sale de este agujerito como si nada.
Antes hacía un montón de cosas, ¿sabes? Iba más al cine, a comer fuera, iba a los teatros de Broadway. Me gustan las obras de Broadway. Están bien, tío.
Cuando llegue 1997, ahora estamos en 1996... ¿no?, 17 o 18 de agosto, o lo que sea, venís con vuestras cámaras y seré una persona totalmente diferente.
Triunfaré.
Me jugaría la vida.
Sobreimpresión: Heroína.
¿Quieres un poco?
Partnership for a Drug-Free America.
(Asociación para una América sin Drogas).

Surfing Monkey, p. 117
Voz en off femenina: Una vez más, el artículo J343 es la hucha del mono surfista. Estupenda para graduaciones y regalos de boda. Creo que la última vez se agotaron, o sea que no dejes pasar esta ocasión. Vamos a contestar la llamada: Scott de Nashville.
Bueno, Scott, creo que acabas de comprar quince de nuestras huchas mono surfista. ¿Es verdad?
Scott: ¡...sí!
(ruido de fondo y risas)
Scott: Chist, callaos. Estoy en televisión.
Sobreimpresión: Marihuana. Un hábito muy caro.
Partnership for a Drug-Free America.

Celebrities, p. 118
Titular: En publicidad se dice que una de las formas más eficaces de hacerte llegar un mensaje es a través de personas famosas.
Partnership for a Drug-Free America.

Nose, p. 119
Voz en off femenina: Un gramo de cocaína cuesta lo mismo que un radiocasete.
Tres gramos cuestan lo mismo que un televisor.
Siete gramos, un viaje a París.
Un gramo a la semana durante un año, un coche nuevo.
Si estás enganchado a la coca, todo aquello por lo que has trabajo se te va por la nariz.
Sobreimpresión: Partnership for a Drug-Free America.

Elephant, p. 121
Efectos especiales (todo el tiempo): Pisadas de elefante
Voz en off masculina: Una de estas mujeres rindió homenaje a la naturaleza donando parte de su paga a la Environmental Federation of California (Federación Medioambiental de California).
La otra no.
Puede que tú no sepas cuál de las dos hizo una donación para el medio ambiente, pero un elefante nunca olvida.
Colabora en la conservación de la naturaleza haciendo tu donación para el medio ambiente con el plan de deducción de nóminas.
Sobreimpresión: Environmental Federation of California (Federación Medioambiental de California).
Para más información llama al teléfono 1 800 368 1819.

The Only Fur, p. 124
Titular: La única piel que no me avergüenza llevar.
Texto: International Fund for Animal Welfare (Fondo Internacional para la Protección de los Animales).

Hatchet, p. 125

Whales, p. 126
Voz en off: Las ballenas sólo quieren lo mismo que nosotros. Ser libres y vivir en paz, reproducirse sin problemas. Pero ahora más que nunca su supervivencia está en peligro. Greenpeace ha luchado siempre para evitar su extinción.
Colabora con Greenpeace. 06 57 82 484.

Water Cooler, p. 128
Titular: Salva a 100 víctimas del huracán Mitch de la deshidratación por tan sólo 12 $.
Texto: Colabora con Unicef para ayudar a los niños que están en situaciones de emergencia. Llama al 1800 025 192.

Year of the.., p. 129
Titular: El Año de...
Texto: El tigre está desapareciendo.
La extinción total es un peligro real.
El WWF (World Wide Fund For Nature, Fondo Mundial para la Naturaleza) trabaja intensamente para proteger a los tigres de todo el mundo del peligro que supone la desforestación y el comercio ilegal de las partes de su cuerpo. Este año, el Año del Tigre, haz lo que puedas para ayudarnos a mantener viva la causa del tigre, para que vuelva a los titulares.
Para más detalles, llama al teléfono 703 3772.

Last Water in Rwanda, p. 130
Titular: La única agua que queda en Ruanda.
Texto: Millones de refugiados ruandeses necesitan desesperadamente agua

potable, igual que necesitan comida, medicinas y aire que respirar.

Going, Going, Gone, p. 131
Efectos especiales: Música y tambores africanos con ruido de elefantes
Sobreimpresión: Desaparecen.
Efectos especiales: Los tambores se convierten en disparos
Sobreimpresión: Desaparecen.
Sobreimpresión: Han desaparecido.
Sobreimpresión: La extinción es para siempre. No dejes que ocurra.

Zaire, p. 132
Efectos especiales (todo el tiempo): Gotas de sangre.
Voz en off: Zaire. Zaire se está desangrando.
Somos Médicos sin Fronteras. Ayúdanos.

War on Hunger, p. 134
Sonido: Ruido de una batalla
Sobreimpresión: Declara la guerra al hambre.
Telefood '98.

Speed Kills, p. 138
Texto: La velocidad mata.

Glasses, p. 140
Efectos especiales: Alguien deja copas sobre una mesa, una a una.
Sobreimpresión: Cada copa que tomas antes de conducir perturba tus facultades.
Efectos especiales: Frenazo
Sobreimpresión: Si bebes, no conduzcas.

Ash, p. 142
Sobreimpresión: La ceniza de un sólo cigarrillo.
Texto: No trates el borde de la carretera como un cenicero.

Stripes, p. 144
Titular: Sólo un buey no cede el paso a una cebra.
Texto: La conducción irresponsable mata.
(Llamar «buey» a alguien en checo equivale a llamarle imbécil.)

Just Sit There, p. 145
Titular: Prueba a sentarte ahí todo el día cada día.
Así es la cárcel.
Madres contra la conducción en estado ebrio.

The Censor, p. 146
Sobreimpresión: El censor
Hombre: ¡Pare!
Muéstreme esa pieza otra vez.
Vamos... de prisa.
No, no, no, no, eso fuera.
No puede hacer esto.
No, no, no. Esto no está permitido.
¡Deténgase!
Suprima esto.
Suprímalo.
Esto no está permitido, ya lo sabe.
Suprímalo.
¡Esto... esto... y esto!
Bueno, adelante... adelante, baile.
¡Deténgase! ¿Por qué no baila?
¿A eso le llama bailar?
¡Deténgase! No admitiré ninguna indirecta.
Voz en off masculina: Esta pequeña obra del escritor checo Ivan Kraus, censurado en su propio país, fue publicada en *Index on Censorship*, una revista que pone de relieve la represión que sufren los artistas de todo el mundo y que ofrece una plataforma desde la cual expresarse. *Index* es para el artista censurado, y para ti.
Sobreimpresión: Index on Censorship.

Free Press, p. 148
Titular: Prensa libre.
Artículo 19.

Spaniel, p. 149
Texto: No levantaré la pata contra tu Mercedes Benz.
No morderé al repartidor de pizzas.
No esconderé mi hueso bajo tu almohada.
No escarbaré bajo la almohada en plena noche para buscar huesos.
No lameré tu cara justo después de lamer mis partes privadas.
Adopta un animal doméstico con pedigrí del SPCA. Llama al 287 5355.

Dog and Gun, p. 150
Efectos especiales: Una niñita cantando durante todo el anuncio: ¿Cuánto vale ese perrito del escaparate, el que menea la cola? ¿Cuánto vale ese perrito del escaparate? Espero que esté en venta...
Sobreimpresión: 92 p al día
£6,44 a la semana
£27,50 al mes
£330 al año
£3.630 toda la vida
Voz en off masculina: Antes de regalar un perro estas Navidades, piensa primero en los gastos que comporta.
Sobreimpresión: RSPCA (Real Sociedad para la Prevención de la Crueldad con los Animales).

Light Bulb, p. 151
Voz en off masculina: Si vas en bicicleta y no llevas casco puede pasarte esto.
Pero si llevas casco, no te pasará.
Ponte el casco. No pierdas la cabeza.
Sobreimpresión: Ayuntamiento de Barcelona
Barcelona... más que nunca.

Don't Piss..., p. 152
Titular: No malgastes tu vida.
Madres contra la conducción en estado ebrio.

Vote No, p. 153
Titular: El cielo del No.
Texto: Míralo. Éste es el cielo de los que matan a miles de animales cada año, por deporte. El cielo de los que tratan de bloquear el referéndum sobre la caza. Pero también es el cielo de todas las personas perezosas o indiferentes que no votan el 3 de junio. Así que míralo bien. Si hoy gana el No, mañana este cielo desierto será tu cielo.

Vote Yes, p. 153
Titular: El cielo del Sí.
Texto: Vota Sí, el 3 de junio, para prohibir la caza. Verás los resultados en el cielo. Míralo. Éste es el cielo de los que trabajan cada día para defender la naturaleza. El cielo de los que comprenden que prohibir la caza en Italia significa el comienzo de una maravillosa etapa. Da alas a los valores en los que crees: vota Sí el 3 de junio. Verás los resultados en el cielo.

Poached Elephant, p. 154
Efectos especiales: Música clásica.
Sobreimpresión: Pescado a la cazadora.
Sobreimpresión: Huevos a la cazadora.
Sobreimpresión: Elefante a la cazadora.
Efectos especiales: La música se detiene.
Efectos especiales: Disparo.
Sobreimpresión: Marfil.
Sobreimpresión: No permitas que la masacre vuelva a empezar.
Sobreimpresión: No lo compres. No lo vendas. No te lo pongas. No lo uses.

Power of One, p. 155
Sobreimpresión: No hace mucho, una mujer de Alabama quiso sentarse en la parte delantera del autobús.
Sobreimpresión: Y un apacible señor de la India quiso que la gente adquiriera una mayor conciencia sin elevar el tono de voz.
Sobreimpresión: En Alemania del Este, un hombre quiso liberarse.
Sobreimpresión: Y una mujer viajó por el mundo dando esperanza a los que no la tenían.
Sobreimpresión: Una sola persona puede.
Sobreimpresión: Proteger tu hogar en la Amazonia.
Sobreimpresión: Impedir la caza del gorila de montaña en África.
Sobreimpresión: Salvar las focas de Groenlandia en Finlandia.
Sobreimpresión: O cuidar del medio ambiente de tu propio jardín.
Sobreimpresión: El poder de cada persona consiste en hacer algo.
Sobreimpresión: Lo que sea.
Sobreimpresión: Earth Communications Office (Oficina de Comunicaciones de la Tierra)

Abbandono, p. 156
Voz en off masculina: ¿Qué pasaría si fueran ellos los que nos abandonaran? ¿Si nos condenaran a pasar un verano de perros?
Sobreimpresión: ¡El que abandona un animal es un animal!

Brains, p. 163
Texto: Africano
Europeo
Asiático
Racista
Campaña de los Jóvenes Europeos contra el Racismo – con la colaboración de la Commission for Racial Equality (Comisión para la Igualdad Racial).

Scars, p. 164
Titular: En Asia
En África
En América
En Europa
Texto: Allí donde hay guerras, epidemias y desastres naturales, nosotros también estamos. Cada día, durante 25 años, suturando las heridas del mundo.
Medici Senza Frontiere
via Ostiense 6/E, Tel. 06 573 009 00,
Fax 06 573 009 02, Roma c.c.p 874 86007.

Them, p. 166
Hombre 1: Perdone.
Hombre 2: No pasa nada, hombre. Deberíamos mandarlos a todos a su país, ¿no crees?
Voz en off femenina: Sólo por una vez le concederemos el deseo.
Hombre 2: Paquistaníes, judíos, italianos...
Voz en off femenina: Y veremos qué pasa con Gran Bretaña cuando miles de «ellos» abandonen nuestros hospitales.
Cuando miles de «ellos» dejen el sector del transporte.
Cuando cientos de «ellos» dejen el periodismo.
Cuando miles de «ellos» dejen la construcción.
Cuando miles de «ellos» dejen la enseñanza.
Cuando miles de «ellos» cierren sus tiendas.
Cuando cientos de «ellos» cierren sus fábricas dejando a miles de personas en el paro.
Cuando cientos de «ellos» dejen de competir por Gran Bretaña.
Cuando miles de «ellos» abandonen la industria de las finanzas.
Y cuando se olviden los sacrificios que han hecho millones de «ellos».
Hombre 2: Mandarlos a su país... Estaría bien, ¿no?
Hombre 2: ¿Te apetece un curry?
Sobreimpresión: ¿Ellos? Ellos son nosotros.

Openings, p. 168
Titular: ¿Quién dice que las minorías étnicas no pueden conseguir trabajo? Hay oportunidades en todas partes.
Texto: Encargado de lavabos. Trabajador de la limpieza para oficinas. Alguien tiene que hacer todo el trabajo mal remunerado y de baja categoría, ¿pero por qué con tanta frecuencia son personas de las minorías étnicas?
El prejuicio, la discriminación y la hostilidad raciales están negando a la gente la elección del trabajo que se merecen. Es injusto e injustificado. Más que eso, es un terrible desperdicio del talento británico.

Lograr una profesión cualificada es muy difícil para cualquiera hoy en día.

Pero lo es incluso más para las minorías étnicas.

De entrada, el currículum cuenta, pero la mayoría de las minorías étnicas aún tienen más posibilidades de estar en el paro que las personas blancas.

Tienen que presentarse a más trabajos antes de conseguir uno. En una investigación reciente, una de cada tres compañías estudiadas no concedía entrevistas a los solicitantes negros y asiáticos.

Pero ofrecían entrevistas a los solicitantes blancos con la misma preparación.

Si encuentran trabajo, las minorías étnicas casi siempre lo tienen más difícil para acceder a un ascenso que sus compañeros blancos.

Hay un número desproporcionadamente bajo de minorías étnicas en cargos directivos.

Por ejemplo, en una gran compañía de transporte el 30% de toda la plantilla procede de las minorías étnicas, pero éstas sólo ocupan el 3% de los cargos directivos.

Y, para colmo, las minorías étnicas sufren la hostilidad racial en el lugar de trabajo.

Si se quejan de ello, a menudo se les dice que deben aceptarlo como parte de su trabajo.

Lamentablemente, la mayoría de la gente lo acepta.

Aquéllos que quizá no puedan llevar a su empresa a la magistratura de trabajo, donde deben presentar pruebas sólidas para basar su reclamación.

Tanto si ganan como si no ganan el caso, es probable que tengan que empezar de nuevo todo el duro proceso de buscar un trabajo.

No es de extrañar que para las minorías étnicas haya sido tan difícil progresar en Gran Bretaña.

Sin embargo, a pesar de lo mala que parece la situación, algunos aspectos han mejorado.

Un antillano que vino en los años cincuenta a trabajar para la British Rail recuerda.

«Era horroroso. Durante los primeros diez años nadie se sentó a mi lado en la pausa de la comida. Te daban el peor trabajo, te pagaban menos y no te daban formación. Te insultaban. Había letreros de 'No se admiten negros' en todas partes. Entonces era muy diferente. No había leyes que prohibieran todo esto.»

Afortunadamente, la legislación ha cambiado.

En 1976 se aprobó la Ley de Relaciones Raciales, que hacía ilegal que las empresas discriminaran por razón de color, raza, origen étnico o nacional.

Los que discriminan tienen que afrontar gastos brutales por compensación y costos legales, así como el hecho de que se airee su culpabilidad en público.

La ley, sin duda, pone fin a una flagrante discriminación como la que suponían los letreros de «No se admiten negros».

Pero no puso fin a la discriminación más sutil que hoy todavía existe.

Como cuando un empresario dice: «Lo siento, hay alguien más cualificado para el trabajo», cuando no lo hay.

Cuando un directivo «se olvida» de mencionar una promoción a alguien.

Esto es discriminación.

Es sutil, quizá incluso involuntaria, pero puede ser muy desmoralizante.

Imagínate que se te dijera una y otra vez que no estás cualificado para un trabajo cuando sabes de sobras que sí lo estás.

¿Qué podrías hacer al respecto?

Si tu caso es lo bastante evidente podrías hablar con la Commission for Racial Equality (Comisión para la Igualdad Racial).

Somos el organismo independiente financiado por el Ministerio del Interior encargado de eliminar toda clase de discriminación racial.

Con este fin damos apoyo a las víctimas de la discriminación en las magistraturas de trabajo. (No siempre son minorías étnicas. Hemos tratado casos de trabajadores blancos que han sido tratados injustamente por jefes negros o asiáticos.)

También estamos trabajando con los sindicatos para ayudarles a combatir la discriminación y hostilidad raciales, tanto en sus propias organizaciones como en el lugar de trabajo.

Muchos sindicatos ahora tienen dirigentes especialmente designados para ofrecer apoyo y asesoramiento práctico a las personas que han sido discriminadas.

Encontrarás agentes igualmente cualificados en el Racial Equality Council (Consejo de Igualdad Racial) de tu población y en el Citizens Advice Bureau (Oficina de Asesoramiento a los Ciudadanos).

Es más, con nuestra ayuda las empresas están adoptando políticas para la igualdad de oportunidades. Esto previene la discriminación antes de que ocurra, dando a todo el mundo una oportunidad justa.

Si quieres hablar con alguien sobre la aplicación de esta política en tu empresa, escríbenos a la dirección de abajo.

De este modo venceremos el racismo.

No mediante la violencia, sino aceptándonos mutuamente como iguales.

Abriendo nuestras mentes.

Por nuestro propio bien y por el de las generaciones futuras, ésta sería la mejor oportunidad.

Criminal Isn't It? p. 170
Titular: Criminal, ¿no?
Texto: Robo de coche 9 meses
Robo de coche 1 año y medio.

Junk Mail, p. 171
Titular: Y te enfadas por el «correo basura».

Ethnic Cleansing, p. 172
Titular: Discursos sobre la limpieza étnica, ¿te suenan?
Texto: Pon fin a los crímenes nacionalistas serbios contra la humanidad.

Next Generation, p. 173
Titular: Puede que a ti no te importe que la vida judía sobreviva a la próxima generación. Pero a él sí.
Texto: La vida judía ha sobrevivido durante miles de años. El fascismo ha sobrevivido setenta años. Pero en todo ese tiempo ha sido devastador. Las señales de alerta todavía están aquí y cada una de ellas lleva el mismo mensaje: no te duermas en los laureles. Éste es el motivo por el que el JIA tiene un papel tan importante a desempeñar. Tenemos que ser capaces de responder a la persecución de los judíos en cualquier lugar del mundo, en cualquier momento. Tenemos que estar alerta ante cualquier amenaza.

Respondemos a esas amenazas obteniendo fondos para la Jewish Agency (Agencia Judía), ayudándole a salvar judíos allí donde estén y a traerlos a la seguridad de Israel.

Cuando llegan, les ayudamos a construir nuevas vidas con nuevas oportunidades. Israel tiene la llave para todos nuestros futuros.

Ayúdanos a enseñar a las generaciones futuras la importancia de Israel y la necesidad de preservar la vida judía en todo el mundo.

Demuestra tu compromiso con el JIA llamándonos hoy al 0345 585 004 y hablaremos de cómo puedes ayudarnos. Puede que tú no creas que eres necesario. Pero nosotros sí.

Saddam, p. 174
Titular: Si no quieres refugiados kurdos en tu país, envíamelos de vuelta.
Texto: Saddam Hussein, Slobodan Milosevic, Pol Pot, Adolf Hitler.
Los nombres cambian. Sus crímenes contra la humanidad, no. El tratado de las Naciones Unidas de 1951 sobre refugiados fue redactado como respuesta directa al holocausto.

En sus páginas la comunidad internacional reconocía la obligación de proporcionar un refugio seguro para aquellos que huyen de la tortura, la persecución y la muerte.

Gran Bretaña fue uno de los primeros países en adherirse al tratado. Respetar un documento de casi 50 años de edad puede parecer anticuado.
Desgraciadamente, el gas venenoso, los campos de concentración y la limpieza étnica no lo son.
www.refugeecouncil.org.uk
0 0171 820 3055.

No Flag, p. 175
Titular: Ni siquiera una bandera para arroparse.
Texto: Campaña Kurda de la Cruz Roja
Llama al (01) 76 68 77 0 al (01) 76 51 35 para hacer donativos.

Equals, p. 179
Es el trabajo de catorce directores publicitarios a los que se les dio una palabra breve como «comida», «trabajo», «religión», «dormir». Se les pidió que filmaran en ocho segundos, en blanco y negro, qué significaban para ellos estas palabras cuando se aplicaban al término «igualdad».
Sobreimpresión: Commission for Racial Equality (Comisión para la Igualdad Racial)
Sobreimpresión: 1997 Año Europeo Contra el Racismo, con la colaboración del Ministerio del Interior.

Shattered Dreams, p. 180
Sobreimpresión: Puedes hacer algo para evitar la violencia doméstica.
Llama a la policía.

Flowers, p. 182
Texto: David me trae flores.
Me dice que me quiere.
Y quiero creerle.
Mis amigas dicen que soy tonta.
Pero no conocen a David.
David me trae flores.
Y me dice que lo siente.
Cuando pierde la paciencia.
Y me pega sin querer.
Mis amigas dicen que soy tonta.
Pero no conocen a David.
David me pegó anoche.
Todo parece confuso.
Y mis amigas tenían razón.
Pero David me trae flores.
Si eres adolescente y víctima de malos tratos, tienes a alguien con quien hablar.
Simplemente llama al teléfono 213 626 3393.
Somos Los Angeles Commission on Assaults Against Women (Comisión contra las Agresiones a Mujeres de Los Angeles), y podemos ayudarte.

Scream, p. 183
Titular: Los insultos a tus hijos permanecen en la familia durante generaciones.
Texto: Eres un inútil. Eres imbécil. Ojalá nunca hubieras nacido. Profiere insultos como éstos a tus hijos y no sólo los herirás, sino que también les enseñarás a ser padres ofensivos. Rompe el ciclo. Llama al 0800 222 999 para un folleto gratuito sobre cómo educar a los hijos que te será de ayuda.

Vicious Circle, p. 184
Escena 1
Hombre: ¿Crees que salgo con los colegas sólo para amargarte la vida?
Mujer: Cállate.
Hombre: ¿Eso crees?
Mujer: Cállate.
Hombre : ¿Cuándo me abrazaste por última vez?
Mujer: Déjame en paz.
Hombre: ¿Llevo un letrero en la cara que diga que soy invisible?
Mujer: No.
No.
No.
Hombre: ¿Lo llevo?
Mujer: Déjame en paz.
Hombre : ¿Soy invisible?
Hombre: Cállate.
Mujer: Cállate, sólo quiero que me dejes en paz.
Hombre: Óyelo bien, esta noche voy a emborracharme.

Escena 2
Hombre: ¿Crees que salgo con los colegas sólo para amargarte la vida?
Mujer: Cállate.
Hombre: ¿Eso crees?
Mujer: Cállate.
Hombre: ¿Cuándo me abrazaste por última vez?
Mujer: Déjame en paz.
Hombre: ¿Llevo un letrero en la cara que diga que soy invisible?
Mujer: No.
No.
No.
Hombre: ¿Soy invisible?
Mujer: Cállate.

Escena 3
Hombre: ¿Crees que salgo con los colegas sólo para amargarte la vida?
Mujer: Cállate.
Hombre: ¿Eso crees?
Sobreimpresión: Romper este círculo vicioso depende de ti.
Para más información llama al 0800 222 999.

Fading Fast, p. 190
Titular: Mi imagen desaparece con rapidez. Yo también.
Texto: A medida que mis músculos se van atrofiando, cada día estoy más imposibilitado. No hay remedio para mi enfermedad y ninguna esperanza para mí, pero deseo que haya esperanza para otros. Envía una donación para ayudar a las personas a vivir con la E.N.M. y para financiar la investigación.
Motor Neurone Disease Association (Asociación de Enfermedad de la Neurona Motora)
P.O. Box 246, Northampton NN1 1TR.
Sociedad benéfica registrada con el n.° 294354.

Walkies, p. 194
Mujer: ¡Ven aquí, cariño, ven!
¡Vamos!
¡Ven aquí, Roger!
Voz en off masculina: Puede parecer una broma de mal gusto, pero las personas necesitan tanto ejercicio como los perros.
Unos simples paseos serían un buen comienzo.
De hecho, es muy posible que te guste.
Mujer: Vamos, Roger, cógelo.
Voz en off masculina: Una vez empieces, tu corazón, tus pulmones y tus músculos se fortalecerán. Evitarás la depresión y te sentirás como nuevo... o nueva.
Mujer: Corre.
Voz en off masculina: Pondrás más empeño en todo lo que hagas.
Y sacarás mucho más provecho de todo.
Mujer: Roger, vuelve enseguida.
Unos pocos minutos de ejercicio cada día podrían aportar mucho a tu vida.
Cuídate.
Sobreimpresión: ¡Cuídate!

Naledi/Crying Girl, p. 196
Titular: Marcada para siempre por un coche que ni la llegó a tocar.
Texto: Naledi estaba segura en la cama mientras su padre volvía a pie borracho del bar. Él nunca supo qué fue lo que le golpeó, pero ella sufrirá para el resto de su vida.
Anda con cuidado.

Scrambled Page, p. 197
Titular: La esclerosis múltiple mezcla mensajes entre el cerebro y el cuerpo.
Texto: Puede trastocar todas las partes del cuerpo, todos los aspectos de tu vida.
En cualquier momento.
Durante la semana de la E.M., esperamos lograr una mayor concienciación (y es de esperar que algún dinero) para que nos ayudes a combatir esta enfermedad imprevisible.
Para más información sobre la esclerosis múltiple, llama gratuitamente a la Línea de ayuda de la E.M. al 0808 800 8000.
La MS Society (Asociación de la E.M.) da fuerzas para combatir la E.M.

Pin, p. 198
Titular: ¿Cómo es la esclerosis múltiple? Cierra los ojos y clava un alfiler en esta página cada día durante el resto de tu vida.
Texto: Hoy te duele todo el cuerpo.
Hoy no puedes sentir los dedos.
Hoy tienes espasmos musculares.
Hoy no puedes mover la pierna izquierda.
Hoy no puedes conducir.
Hoy no puedes subir las escaleras.
Hoy te sientes bien.
Hoy eres impotente.
Hoy ves borroso.
Hoy no tienes equilibrio.
Hoy no puedes mover la pierna derecha.
Hoy no puedes sentir los dedos.
Hoy no te puedes concentrar.
Hoy te duele todo el cuerpo.
Hoy te sientes de maravilla.
Hoy te sientes como si tuvieras peces nadando por dentro del cuerpo.
Hoy no oyes bien.
Hoy no te puedes mover.
Hoy no puedes dejar de temblar.
Hoy no puedes hablar.
Hoy no puedes sentir los dedos de los pies.
Hoy no puedes mover el brazo derecho.
Hoy tienes incontinencia.
Hoy estás sordo.
Hoy no puedes sentir los pies.
Hoy te sientes bien.
Hoy no te puedes mover.
Hoy no puedes dejar de temblar.
Hoy no puedes hablar.
Hoy no puedes sentir los dedos.
Hoy te sientes cansado.
Hoy no puedes subir las escaleras.
La esclerosis múltiple (E.M.) es una enfermedad que ataca al sistema nervioso central. Nunca sabes a qué parte de tu cuerpo afectará al día siguiente, y con cuánta gravedad. Cualquiera puede sufrir E.M. y queremos que sepas más sobre esta enfermedad. Para más información o para hacer una donación, llámanos las 24 horas del día al 0800 100 133.
La MS Society (Asociación de la E.M.) da fuerzas para combatir la E.M.

Me No Fry, p. 200
Titular: Yo no querer freírme.
Texto: NSW Health (Sanidad de NSW).
Para un estado más saludable.

Eclipse, p. 201
Titular: Es una oportunidad única en la vida. Piérdetela.

Come and see us, p. 202
Titular: Ven a visitarnos
Texto: El remedio para el cáncer de mama es la prevención.

Flies on Food, p. 204
Texto: Esto es lo que ocurre cuando una mosca aterriza en tu comida.
Las moscas no pueden ingerir comida sólida, por lo que para ablandarla vomitan encima. Después meten el vómito dentro hasta que la comida se vuelve líquida, con lo que suelen estampar unos cuantos gérmenes, por si fuera poco.
Luego, cuando la comida ya está buena y líquida, lo vuelven a chupar todo, probablemente dejando caer algún excremento al mismo tiempo.
Y finalmente, cuando han acabado de comer, llega tu turno.
Cubre la comida. Cubre los utensilios de comer y beber. Cubre los cubos de basura.

Scrub your Lungs, p. 205
Titular: No puedes limpiar tus pulmones a base de fregar
Texto: El cáncer de pulmón mata trece veces más a los fumadores que a los no fumadores.

Lethal Weapon, p. 206
Titular: Tu coche es un arma letal.
Texto: Conduce con cuidado.
Publicado en beneficio del medio ambiente de los EAU.

3 More Days, p. 207
Titular: Sólo faltan tres días para el «Día contra las minas terrestres».
Texto: Cifras desesperanzadoras: 110 millones de minas terrestres en 64 países de todo el mundo; una víctima cada 20 minutos; de 5 a 10 millones de minas fabricadas cada año; 100 millones más disponibles en el arsenal mundial; el 90% de las víctimas son mujeres y niños.
Números esperanzadores: cuenta postal n.° 189241, Mani Tese, Campaña Italiana Contra las Minas Terrestres, via Cavengahi 4, I–20149 Milano. El sábado, 13 de abril, ven a la Piazza Santi Apostoli a firmar nuestra petición y a hacer tu contribución.

Landmines in Cambodia, p. 208
Titular: ¿Puede una mina terrestre de 3 $ paralizar toda una economía?
Texto: Puede hacerlo cuando los agricultores están demasiado asustados para arar sus campos; cuando los niños tienen demasiado miedo para ir a la escuela; cuando las actividades cotidianas más simples se convierten en un juego de ruleta rusa. Y además de los 110 millones de minas terrestres todavía enterradas en el Tercer Mundo, se colocan otros 2 millones cada año. Ayúdanos a abolir las minas terrestres. Es la única forma de que el Tercer Mundo pueda dar un paso adelante. Para saber cómo puedes ayudar, escribe al gobierno de tu país o a la Mine Clearance and Policy Unit, Department of Humanitarian Affairs, United Nations, New York, N.Y. 10017.

Unleaded, p. 209
Titular: No acribilles a plomadas a nuestros niños.
Texto: Usa gasolina sin plomo.
Publicado en beneficio del medio ambiente de los EAU.

Pavement, p. 210
Titular: Es incluso más asqueroso en la acera.
Texto: Si tu perro hace caca en la calle, recógela.

Atomic Bomb, p. 211
Texto: La cooperación internacional ha realizado una labor excepcional en cuanto a la amenaza de la aniquilación se refiere. Ahora quizá pueda distender la situación. Si alguna vez has querido cambiar el mundo, ésta es tu oportunidad. Únete al debate a través de nuestra página web entre el 27 de octubre y el 1 de noviembre. www.worldforum.org.

Leaf/Match, p. 212
Titular: No dejes que el peligro de incendio ronde por casa.

Off Duty, p. 213
Marido: Hace 18 años que estamos casados.
Mujer: En general, hemos tenido una vida tranquila.
Marido: Nos ocupamos de nuestras cosas.
Mujer: El día a día es el trabajo, la casa y el niño. Nada fuera de lo corriente.
Cuando le despidieron...
Marido: Ocurrió tan de prisa. La mente se me quedó en blanco...
Mujer: Parecía tan asustado. Los ojos se le llenaron de lágrimas.
Marido: Lo primero que perdí fue la autoestima. Sólo podía pensar en ahogar mis penas en alcohol.
Mujer: Necesita mi apoyo.
Marido: Me ha ayudado mucho.
Mujer: No te preocupes. Todo saldrá bien.
Marido: Que me despidieran ha sido lo mejor que nos ha pasado durante mucho tiempo...
Mujer: Nunca habíamos estado tan unidos.
Marido: Para mi cumpleaños...
Mujer: Le compré unos zapatos.
Marido: Unos zapatos nuevos.
Mujer: Para que puedas explorar un nuevo mundo de posibilidades.
Marido: Me emocioné tanto que me saltaron las lágrimas. Mi nuevo empleo es mejor. Al menos mejor que rondar por casa. Mientras nuestros corazones estén unidos, lo demás no importa.
Sobreimpresión: Tu apoyo es su fortaleza.

Chain Letter, p. 216
Texto: Querido Eric,
Hay un virus que se está extendiendo en nuestra comunidad y que se cobra una vida semanal. Se propaga a través de la sangre contaminada o el contacto sexual. Seguro que sabes de lo que te estoy hablando: VIH y, a la larga, SIDA.

El único modo en que podemos detener su propagación es difundir el mensaje con más rapidez que el virus.

Y el mensaje es condones. Practica sexo seguro y úsalos. Así de sencillo.

Ahora coge esta carta y cópiala seis veces. Mándala a personas que creas que hacen que el mundo sea un sitio mejor. No te dé vergüenza, a todos nos viene bien un recordatorio.

Si mandas la carta a seis personas esta semana, y cada una de ellas hace lo mismo, al final del mes 7.776 personas estarán mejor informadas. Si optas por no hacer nada, al final del año varios millones de personas no habrán recibido nuestro mensaje.

Debemos difundir el mensaje y vencer al virus por el bien de todos.

Firmado: Alguien que se preocupa P.D. Si te alcanza para enviar una donación a la Fundación del SIDA, te lo agradecerán enormemente. Su dirección es:
NZ AIDS Foundation
(Fundación del SIDA de Nueva Zelanda)
PO Box 7287,
Wellington,
New Zealand.

Slow Poison, p. 217
Titular: Veneno lento.
Texto: Publicado en interés público por Tata Tea Limited.

Clean Up, p. 220
Música; Morning Has Broken
Hombre: ¡Buenos días!
Vuelve a hacer un buen día...
Efectos especiales: Ruidos de chapoteo y resbalones
Sobreimpresión: Tú no lo harías.
Sobreimpresión: No dejes que tu perro lo haga.

Anybody Out There? p. 222
Voz en off masculina: ¿Hay alguien ahí?
¿Hay alguien ahí?
¿Hay alguien... ahí?
¿Hay alguien ahí?
Sobreimpresión: SÍ.
The Samaritans.

Die and Live, p. 224
Titular: Ron estaba listo para morir. Entonces vino la peor noticia de todas. «Vas a vivir».

Devastado, y ¿quién no lo estaría? Se te ha asegurado que tienes un cáncer terminal cuando, como un acontecimiento inesperado, tu doctor asesta el golpe asesino. «El tratamiento ha funcionado. El cáncer ha sido erradicado. Vas a vivir». Devastador. La perspectiva no podría ser peor.

Ahora tienes que recordar que la historia de Ron es bastante excepcional. La mayoría de la gente no reaccionaría como él. Pero lo importante sobre morir (o en el caso de Ron, no morir) es que no hay dos personas que reaccionen del mismo modo.

Cuando se le diagnosticó el cáncer, Ron, naturalmente, se quedó de piedra. Era lo peor que jamás le habían dicho. Pero con el tiempo su actitud cambió. Aceptó su destino. Incluso empezó a prepararse para ello, encauzando toda su vida hacia la muerte. Y aquí es donde empezaron los problemas. Ron estaba tan preparado para la muerte que llegó a un punto de satisfacción. Normalmente, en nuestro campo, esto es lo mejor que puede ocurrir. De hecho, es positivo cuando un paciente terminal alcanza este grado de aceptación, pues es muy poco habitual. En el Mary Potter Hospice (residencia de enfermos terminales) sentimos que hemos realizado nuestra labor lo mejor que podemos si somos capaces de ayudar al paciente a llegar a este punto.

«Vas a vivir, Ron». Guarda las coronas de flores para otra ocasión. Anula el coche fúnebre. Seguro que es la mejor noticia que podía recibir, ¿no? Pues no. Su vida estaba tan preparada para la muerte que, de manera un tanto curiosa, se había convertido en su razón de vivir. Había comenzado a despedirse de la gente, todo conducía agradablemente hacia un final bien trazado; ya se había ido.

Y entonces, de golpe y porrazo, esa razón de vivir le fue cruelmente arrebatada. La puerta de la muerte le dio en las narices. De repente, todas las preparaciones y angustia mental por las que había pasado no habían servido de nada. Tambaleándose en su vuelta a la vida, Ron empezó a imaginar enfermedades. Tenía una afección cardíaca. Estaba convencido de ello. Por supuesto, no la tenía; en realidad era una afección psicológica y, siendo la mente el órgano más poderoso, se encargó del resto. Ron se convirtió en un hombre imposible empeñado en encontrar una excusa para deleitarse con una muerte inminente, la situación en que ahora se encontraba más cómodo. Había llegado a depender de todos los servicios de apoyo a los enfermos terminales recientemente descubiertos. Se había adaptado demasiado bien a toda la atención y compasión. Eso no significa que le divirtiera, pero las necesitaba. Y en este estado vivió el resto de sus días.

El destino fatal de Ron fue principalmente voluntario. Y aunque nunca fue un paciente del Mary Potter Hospice, es un caso verdadero que nos contó nuestro director médico (Ron fue uno de sus pacientes cuando trabajó en Inglaterra) que ilustra el tipo de problemas con que nos encontramos habitualmente.

Y tiene ramificaciones importantes para el Mary Potter Hospice en lo que se refiere al trato que reciben los pacientes. Porque a veces incluso cuando las cosas cambian para mejor, las situaciones en realidad empeoran mucho. Así de impredecible es nuestra jornada laboral. Éste es el motivo por el que esperamos no dejar nunca de aprender de los Rons de este mundo para que situaciones como la suya no se repitan.

Se dice que sólo dos cosas en la vida son seguras: la muerte y los impuestos. Mientras que los impuestos son terriblemente previsibles, la muerte no lo es. La historia de Ron es testimonio de ello, así como la de Nell. Pero su historia está justo al otro extremo del espectro. Posiblemente la muerte perfecta. Petronella, Nell para los amigos, vino de Kapity. Estuvo hospitalizada en el Mary Potter, pero por muy poco tiempo. Nell tenía sesenta y pocos años cuando nos llegó como paciente en mayo de 1994. Tenía tumores en el hígado, el riñón, el páncreas y el estómago. No era su primer contacto con el cáncer. En 1989 ya se le tuvo que extirpar un riñón. Pero en el diagnóstico que se le hizo esta vez, se le dijo que sólo le quedaban dos meses de vida. Nell ingresó en la residencia con grandes dolores y vómitos constantes. Nosotros también estábamos convencidos de que no le quedaba mucho tiempo de vida, aunque no le pondríamos una fecha límite. Si una cosa hemos aprendido es que poner fecha a la muerte de una persona puede ser una de las peores cosas que se pueden hacer. Para empezar, es prácticamente imposible ser exacto. Pero, aún más importante, puede llevar a situaciones como la de Ron.

Al principio creíamos que el cáncer de Nell estaba fuera de control, pero ella no lo creía así. Estaba segura de que tan sólo se había desgarrado un músculo y que eso era lo que le provocaba dolor. Estaba equivocada. Pero también creía que las drogas que tomaba podrían ser la causa de sus problemas, y en esto tenía razón. En las dos semanas que pasó en la residencia conseguimos aplicarle una terapia de control del dolor para evitar los vómitos. Marchó a casa libre de dolores y lista para seguir viviendo. Todavía tenía cáncer, todavía era incurable, pero tenía mucho por vivir.

Cada vez más nos encontramos con que nuestros pacientes son más felices al ser tratados fuera del recinto hospitalario. Aún son hospitalizados, y nuestras camas todavía están llenas, pero suelen venir periódicamente para tratarse y hacer un seguimiento del control del dolor, y después regresan a casa, donde se sienten más cómodos. Nosotros les animamos a hacer esto en la medida de lo posible. Existe el peligro de que si los pacientes ingresan en la residencia demasiado pronto, puede que se resignen a morir demasiado pronto. Pero en casa, suelen seguir adelante, como hizo Nell.

Pasaron dos, tres y seis meses. Nell continuaba sintiendo deseos de vivir. Consultaba con regularidad a su médico de cabecera, y nuestro doctor de la residencia la iba a visitar a la costa cada dos meses. Usaba también remedios naturopáticos. Pero era su actitud lo que más la beneficiaba. Si se hubiera creído su sentencia de muerte inicial, si hubiera decidido quedarse en el Mary Potter, pudiera muy bien haber dejado de vivir. Por suerte, no lo hizo. Quería estar en casa con su esposo.

También quería marchar de casa con su esposo, lo que hacían a menudo. Enganchaban la caravana y realizaban largos viajes por toda Nueva Zelanda. Lejos de ser como Ron, lejos de consumirse por la muerte, Nell se dejó consumir cada vez más por la vida. A finales de 1995 surgieron complicaciones. Nell tenía una oclusión intestinal. Pero incluso esto no la detuvo. Se le practicó una operación que la llevó a una excelente recuperación. Continuó siendo una mujer de gran vitalidad unos dieciséis meses después de su supuesta fecha de muerte. Pero en mayo de 1996 su enfermedad finalmente empezó a apoderarse de ella. Estaba cansada y volvía a sentir dolor. La propia Nell se dio cuenta de que su vida se estaba acabando. Ya no podía tragarse las pastillas, por lo que se le tenían que administrar los calmantes por vía parenteral. Sólo en este momento, unos dos años después de su primer diagnóstico, Nell decidió volver a la residencia para morir.

Como ya hemos dicho, tratamos de no decir cuándo van a morir las personas. Lo que ocurre a menudo, sin embargo, es que nos lo dicen los propios pacientes. Algo en su interior les avisa de que está a punto de ocurrir. Así es como le sucedió a Nell. La mañana del día en que murió sabía que sería la última. Llamó uno por uno a todos los miembros de su familia para despedirse, y cuando terminó todos se reunieron a su alrededor, y murió en paz.

Nell era una mujer increíble, siempre positiva y risueña, a pesar de haber padecido la amenaza del cáncer durante siete años. Su recuerdo sigue muy vivo entre los miembros del personal de la residencia y otros enfermos terminales a los que dio apoyo y coraje. De manera extraña, lejos de encontrar su enfermedad espantosa, la encontró liberadora. No sabía por cuánto tiempo viviría, pero estaba absolutamente decidida a aprovecharlo al máximo. Como un miembro de nuestro personal remarcó después, afrontó la muerte a lo Frank Sinatra. Lo hizo a su manera.

En la residencia Mary Potter tenemos un lema: aprovechar la vida al máximo. Como Nell demostró, a menudo esto se puede lograr fuera de la residencia. Por este motivo estamos extendiendo nuestros servicios a la comunidad. También por eso, con un gran apoyo local, acabamos de construir una unidad de pacientes externos en la región de Kapiti. Y con tu ayuda durante la campaña de este año en la calle para recaudar fondos podremos hacer incluso más para ayudar a los enfermos terminales (y a aquéllos que descubren, después de todo, que en realidad no se están muriendo) a aprovechar la vida al máximo.

Start Again, p. 227
Sobreimpresión: Un ataque de apoplejía no es el final. Es cuestión de volver a empezar.

Texto: Tienes una posibilidad entre ocho de sufrir un ataque de apoplejía. Por supuesto, si eres fumador, tu riesgo se multiplica por cinco. La alta presión sanguínea incrementa cuatro veces el riesgo. Y si eres un fumador con una alta presión sanguínea entonces has hecho diana. Tu posibilidad de sufrir una apoplejía es 18 veces mayor. La apoplejía se produce por una súbita interrupción del suministro de sangre a parte del cerebro y causa lesiones cerebrales. Sufrirás algunos o incluso todos los síntomas siguientes. La muerte (la peor consecuencia, así que pensamos en dejarla de lado en primer lugar). Pérdida de conciencia. Parálisis o debilidad en la mitad de la cara, en un brazo o una pierna. Es probable que no puedas comunicarte. Quizá tengas dificultades para tragar o comer. Puede que padezcas una pérdida de control de la vejiga o el intestino. Es muy posible que sufras problemas de visión. Pérdida de memoria y del control emocional. Tu capacidad de aprender es probable que se venga abajo. Y ni que decir tiene que la depresión es muy común. A menudo te quedas con un cuerpo que tiene dos mitades absolutamente diferentes.

Una parte puede ser bastante igual que antes. Pero tendrás que enseñar a la otra a moverse, coordinar, hablar, comer y andar empezando desde cero. Tras todo esto, no es de extrañar que la percepción común sea que si eres lo bastante afortunado de sobrevivir a un ataque de apoplejía, en realidad no seas nada afortunado. Te podemos decir con cierta satisfacción que no es así. Es muy probable que puedas llegar a recuperarte parcialmente o hasta totalmente. Una terapia intensiva, un servicio de enfermería bien cualificado y el tiempo pueden ayudarte a volver a adquirir un control absoluto del cuerpo. Otra cara positiva de la apoplejía es que a medida que conocemos mejor sus causas, podemos disminuir de manera significativa las posibilidades de que lo sufras. El exceso de alcohol, el tabaco, un alto nivel de estrés, la falta de ejercicio, un alto nivel de colesterol en la sangre, los problemas cardiacos, la diabetes y la obesidad son factores de riesgo. Muchos de ellos pueden controlarse con medicación, cambios de dieta o hábitos de trabajo, o en el caso de un consumo excesivo de alcohol, por ejemplo, con una dosis saludable de autocontrol (no te preocupes, no somos abstemios, sólo fomentamos una cierta moderación). La Stroke Foundation (Fundación de la Apoplejía) es el único organismo de Nueva Zelanda exclusivamente dedicado a ayudar a las víctimas de la apoplejía, a sus familiares y amigos. Pero... sorpresa, sorpresa, no somos una organización rica. A fin de proseguir nuestra labor, nuestra investigación, nuestros servicios de apoyo y nuestros programas de educación preventiva, necesitamos tu ayuda.
Puedes hacer una donación a la Stroke Foundation.
PO Box 2320
Wellington,
o comunicánosla por teléfono al 0800 Stroke (0800 787 653).
Sea cual sea la cantidad que puedas aportar, nos ayudará a divulgar cómo prevenir una apoplejía y a garantizar que más personas se den cuenta de que no es una historia con una sola cara.

Para más información, dirígete a la Stroke Foundation of New Zeland inc.
PO Box 2320,
Wellington.
Teléfono (04) 472 8099,
Fax (04) 472 7019.

Blind, p. 228
Titular: Ciego, ga adj. y n. 1 Incapacitado fisiológicamente para ver.
Ciego, ga adj. 2 Se dice de la persona que no percibe cierta cosa patente.
Texto: Pasa un día con los ciegos. Verás las cosas de otro modo.
Publicado en interés público por Tata Tea Limited. Marcando la diferencia... cada día.

Matches, p. 229
Voz en off masculina: Cuando una vida se apaga, algo en su interior puede encender otra.
La vida te llama. Dona tus órganos.
Voz en off masculina y título: La vida te llama. Dona tus órganos.
Voz en off masculina: Este es un mensaje público de Antena 3 TV.
Creado por Saatchi & Saatchi Advertising

Prisoner, p. 230
Voz en off masculina: Algunos encarcelados disponen de electricidad y comen tres veces al día.
Algunos encarcelados disponen de agua caliente y televisión.
Otros no...
y su único crimen fue sobrevivir a sus ingresos.
Colabora, ayuda a Rand Aid a marcar la diferencia 011 882 2510.

Punch These, p. 232
Sobreimpresión: ¿Enfadado, frustrado, confundido?
Márcalos.
The Samaritans Tel. 366 66 76.

Bus, p. 286
Texto: Samaritans. Tel. 4 739 739.

讀這篇文章，你他媽的 [Read This You Piece of Shit]，第7頁

大字標題：讀這篇文章，你他媽的。

廣告文字：如果這廣告冒犯了你，這是應該的。

無人應該得到如此的對待，但不幸地，世界各地有數以百萬計的人就是如此的對待。對很多人而言，言語上的粗糙是最少令他們關注的一回事，例如在巴西亞馬遜河流域從事開發莊園地產工作的工人要承受一種稱為「樹幹」[the trunk] 的刑罰，未能砍下足夠限額的樹木的工人會被脫光衣服，然後綁在挖空的樹幹上三天，似乎這種刑罰還不夠，施刑者還在樹幹上塗抹蜜糖來吸引螞蟻和其他昆蟲。

在印度的兒童亦要承受同類型的可怕事件，年幼得只有六歲的兒童被賣到地氈廠工作，若織氈老板找不夠兒童購買時，他們便綁架擄拐孩童，兒童被迫整天工作，如果他們稍為手慢，晚上便不准睡覺，如果他編織錯誤便會被鞭打。有一名孩童更因為要求休息時間而被淋潑煤油，然後燒燬。另外六名兒童就只因為玩耍而被恐嚇毆打，其中一名更因此而死亡。

在尼泊爾，奴隸問題一樣的普遍，十歲小的女孩被擄，然後被賣往印度的色情賣淫組織。她們首先要渡過一段「修飾」期，她們會被脫光衣服，再被鎖在一個細小的房間數日，沒有任何食物，更被人用煙頭燒灼、毆打和強姦至她們終於變得完全順服，這時他們才會取得孟買妓院付出的最高賣價。

色情賣淫是一種奴隸活動，婚姻亦會是一樣。

世界上很多地方的父母仍然操縱他們的女兒的婚姻，為她們選擇配偶，他們所選擇的對象多數是視乎男方家庭提出的交易條件是否豐厚而定，極少會為新娘的福利著想。

因此，很多婦女被迫婚，有些更只得九歲。有一名十二歲的尼日利亞女孩對她的丈夫憎恨得多次欲逃走，而她的丈夫為了制止她而將她的雙腿砍掉。正如所見，奴隸並非是以往的問題，亦並不只是第三世界的問題。

就在英國，由1987年至今已有1700宗虐待家傭的舉報，她們大多數是來自海外貧窮背景，她們以為在英國工作便可解決她們的問題，但當她們抵步後，便受到像畜生一樣的對待，很多都要睡在地上和吃殘羹剩飯，每天工作18小時，稍有埋怨便會被鞭打，有些甚至不准外出，有些更被強姦。

暴虐例子多不勝數。

世界上仍有超過一億奴隸，每一個可能都有著同樣悲慘痛苦的故事。

國際反奴隸組織 [Anti-Slavery International] 呼籲終止奴隸活動，我們知道如要肅清奴隸活動，唯一途徑便是將這些人的境況事實公諸於世。

當然，透過呼籲活動，提醒世界各地有關這些問題的存在，我們已說服多個政府和聯合國去對付這些問題。

我們更在一些國家竭力爭取更改法律，例如泰國、印度和巴基斯坦。沒有我們的擁護者的支持，我們根本沒可能做得到，他們曾致函世界各地向個別人士、公司和各政府機構查詢有關問題。

為了繼續向這些人施加壓力，我將來的廣告運動需要你的協助。

如果你不想參與，請填妥下面的表格成為會員。始終會有一天，我們會確保無人知道作為奴隸的感受。

Anti-Slavery International,
Stableyard, Broomsgrove Road,
London SW9 9TL
電話：0171 924 9555 傳真：0171 738 4110

嬰兒車／家庭計劃 [Pram/Family Planning]，第18頁

母：你無須理會那些家庭生育計劃的問題，

阿葛，停止呀。

我的意思是有少許醫生和診所能告訴你，任何有少許認識的人都不能自己去解決問題嗎？

問你的朋友，我，就是這樣的呀。

阿嫻，不要騷擾啤啤 - 我要講多少次呢？

如果你不想懷孕，你便應該 - 你知道的意思是小心之類。

用你的腦...

男聲旁白：切勿聽有關家庭計劃的荒唐故事。

你的醫生或診所會歡迎你，不論已婚或單身，他們提供友善和正確的指導。

在電話中查找家庭計劃 [Family Planning]。

標題字幕：在電話中查找家庭計劃 [Family Planning]

母：... 有這麼多個孩子，我又怎能負擔避孕用品呢？

男聲旁白：你無須支付任何費用

剪下這票 [Clip this Coupon]，第22頁

廣告文字：剪下這票，就好像將你的照片放在這裡一樣。

婦女及兒童優先 [Women and Children First]，第24頁

大字標題：而各核子國家說：婦女及兒童優先。

廣告文字：不，這不是細緻的畫面繪圖傑作，這是一個圖像哈薩克 [Kazakhstan] 的小孩，生來便有腦積水，由於他的母親感染至崩角，結果便形成這種畸形。他們向你展示這圖片而對我們勸說，你應該向隱瞞事實和堅持核實並不危險的人動氣。

別看 [Can't Look]，第26頁

聲音：嬰兒哭聲

第一幕

女人：住嘴，如果你再不停止叫喊，我便掌摑你往那個門口。

第二幕

男人：過來這邊坐。

第三幕

男人：你沒有腦袋的，你真蠢，你絕不是我的孩子。

第四幕

小童：媽咪，你在那裡？
我不喜歡孤獨一個人。

第五幕

男人：不要告訴任何人，這是我們小小的秘密。

有時我們連者也忍受不住。

虐待兒童是可以制止的，而你的幫助更可以永遠制止它。

女聲旁白：請支持國家防止虐待兒童協會 [NSPCC] 最新的全面終止運動

標題字幕：國家防止虐待兒童協會 [NSPCC] 對兒童的虐待必須終止。
全面終止。

懷孕男人 [Pregnant Man]，第28頁

大字標題：如果是你會懷孕的話，你會小心一點嗎？

廣告文字：任何已婚或單身人士都可以向家庭計劃協會 [Family Planning Association] 索取有關避孕的指導，

Margaret Pyke House, 27–35 Mortimer Street London W1N 8BQ。電話 01 636 9135。

有些父親 [Some Fathers]，第29頁

大字標題：有些父親令他們的孩子改變。

廣告文字：你 可以看到孩子頭上所受的損傷。你真的見到嗎？

但實際上，肉體損傷會慢慢痊愈，但精神上的疤痕會持續一生，令一個開心、正常的小孩變到落魄不安。

每一年都有數以千計的兒童受到他們的父親和母親的虐待，但如果你懷疑有小孩受到虐待，不論是任何人，你都要負責任，因為假如你不將虐待事件舉報，你就好像是施行虐待。

如果你有任何關於虐待兒童的資料，請在9月4日打電話給我們，1 800 011 233。舉報虐待及制止虐待。新南威爾斯警察服務部 [NSW Police Service]

同一個父親 [Same Father]，第30頁

大字標題：我們有同一個父親
廣告文字：這是莎莉的故事。

「我十二歲時媽媽死了。有一天晚上我造了一個噩夢，我的爸爸說我可以到他的床上睡。開始時他只是擁抱我，但跟著他便強吻我事，我想他停止，但他還繼續，我憎恨那回事，它實在令我很痛。爸爸說那表示他愛我。

第二天我離家上學時，他說絕對不能告訴任何人發生過的事。

之後每天晚上他都要我跟他睡，他說這是我們的小秘密。後來當我的經期停止時，我的爸爸不讓我上學，並告訴學校我生病了。

有時我也感覺到啤啤在我的身體內郁動，這感覺實在太可怕」。

很幸運地，莎莉的學校因為她姊妹而提出舉報，現在她可以獲得所有她需要的援助了。

當然，她所受到的虐待是不止於受孕的，她會需要長期的輔導，以及處理情感上的損傷，例如內疚以及喪失組織關係的能力。

其實，各種形式的虐待都會導致情緒上的損傷，並不單止是牽涉到性侵犯和肉體暴力這些較為明顯的形式。

例如，迴避任何愛慕的表示、不理孩子、經常地批評他們或對他們喝罵都能導致持續一生的感情疤痕，有時孩子更可能被驅使到自殺。

因此，國家防止虐待兒童會 [NSPCC] 展開「為兒童呼籲」運動 [A Cry for Children]，呼籲所有人停下來想一下他們對待兒童的態度，確定任何形式的殘酷所能帶給孩子能影響他們的一生。

請對呼籲作出回應。

如果你或你認識的人正在受到虐待，請致電國家防止虐待兒童會 [NSPCC] 的保護兒童援助電話 [Child Protection Helpline] 0800 800 500。

或者，當你讀完這廣告後想索取更多資料的話，請電 071 825 2775。國家防止虐待兒童會 [NSPCC]：為兒童呼籲 [A Cry for Children]

太空人 [Astronaut]，第31頁

大字標題：這世界是否將問題重點的次序處理得當呢？

廣告文字：世界狀況論壇 [State of the World Forum] 將很多全球最有影響力的人士聚集在一起，討論人類要面對的各種實際問題。解除核子武裝軍備... 終止戰爭紛爭。婦女與兒童的發展任務，這都是與適當地處理將來的問題有關，請在10月27日至11月1日在我們的網址參加討論，這是你改變這個世界的機會。

面孔 [Face]，第32頁

標題字幕：這個少女想聊天。
標題字幕：沒有耐性忍受了嗎？
標題字幕：護士羅賓遜 [Robinson] 知道這很快便會是雙向的會談
護士：嗨！麗珠，我們又一齊了。又一個女孩子之夜嗯？
標題字幕：新的國家保健服務 [NHS] 需要更多護士。
女聲旁白：護士能造成相當的改變，有關擔任護士或重投護士行業，並獲得改善的工資和工作條件之資料，請電0845 60 60 655。

小兒臥床 [Cot]，第36頁

男聲旁白：每10宗殺害中便有1宗是在這裡發生的，每星期有1至2宗死亡，一年有超過 5,000宗毆打和超過1,700宗性侵犯。
標題字幕：在英國每天有 36,000 名兒童過著受到虐待威脅的生活。
標題字幕：國家防止虐待兒童協會 [NSPCC] 為兒童呼籲 [A Cry For Children]

這個世界很容易便能終止這個 [The World Could End This Easily]，第40頁

標題字幕：這個世界很容易便能終止這個。
大膽說出反對核子試驗
綠色和平 [Greenpeace] 0800 22 33 44

繼續受教育 [Stay In School]，第42頁

標題字幕：繼續受教育。

餓餓 [Hungry]，第44頁

男聲旁白：假如我說粗言穢語，可能會令你不安，如果我告訴你我肚餓，可能不會令你不安，她媽的，我好餓啊！
標題字幕：切勿浪費食物。

反暴力日 [Day Against Violence]，第46頁

標題字幕：似乎是不可能的。
在1995年2月12日發生。
世界各地十七億人都看到。
這是第一次。
意大利足球隊進場時穿著對手球隊的球衣。
它們上面的信息是足球必須團結，不要分歧。
今日，這概念屬於所有人。
沒有事是不可能的。

最差的印記 [Worst Marks]，第50頁

大字標題：來自少數民族的兒童通常在學校獲得最差的印記。

老師考試合格 [Teacher Passing an Examination]，第51頁

廣告文字：他努力掙扎試圖學識乘法計算，他根本不懂得怎樣做乘數，直至他的老師用另一種方法解釋。

大字標題：老師考試合格。

廣告文字：當一個學生掌握到困難問題的竅門時，這可能是教書最喜之處，這表示老師已找到一個有道理的方法，這是很有意義的。

令學生領悟到竅門是教書的缺

窮，這是知識的傳授和領悟之間的連結，對老師和學生來說，這是雙方分享的成就。

可能就是這一點令你對教書行業感興趣，如果是的話，那麼你會高興和知道其他的報酬亦是很有價值的。

有十二月開始，倫敦內區擁有良好榮譽學位的中小學教師只起薪是14,000英鎊（包括倫敦內區津貼和增補）。

一個在倫敦內區大型中學的校長的薪金可以高達48,000英鎊。

當然，這不是容易及賺的錢，教書畢竟不是機械化的過程，亦不可能是。

每一班都包括各類學生，有各種才能、興趣、觀點態度和背景。

作為一個老師，你要對這些分別有認識，並對它們和對它們作出當的反應。

例如，各兒童在各種科目的學習速度都是不同的，而老師卻要全部適應通達。

當遇到毫無反應時，可能需要改用全行的方法去解釋，通常創新的處理和探討會有奇妙的效果，並會提高教室的氣氛。

在某種意義上，一個教師每天都在考試，而且必須要合格。

一種令人膽怯的狀況，抑或是一個令人鼓舞的挑戰呢？

如果你認為是後者，訓練可以接納你對教書的衝勁，以及磨練你的本能技巧去應付這每天每天的考試。作為一份職業，這便有雙倍的價值。

欲知有關怎樣成為一教師，請電0345 300121，說明部門代號 IS/4/A 或郵寄下面表格。

教書能顯露才華。

決心 [Resolution]，第52頁

標題字幕：每年在菲律賓有數以千計的兒童是在醫院渡過新年元旦的，因為低劣粗製濫造的爆竹令他們失去手指和手掌，這廣告目的是終止這壞的循環。

老師：各位同學，你們有甚麼新年決定呢？

兒童：老師，我不再玩爆竹了。

標題字幕：這個新年切勿接觸爆竹。

妓女 [Prostitute]，第54頁

大字標題：你想在歐洲做妓女嗎？

廣告文字：有數以百萬計的婦女是無從選擇的，就好像那些受到國際販賣色情組織欺騙的移民婦女，她們成為被利用剝削的受害者，不能為自己的生命作抉擇。

當你認識到現今用來貶低人類的各種手法時，你會感到驚訝，Manos Unidas希望終止這些虐待行徑，協助我們廢除奴隸狀況。

注意：在左邊的插圖你可以看到在西班牙主要報章的分類廣告（就業機會專欄）刊有這些運作。

採礦兒童 [Mining Children]，第55頁

大字標題：冶金公司 [Metallurgical Company] 需要採礦兒童。

廣告文字：有數以百萬計的二桶是無須找工作做的 - 工作是會強加在他們身上。

就好像被聘請做廉價勞工的兒童，他們成為被利用剝削的受害者，不能為自己的生命作抉擇。

當你認識到現今用來貶低人類的各種手法時，你會感到驚訝，Manos Unidas希望終止這些虐待行徑，協助我們廢除奴隸狀況。

注意：在左邊的插圖你可以看到在西班牙主要報章的分類廣告（就業機會專欄）刊有這些運作。

虐待兒童 [Child Abuse]，第56頁

男人1：靚女嗯？
男人2：她是處女嗎？
男人1：當然，她是我的女兒。
男人 2：多少錢？
男人1：只是$100元。
男人2：她可以做甚麼？
男人1：甚麼都做 - 但不要弄死她。
... 來吧，愛人。
旁白：假如這是發生在你的女兒身上，你會驚恐，對嗎？
在世界任何地方，切記這一點。
在全世界任何地方，兒童就是兒童。
標題字幕：Centro Italiano per L'adozione Internationale (意大利國際收養中心 [The Italian Centre for International Adoption])

三歲時被污辱 [Raped as a 3 Year Old]，第58頁

大字標題：在三歲時被強姦的感受是怎樣的呢？
一名受害者解釋。
廣告文字：我最初記得我被我的父親性虐待時，我大概是三歲，可能之前已發生，但我不知道。

我現在可以看到自己睡在床上，那張大臉漸漸移近我，他吻我，說晚安，但也不停的吻我。

他告訴我這是我的秘密，如果我告訴任何人，我便會被送走。

但即使當時我只是一個小孩，我知道事情原先只是那麼可怕，「我會保護你的。」他又怎能保護我呢？他令我很痛呢？

其實很奇怪，他是我的敵人，但同時亦是我在這世界中唯一的朋友，他令我很依賴他，控制我，我的身體成為他的玩物超越九年。

在學校我發覺很男人別人結交，我覺得我與別人在一起時我便不讓任何人接近我，我對別人在更衣室內看到我的身體，我覺得很羞恥，我討厭別人看到我和叫我做「基佬」。

即使別人說我到女朋友時，我仍然不能肯定自己是否異性戀者。我對她非常粗暴，我想這是因為我要控制別人，像我的父親對我一樣。

性愛令我感到可怕，達到高潮時又令我想到我父親在我的體內做甚麼，以及那張大臉。

後來我遇到另外一個人，我們結了婚，兩年後，她離開了我，她說我冷漠和不了解她。

我就是那樣，就是不知道自己感覺到或導致別人精神的痛苦，我有些東西在很久以前被閉了，有很多次其實我是可以用刀割自己而不了解那些。

離婚之後，我轉向酒精，那是一種逃避的方法，但我仍然有時感到極之消沉。

去年，我的父親終於死了，我想就是他的去世促使我聯絡國家防止虐待兒童協會 [NSPCC]，我53歲，這是我第一次向別人講述我兒時的經歷。

六個月期間，有一位保護兒童主任每星期與我一起工作一次，他使我把我的創傷和盤托出，這過經歷是很痛苦的，我對四十多年來一直嘗試不去想它。

最後終於生效，他令我明白到以往發生的一切都不是我的錯。

我記憶所及，這是我首次真正對自己有好感，就好像在黑暗和孤獨的小室被鎖出來一樣。

我永遠不會忘記在我身上發生的事，但最低限度我可以開始我的新生活。

欲知有關國家防止虐待兒童協會 [NSPCC] 的工作詳情或捐款，請致函：NSPCC, 67 Saffron Hill, London EC1N 8RS 或致電 071 242 1626。

如欲舉報懷疑是虐待的事件，請電國家防止虐待兒童協會 NSPCC 的保護兒童援助電話 0800 800 500。

善惡雙重性格的杰基爾醫生和海德先生 [Dr Jekyll, Mr Hyde]，第59頁
大字標題：善惡雙重性格的杰基爾醫生 [Doctor Jekyll] 和海德先生 [Mister Hyde]
廣告文字：你是一個可靠、有感情、股勤體貼和人家敬重的男人，你有一個漂亮的妻子和一個可愛的九歲女兒，你的溫馨家庭是你最大的賜福，但是，有一次，你要出外處理業務，要去一個富異國風情的目的地，例如曼谷，一個「有不同傳統和風俗」而又容忍任何事的地方，在那裡市集醞著售賣槍枝和紀念品外，還向你兜售小女孩，她是一個美麗的九歲女孩，有少許像你的女兒，只是她有著較像一個成年女人。你以為這是那裡的風俗習慣，於是你開始轉變，搖身一變成為另一個人，世界雛妓市場是一個有和勢力大的死亡市場，它正在點數你另一個囚禁，他們大部分的利潤其實並非有罪犯和變態的，而是來自普通人，像你一樣的普通人。CIAI意大利國際收養中心 [Italian Centre for International Adoption] 多年來一直爭取堅持維護一個簡單的概念，那就是所有人都不應忘記，特別是到國外旅行時：不論你在世界任何地方，一個孩子就是一個人。
可用信用卡支付你的捐款，請電 +39-2-55-01-20-11，意大利米蘭的 Cariplo [A/C No.10837 at Cariplo, Branch 15, Milan, Italy]。

每八個便有一個 [1 in every 8]，第60頁
大字標題：每八個走過這海報的人便有一個曾在小時受到虐待。國家防止虐待兒童協會 [NSPCC]，為兒童呼喊。

禁制鎗械 [Ban Guns]，第64頁

子彈 [Bullet]，第66頁
大字標題：沒有避孕套的陽具。

廣告文字：索取免費避孕套，請電 250 8629。

不致要命 [Less Dead]，第68頁
廣告文字：如果 .22 口徑手鎗並不那麼致命，為何要他的命？請立即廢除 .22 口徑手鎗的禁止鎗械法例。

邋遢天使 [Grunge Angels]，第70頁
男聲旁白：作為我後世的娛樂，我們為你帶來 Whitney Houston 最著名的情歌。
聲音：尖聲叫喊。
標題字幕：死亡是極可怕的一回事。請扣安全帶。

橡皮女人 [Rubber Woman]，第74頁
大字標題：橡皮套，最新睡房裝束。

橡皮男人 [Rubber Man]，第75頁
廣告文字：穿橡皮套的男士時常都比較好看。

方言 [Tongue]，第76頁
大字標題：她想將她的方言放進你的嘴巴。
廣告文字：令學習廣東話或國語更容易，請致電香港語言學習中心 [Hong Kong Language Learning Centre] 2385 5331。

母親 [Mother]，第78頁
標題字幕：警告：以下片段可能會令一些觀眾不安。
男聲旁白：你跟看到的會令你震驚，這是一個七歲女孩坐在一架正在以時速50公里行駛的汽車後面座位而又沒有扣安全帶的結果，請細心觀察情形。
沒有安全帶的座椅是不安全的，必須扣上安全帶。
標題字幕：馬路死傷人數一定要降低。

工作滿足感 [Job Satisfaction]，第81頁
大字標題：當你要遺送別人回家去死時，如何能從中取得工作滿足感呢？
廣告文字：當抵達醫院時，阿力的病疾已差不多要了他的命，呼吸和吞嚥都困難且痛楚，任和較為有力的動作都極艱苦。
即使如此，83歲的阿力依然決定在家中渡過餘下的日子，但直至他的護士今有足夠力量，他甚至地方也不能去，氧氣、藥物療法和人工餵食漸漸令阿力稍覺舒服。
護士一定會為阿力的和他的家人騰出時間：指導他們，令他們安心，或只是聽他們的說話。
三個星期後，他的病徵已穩定得可以回家了。
當阿力和護士最後告別時，他們已成為朋友。
照料老年人並不容易，你需要精力充沛，有同情心，以及有啟發的創意，當你能滿足一個快將死去的人的意願時，你究竟想你所得到的工作滿足感是沒有任何其他職業能及的。
請在任何時間致電 0345646464，指明是2J。護理服務，你有否所需的條件呢？

一個鄉村故事 [A Country Story]，第82頁
第一集
廣告字幕：在8月24日，丹尼將會與特莎結婚。
媽媽：早餐來啦！
彼德：挺好呀！煙肉！
特莎能煮菜嗎？
爸爸：那真有趣 - 她的母親不懂得煮菜。
媽媽：布魯斯！
男聲旁白：如果你想寫信給這一家人，你要寫給卡特斯，由 Central Hawkes Bay 轉交。
這農場屬於卡特一家有八十多年了，是下一個繼承人，在婚禮之後不久，他將會入住農舍，而另一代將會被訓練在這片土地工作，這將會如此繼續下去。
丹尼：爸爸，如果你喜歡的話，今年你在練足球會先去拿取那些x。
爸爸：那就好啦。
丹尼：我們大概在下午四時便走了啦，彼德。
彼德：好呀。
媽媽：不要整晚留在那裡。
廣告字幕：待續。

第二集

還有五個星期，丹尼便會與特莎結婚。
男聲旁白：就像過去數年一樣，丹尼和彼德在足球訓練完畢後，在回家途中先去酒吧去。
布盧：嘿，四星期新郎，你好，彼德？
彼德：你今晚好呀，布盧？
布盧：看誰回來了。
丹尼：嘿，馬修，你去了哪裡？
馬修：啊，去了 Palmy，去看那個A & P農展。
丹尼：看到好東西嗎？
馬修：得獎的公牛，$5看一看。
丹尼：我說全家都可以減價嗎？他說你有多少人，我告訴他... 只是我和我的太太以及你的十三個孩子，他對我說，你在這裡等著，我帶我的公牛出來看看。
男聲旁白：這已成為一個受歡迎的習慣了，馬修總是由此處回來，而且他總是有故事說的，人們稱這為貓頭鷹，應為如果它整晚留在那裡，它是不會叫的，但可能是有其他原因的。
廣告字幕：待續。

第三集
標題字幕：還有四個星期丹尼便會跟特莎結婚。
丹尼：在想甚麼？
彼德：弟弟，我只是在想我們是多麼的幸福，每星期一，無憂無神的日常工作，無須握緊錢財。
彼德：那好像很深奧。
丹尼：算了吧，你還欠我一個仙呢？
彼德：在這兒呀！
丹尼：他們一直都非常要好，而再過數星後，彼德便會是婚禮中的伴郎。
彼德：夠了嗎？
丹尼：這就要看了。
彼德：看完嗎？
丹尼：我是伴郎，對嗎？
彼德：對。
丹尼：我要演講，對嗎？
彼德：對。
丹尼：有關數年前你在 Massey 認識的女人，你究竟想我講多少？
彼德：要幫手嗎？
好帥的名字。
彼德：她叫甚麼名字？艾琳呢。
丹尼：不要欠那一個仙了！
彼德：(唱) 艾琳，晚安，艾琳，晚安...
標題字幕：待續。

第四集
標題字幕：還有三個星期丹尼便會跟特莎結婚。
教練：OK，各位球員，我們無可能再讓那些城市球員打敗我們的，我們一定要在哨子盪響前做出來，我們要讓他們知道誰是大阿哥，講起大阿哥，因為丹尼和特莎OK，就這樣吧。
隊長：是一次，各位，我只要說恭祝丹尼一切順利... 還有，總之祝丹尼和彼德...
隊長：噢，對... 丹尼和特莎... 祝好運。
丹尼：你好！
馬修：還有多久？
丹尼：兩個星期。
馬修：我那年老的叔父在前幾天再次結婚。
馬修：91
丹尼：91！怎麼他這把年紀仍想結婚呢？
馬修：他不想的 - 但一定要。
廣告字幕：待續。

第五集
標題字幕：還有兩個星期丹尼便會跟特莎結婚。
丹尼：媽，你好！
媽媽：你那麼遲，試試這些... 造的。
特莎：彼德呢？
丹尼：精美的糕點呀，特莎。
特莎：是鬆糕。
丹尼：精美的糕點，鬆糕。
彼德：是否重要人物？
男聲旁白：這裡充滿著最重要的年青人，來自農場工人工會。
他們知道各人的薪酬待遇。
丹尼：爸爸如果他有家牛主管每星期有兩百元和免費住屋等，跟曾經是雜工，每星期有一百六十元和免費住屋。
他會着問請有誰人，我說有一名遲鈍的，他在這裡擔任大部份的工作，每星期有$40一星期四十元！那知是我要跟他談的人。於是我說是你，他便走了。
廣告字幕：待續。

第六集
標題字幕：這個星期丹尼會跟特莎結婚。

婚結。
男聲旁白：丹尼和特莎這個星期便會成為卡特先生和太太... 這個家庭農場再一次轉手讓較年青、較強壯的人打理。
布盧：嘿！丹尼...
等等，乃尼，要聽這個...
說吧，馬修
馬修：我正在告訴他們有關那天那個來自城市的人，那個「生活作風」的人間瘦鬼，他說很有害害，你給他甚麼？」瘦鬼說：「我給牠苯基 [phenyl]」過了兩天那城市人回來對瘦鬼說：「瘦鬼，我給你的馬服用苯基，牠跟著死了！」瘦鬼：「我的也是呀。」
布盧：丹尼，有個口信給你，特莎有一個... 有關婚禮的細節。
丹尼：噢，OK，謝謝，我們走了，來吧，彼德，要載你一程嗎？
馬修：來一杯，我們便走。
標題字幕：待續。

第七集
標題字幕：這個星期丹尼便跟特莎結婚。
丹尼：喂，你們靜一下... 這可能是軍部打來的。
喂，貓頭鷹... 你好，布魯斯... 不，他們的確是來過。
爸爸：謝謝你，布盧，謝謝。
丹尼：一定是... 跟土著有麻煩... 我出去找他們。
彼德：那好像很深奧。
爸爸：跟土著有麻煩？... 他們怎麼不打電話回來？
丹尼：算了吧，你還欠我一個仙呢？
彼德：在這兒呀！
丹尼：他們一直都非常要好，而再過數星後，彼德便會是婚禮中的伴郎。
爸爸：噢！媽媽！噢！媽媽！
標題字幕：待續。

第八集
標題字幕：丹尼死了
男聲旁白：馬修和年輕的丹尼都在那晚的汽車意外死去。鄉村人是會死在鄉村道路的。
以前一樣 他現在克賴斯特徹奇 [Christchurch] 的一間脊椎診所，他不能行，永遠不能了。
特莎：媽媽，他們有否就農場的作出投訴？
媽媽：我想有的。
爸爸：有一或兩個人有興趣。
媽媽：告訴布魯斯。
特莎：我要離開，不是永遠的，只是暫時，但我會保持聯絡。
爸爸：去哪裡？
特莎：去北部我的姑媽處。
爸爸：真的。
媽媽：她要走了，爸爸，她懷著丹尼的孩子。
爸爸：這永不停止的，媽媽，對嗎？永不停止。
標題字幕及男聲旁白：以後都沒有鄉村人是會死在鄉村道路的。

它的高度 [The Height of It]，第93頁

計程車自白 [Taxi Confessions]，第94頁
司機：你要告訴我甚麼街道，因為如果你睡了，我便不知道送你往那裡去。
男人：啊！的士！
男人：對呀！你去所有這些酒吧，卻從來找不到他們，對呀，你去是...
女人：他擧高他的手，他的手有手銬。
是手銬。
男人：我不要回家。
男人：這是你要去的地方呀。
男人：哦！我們到啦！
男人：這些肉飽，他們就只給豬皮，你知道嗎？時時都是這的。
男人：這一刻他在我的後面，但轉眼間他便不見了。
司機：Herne Bay，謝謝。
司機：Herne Bay？大概在那一帶？
情侶：這裡是否有 White Lady 或之類在這兒？
有呀。
對呀！就在下面。
你今晚真的是漂亮。
男人：他去這些海外酒吧，他時常迷途的。
男人：不，不，不，因為不是那裡，不要去那裡的地方。
我們是由那裡來的。
男聲旁白及標題字幕：如果你飲酒，然後叫計程車，那你便是個大天才了。

天災橫禍 [Disaster]，第96頁
大字標題：無論我們到那裡，都是天災橫禍。
廣告文字：我們並不是想逃避災難，但我們需要為隨時隨地都突然發生的災禍作好準備，例如盧旺達 [Rwanda] 的天災，是于 Ruahire 大飛機墜毀事件。以百萬計的人而言，紅十字會的標記徽號已成為災禍非常見和安定人心的標誌。我們為緊急反應作好準備，透過我們的急救和救援課程，我們亦讓你作好準備。我們可能有時向你求援，但有一天才可能需要我們的援助。

打仗 [Fight]，第98頁
大字標題：我們教他們如何打仗。
廣告文字：我們的戰爭中，打仗的手段是公平合理的嗎？是否不對的，即使在戰場中也有規例的。紅十字會在世界各地的戰爭中都會執行人道工作過程時遇到很多軍人，他們在對囚犯、平民或敵人的義務中，是毫無概念的。
如果我們能夠教導這些軍人日內瓦公約 [Geneva Convention] 所要求他們需要具備的操守的話，那麼我們便能救授人命的。你對一些紅十字會的操守的工作可能感到驚訝，但無論是任何工作和在任何地方，我們都需要你的協助。

350種語言 [350 Languages]，第99頁
大字標題：怎樣用35c種語言說「別射殺我」。
廣告文字：紅十字會的標記徽號來自1859年在Solferino的戰場，今日你們將軍隊和軍人以及生命與死亡分隔開，它是受到日內瓦公約 [Geneva Convention] 保護的，誤用它會被視作抵觸法律處理。它不應是急救箱，也不是標籤診所或醫療中心，它是包庇掩護、中立和人道的象徵。紐西蘭紅十字會有責任去保護它，因為沒有它我們便不能保護你。

切勿忘記 [Don't Forget]，第100頁
大字標題：飲過酒後切勿忘記如何進行性愛。
廣告文字：酒後容易忘記事物。保護自己，提防愛滋病疫，使用避孕套，只需記得你將它放在那裡。

預防疾病 [Prevent Sickness]，第101頁
大字標題：帶備所需以防感染後染病。
廣告文字：飲酒可以導致不安全的性愛，避孕套保護自己，因為愛滋病令你生病，永久的病。

睡帽 [Night Cap]，第103頁
大字標題：不論你飲了多少酒，記得帶備睡帽。
廣告文字：你飲酒越多便越容易忘記。降低感染愛滋病的威脅，帶避孕套上床。

適當的套包 [Right Package]，第102頁
大字標題：如果你想保留你的僱員，給他們適當的套包。
廣告文字：你的僱員在床上做甚麼是不關你的事，但這可能會對你公司的業務有很大的影響。
假如有一位員工受到HIV病毒感染，而後來演變成為愛滋病，你便要另請別人代替他。
在現實中，你和你其他的僱員可能都擔心若果有HIV病毒的人在你們之間工作時是否安全，幸運地這是安全的。
你亦可能想知道個中所涉及的法律問題和究竟該員工是否受到保障，又或者該公司是否需要負責。
為這些問題尋求答案是很重要的，因為如果你的業務還未受到愛滋病的影響的話，它很快便可能。
到2000年，這傳染病問題在亞洲這個比非洲現在現時受到影響的地區加劇重，當愛滋病在此發生 - 除非你現時就採取行動去阻止這疾病的發展。
首先是與你本區的愛滋病行動組和政府醫務衛生處接觸，他們應能夠為你解決問題。
他們亦會指導你防止愛滋病在你的公司蔓延所需要的措施，例如請一位健康專業的員工講解，在佈告板上張貼有關預防愛滋病的海報，甚至在廁所設置避孕套自動配給機，向有關方面索取聯合國發展計劃辦事處 [United Nations Development Programme Office] 和在新德里的UNDP (請看下面地址) 查詢最近的愛滋病行動組在那裡。
立即採取行動，表示你的關心會提高員工的士氣。
別讓你避免因為愛滋病而損失可貴的員工。

預防 [Preservativo]，第105頁
旁白：避孕套，避孕套，避孕套，避孕套，避孕套，避孕套，避孕套，避孕套，避孕套，避孕套...
標題字幕：我們永不會討厭重複的。
避孕套是預防愛滋病可靠的武器。
說服你的伴侶，要他使用它。
ANLAIDS。

晚間的陌生人 [Strangers in the Night]，第106頁
這廣告的音樂是Strangers in the Night。在廣告中，音樂由原本的流暢弱拍轉為較零碎的悲哀版本，反映音符變化成十字架。

愛情故事 [Love Story]，第108頁
音樂：Love Story
男聲旁白：這個夏天很多好像他們這樣的人在沙灘上造愛。
紅十字會。
造愛！
標題字幕：紅十字會義工

蘭尼 [Lenny]，第113頁
蘭尼：你知道的，我只是覺得...好像...好舒服。你知道的，我不是在勁678，不是在狂快，我好像是柔和成熟。
我第一次嗑，你怎麼知道啦，嗑完之後，我說，這東也他媽的好。對。
你知道嗎，當你坐快車時，你的腎上腺索抽動，你知我說甚麼的，是那種感覺。
就像那樣。
我的大腿有蜂窩織炎，我有一個這麼大的疤痕，真是難以置信。
我差不多了... 我的腳在壞疽，它們差一點要了我的腳。
我認為我頗聰明，我可以去做我想做的事，無論我想做甚麼，我都能夠做。
我把五萬都花啦，當我想做，就好像他媽的，這媽的就是我想做的呀。
我是想做一個好人 - 只是這樣。為什麼不能這樣做呢？或者每一個人都應該吸毒，然後變得溫和。
我全身佈滿這些疤痕，腰下面都是小孔洞。
我以前做很多事，好像看電影和去餐廳吃東西，我時常去看百老匯歌舞劇，我喜歡百老匯歌舞劇，它們實在很好看。
到97年時，現在是1996年，對嗎？1996年8月17日，那一天也好，你們你的照相機來，我會是一個完全不同的人。
我會很成功，我可以用我的生命作賭注。
想要嗎？
沒有毒品的美國合辦 [Partnership for a Drug-Free America]

滑浪猴子 [Surfing Monkey]，第117頁
女聲旁白：各位，再一次，J343是滑浪猴子錢箱。畢業或結婚的最佳禮物，我記得上一次全賣掉，因此，不要錯過這機會。
現在我們與打電話來的人說話，來自納什維爾 [Nashville] 的史葛。
史葛，我知道這是你想要的。
史葛，我知道這是你想要的第十五隻我們的滑浪猴子錢箱，是真的嗎？
史葛：...對呀！
(聲浪及笑聲背景)
標題字幕：大麻，一種非常昂貴的嗜好。
沒有毒品的美國合辦 [Partnership for a Drug-Free America]

知名人士 [Celebrities]，第118頁
大字標題：在你的行業中，有人說最能將信息溝通的方法是讓名人士在你的廣告出現。
沒有毒品的美國合辦 [Partnership for a Drug-Free America]

鼻 [Nose]，第119頁
女聲旁白：一克可卡因的價值等如一個收音機。
三克可卡因的價值等如一個電視機。
七克，一次巴黎假期。
如果你服用可卡因，你工作所獲得的一切都會漸漸在你的鼻子下消失。
標題字幕：沒有毒品的美國合辦 [Partnership for a Drug-Free America]

大笨象 [Elephant]，第121頁
聲音：(由始至終) 大笨象的腳步聲
男聲旁白：這兩名婦女其中一個表示對大自然的尊重而將她部份薪酬捐給加州環境協會 [Environmental Federation of California]。
另一個沒有。
你現在可能不知道誰曾捐贈給環境，但大笨象永遠都不會忘記。
在辦公室支持大自然，捐贈給環境的薪酬扣減計劃。

今天你不能郁動。
今天你不能停止發抖。
今天你不能講話。
今天你的手指沒有知覺。
今天你覺得疲倦。
今天你不能上樓梯。
MS多發性硬化症是一種侵襲中央神經系統的疾病，每一日你都不知道身體哪一部份會受到影響和嚴重程度。任何人都會患上 MS多發性硬化症，我們希望你能對它更加認識。如欲索取更多資料或捐贈，請電0800 100133，24小時服務。MS協會提供力量抵抗MS多發性硬化症。

我不煎炸 [Me No Fry]，第200頁
大字標題：我不煎炸。
廣告文字：新南威爾斯健康衛生[NSW Health]。增進健康的州。

日蝕 [Eclipse]，第201頁
大字標題：這是一生只得一次的機會。錯過它吧。

請來見我們 [Come and see us]，第202頁
大字標題：請來見我們。
廣告文字：乳癌的治療方法是預防。

食物上的蒼蠅 [Flies on Food]，第204頁
廣告文字：當一隻蒼蠅飛到你的食物上時會怎樣？
蒼蠅不能吃固體食物，因此他們先在食物上嘔吐令其軟化，然後將嘔吐物踩踏進去直至食物變成流質，通常踩踏時加入相當成份的細菌。當食物變成流質時，它們便再次吮吸入其體內，同時可能放下一些排泄物。
當它們吃完時，跟著便到你。
蓋上食物。蓋好飲食器皿。蓋好垃圾桶。

擦淨你的肺 [Scrub your Lungs]，第205頁
大字標題：你不能將你的肺擦得乾淨。
廣告文字：肺癌殺害吸煙者比不吸煙者多出十三倍。

犀利武器 [Lethal Weapon]，第206頁
大字標題：你的汽車是犀利武器。
廣告文字：小心駕駛。
在阿拉伯聯合猶長國 [UAE] 為道路安全利益而發行。

還有3日 [Three More Days]，第207頁
大字標題：只有三天便到「反對地雷日」[Anti-Landmines Day]。
廣告文字：絕望的數字：有一億一千萬個地雷遍佈地球六十四個國家；每二十分鐘便有一名受害者；地雷每年的生產數目為五百萬至一千萬；另有一億個地雷足夠如世界的軍火庫；90%的死傷是婦女和兒童。
希望的數字：郵遞資料
No.189241, Mani Tese, Italian Campaign Against Landmines, via Cavengahi 4, 20149 Milan。
四月十三日星期六請到Piazza Santi Apostoli參加我們的簽名請願和慷慨捐輸。

束埔寨的地雷 [Landmines in Cambodia]，第208頁
大字標題：一個3$的地雷能否另整整一個經濟體系癱瘓？
本文：當農夫害怕不敢去犁田時；當兒童害怕不敢步行上學去時；當日常最簡單的活動變成一個俄羅斯輪盤遊戲時，它是能夠癱瘓一整個經濟體系的。然而，除了現時仍然埋在第三世界的一億一千萬個地雷外，每年依然有二百萬個被埋在泥土中。協助廢除地雷是第三世界唯一可以向前邁進的途徑。欲知你們如何協助，請致函你的本地政府或紐約的聯合國人道事務部的地雷清理及政策科 [Mine Clearance and Policy Unit, Department of Humanitarian Affairs, United Nations, New York, NY 10017]。

無鉛 [Unleaded]，第209頁
大字標題：別讓我們的兒童充滿鉛，
廣告文字：使用無鉛汽油。
在阿拉伯聯合猶長國 [UAE] 為環境利益而發行。

行人路 [Pavement]，第210頁
大自標題：在行人路上更加令人厭惡。
廣告文字：如果你的狗在街上大便，請善後清理。

原子彈 [Atomic Bomb]，第211頁

廣告文字：國際合作出色地以殲滅威脅大眾，現在或者可以紓情況調解。如果你想改變這個世界，這便是你的機會。請在10月27日至11月1日在我們的網址參加討論。www.worldforum.org

樹葉／火柴 [Leaf/Match]，第212頁
大字標題：別在家中留下易燃火種。

解僱 [Off Duty]，第213頁
丈夫：我們結婚已有十八年。
妻子：生活一直都平靜。
丈夫：我們各自忙碌。
妻子：日日如是，工作、家庭、孩子，沒有甚麼不平凡。當他被解僱時...
丈夫：發生的很突然，我的心變成一片空白。
妻子：他像很害怕的，眼睛充滿淚水。
丈夫：首先消失的是我的自尊，我只會想到用酒精來掩著我的痛苦。
妻子：他需要我的支持。
丈夫：她一直都鼓勵我。
妻子：不要擔心，會好轉的。
丈夫：被解僱是我們之間所發生的最好一件事。
妻子：我們從來沒有那麼親近。
丈夫：我生日那天...
妻子：我買了一雙皮鞋給他。
丈夫：新皮鞋。
妻子：送給他，讓他去探索整個世界的新希望。
丈夫：我感動得流淚。這份工作比較好，總比坐在家裡好。只要我們二人同心，甚麼都不成問題。
標題字幕：你的支持便是他的力量。

連鎖書函 [Chain Letter]，第216頁
廣告文字：
親愛的艾力
我們的社區中有一種病毒正在蔓延，它每星期都奪去一條生命，它是透過污血或性接觸而傳播的。我肯定你知道我說的是甚麼 — HIV 及最終的 愛滋病。
我們唯一能制止它蔓延的方法就是將信息傳播得比它快。
這信息是安全避孕套，實行安全的性活動，使用避孕套，就是那麼簡單。
現在把這封信抄六次，然後將它們寄給你認為能夠改善這個 世界的人。不要覺得尷尬，我們都需要提醒的。如果你在這星期內將這封信寄給六個人，而他們每人都照樣做，到月底便會有 7,776個人知道這信息；如果你不照樣做的話，到年底便會有數百萬人錯過了我們的信息。
這是我們對其他每個人的責任。為每個人將這信息傳播，消滅這病毒。
簽名：關心的人。
再者：如果你們能負擔一些捐款給愛滋病基金會 [Aids Foundation]，他們會很感激的。
他們的地址是：
NZ AIDS Foundation, PO Box 7287, Wellington, New Zealand。

慢性毒藥 [Slow Poison]，第217頁
大字標題：慢性毒藥。
廣告文字：由 Tata Tea Limited 為公眾利益而發行。

清除乾淨 [Clean Up]，第220頁
音樂：Morning Mood from Grieg's Peer Gynt suite
男人：早晨！
今天天氣是很好呢。
聲音：格喳格喳響和滑動聲。
標題字幕：切勿讓你的狗。

外面有人嗎？[Anybody Out There?]，第222頁
男聲旁白：外面有人嗎？
外面有人嗎？
外面... 有人嗎？
外面有人嗎？
標題字幕：有
撒瑪利亞防止自殺會的人
[Samaritans]

死與生 [Die and Live]，第224頁
丈夫從一切準備妥當，等待死亡，跟著接到最壞的消息，「你會活下去。」
反感失望，你都會的，對嗎？當你確定是患有末期癌症時，醫生卻送來一個震耗，這說好像晴天霹靂，「治療生效，癌症得以根治，你可以繼續活下去。」打擊實在太大了，前景簡直不能再差。
你要記住羅恩的故事是頗為獨特的，大多數人不會有像他這樣的反應，但對於死亡 (或羅恩的個案是不死) 沒有人會有同一反應。

然像開籠雀。到了1996年5月，她的疾病終於開始跟她趕上。她變得疲累，痛楚又再出現，妮娜知道她的時日無多，她開始吞藥丸，可以靠皮下注射來接觸痛楚，直至此際返回善終院舍等待去世。
正如我們剛才說過，我們盡力不說病人何時會去世，但通常病人自己會告訴我們，他們內心知道會發生甚麼事情。妮娜就是這樣，在她去世的那天早上，她知道她會在那天去世，她把她的全家召來，逐一向他們道別，告別完畢後，他們圍繞著她，妮娜便安靜地去世。
妮娜是一個與別不同的女人，即使受到癌症的影響了七年，但她的面上永遠掛著笑容，時常都抱著積極態度，充滿自信。她的印象深刻地留在善終院舍的員工及那些患有不治之症而又曾受過她的支持和鼓勵的人的心中。不可思議地是她地疾病沒有令她害怕，反而令她終於解放，她不知道她還生存多久，但她完全堅持要盡量享受餘生，正如她其中一個同事說，妮娜採取法蘭仙納度立 [Frank Sinatra] 的做法，她以她的方式去世。
在Mary Potter Hospice善終院舍裡，我們有一個座右銘：盡量生活得最好。王如妮娜的例子，當離開善終院舍生活時，這是通常可以達到的，因此我們將服務延至至社區，亦因這樣，我們獲得Kapiti地區大大的支持，在當地建立了一個門診部，而你在今年的街頭勸捐的資助亦會使我們能夠將服送出去 (和那些發覺其實不會那麼快死) 的人做更多事，讓他們盡量生活得最好。
羅恩悲劇性的命運是他自己強加的，雖然他不是Mary Potter Hospice善終院舍的病人，但這個來自我們的院友 (羅恩是他在英國工作的病人) 的真實故事強調我們在日常工作中所遇到的問題。
這故事對我們在Mary Potter Hospice善終院舍處理病人的手法帶來重要的後果，因為有時即使當所有事情都好轉時，情況其實往往變得更壞，我們一日的工作是這麼難預料的，因此我們經常向世界各地的羅恩學習，免致像他這樣的情況再出現。
聽說人生有兩件事是肯定的：死亡和稅項，稅項可以預測，但死亡卻不是，羅恩的故事就是確實的證明，妮娜的也是。但如果說妮娜只是扯壞了肌肉，因而引致痛楚，這點她是錯的，但她亦覺得她所服用的藥物可能是問題的起因，這點她卻是對的。 在她住院的兩個星期，我們給她一種不會導致嘔吐的止痛藥，她出院回家時已毫無痛楚，準備繼續她的生命。她仍然有不治之症的癌症，但她仍有很多日子要活呢。
我們發覺我們的病人越來越喜歡在院外治療，他們依然會回來，而我們的病床依然是滿額的，但他們會定期回來接受治療和接受控制病痛的評核，之後他們便會覺得最舒適，我們盡量鼓勵病人這樣做。如果病人太早入住善終院舍，這未必太好，但可能會過早放棄，束手待斃，但在家裡，他們會像妮娜一樣繼續生活。
過了兩個月，跟著第三個月，跟著第六個月，妮娜只是熱烈地追求生命，她定期諮詢她的家庭醫生，而我們善終院舍的醫生亦會每兩個月去探訪她一次。她亦採用物理治療，並收到積極的觀想和展望對她有最大和有益的影響。假如她相信最初的生命時限，假如她決定留在Mary Potter 善終院舍，她便早已停止生存了，最欣慰的是她並沒有這樣做，她選擇留在家中與丈夫一起。
她更想與丈夫一起出門，他們亦真的經常出門，他們會裝備好旅行車，在紐西蘭到處作長程旅行。遠遠不像羅恩，她不讓死神毀滅，反而激活力。終於在1995年年期，併發症開始，妮娜的腸臟閉塞，這也沒有令她停下來，她接受腸工手術後痊愈得很好，在她被診斷即將不治的十六個月後，她依

生命。
生命呼喚你，捐贈你地器官。
男聲旁白及題目：生命呼喚你，捐贈你的器官。
男聲旁白：這是Antena 3 TV的公共服務信息。
由Saatchi & Saatchi廣告公司創

犯人 [Prisoner]，第230頁
男聲旁白：有些犯人有電力供應和一日三餐，有些犯人有熱水供應和顏色電視，其他犯人沒有...
而他們唯一的罪行就是生活支出超過他們的收入。
因此請協助Rand Aid令生活有所改變。
011–882 2510。

打這個 [Punch These]，第232頁
大字標題：憤怒，挫敗，慌亂？
打這個。
廣告文字：撒瑪利亞防止自殺會[The Samaritans] 電話 366 6676

公共汽車 [Bus]，第286頁
廣告文字：撒瑪利亞防止自殺會[Samaritans] 電話 4 739 739

重新開始 [Start Again]，第227頁
大字標題：中風並非是終結，你只需要重新開始。
廣告文字：你有八份之一的機會中風，當然如果你是吸煙的話，你會中風的威脅會增加五倍，高血壓令你的機會增加十倍，但如果你是吸煙的，又有高血壓的話，你的中風機會便多出十八倍。
中風是由於輸往腦部的血液突然中斷，令擲部受損所致。你會有以下一些或全部的病徵。死亡 (最壞的結果，所以我們先列出這個)，失去知覺，一邊面部、手臂或腿部癱瘓或軟弱，不能與人溝通，又或者在吞食時有困難，你可能失去膝頭或腸臟的控制，視覺或受損，失去記憶，你不能控制情緒，你的謀生能力繼而消失，不用說消沉是很普遍的，通常的接通是你的身體兩邊變成完全不同。
一邊跟以前差不多，但你要重新教導另一邊怎樣去郁動、協調、說話、吃東西和走路。正因為如此，你中風後雖然生還但也不算是幸運這等普遍的概念是錯誤的，但我們可以樂意告訴你這並不對，你能夠部份或甚至完全康復的機會很大。深切治療、有技巧的護理和持之有恆的決心，以及我們善終院舍可以協助你們再次全面控制身體。中風的另一個正面意識是當我們對它更加認識時，我們亦能大大地降低你會中風的機會。過量的酒精、吸煙、緊張壓力太大、缺乏運動、膽固醇過高、心臟病、糖尿病和肥胖都是起因，這些病原很多可以用藥物控制，改變飲食或工作習慣，或者假如是過量酒精的話，便停止自控 (切勿擔心，我們的親友不會老古板，只是想鼓勵節制而已)。中風是紐西蘭唯一全面至誠協助中風者和他們的親友的機構，但我們並不是一個富有的機構，為了繼續我們的工作、我們的研究、我們的支援服務、以及我們的各種預防教育課程和計劃，我們需要你的幫忙，你可以捐款給中風會，PO Box 2320 Wellington，或以電話捐贈給0800 Stroke (0800 787 653)。你所捐贈的任何數目都會協助我們將有關預防中風的信息開去，確保更多人對中風的認識不止於單方面。
如有查詢，請聯絡紐西蘭中風會 [Stroke Foundation of New Zealand inc. PO Box 2320, Wellington]。電話 (04) 472 8099，傳真 (04) 472 7019。

失明 [Blind]，第228頁
大字標題：失明 形容詞，動詞，名詞和副詞 – 形容詞1缺乏視覺力量。
失明 形容詞，動詞，名詞和副詞 – 形容詞2不願意或不能體會 (因素，情況等等。)
廣告文字：與失明人士消磨一日時間會令你對事物有不同的看法。
由Tata Tea Limited 為公眾利益而發行。令每日... 都有所分別。

火柴 [Matches]，第229頁
男聲旁白：當一條生命熄滅的時候，內裡的東西卻可以燃亮另一條

Samaritans, New Zealand, 1996

Acknowledgements

The work in this book spans more than thirty years.
Thousands of people have contributed to it, at all
levels, during that period.
The publishers and Saatchi & Saatchi gratefully
acknowledge all those who have been involved in
any way with the campaigns featured here.

Additional photography by Anthony Oliver.